THE OTHER AMERICANS

THE OTHER AMERICANS

Sexual Variance in the National Past

EDITED BY

Charles O. Jackson

Westport, Connecticut
London

Library of Congress Cataloging-in-Publication Data

The other Americans : sexual variance in the national past / edited by
Charles O. Jackson.
     p.   cm.
   Includes bibliographical references and index.
     ISBN 0–275–95550–8 (alk. paper). — ISBN 0–275–95551–6 (pbk. :
alk. paper)
     1. Sexual deviation—United States—History.   2. Sex customs—
United States—History.   3. Sexual ethics—United States—History.
I. Jackson, Charles O.
   HQ72.U53O86   1996
   306.77'0973—dc20   95–52995

British Library Cataloguing in Publication Data is available.

Library of Congress Catalog Card Number: 95–52295
ISBN: 0–275–95550–8 (hc)
       0–275–95551–6 (pb)

First published in 1996

Praeger Publishers, 88 Post Road West, Westport, CT 06881
An imprint of Greenwood Publishing Group, Inc.

Printed in the United States of America

The paper used in this book complies with the
Permanent Paper Standard issued by the National
Information Standards Organization (Z39.48–1984).

10 9 8 7 6 5 4 3 2 1

Copyright Acknowledgments

To Mandy
for her friendship and her faith in alchemy

Contents

Preface

In practice, if not in theory, every society has had to confront the issue of sexual expression or behavior. Sexuality is a basic management issue that must be addressed. Theorizing about it is a relatively recent phenomenon in American history. It dates from no earlier than the beginning of the twentieth century. In recent decades this interest has produced an enormous outpouring of literature on sexuality, dealing largely with what we do, how we do it, why we do it, and how to do it better. Such inquiry has been, however, essentially the province of anthropology, psychology, and sociology. The historical perspective on sexuality has been less well treated. Some recognition of and attention to this omission has occurred over the past decade or so. Yet, in this recent scholarly historical concern minimal attention has been given to practices beyond the boundary of "acceptable" sexuality. This is to say sexual deviance or stigmatized sexual behavior. Deviance is also a basic management issue. The omission of scholarly concern is all the more important because such variance reflects well other larger currents of the national past. Deviance has also acted to facilitate and make clear the boundaries beyond which respectable America must not journey either sexually or socially. In this sense, and like the role of all behavioral variance, sexual deviance serves the social purpose of helping to provide cohesion in the larger culture.

The primary aim of this volume is to provide a compact and manageable, thus of necessity, selective perspective on sexual variance as one dimension of American social history. If successful, the chapters should speak collectively as much to the history of American culture as they do to a national history of deviant practice. Accordingly, the volume does *not* occupy itself especially with the currency of scholarship. This is not the primary selection criteria. It is less concerned also with ethnic/racial or even social-class diversity in sexual deviance than it is with commonality of American management of, interaction with, and response to practice beyond the defined boundaries of "respectable" sexuality. This basis of organization is both the strength and admitted weakness of the volume. In addition to a general audience the collection should be valuable as a text that provides a very different, even unique, perspective on the American past. As such it should find use in undergraduate American studies, history, sociology, sex education and other related courses.

The collection draws on a variety of cross disciplinary sources, largely, though not exclusively, on articles published in scholarly journals over the last twenty-five years. A curiosity of such historical coverage is that it clusters essentially in the decades of the 1970s and 1980s. Little is done before the former decade, except on the issue of dating the "sexual revolution." Insofar as journal essays, pertinent material on sexual deviance beyond 1990 addressed to the American cultural context is meager. "Pertinent" is the operative word here. Search for appropriate material began with the 1960s and was carried through 1995. Choices of essays for this volume were then made based solely on their useful insight into American social history. Organization of the volume takes two approaches. One is chronological; chapters are divided into three sections corresponding roughly to Early America, Victorian America, and the twentieth century. The second approach focuses on specific categories of deviance. Because more historical attention has been paid to what may be labelled "conventional" deviance, e.g., disapproved heterosexual behavior, these practices obtain lesser attention in categorization than more controversial and more highly stigmatized forms. Categories of sexual deviance to receive more emphasis here, though not exclusively, are prostitution, sexual assault, and same-sex relations.

The window-on-larger-culture technique taken in this volume claims no uniqueness. I have used it to my satisfaction previously in dealing with death ritual and attitude, e.g., *Passing: The Vision of Death in America* (1977). I do consider this sexual variance "window" or perspective to be quite an important one here in that it is especially fruitful and it has not been done. Moreover, sexual deviance lends itself well to perspective on larger culture since many aspects of such stigmatized behavior have gradually been incorporated, if not always with applause, into acceptable sexual normality in this century. That occurrence should remind the reader that deviance and normality are not polar opposites but parts of a continuum, and a shifting one at that. Sexual deviance is a social construct at any given time. Stigmatized practice is not a property *inherent* in any particular behavior. It is *conferred* upon behavior by people who come in contact with it, directly or indirectly. Social groups or societies then respond to it by punishment, toleration, or forgiveness. Societies create their own particular brands of deviance. Thus social groupings that place a high premium on private ownership will quite likely see theft as very serious business. Those that stress a strict conservative political orthodoxy will very likely stigmatize heavily alternatives such as socialism or communism. Nineteenth-century America was committed to a human physiology that conceived of the body as a relatively closed energy system in which creativity, indeed national destiny, was dependent on proper use of vital powers. "Waste" of that vitality (i.e., male semen) for other than procreative purposes could be viewed only as a most grievous and destructive perversion. In the period this was surely "deviance" in its most derogatory connotation.

The present volume is concerned primarily with time-related definition and social organization of sexual deviance. It is concerned also, however, with the social mechanisms employed against deviant activity. The volume postulates that sexual deviance, indeed social deviance in general, is a constant presence in societies. It will not be banished. It is possible to argue here that deviance is a product of normative structuring. In this sense it may be observed that if deviance did not exist social imperative would require that it be created. Finally, hope is that the volume title, "The Other Americans," will be understood as at least a nod to irony. Reflecting on the use of this appellation, the editor begs to remind readers of a line from a popular comic strip some years back on the occasion of Earth Day— "We have met the enemy and it is us."

To the extent that this volume has scholarly merit and is successful in its purposes, I owe thanks to many different people. I am able to take note here of only a few. A first bow is of course to the authors of the chapters included in this volume, some of whom have been personally helpful. Beyond this I limit my acknowledgments to several most important local sources of assistance. One is a very able research staff in the John Hodges Library at The University of Tennessee, Knoxville. I offer special thanks to four university colleagues for their critique of material in this volume and their frankness in forcing me to clarify in my own mind issues that they raised. They are professors James Black, Department of Sociology, and Charles Johnson, Milton Klein, and Larry Ratner, Department of History. The latter was dean, College of Arts and Sciences, during the period in which this volume was developed. As such he provided me office services and the necessary time to complete the work. Amanda Smartt gave me her encouragement, patience, and her confidence that this book would reach fruition. I received invaluable aid in the physical preparation of the manuscript from two graduate student assistants, Kristin Russell and Theresa Swanson, as well as from my office colleague Linda Brooks. Linda's grace, equanimity, and occasional solicitude toward me kept a temperamentally manic-depressive author/editor largely civil through the day. Tyler Ludlow should be included here simply because he is important. My greatest debt as always is to my wife, Emma, who has chosen to care about me for over forty years.

Needless to say, I am grateful to Praeger Publishers for their interest in my project and to my production editor, Desirée Bermani, for her work in bringing that project to publication. Finally, I owe thanks to Dr. James Sabin of the Greenwood Publishing Group who has now seen me through two manuscripts.

Charles O. Jackson
Knoxville, Tennessee

A Beginning: On Sexual "Normality" and "Deviance" in America, a Perspective in History

Sexual expression represents a fundamental management issue that must be met and at least functionally resolved by every society. Resolution is never final, however; constant maintenance and modification are required. Sexual concerns have generated an enormous body of literature over the past fifty to sixty years of this century. It has mainly informed Americans what they do, how they do it, why they do it, and suggested ways to do it better. Such inquiry has been largely the province of anthropology, medicine, psychology, and sociology, and has tended also to be ahistorical. Sexual deviance is a related and similar management problem that has been treated essentially by the same disciplines and characterized by the same approach.

This volume provides a collection of thirteen chapters on episodes of sexual deviance as dimensions of American social history. If the volume is successful, content should speak collectively as much to the history of American culture as it does to a history of deviant practice. Selections are included here less because of their publication currency than because of useful insight into the American social record. The volume is more concerned with American commonality in management of, interaction with, and response to practice beyond the defined boundaries of "respectable" sexuality than with discovery and examination of ethnic/racial or even social-class diversity. This perspective is both the strength and admitted weakness of the collection.

As noted, the chapters that follow are structured to examine in historical perspective issues of sexual normality versus sexual deviance, and the relationship between the two in American culture. Norms are defined simply as a set of standards that inform and characterize behavior in a given social group. Deviance is used here to mean behavioral practices that diverge from accepted norms and which are then stigmatized by a majority of those who comprise a social group or society. In popular usage the term deviance commonly carries some pejorative connotation. This is not the case here where it is used as a synonym for the more value-free term, variance. Both labels point directly to the origin of the phenomenon. Not unlike normality, deviance or variance is a social construct. It is not a property *inherent* in any particular kind of behavior. It is property *conferred* upon that behavior by people who come into direct or indirect contact with given activity.

Societies create their own particular brands of deviance, and those brands serve important social purposes in a society. As Kai Erikson has pointed out in his still very useful work, *Wayward Puritans* (1966), the presence of deviance draws people together in a common anger and indignation toward it. In this process, they develop a tighter bond of cohesion and solidarity than existed before. Unless the rhythms of group life are punctuated occasionally by outbreaks or heightened visibility of deviance (because it is always present), maintenance of social organization would be extremely difficult. Moreover, it should be observed that what constitutes deviance may change drastically over time. Definition of it is never a fixed property in a society. It is always shifting as members of the group find new behavior forms to set the outer limits of respectability. Finally, as Erikson has observed further, every community or society tends to develop its own characteristic forms of deviant behavior. Societies that place a very high premium on ownership of property are likely to experience a greater volume of theft than those that do not hold it in such high esteem. Societies that stress conservative social orthodoxy in expressions of sexuality, and feel seriously jeopardized by deviance in this area, will very likely impose more severe sanctions against it, and will devote more energy to the task of rooting it out. Such has been the case for much of the American past.

A clearer understanding of the origins of modern sexual deviance as a distinct category of "disorder" is now possible given significant explorations of Michel Foucault in his *The History of Sexuality, Volume One: An Introduction* (1978). Foucault's general concern is to describe how and why certain forms of sexual discourse and knowledge have taken shape in the West since the close of the sixteenth century. He contends that contrary to the notion that sexuality was repressed during that period all social relations became drastically sexualized. Sexuality was "deployed" into every area of life. One consequence of organization begun in the seventeenth century was the "perverse implantation." This label is used to describe a development in which sexual deviance was singled out as a distinct category of socially stigmatized behavior. Previously such practice was scarcely noticed or at least counted as merely one component in the overall human potential for perversion. There was in the seventeenth and eighteenth centuries, however, a separating out of sexual acts "contrary to nature" as especially abominable. Rather than repression, there followed a multiplication of identifiable disparate and stigmatized sexualities. While Foucault's full thesis not pursued here remains arguable, the present volume does accept his explanation for the modern invention of sexual deviances.

Several assumptions about sexuality and its variant forms are either explicit or implicit in this collection and so should be made clear. They are largely matters that by now are the common corpus of professional sociology. A first set of such observations hold that while sexual gratification (at least beyond adolescence) cannot be entirely suppressed, such gratification is not required for survival in the same way that release for other basic needs—hunger, thirst, fatigue—is required.

The sex drive can accept and operate within a context of substantial social conditioning. Secondly, and compared to other basic drives, sexual needs are capable of an extraordinary variety of expressions. This means that potentially there is a wide range of behavior that is the legitimate domain of sexual norms. A substantial amount of otherwise normally nonsex related activity exists, which can be, and has been, sexualized sufficiently to the point where it could be deemed appropriate for application of sexual concern, e.g., current erotic innuendo in advertising that sexualizes products. Finally, the human sex drive is inherently unstable and anarchic. It is, therefore, very difficult to regulate effectively, *but* must be conditioned if a stable social order is to be maintained. So-called "free sex" settings, such as the Oneida Community in nineteenth-century America, turn out to be social groups "marching to a different drummer," but quite clearly there is a "drummer."

A second observation drawn from the general corpus of sociology and for which there is no claim of originality is on the force of modern science in defining and conceptualizing sexual deviance. With sexuality, as in other areas of human existence, there have been gradual changes in what society has learned to accept as the authoritative standard for definitions of self and others. Basically, that shift has been from an ideology based on religious doctrine to one based on scientific knowledge. This does not mean that religion no longer has force in life decisions, or has no effect in determination of sexually acceptable behavior. It does mean that religion or the sacred retains no longer the authoritative position it once held. While the beginnings of this transformation were perceptible by the late eighteenth century, it has been most pronounced in the present century. Even at the inception of the 1900s, it is fair to assume that most Americans were taught to conceptualize their sexuality in terms of religious doctrine and standards. To do otherwise was to endanger their moral, mental, and physical health.

The religious tradition, as transported to the British Colonies of North America, embodied a sharp dichotomy between body and mind, the flesh and the spirit. As commonly understood, the latter was the focus of physical desire, which at best was a hinderance or obstacle to progressive spiritual development by the mind. Morality was understood in terms of an absolute standard toward which one should strive even though an individual might fall short of the goal. With some regional variation through the eighteenth century, largely related to sexual contacts by white masters with black slaves in the southern colonies, sexual norms were clear, as were defined forms of stigmatized deviation.

While any chronology is arbitrary, it is surely possible to conclude that from the mid-eighteenth century forward, popular confidence in physical science as a source of "truth" was growing substantially and would continue to grow through the nineteenth century. This new confidence in science was encouraged all the more because, and contrary to what is often currently assumed, the new science generally gave its imprimatur to explanations that tended to reconfirm older religious "truths." While the nineteenth century would bring some challenges to orthodox religion, notably of course Darwinian evolution (which was gradually compromised at least at higher theological levels), the conflicts were not serious. Moreover, in that century, the sciences never investigated *all* aspects of human behavior at more than a cursory level. Science tended more often to accept religious assumptions without much evidence and incorporate them into the former's purview of expertise.

One corollary of the growing authority of science has been that interpretation of sexual behavior gradually moved away from religious definition, toward what may be labelled a "medical model." From the standpoint of sexual liberality, this brought limited advantage in the short run. A conservative medical establishment did operate to discourage references to sin and satanic evil, which had previously been applied to some expressions of sexuality. But it tended also to substitute words such as *pathological,* and by implication suggested that this behavior be defined as "illness." Masturbation was a case in point.

In the long term, this transition had great advantage with respect to stigmatized sexual behavior—at least in the present century. Even sexual deviance would move in its explanation from moral judgment to psychiatric judgment. This meant also a change in perspective on deviant actors, though the two responses toward them might be hard to tell apart. Increased rationality, which accompanied the new medical concept of rehabilitation, worked to promote greater tolerance and less severe negative sanctions in social response to so-called deviant behavior. This trend was reinforced in the late nineteenth century through what may be labelled "sociological morality." As held by reform-minded behavioral thinkers such as Jane Addams, this notion meant essentially that human beings and their actions were products of given social environments in which they were nurtured. At its sociological extreme, this view perceived deviants as victims. The consequence of the logic was simply that "I am depraved because I am deprived."

The medical model for sexual expressions finally had other significant advantages over religious interpretation. While the latter in the eighteenth and much of the nineteenth century appeared to advance an absolute standard of behavior, the former could take a relative posture and was readily capable of change. When new findings appeared, they could be more easily incorporated into older knowledge and produce ultimately new definitions of normality. A dramatic instance of this potential was a 1974 decision by the American Psychiatric Association that removed homosexuality from the category of pathological illness. The emergence of the medical model as an aspect of the growth of scientific authority was not the only benefit to understanding of sexuality and its expressions. As science became gradually the dominant authority on sexual matters in this century, sexuality became legitimized as a field of study by natural and social scientists. The assignment of scientific status to the study of sexuality has given it new social importance and has encouraged, moreover, production of a large body of what has been called "sexology" literature. It was a significant departure. Theorizing about sex, unlike having it, was all but unknown until the last one hundred years.

In his 1976 volume on this subject, Paul Robinson (*The Modernization of Sex*) has argued that "sexology" clearly deserves serious attention because it is now a solid part of American intellectual history. The assertion may well be correct. The more important justification, however, is that at least since the publication of findings by Alfred Kinsey and colleagues, sexology provided in laymen's prose, has made its way into American popular culture. It has become not merely a facet of intellectual history, but guides to which the general public has turned for definitions and measures, as well as answers about sexual normality. Especially in such participant report studies as that of William Masters and Virginia Johnson or even Shere Hite's *The Hite Report* (1976), now primary types in sexology literature, readers are essentially invited to measure their own sexual attitudes and practices against a standard of normality that was provided by behavioral data presented in the studies themselves. It is granted, however, that more scholarly work such as that of Kinsey or even Masters and Johnson, not unlike the sexual wisdom of Sigmund Freud as dealt with popularly in the 1920s, was much more discussed and quoted than actually read by the public. Yet in any event, popular sexology in scientific garb has gone far, if only by publicizing the extent of participation in previously stigmatized sexual behavior within the general public, to make more acceptable if not completely legitimize, much previous deviant behavior. Oral sex, masturbation, pre- and extramarital coitus are prime examples.

Sexology in all its forms has tended generally to approach "deviant" behavior, at least where there was no identifiable victim, in terms of a liberated pleasure-oriented morality and/or a philosophy of sexual relativism. There were no homosexuals, only homosexual acts, Professor Kinsey once observed after having reported that over one third of all American males had one or more homosexual experiences. While hardly "scientific" sexology, fellow travelers such as "J" in the *Sensuous Woman* (1969) or Alex Comfort's *The Joy of Sex* (1972), prototypes of later works that capitalized on the popularity of the legitimate genre, urged upon readers the practices of anal sex, group sex, fellatio, and cunnilingus as well as virtually every other form of sexual expression open to the imagination. Notably and significantly this genre has advanced heterosexual variation while marginalizing other forms. In the midst of such large-scale pronouncements to the public, words like *normality* and *deviance* have blurred and have lost much meaning.

Another useful distinction here is between what may be labelled "conventional" versus "radical" deviance. The former refers to forms of behavior that, while officially disapproved in American society, are characterized by limited intensity of disapproval and by limited instances of applied sanctions against them. In part, "limited intensity" is a consequence of high occurrence within the general public. Limited "sanction occasions" occur because the behavior has such low social visibility that only a small number of actors are ever put in a position where punishment may be applied. Examples would be pre- and extramarital coitus as well as heterosexual oral and genital contact. Radical deviance would be behavior beyond the previous category that obtains much stronger denunciation and commitment to negative sanction. Occurrences are less than in the conventional deviance category but are perceived popularly as more overt and dangerous challenges to the established sexual order. Examples would be sexual assault, homosexuality, and, though arguable in contemporary America, prostitution. The present volume is more concerned with the latter category than the former.

Beyond matters of definition or conception of deviant practice, the present volume is concerned also with social mechanisms used historically to enforce sexual normalcy and suppress deviance. There have been four primary means: elevation-to-the-sacred, community pressure, application of social taboos, statutory law. The first has been the most effective in social groupings, oriented toward a sacred understanding of life, for these purposes the traditional Judeo/Christian perspective. Here sexual standards were surrounded in mystery and given divine purpose. Enforcement and negative sanction for failure to conform were left to the Godhead. Communities may not know of indiscretions but higher powers did, and retribution was certain to follow sooner or later. This mechanism was at its maximum effectiveness from the Colonial period through circa the first half of the nineteenth century.

While any attempt to establish a beginning point for the process of secularization in American culture would be arbitrary, that trend was clearly evident in the late nineteenth century and went far to destroy the effectiveness of "elevation to the sacred" as an enforcement mechanism. A part of that process has been, as noted, the rise of scientific authority. Its elevation was not meant as observed previously—that the "sacred" no longer had force in the moral or sexual realm, but did mean that this force did not carry the level of authority it had a century or so ago. What it has retained has been purchased at heavy cost. First was the softening (if not the elimination) of rhetoric about hell and damnation for carnal offenses. More recently situational ethics have obtained increasing, if grudging, general acceptance. Both matters dealt severe blows to the vitality of the "elevation-to-the-sacred" enforcement technique. The breakdown of this mechanism has meant that standards of sexual practice have been removed from the hands of God and placed in the hands of mere mortals.

A second and more recent enforcement technique in the American past, and not without authority today, has been community pressure. This measure was particularly forceful throughout the nineteenth century when the worship of respectability became epidemic at least in the middle class and those who aspired to it. Central to that behavior was a highly restrictive sexual code that went further than did that of the eighteenth century. Previously accepted practices such as "bundling" became a shocking ancestral failing to be condemned and forgotten. Existing stigmatized practice such as premarital coitus became escalated to the scale of sexual-behavior outrages. Such practice was an act of defiance to be deterred swiftly and strongly by more direct supervision than previously, of unmarried couples in particular, by introduction into that relationship of the chaperon. A major new potential category of behavioral deviation was created by the societal pronouncement that "normal" women did not experience sexual desire. The weapons of community pressure were often subtle but effective. They began with general collective surveillance of individual behavior by the community, and with the implicit threat toward observed deviants of gossip, loss of face, ostracism, and other informal techniques of social retaliation.

Community pressure was only effective, however, where the surveillance system operated in a fairly static environment, homogeneous in population, cohesive, and with limited in-out migration. Effective pressure also requires a setting where social judgment by the group was deemed of importance to potential deviant actors, implying an intimate small-town setting. Increasing geographical mobility, rapid urbanization, and specialized role bureaucratization in the late nineteenth century steadily took its toll on community pressure as a norm enforcement mechanism. The city meant anonymity and heterogeneity in the population. Bureaucratization also encouraged a setting of secondary relationships where individuals related to and were recognized by most social "others" less as total beings than through a variety of segmented social roles, e.g., church member, milkman, or co-worker. Mobility not only encouraged anonymity, but in the absence of immediate kinship, promoted greater freedom (and greater burden) to make one's own judgment of what was accepted sexual practice. Decisions would be made in an atmosphere of substantial tolerance, even peer impersonal disregard toward behavior of others. Under such circumstances surveillance as an effective social process lost force in the twentieth century.

A third mechanism for defending traditional sexual norms was to make the topic of deviance and even sexuality a social taboo. This too was a norm enforcement mechanism of the nineteenth century. Taboo was not employed prior to that period in any substantial degree, and was crumbling by the second decade of the twentieth century. While it lasted, the Victorian code of "delicacy" (defined as an aversion to and evasion of what was considered morally distasteful or morally injurious) surrounded all sexual practice with an aura of mandated silence. If forced into public conversation, Victorian Americans did so only within a context of vagueness, ambiguity, and euphemism. The latter was not only applied to discourse specifically related to sexual activity (adultery became "criminal" conversation and masturbation the "solitary vice") but deployed even to bodily parts (legs became "nether limbs," the stomach, "lower parts").

The "taboo" technique made no pretense of ending deviant behavior but rather simply denied its reality or existence. Victorian culture itself involved a substantial degree of hypocrisy in this regard. On the one hand, for example, it condemned prostitution, and on the other, it tacitly accepted that activity as an outlet for base male desires that might otherwise be pressed upon virtuous women. The effectiveness of the taboo technique in even slowing down the growth of deviant behavior in the century is open to debate. Contraceptive practice provides a case in point. Despite substantial disapproval of it even by physicians (such to classify it in hind sight as "normal" deviance), as well as belated state and federal legislation to halt the spread of information about such practice, the fertility rate for women fell steadily across the nineteenth century. It was generally asserted in the period (usually in outraged fashion) that the decline was a result of widespread use of birth-control methods, and that perception probably had substantial substance.

A final means of enforcing sexual norms has been through passage of law. An initial observation here is that the relationship between given sexual behavior and its declared criminality has been historically a complicated one, at times impossible to maintain rationally. Application of criminal sanction has been clearly situational. Thus matters such as degrees of consent, the right to submit, physical setting, or gender/age of actors are major variables in the application of law. The right to participate in incest versus simple fornication are two very different matters. Legal sanction against sexual solicitation in public versus in private vary substantially. Legal significance given to same-sex relationships has been quite different than that ascribed to heterosexual infractions. Such examples make the point. Historically what these applications of criminality to behavior have had in common, however, is their grounding in moral condemnation by a community. Presumably this connection is not an imperative. An alternative and more rational approach, and one advanced in the American Law Institute's 1959 Model Penal Code, is legal sanction only where behavior is socially dangerous or injurious, independent of its "moral" content. Alas, the approach has yet to obtain serious precedent in law.

An additional observation on control of sexual deviance through law is that, excepting perhaps the technique of silence and taboo, it was clearly the weakest of traditional enforcement mechanisms. For one thing, a significant amount of stigmatized sexual practice, particularly in the category of "conventional deviance," had such low visibility that effective application of legal sanctions was virtually impossible. For another, statutory law had not uncommonly been an artificial substitution in a community that had lost its authority within a significant segment of the social group. Authority could no longer be effectively enforced by more traditional and less formal mechanisms. Beyond these considerations laws were simply collective actions by a legislative body. They were subject to modification or repeal by that body should it have a change in mood or composition. Moreover, statutes have always been open to judicial challenge and judicial interpretation. At best they were tentative statements, temporal and problematic. Never could they carry the force, for example, of Biblical decree—God's will. Finally, application of law required not merely identification of deviant actors. There was also the more difficult task of proving legal guilt. The latter has not been without substantial significance. Statutes dealing with issues of sexual deviance have tended historically to be notoriously vague and ambiguous, making them extremely hard to enforce even with the best of intent and commitment.

Basically laws in the United States, especially in the nineteenth century, began with the old belief that certain sexual acts were "natural" and others were not— indeed they were "against nature." In determination of which phenomena were deviant, the test of procreation was applied. If it did not serve that purpose it was stigmatized. But so-called "crimes-against-nature" legislation was, as noted, rarely precise. It was as if law-making bodies were reluctant to spell out the exact nature of such activities, preferring to stay with fuzzy labels such as "sodomy" or "buggery," each of which were applied to a variety of sexual sins. This lack of clarity in language has never gone away, and has often meant that given acts of deviancy could not be prosecuted. Such ambiguity continues to plague discussion and law enforcement even today.

In any event, by the later nineteenth century, earlier forms of enforcement mechanisms used against stigmatized sexual practice—elevation-to-the-sacred, community pressure, application of taboos—were in stages of faltering effectiveness. In this situation anxious Americans moved to keep norms visible and viable by writing them into law. Some statutory action against deviant behavior had always existed in America, for example, dealing with "bestiality" or adultery. Such generalizations do also have their limitations, but a very good case can be made for this thesis as applied to the later nineteenth century in the United States. These were years in which purity forces began an all-out assault on prostitution and white slavery. These were years that saw a proliferation of sexuality-related censorship laws, for example the federal Comstock Law (1873) and similar statutes enacted in twenty-four states. Such legislation sought mutually in various ways to halt distribution of "obscene" material, including information on contraceptive techniques. All abortion became a legal crime in this period as well. Previously, there were no restrictive statutes, at least with reference to the early months of pregnancy. Finally, the late nineteenth century witnessed a rash of purity reforms that sought legally to protect and preserve female virginity in the young by raising the age of consent. Between 1886 to 1895, legal age increases were obtained in thirty-six states. Whatever public hopes, the legislative assault on stigmatized sexual practice fared no better than other enforcement mechanisms previously discussed.

What then can be said in the end of sexuality and deviance in the American past and present? A final pronouncement is simply that both are here to stay. The former is self-evident. The latter requires further comment. Kai Erikson has argued aptly in his previously noted classic examination of social deviance in Puritan Massachusetts that the volume of deviance encountered in a community tends to remain constant over time. He was quite correct. If it were indeed suddenly possible to banish from society its most unacceptable population segment, very little would change. Either new ranks of deviants would soon move in to fill the vacuum; agencies of control, if only out of self interest, would seek more diligently and in more sophisticated fashion to fill the void; or targets of concern would shift and/or new categories of deviance would be developed. The fact remains that deviant actors, as noted, supply important services to societies by marking clearly the outer limits of acceptable conduct. They provide a needed contrast with normality, which gives the latter some scope and dimension. In this sense, it is possible to argue that in a very significant way, social deviance is a product of normative structuring. Of deviation as a whole and stigmatized sexual practice specifically, it must be concluded finally that if they did not exist, social imperative would dictate their creation.

GOD, FLESH, AND DESIRE: EARLY AMERICA

Introduction

Properly perhaps, historical consideration of sexual deviation on this continent should begin with the New World's European explorers. Whatever the Christian mandates and sexual mores on the continent, and they were loosely applied in the fifteenth and sixteenth centuries, they were less effective in the opening of the New World. Thus even as Columbus' crew was planting the cross on an island in the Bahamas, members of that crew also set out to sample the sexual charms of the natives, by force if need be. The cost to Europe of those infractions, the wages of sin, as it were, came high as Alfred Crosby has documented (*The Columbian Exchange* ... ,1972: See Bibliography Cit., Chapter 4). Sexually transmitted syphilis was introduced onto the continent and in limited time a deadly epidemic ensued.

This volume proposes to begin, even if somewhat arbitrarily, with the permanent British settlements of North America. Despite diversity in other aspects of lifestyle, there was in these colonies essential agreement on what was and what was not proper expression of sexuality. The consensus held that marriage was a sexual union. Coital capacity was a gift from God and therefore could not be evil or sinful per se. Contrary to assertions in the nineteenth century, female desire was a reality. Sexual intercourse inside marriage was supposed to be pleasurable for both parties. The hopeful outcome of the sex act was procreation of children. Yet even married partners were cautioned that the level of such activity must be in moderation. Overindulgence or excess was harmful and led to a variety of bodily ills including premature death.

Hardly had God's order been established, however, than signs of backsliding began to appear. Response of the colonists to sexual deviance was quick and, at least in theory, harsh. Behind that zeal and fueling it was a clear understanding as well as mandate that the state play a significant role in the regulation of personal life. Through their response to sexual transgressions colonists reaffirmed the boundaries of acceptable behavior. Retribution served the larger function also of reminding the community that sexuality belonged within marriage and its purpose was procreation. Gender tended to shape reaction to specific deviance. Sodomy and bestiality were male crimes and all the more heinous because of their "unnatural" and "illegitimate" use of sperm. Lesbianism was not recognized at all, even though male homosexual behavior (and bestiality) carried the death penalty. Adultery, fornication, and bastardy involved couples, though women were more likely than men to be prosecuted and convicted. In such behavior the woman was not viewed a priori as a victim. Female lust was considered almost insatiable.

Colonial consensus on sexuality condemned all forms of sexual practice outside marriage. Fornication was a sin. Adultery was worse than fornication because it not only violated the sanctity of marriage but was also a breach of the covenant consecrated by God. Homosexuality, "bestiality," or "unnatural acts" were not to be tolerated. Laws promulgated at Jamestown, Virginia, in 1607 provided the death penalty for "sodomy," adultery, and rape. In New England early laws required execution for "sodomy," "bestiality," and adultery though not rape because it carried no scriptural injunction. The "solitary vice" (masturbation) was of moral though not legal concern. In the eighteenth century it became also a medical concern.

Beyond injunctions against such traditionally defined "perversions" an early and unique brand of deviance to the colonies at least in volume was interracial sexual contact. When Europeans met Africans in the new world such unions were inevitable. The presence of a large black female population in debased condition was simply too tempting an opportunity for irresponsible sexual exploitation. With degrees of variation between North and South, few colonists thought intermixture was a good thing. One issue was fornication. Another was race. But physical antipathy to such contacts was more than a concern over long-term discoloration. The colonial English were convinced they held a charge to sustain a "civilized" condition (i.e., British) in the new world. This alone rendered sexual union and certainly miscegenation a threat to this underlying and ordained plan for settlement of North America. Public feeling against such contacts was sufficiently strong to promote stringent legal penalty for miscegenation and carnal liaisons in general. Still, both persisted and flourished in the colonies, apparently increasing substantially in the eighteenth century.

In significant ways the moral order of Colonial America seems consistent with Michel Foucault's recent view (see introductory essay) at least of early seventeenth-century Europe. He sees it as a watershed period in sexuality discourse, and the development of modern sexual deviance as a distinct category of human perversity. The language of sexuality was open and blunt. Little was hidden even from children. Custom provided substantial opportunity for easy mingling of the sexes without supervision or a great deal of formality. What Foucault has spoken of as the "sexualization" of social relations was not extensive by contrast with the next two centuries. "Bundling" was accepted social practice in the northeast colonies. Intimacies such as kissing, pinching, or even fondling of women were not regarded as social breaches. Nor did sexual deviance have yet a firm *distinct* place in law or other sanction forms. It was difficult for early Americans to make distinctions in gradations within stigmatized behavior. Evil was a capability of all human beings even though punishment might vary among them. There was no reason to separate out specific evils or sins, e.g., sexual transgressions, for special concern. Use of social deviance as boundary of respectability for the larger society was less sophisticated than today. The boundary was bipolar and absolute.

The relationship between law and morality as well as the actual enforcement of morals' legislation in Colonial America is the issue under discussion in the first chapter of this section. In the seventeenth century divine moral law was held to be necessarily binding on all persons in all time. Moral law was the basis of civil law. Sin and crime, divine moral law, and secular law were tightly intertwined. Enforcement of moral law was a primary obligation of Colonial governments. Various statutes across the colonies were designed to regulate public morals. Typical were those related to drunkenness, fornication, blasphemy, adultery, bastardy, and rape. In fashioning the structure of law enforcement apparatus the British settlements faced, however, a particular structural problem. In England, enforcement of morality was primarily the responsibility of ecclesiastical courts of the established church. None ever existed in the North American colonies. Responsibility for development of such regulation and its enforcement were passed, therefore, to secular authority. That merger continued to exist through most of the eighteenth century. In that century, however, new statutes and law-enforcement practice increasingly pointed toward a separation of law and morality. In the period circa 1760 to 1810 a gradual shift of legal emphasis in the laws' basic function took place. Concern became less with morality and more with protection of property. This is to say criminal law consciously became more concerned with preservation of social order than salvation of souls and maintenance of moral purity.

In the text presented here, David Flaherty is concerned with actual enforcement of moral codes in the colonies through essentially the first six decades of the eighteenth century. His thesis is that effort to enforce morals through statutory law was a relative failure in terms of its original expectations. What is striking in the period is the prevalence of sexual immorality especially as evidenced by fornication resulting in childbirth. Prosecuted cases were only the visible edge of sexual misbehavior. By the eighteenth century secular courts became decidedly lenient in punishment, whatever laws stated. Flaherty puts forward a series of considerations and experiences that weakened gradually the inclination among early colonists toward strict enforcement of morals. Central to them was that the frequency and volume of such infractions made all too clear and acted well as a constant reminder of an already healthy respect for Satan and the reality of human depravity. Tolerance was encouraged in part because little real control, especially of "conventional" deviance (see introductory essay definition), could be obtained. Lack of public zeal for legal action against this type deviance negated strict enforcement especially in personal and private affairs. Legislative bodies only created law, after all, but not the ability or instruments to enforce them. In the end, Flaherty's conclusion is that moral considerations in these societies generally did prevail but less from enforcement by law than by other extra legal mechanisms: Invocation of the divine, peer pressure, and conscience.

Some historical studies have been done especially on New England that have included investigation of heterosexual deviance such as adultery and premarital intercourse. Very little has been done, however, on more variant sexual activity such as homosexuality (sodomy) and bestiality (buggery), that is, so-called unnatural acts or acts against nature. While court records provide the major source for investigation of the latter, they do not tell the whole story, and often may obscure the presence of these episodes under vague labels such as "unclean practice" or "lude carriage." In addition, the private nature of such behavior would naturally render indentification difficult and so opportunity for prosecution was quite limited. Frequency levels remain therefore a matter of debate. On the other hand it is clear that the extent of public outrage and condemnation of "sodomy" and "buggery" was substantially disproportionate to actual occurrence of these crimes. In the case of homosexuality, Roger Thompson has argued ("Attitudes Toward Homosexuality in Seventeenth Century New England," 1989: See Bibliography Cit.) that the extreme hostility in the Colonial New England social environment toward that practice was such to make it a rarity—virtually unknown in everyday life. Central to the fury of condemnation was the fact that homosexual practice ran directly against the Puritan ideal of masculinity. Any signs of "effeminacy" among males were unacceptable.

The chapter included in this section by Robert Oaks reaches a rather different assessment. He suggests that homosexual episodes in Colonial New England were significantly greater in frequency than what Thompson would allow. The former argues also that homosexuality, while considered reprehensible, did obtain in fact some level of toleration within the Puritan community. "Sodomy" was a capital offense and yet only one execution for that crime actually took place. More commonly, when convictions occurred severe punishment was simply "remanded." A complementary observation by Oaks is that legal sanction against or punishment of lesbian activity was almost nonexistent. For this author what is equally interesting is the significant disparity in stringent prosecution of bestiality cases over those of sodomy. Both were death penalty crimes linked together in Biblical and Puritan legal interpretation. The community seemed willing to bend over backward in application of legal caution in alleged episodes of sodomy. On the other hand there was much quicker and harsher judgment in cases of bestiality, despite the fact that incidents of the latter were likely less prevalent than those of the former. Oaks discusses the disparity in reaction, suggesting finally that "buggery" was the more heinous because in part of a popular belief that sexual intercourse could result in human impregnation of animals.

Historical documentation of sexual violence and cruelty has also been a neglected area. This is clearly true of rape, which was commonly defined in early America with minor variations as "carnal knowledge of a woman, forcibly and against her will." Sexual assault is not, however, a straightforward matter. For one thing, in the period under consideration, women were held to be dominated by sexual desire more than males, generally wanton, and largely unable to control their "lustful" insatiability. This fact tended to encourage a sense of male entitlement to women's bodies. In cases of alleged rape, proof of nonconsent was necessary on the part of the woman, or she risked punishment for the assault. For another, rape was conceptualized essentially as a violation of a male's property. The crime, if there was one, was against a father or husband rather than against the woman. Her immediate well-being was at least a secondary concern. Finally, it is noteworthy that the rape cases most likely to reach court were those in which the perpetrator was from a lower social class than the victim or was married. Whatever these beliefs, Barbara Lindemann's chapter in this section on rape in eighteenth-century Massachusetts suggests that conditions of that day kept the rate of such assaults quite low.

Conventional explanation for the frequency of rape in a society has been that it will change over time as a consequence of certain historical variables, e.g., strength of patriarchy, enforcement levels of repressive mores, relative proportions of root-less strangers (i.e., military troops around Boston), population growth, or economic fluctuations. This was not the case in eighteenth-century Massachusetts. The most striking finding of that period was that so few rape or attempted rape cases reached the courts. There is no way, of course, to know how many such acts actually occurred in the century, anymore than there is today. Unless one is willing, however, to allege that the level of cases reported officially bore no relationship to the real commitment of these crimes, the conclusion must be that the number of rapes or attempted rapes was much smaller in this eighteenth-century locale than today in proportion to population.

Strikingly, rape or attempted rape, at least as related to prosecutions, remained surprisingly low, even with conditions such as high-troop concentration, loosening of sexual-mores enforcement, and high presence of rootless poor or economic fluctuations. Lindemann might find this constancy less striking, however, had she considered Kai Erikson's thesis (noted earlier) regarding the social necessity of deviance. Her explanation, and clearly one seemingly might apply to other British colonies as well, was in deterrence factors that were deeply ingrained in eighteenth-century culture. For one thing, there was the existence of a strong sexual bias supportive of male prerogatives, which meant that some assaults recognized today as rape probably would not be so viewed by the victim at that time. Moreover, the fact that rape was a capital offense surely meant some reluctance to prosecute it as such. More significantly, however, there existed in the culture very strong moral prohibitions on all extramarital sexual contacts, such as to minimize the seriousness of criminal rape. Family and community structure effectively upheld sexual mores. Communities were small, residents knew each other, strangers were readily identified, and surveillance applied. Most women lived under the immediate protection of a male—husband, father, or master—thus lessening the opportunity for sexual assault. In brief, Ms. Lindemann argues with force that the culture discouraged rape and community structure minimized opportunity for occurrence.

In a general way, the conditions that deterred sexual assault as described above by Lindemann acted also to place limits on the growth of prostitution, at least in the seventeenth century. The climate of opinion stigmatized heavily the patronization of prostitutes. That practice was not considered endemic to society. The "fallen woman" was rather an individual's sin and personal moral failure. Eradication of prostitution as an institution was not only desirable but possible. Communities were relatively small. Purveyors of commercial sex were readily identifiable and effective social surveillance was easily attainable. Most women who migrated into "sinful" urban centers, the most active locales of prostitution, did so within the protections (or confines) of conventional marriage. Finally, and more related to the attraction of prostitution as a livelihood in an economic market of gender discrimination, scarcity of women meant that marriage was a generally available alternative to a brutalizing life on the streets. The greater presence of commercialized sex in the seaport cities in particular by the mid-eighteenth century was testimony to decline in effectiveness or traditional regulation of morality. Essentially for the first time in those cities, client location of prostitutes could be done with ease. Moreover, by the latter years of that century, the symbolic importance of prostitution became quite disproportionate to the actual reality of it on the streets of urban centers. Prostitution was all the more a threat to the social order by the end of the century because individual purity had become essential and central to the important matter of "Republican Virtue."

Scholarship on prostitution considered historically has in general approached the subject on moral or sociological grounds. Timothy Gilfoyle, in his chapter on commercial sex in New York City, 1790–1860, does so from the standpoint of evolutionary geography. That urban center was viewed as the sexual opprobriums of the nation. This final chapter in the section attempts to explain why specific physical and spatial patterns—the city's "moral geography"—changed and evolved in the period. The city passed through three distinct phases. The first was roughly 1790–1820 in which commercial sex was confined to three areas. In this time New York was primarily a seaport, and prostitution flourished near the waterfront. The second phase was 1820–1850 wherein prostitution was "suburbanized" and spread from the docks into most residential areas of the city. Finally, in the period after 1850, prostitution was "resegregated," becoming identified with specific geographics in the city. Gilfoyle examines in some detail causes behind this pattern, principally in phases one and two. In the former case one factor was rapid population growth in which the city was unprepared to cope with the social problems, including population created by that growth. Specially with regard to commercial sex, the influx produced a surplus of males, in particular a constant stream of transient and rootless men, who constituted a ready clientele. Gender discrimination in the "free market" encouraged impoverished working class women to enter prostitution. In phase two the residential configuration was redefined by industrialization. The middle class moved out of the downtown to areas peripheral to the city center and prostitution followed, mirroring the clients they served. This pattern was provided additional support because of lax law enforcement by police. Aside from unique approach Gilfoyle's piece is all the more valuable because most scholarship on prostitution in the nineteenth century was with the post–Civil War period.

2

Law and the Enforcement of Morals in Early America
David Flaherty

The Enforcement of Morality

In seeking to explore the experience of a society where law and morals were intimately intertwined, it is essential to examine the realities of everyday behavior. What was the fate of the attempt to enforce morals once the state assumed that responsibility? While one must exercise caution in rendering judgments about the general state of morality in the colonies, most scholars have been impressed with the formal evidence of sexual immorality in the court and church records. The prevalence of such immorality was a problem in colony after colony, normally in the form of fornication that resulted in childbirth. The prosecuted cases were only the most visible manifestations of illicit sexual activity. Most immoral acts escaped the attention of the law. While considerable further research can be carried out in this area, the general sense of the situation, if not its explanation, seems adequately established.

There is substantial historical discussion of the prevalence of sexual offenses in New England, perhaps because such information is so much at odds with the popular conception of the Puritan lifestyle. Practically every scholar who has studied this subject has commented on the existence of widespread sexual irregularities.[1] A random examination of county court records in any of the New England colonies would illustrate this situation. New England legal machinery prosecuted many breaches of the moral laws, but the violations remained numerous. Legislative repression of sexual misbehavior did not succeed, despite the continued experiments with types of laws and punishments. Perhaps the most startling evidence comes from the disciplinary records of the Congregational churches, where prosecutions for incontinence were routine. The author of the leading study of this subject simply concluded that "the suggestion that Puritanism was sexually ascetic . . . is not supported by the evidence."[2] By the eighteenth century the secular courts treated cases of fornication and bastardy with considerable leniency and often did not prosecute the men involved.

The situation with respect to the enforcement of morals was not very different in Pennsylvania. The Quakers' apparent goal was to stamp out breaches of the moral law by strict enforcement. By the beginning of the eighteenth century the court records were already full of cases of bastardy, fornication, and adultery.[3] Fornication was common in the select Society of Friends: it followed marriages that breached certain prohibitions in the order of most common offenses. Yet the vigorous prosecution of Quakers for fornication did not improve the situation. "During the colonial period fornication and illegitimate births increased while membership remained stable. By the disownments it produced, prosecution of fornication decimated the membership of Friends."[4]

In Virginia there were many complaints that the laws against immorality were not being enforced. General Assemblies, vestries, and county courts joined the lament at recurrent intervals. Sex offenders were among the most common criminal offenders before the county courts. Although adultery and fornication were punished only occasionally, "prosecutions for bastardy form the most important single group of cases which came before the county courts."[5] Far more women than men were prosecuted. Commissary Blair would not have initiated his ill-fated plan for the establishment of ecclesiastical courts in 1690 had the state of the enforcement of morals in Virginia been satisfactory.

In Maryland in the seventeenth century calls for the enforcement of the moral laws became a regular feature of the political landscape. In 1658 officials, alarmed at the number of unmarried servants who were becoming pregnant, instituted more severe punishment of bastardy.[6] The offense remained a common one in the county court records. The governor closed the 1696 session of the Maryland legislature by reminding his listeners "that the making of good lawes was altogether ineffectuall unless they were duly put into Execution. Therefore since most parte of the house were Magistrates in their Severall Countys he Straitly charged them to put in Execution all the good lawes against Sabbath-breaking, Prophane Cursing and Swearing, Adultery, and fornication, etc."[7] There is no evidence that this or any other colonial governor was ever very successful in such endeavors.

Despite their good intentions about upholding public morality, the colonists were duplicating English experience—immorality had been and continued to be a significant problem. Sexual offenses were exceedingly common in the English ecclesiastical courts prior to the Civil War.[8] Immorality had become such a problem in the early Stuart era that the Civil War Parliament passed an act making adultery and fornication secular offenses in 1650. Adultery became a capital offense, while fornication was punishable with three months' imprisonment. Yet even amidst the revolutionary fervor of the 1650's any initial rigor in the enforcement of this act was soon relaxed. As public opinion proved increasingly unsympathetic, it became difficult to obtain convictions, especially for adultery.[9] Cromwell himself failed in his efforts to stimulate the act's enforcement. It lapsed at the Restoration, when jurisdiction was restored to the ecclesiastical courts. By the early eighteenth century many of the English laws regulating morality, especially those against adultery, had fallen into desuetude.[10] Thereafter the English abandoned the legal regulation of adultery and fornication.

A series of considerations and experiences gradually weakened the initial inclination of the early colonists toward the enforcement of morals. This can be seen
most readily in the extent to which colonial officials turned away from their original
goals. The initial shock of a Governor Bradford at the kinds of cases that appeared
in the courts soon gave way to a much less surprised attitude on the part of colonial
magistrates. Recurring moral offenses reinforced their respect for Satan and their
conviction of the depravity of man in ways they had not expected in the New
World. Their attempts to use law as an instrument of social control were too am-
bitious.

Yet most colonial authorities did not consider their enactments on moral matters
to be mere ideals for the edification of the weak. In many ways they never gave
up the enforcement of morals as a lost cause. Prosecutions for fornication continued
into the late eighteenth century in one form or another. The authorities did not
abandon the search for better laws that might actually improve public behavior or
at least reduce the economic burden. As Arthur Scott noted in studying moral
offenses in Virginia, "the great number of laws and amendments which the Assembly found it necessary to pass bear eloquent testimony to the perplexities encountered in devising suitable penalties and an adequate machinery of law
enforcement." As early as 1658 Virginia sought to encourage the enforcement of
laws to suppress odious sins by declaring those convicted of adultery or fornication
incapable of being a witness or of holding any public office. This applied to "persons of what degree or qualitie soever." Later acts against vice did not repeat this
provision. A Virginia enactment in 1727 illustrates another problem in the enforcement of the moral law. It imposed fines on householders who did not report bastards
born in their homes to the authorities. Scott concluded that the gradual diminution
in prosecutions for such moral offenses as adultery and fornication "was more
probably due to an increasing indifference on the part of the public, or at least to
a growing hopelessness of dealing with such offenses by coercive measures, rather
than to an actual diminution in the frequency of these moral lapses."[11] Perhaps
there was a sense that to stop enforcing the laws on sexual morality completely
would be to countenance such misbehavior.

Some of the reluctance to enforce certain statutes and some of the effective limits
to the implementation of legislation concerning morals also helped to maintain a
livable situation for the inhabitants of the colonies. The Massachusetts magistrates
seem never to have carried out the explicit threat in the fornication law of 1665 to
disfranchise a freeman for fornication.[12] Persons convicted of capital sexual offenses such as adultery in early New England did not suffer capital punishment.
The early New England courts demonstrated appropriate leniency in fornication
cases that eventuated in a marriage. The growing leniency in punishments for fornication in all of the colonies as the seventeenth century progressed bore testimony
to the increasing tolerance for sexual deviance in the New World and the slackening
commitment to the strict enforcement of a moral code. The goals of the colonial
criminal law were not stated with the sophistication of a twentieth-century *Model
Penal Code*, but in practice some of the basic aims were similar. The maintenance
of law and order in the local setting and the prevention and punishment of acts

that hurt other persons were the primary goals of colonial magistrates. Sexual acts that were illegal and immoral but not harmful to anyone did not have a high priority among the tasks of most persons charged with law enforcement. This did not, however, prevent periodic enforcement to reassert the moral condemnation of the community.

One has a sense of an increasing official tolerance of private immoralities, if only on the ground that little could be done about them anyway. Legislatures did not create a law enforcement apparatus that could effectively prosecute private immoral conduct. In 1731 the Monthly Meeting of Philadelphia Quakers in voicing its long-standing suspicions that one of the brethren was engaging in fornication, lamented that since "such secret works are often difficult to prove, nothing more could be done for a long time, but frequent admonitions."[13] In practice private illicit behavior was almost untouchable by the available means of enforcement. As a magistrate in the town of Boston in 1714, Samuel Sewall asked a crowd drinking in a tavern on a Saturday evening after the Sabbath had begun to leave such public premises, but he did not intervene when someone invited the group to move to the privacy of his house.[14] The concept of the home as a castle provided privacy for individuals. In practice the authorities followed a policy of noninterference in the personal and private affairs of others that were not publicly recognized as seriously harmful or that required extensive surveillance for prosecution. Public offenses that challenged the honor and reputation of the society demanded prosecution, but undetected behavior that avoided scandal in the community was felt to be less pressing.

Another motive that operated in the selective enforcement of moral legislation by colonial authorities was much less idealistic than concern for personal privacy. Especially in Virginia, where the trend was much in evidence, economic considerations came significantly into play in prosecutions for sexual offenses. Moral offenses had a low rating among the priorities of concern of the Virginia gentry except when their interests were at stake. This accounts for the frequency of bastardy prosecutions alone without an accompanying presentment for fornication or adultery. In any colony a bastard child represented a significant drain on the parish poor fund unless the authorities discovered a source of financial support. This was particularly true in cases of pregnant servants in Virginia. Their terms were extended to the benefit of the master, and efforts were made to apprehend the responsible male. Out of 490 York County criminal cases studied by Scott, 73 involved servant women having illegitimate children, 8 of men for fornication with servants, 9 adultery cases, and only 35 cases of fornication.[15] Virginia did not prosecute the reputed father of a bastard, if he tendered security to a churchwarden. In addition, the law stated that "a Bastard of a Person able to keep it, and not likely to be chargeable to the Parish, is not within the Statute of 18 Eliz. cap. 3."[16] Scott concluded that in Virginia "the relentlessness of the prosecutions for bastardy indicates that it was the birth of the child rather than the breach of the moral code involved which was the real offense in the eyes of the ruling classes."[17]

Such an economic motive also figured prominently in cases in other colonies, since the need to find support for the illegitimate child was always a major consideration. Massachusetts introduced a bastardy law in 1672 to relieve the economic burden of a town where bastards were born of poverty-stricken persons. In future a man accused by the female during labor would be held legally responsible for the support of the child, however much he himself might deny paternity, unless he had excellent proof. Although laws against fornication were already in existence, this was the only punishment to which the male was liable under this statute. Gentlemen normally received more lenient treatment at the hands of the law.[18] Although South Carolina did not enact statutes forbidding fornication and adultery, it did formulate an act against bastardy in 1703. The sequence of motives in the preamble was revealing: "Whereas great Charges ariseth upon many Places in this Province by Reason of Bastardy, besides the great Dishonour to Almighty God, and the evil Encouragement of lewd life. . . ."[19] The punishments inflicted were purely of an economic nature.

The association of law and the regulation of morals in the hands of the state in America considerably weakened the entire relationship. The abolition of ecclesiastical courts had broader consequences than anyone had anticipated as the state took over from the church almost complete control of the enactment and enforcement of statutes. An English cleric, who had been living in Virginia, commented that as a consequence of the absence of an ecclesiastical court there, "Vice, Prophaneness, and Immorality are not suppressed as much as might be: The People hate the very name of the Bishop's Court."[20] His suggestion that an ecclesiastical court might perform better struck close to an important point. The state lacked the essential long-term moral commitment to the enforcement of the sexual code that the church possessed. The gradual process of secularization of society that began in America in the latter half of the seventeenth century made the infusion of the state with moral fervor less and less likely. The secular aims of government took permanent precedence over more noble but less relevant ones.

Christopher Hill has made the related point that the abolition of church courts in England represented an intellectual and moral revolution. He identified three basic consequences flowing from this act: the absence of an alternative source of discipline, a reliance on individual conscience, and the increasing distinction between sins and crimes. Perhaps most important, the justices of the peace did "not appoint themselves residuary legatees of the church courts."[21] If abolition dealt a mortal blow to the enforcement of the sexual code in England, and represented an important step in the separation of law and the enforcement of morality, the implications of American inaction in this sphere were similar. In some colonies, where a movement such as Puritanism provided temporary impetus to the enforcement of morals, it took longer than a generation of New World experience for the serious weakness of the existing mechanisms for the enforcement of morals to become apparent.

As this process of secularization continued, the civil authorities almost abandoned responsibility for the upholding of sexual morals to the various churches. This occurred without an accompanying grant of secular power in the form of a separate court system that would permit churches to implement their real desires. Secular authorities had enough problems without trying to uphold the moral law for its own sake. Perhaps this was the implication of Richard Henry Lee's statement to Madison in 1784 that "the experience of all times shows Religion to be the guardian of morals."[22] Such developments encouraged the selective colonial churches, such as those of the Puritans and Quakers, to turn inward even more and focus on disciplining their own adherents rather than the general population. Their existing frustration in trying to control the sexual activities of current church members made such a response predictable. The Quakers made matters worse by speedily disowning individuals who were disciplinary problems in the sexual realm, unlike the Puritans who labored for the reform of offenders.

Popular attitudes made a substantial contribution to the failure of the attempt to associate law and morals in the interests of high moral standards in society. The tolerance of moderate immorality, the lack of popular zeal for the enforcement of morals, and the opportunities for immorality in a rural environment constituted elements of this picture. The twentieth century has forgotten that the colonists were pre-Victorian in their attitudes to sexual matters. They did not attempt to hide the reality of sexual urges or of nature. The actualities of houses of prostitution and sexual lapses were much in their traditional and current experiences.[23] An agricultural society that was close to nature and marked by serious violence in many forms did not view the offense of premarital sexual involvement or illicit activity generally with much alarm. Americans seem to have been informally tolerant of women who gave birth out of wedlock.[24] Glimpses into standards of personal behavior suggested a generally relaxed atmosphere, especially by the eighteenth century. In 1698 a leading resident of Virginia explained to an English friend why he had never had the gout, in terms that made clear his behavior was considerably above average among his peers: "I never courted unlawfull pleasures with women, avoided hard drinking as much as lay in my power, and always avoided feasting and consequently the surfeits occasioned thereby."[25] There are similar implications to the disclaimer entered by John Adams in his autobiography, after discussing his intensive preoccupation with young women before his marriage: "My Children may be assured that no illegitimate Brother or Sister exists or ever existed. . . . I presume I am indebted for this blessing to my Education. My Parents held every Species of Libertinage in such Contempt and horror. . . . My natural temperament was always overawed by my Principles and Sense of decorum. . . . I have seen enough of the Effects of a different practice."[26] Adams did not mention the deterrent effect of existing laws.

Contrary to the practice of such virtuous men, there are innumerable examples of notable individuals who engaged in illicit sexual activities. Benjamin Franklin was also afflicted by "that hard-to-be-governed passion of youth," but allowed it to lead him into sexual adventures in both Philadelphia and London. He sired an illegitimate son who in turn imitated his father.[27] The heroic sexual exploits of William Byrd II (1674–1744) of Virginia are much better known than those of any other colonist because of his explicit shorthand record. His Virginia diary from 1709 to 1712 records his illicit inclinations and attempted seductions.[28] In London after the death of his wife, Byrd kept a succession of mistresses and cavorted with streetwalkers.[29] As a judge of the General Court of Virginia, the supreme judicial unit in the colony after 1708, Byrd was unlikely to begin a movement for moral reform. Colonial ministers who became personally involved in misbehavior were in a somewhat similar situation. Like Franklin, Byrd had recurring pangs of guilt about such illicit activities. No colonist considered such actions a positive good, but, as Louis Wright has suggested, the moral code of the first gentlemen of Virginia included ready forgiveness for sins of the flesh, so long as one was not gross, did not seduce the innocent, and provided for one's illegitimate offspring.[30]

The presence of the well-known madam, Alice Thomas, in seventeenth-century Boston makes clear that Puritan New England was not immune to the pleasures of the flesh.[31] In 1712 and 1713 Cotton Mather sought a "list" of all whorehouses in Boston and a "catalogue" of men who patronized them: "I am informed of several Houses in this Town, where there are young Women of a very debauched character . . . ; unto whom there is a very great Resort of young men." His resolutions to extinguish the mischief through his Societies for the Suppression of Disorders do not seem to have matured.[32] A British officer visiting Newport at a later date made a comment about his encounter with a local prostitute that was most revealing of local attitudes: "She keeps a house of pleasure and has done so for a good many years past in a more decent and reputable manner than common, and is Spoke of by every body in Town in a favourable manner for one of her Profession. . . . This place must have arrived to a tollerable degree of modern luxury when houses of that kind were publickly allowed of, and the Manners of the People by no means rigid when subjects of that sort become family conversation."[33] Such episodes lend credibility to the comment of a historian of Western morals on American moral attitudes: "As far as externals go, it is clear that the twentieth century permits much the nineteenth century forbade. Whether we have got back to eighteenth-century standards is a nice point for critical discussion."[34]

A penal law that seeks to repress behavior which the community does not generally regard as a serious offense "will neither be accepted nor respected."[35] To a limited extent such a situation developed in the American colonies with respect to the fornication laws. Many colonists were not deeply disturbed or surprised when someone infringed on the moral code in sexual matters, especially if the offense was fornication or bastardy. Prosecutions for such offenses were so common that they could not long remain shocking to the average citizen. Many residents viewed the usual offender against the moral code with a mixture of tolerance, amusement, and titillation. Such episodes temporarily fueled the local fires of gossip. Although the majority of the population formally discountenanced immorality, the general moral climate, the prevalence of gaming and drinking, for example, created a situation where a person could not do much more than discourage sexual vices officially and in his family. In 1698 the young minister of a rural Massachusetts town blamed the "prevailing, growing evil" of fornication on parents who allowed their children and servants to roam at night and on common inducements: "Such are, over costly, light garish attire, filthy communications, idleness, intemperance, by which the body is inflamed, and modesty banished."[36]

The total situation in the colonies was of a type to discourage the successful association of law and morality. Incidents of illicit behavior occurred, especially among younger persons and the lower classes, including servants and slaves. Custom permitted courting couples to bundle in some regions. Some colonists blamed the arrival of various European immigrant groups in the eighteenth century for an increase in vice and immorality. The levels of adherence to asceticism of these groups of newcomers surely differed. In actual fact the flow of British immigrants was a more constant source of moral standards and patterns of behavior somewhat at odds with the expectations of the founders of the colonies. Many colonists themselves held liberal views with respect to some of life's pleasures. Sexual immorality in moderate doses was not the great offense to the residents of colonial New England that it became for some of their descendants.[37]

A zeal for successful implementation of moral legislation was not pervasive in colonial society. The colonists recognized moral standards, just as they were not startled by deviations from the norm. They expected known breaches of the moral order to be punished, as in the inevitable situation of a woman who had a child out of wedlock, or soon after her wedding day. But the colonists were not attuned to involving themselves in the search for moral offenders. The process of informing never attracted popular support. Virginia hardly encouraged the practice by making the informer pay the court costs, if the verdict was for the defendant.[38] In small communities few private individuals actively concerned themselves in the prosecution of offenses against morality. This was a major source of frustration to a New England minister like Solomon Stoddard, despite his excellent grasp of the sociological reasons for this situation.[39]

The failure of secular and clerical leaders to stimulate a moral reform movement testified to the general reluctance of the ordinary person to involve himself in the enforcement of morality. Beginning in the 1690's and continuing into the nineteenth century at sporadic intervals, Englishmen witnessed a series of movements for the reformation of manners in the face of Restoration decadence.[40] The central goal of participants was the effective enforcement of the existing English moral laws, especially against sexual offenses, drunkenness, and cursing. They proposed changes in the statutes and law enforcement procedures to Parliament and organized themselves in small groups to support law enforcement. The objections that arose to this movement mirrored colonial problems with respect to the enforcement of morals. Critics objected to the effort to impose a moral code on the poor, the attempt to use informers, and the corruption and lack of zeal of magistrates themselves.[41]

This English movement had notably little reflection in America. Colonial authorities were aware that the moral laws were not well enforced and that many in the populace believed immorality to be on the increase. The colonists did lack one center such as London to epitomize the degree of degeneracy and spark the impetus to reform. Certain colonial governors, however, became advocates of enforcing morals in the 1690's, at least to the extent of issuing calls for enforcement. This was in specific response to the example of English private societies organized for this purpose. Perhaps Blair's attempt to establish an ecclesiastical court in Virginia was part of this reform phenomenon. In the early eighteenth century Cotton Mather publicly recommended the establishment of societies for the reformation of manners in local communities: "The Society may do considerable things toward the execution of wholesome laws, whereby vice is to be discouraged."[42] Mather referred to the English models and indicated that such societies already existed in Boston. Yet despite this endorsement, societies for the reformation of manners did not make much headway in early eighteenth-century America. Boston's several societies remained small and had died out by 1715.[43]

The frequent opportunities for sexual irregularities helped weaken the impulse to moral reform. The presence of unmarried white servants and black slaves in small communities provided a regular source of, and outlet for, sexual immorality. Indentured servants who were not free to marry accounted for the bulk of the incontinence cases that appeared in the Virginia courts. An overwhelming percentage of these white immigrants to the southern colonies were males, while in New England the percentage of male immigrants was about sixty percent. The economic motive at work in the prosecution of servants should not be discounted, since their terms of service were extended for such offenses. Masters not infrequently seduced their female servants. While the evidence for the explicit use of slaves as sexual objects by the white population is not prominent in the existing records, the possibilities are fairly evident.[44] Slaves were in a permanently debased condition and lacked substantial exposure to the Christian moral code. Whites of any class enjoyed some degree of authority over the slaves by reason of their own color. Younger males found some black females ready prey for their earliest sexual adventures. The practice of allowing younger slaves to walk about naked, the sexual attractiveness of some slave women to the white male, and the relatively defenseless position of female slaves contributed to this situation. In Charleston whites openly kept slaves as mistresses. The statutory responses of some legislatures suggested that interracial sexual activity was common by the eighteenth century. The authorities threatened drastic punishments as a terror tactic to discourage such relationships. In 1715 Maryland decided that any free white man or woman who had a child by a Negro should be reduced to servitude for a seven-year period. White servants had their term extended by seven years. Free Negroes involved in such episodes with whites also were subject to servitude for a seven-year period. Pennsylvania adopted the latter provision in 1726.[45] It is doubtful that such harsh measures were actually implemented.

Virginia passed its first statute against interracial sexual activity in 1662. The "christian" simply paid double the usual fine for fornication under such circumstances. In 1691 the colony imposed a substantial fine or a five-year period of servitude on a free white woman that had a child by a Negro. A white female servant was sold for five years after her current term expired. There were no special provisions against a white man fathering a child on a Negro. The Assembly repealed this act in 1696. A subsequent enactment in 1705 repeated the initial provisions of the 1691 statute. A white female servant was now given the same option of a fine or servitude that a free white woman had previously enjoyed. The Assembly renewed this act as late as 1753.[46]

The presence of slaves and servants was only one aspect of what may be termed the ready opportunities for immorality that existed. In all the colonies courtship was the major preoccupation of the younger elements in the population.[47] In his autobiography John Adams recollected "something which makes an Article of great importance in the Life of every Man. I was of an amorous disposition and very early from ten or eleven Years of Age, was very fond of the Society of females. I had my favorites among the young Women and spent many of my Evenings in their Company and this disposition . . . engaged me too much till I was married."[48] Persons seeking privacy for whatever purpose found it an easy matter to wander off into the fields and woods. In the warmer months young persons gathered for various kinds of outdoor activities. The adventures of young Nicholas Cresswell furnish some sense of what was possible. He attended a reaping frolic on the banks of the Potomac in 1774: "This is a Harvest Feast. The people are very merry. Dancing without either Shoes or Stockings and the Girls without stays." In 1776 in Loudoun County, Virginia, he attended "a very mad frolic this evening. Set the house on fire three times and broke Mr. Drean's leg . . . got drunk and committed a number of foolish actions." In December he participated in a series of debauched evenings with various friends around Leesburg, Virginia.[49] A courting couple on a Virginia plantation found it possible to spend intimate nights together.[50]

The lack of popular enthusiasm for participation in the enforcement of morals infected those officially charged with this task. Governors, reformers, and clerical leaders frequently blamed responsible officials for their unwillingness to enforce the laws. Since legislators were often also justices of the peace in their home community, such accusations evidenced their own guilty feelings. But lack of zeal extended to grand jurors, petty jurors, churchwardens, constables, and deputy sheriffs as well. They exercised a potential veto power over the extent to which morals were to be enforced in any locality. In the eighteenth century this veto reached heights of absurdity when an individual agreed to pay child support in a bastardy case, but a jury refused to convict him of fornication.

Indifference, inefficiency, fear, corruption, the burden of office, and an unwillingness to prosecute friends contributed to the laxity of law enforcement in the area of personal morals.[51] There was no professional force operating in this area. Agents of the law were satisfied if they were able to maintain elementary law and order in an unruly society. The routineness of incontinence cases and the routinized response of the courts in punishing them did not encourage any colonial official to unusual zeal in the prosecution of offenses that did not come readily to his attention. Even ministers of religion were loathe to outdistance their flock in the zealous enforcement of morals. Ministers in the predominant churches of New England and Virginia, for example, were employees of their congregations. Well-informed commentators in Virginia around 1700 remarked on a minister's usual subservience to vestries that frequently entered into annual agreements for his services: "he must have a special Care how he preach'd against the Vices that any great Man of the Vestry was guilty of; for if he did, he might expect a Faction would be made in the Vestry, to be against renewing the Agreement with him for another year."[52]

The Virginia experience with churchwardens well illustrated this situation. The two wardens in each parish were selected from among the upper class members of the vestry. It was their responsibility to enforce the moral order in the parish. Yet in Virginia in 1724, for example, "the average parish of small geographical extent might be about twenty miles long with a scattered population of seven to eight hundred white persons in a hundred and fifty families."[53] At that time there was an average of fewer than two parishes per county and close to thirty counties in the colony. More than a dozen of these parishes did not have a minister, although the situation was often much worse in the seventeenth century. In terms of total population the average parish in Virginia in the 1720's had well over two thousand persons, while the average county had just under five thousand. Although these figures cannot describe varying local conditions adequately, they do provide some sense of the burden of office shouldered by the perhaps four churchwardens in a county. In addition, the negligence of churchwardens in the matter of morals had been a common problem in England.[54] The Virginia churchwardens did not have the threat or prospect of a Bishop's visitation to encourage activism, nor the assistance of a corps of apparitors to generate information upon which to base presentments. Members of a Virginia vestry were either too dignified or too preoccupied to pry into the private affairs of others. After charging churchwardens in 1643 with the burden of reporting fornicators, the Assembly three years later had already found it necessary to provide for the fining of churchwardens who neglected these duties.[55] The assignment of the churchwardens' duties to the youngest and newest members of the vestry testified to the unpopularity of the office. Such new recruits were unlikely to upset settled patterns of lax enforcement. In England the moralistic Root and Branch Petition to Parliament in 1640 had complained about "the imposing of oaths of various and trivial articles yearly upon churchwardens and sidesmen, which they cannot take without perjury, unless they fall at jars continually with their ministers and neighbours, and wholly neglect their own callings."[56] The American Puritans could not have been more demanding of churchwardens or their equivalent in terms of active surveillance of their fellow citizens. The Virginia legislature added further to the burden of office by setting higher standards for convictions of individuals who were not servants or slaves. Churchwardens were reminded that in such instances of fornication or adultery "Conviction must be by Confession, or Oath of Two, or more, credible Witnesses."[57]

The most striking evidence of the failure of colonial authorities in the enforcement of morals occurred in seventeenth-century Massachusetts. It was fitting in the face of previous failures that the Puritans should have made one last effort to support the moral law by instituting the new office of tythingman in the mid-1670's. Each neighborhood in each town was to appoint a tythingman to oversee the morals of ten neighboring families. The tythingman was to be the universal, all-purpose censor of morals and to remedy all previous deficiencies in law enforcement. The system did not fail immediately; in fact it began auspiciously with the magistrates of some county courts openly welcoming this needed assistance. In some instances presentments for offenses against the moral law dramatically increased for a short

period of time. But basically the original system died a gradual death in response
to its unpopularity, in particular the unwillingness of neighbors to undertake such
a burdensome and potentially quarrelsome task.[58] By the early eighteenth century
at the latest the office of tythingman was either a dead letter or had been turned
into an informing system for liquor offenses. If the Puritans could not enforce the
rigors of the moral law successfully, no other group of colonists could.

The thrust of this essay has been to demonstrate the relative failure in terms of
original expectations of laws concerning the enforcement of morals in a setting
where law and morals were consciously intertwined. The upholding and enforcement of morality by extra-legal means was by contrast relatively successful. The
failure of laws and law enforcement did not result in promiscuity or a particularly
low level of morality in the colonies. Alternative methods of social control existed
and have always prevailed in Western society to make up for deficiencies in official
legal processes. While this study cannot explore the extralegal modes of social
control in great detail, several can at least be mentioned. Particularly in the realm
of sexual morals, communities developed a self-generating form of control over
the behavior of the populace. Small population units living in relative intimacy and
collective isolation from other villages induced conformity of behavior in the majority and discouraged conscious imitation of deviant behavior. The force of public
opinion, the prevailing concept of conventional behavior, the threat of becoming a
subject of gossip, the difficulties of shielding from neighbors such unconventional
conditions as pregnancy out of wedlock, and continued acceptance of the sinfulness
of immorality, all served to uphold the moral law much more effectively than
secular laws and law enforcement. Libertinism was not widespread in the colonies,
especially in comparison with London and its environs in the eighteenth century.
Whatever their status as pre-Victorians, most colonists had a sense of modesty and
even prudery in moral matters that helped maintain standards of behavior. Virginity
remained the ideal for unmarried women. Most colonists avoided illicit sexual
activity not because it was illegal but because it was sinful.[59]

Notes

1. See G. E. Howard, *A History of Matrimonial Institutions* (Chicago, 1904), II, 185; James Truslow
Adams, *Provincial Society, 1690–1763* (New York, 1927), p. 159; Arthur W. Calhoun, *A Social History
of the American Family* (New York, 1917–1919), I, 132; George E. Woodbine, "The Suffolk County
Court, 1671–1680," in David H. Flaherty, ed., *Essays in the History of Early American Law* (Chapel
Hill, 1969), p. 203; Edmund S. Morgan, "Puritans and Sex," *New England Quarterly,* 15 (1942), 595–
596; Emil Oberholzer, Jr., *Delinquent Saints: Disciplinary Action in the Early Congregational Churches
of Massachusetts* (New York, 1956), p. 128; Edwin Powers, *Crime and Punishment in Early Massachusetts, 1620–1692: A Documentary History* (Boston, 1966), pp. 404–416; John Demos, *A Little Commonwealth: Family Life in Plymouth Colony* (New York, 1970), p. 152; Geoffrey May, *Social Control
of Sex Expression* (New York, 1931), pp. 244–246; Henry Bamford Parkes presents the only dissenting
view from the above position in "Morals and Law Enforcement," *New England Quarterly,* 5 (1932),
441. The majority conclusion is supported by research on the subject of sexual mores in early America
that I have in progress.
2. Oberholzer, *Delinquent Saints,* p. III, and in general Chapter 5.

3. Herbert K. Fitzroy, "The Punishment of Crime in Provincial Pennsylvania," *Pennsylvania Magazine of History and Biography*, 60 (1936), pp. 262, 259. On the prevalence of prosecutions for fornication and adultery in colonial New Jersey, see Harry B. and Grace M. Weiss, *An Introduction to Crime and Punishment in Colonial New Jersey* (Trenton, 1960), pp. 82–88.

4. Jack D. Marietta, "Ecclesiastical Discipline in the Society of Friends, 1682–1776," (unpub. Ph.D. diss., Stanford University, 1968), p. 59 and in general pp. 49–60. The author did find that prosecutions for adultery were rare in the records of Quaker discipline.

5. Arthur P. Scott, *Criminal Law in Colonial Virginia* (Chicago, 1930), pp. 280–281.

6. Raphael Semmes, *Crime and Punishment in Early Maryland* (Baltimore, 1938), p. 188, and in general on the prevalence of adultery, fornication, and bastardy, Chapter 8.

7. *Archives of Maryland*, ed. W. H. Browne et al. (Baltimore, 1883–), XIX, 497.

8. See Geoffrey May, "Experiments in the Legal Control of Sex Expression," *Yale Law Journal*, 39 (1929), p. 227n; Sumner C. Powell, *Puritan Village: The Formation of a New England Town* (Middletown, Conn., 1963), p. 69; Carol Bridenbaugh, *Vexed and Troubled Englishmen, 1590–1642* (New York, 1968), pp. 40–41, 361–374.

9. See May, "Experiments in the Legal Control of Sex Expression," pp. 240–244 on this whole subject; also May, *Social Control of Sex Expression*, pp. 194–199.

10. Leon Radzinowicz, *A History of English Criminal Law and its Administration from 1750* (London, 1948–), II, 3–4.

11. Scott, *Criminal Law*, pp. 254–255, 291–292; William W. Hening, comp., *The Statutes-at-Large, Being a Collection of All the Laws of Virginia, 1619–1792* (13 vols., 1819–1823; facsimile reprint ed., Charlottesville, 1969), I, 433 (1658), IV, 213 (1727).

12. William H. Whitmore, ed., *The Colonial Laws of Massachusetts, reprinted from the editon of 1660 . . .* (Boston, 1889), p. 231; Whitmore, ed., *The Colonial Laws of Massachusetts, reprinted from the edition of 1672 . . .* (Boston, 1887), pp. 54–55.

13. Quoted in Marietta, "Ecclesiastical Discipline," p. 49.

14. *The Diary of Samuel Sewall* (Massachusetts Historical Society, *Collections*. ser. 5, V–VII [Boston, 1878–1882]), II, 419–420.

15. Scott, *Criminal Law*, p. 281.

16. This statute in 1576 punished both the mother and reputed father of a bastard. George Webb, *The Office and Authority of a Justice of Peace* (Williamsburg, 1736), pp. 44–45.

17. Scott, *Criminal Law*, p. 280. See in particular the major act against bastardy in 1769, in Hening, *Statutes-at-Large of Virginia*, VIII, 374.

18. Whitmore, *Laws of Massachusetts, 1672*, p. 55; for the similar situation in England, see Bridenbaugh, *Vexed and Troubled Englishmen*, p. 370. For the lack of impartiality in the remission of fines and infliction of whipping, see Jules Zanger, "Crime and Punishment in Early Massachusetts," *William and Mary Quarterly*, 3d ser., 22 (1965), 476–477.

19. Nicholas Trott, ed., *The Laws of the Province of South Carolina* (Charleston, S.C., 1736), p. 96.

20. Quoted in George M. Brydon, *Virginia's Mother Church* (Richmond, 1947), I, 404.

21. Christopher Hill, *Society and Puritanism in Pre-Revolutionary England* (2d ed., New York, 1967), p. 343.

22. Quoted by Chester J. Antreau, "Natural Rights and the Founding Fathers—the Virginians," *Washington and Lee Law Review*, 17 (1960), 61. Lee's letter concerned a bill to require support in Virginia for an established church.

23. Writing about England in this same time period, Keith Thomas has pointed out "the tradition of promiscuity" among the lower classes and the widespread practice of prostitution. Keith W. Thomas, "The Double Standard," *Journal of the History of Ideas*, 20 (1959), pp. 206, 198. For evidence of prostitution in the colonies, see Carl Bridenbaugh, *Cities in the Wilderness: The First Century of Urban Life in America, 1625–1742* (New York, 1938), pp. 72–73, 226–227, 388–389; also *Cities in Revolt: Urban Life in America, 1743–1776* (New York, 1955), pp. 121–122, 316–319.

24. Marquis de Chastellux, *Travels in North America in the Years 1780, 1781, and 1782*, ed. Howard C. Rice, Jr. (Chapel Hill, N.C., 1963), I, 120, 228, 288, 358.

25. William Fitzhugh to Henry Hartwell, July 21, 1698, in *William Fitzhugh and his Chesapeake*

World, 1676–1701: The Fitzhugh Letters and Other Documents, ed. Richard Beale Davis (Charlottes-ville, 1963), p. 366.

26. *Diary and Autobiography of John Adams,* ed. L. H. Butterfield et al. (Cambridge, 1961), III, 261.

27. Carl Van Doren, *Benjamin Franklin* (New York, 1938), pp. 91, 290.

28. *The Secret Diary of William Byrd of Westover, 1709–1712,* ed. L. B. Wright and Marion Tinling (Richmond, Va., 1941), pp. 101, 169, 337, 425.

29. In a letter late in his life to Judge Benjamin Lynde of Massachusetts, Byrd reminded his old friend of their activities with ladies of pleasure during student days at the Middle Temple in the 1690's. [Byrd,] *The London Diary (1717–1721) and Other Writings,* ed. L. B. Wright and M. Tinling (New York, 1958), p. 9 and passim.

30. L. B. Wright, *The First Gentlemen of Virginia* (San Marino, Calif., 1940), p. 9.

31. The widow Thomas' exploits can be followed in the records of the Suffolk County Court. Samuel E. Morison, ed., *Records of the Suffolk County Court, 1671–1680 . . .* (Colonial Society of Massachu-setts, *Publications,* XXIX–XXX [Boston, 1933]).

32. *Diary of Cotton Mather,* ed. Worthington C. Ford (Massachusetts Historical Society, *Collections,* 7th ser., VII–VIII [Boston, 1911–1912]), II, 160, 235, 229, 283.

33. Diary of Lt. John Peebles, Dec. 31, 1776, microfilm, Library of Congress, quoted in *William and Mary Quarterly,* 3d ser., 26 (1969), 441.

34. Crane Brinton, *A History of Western Morals* (New York, 1959), pp. 384–385.

35. American Law Institute, *Model Penal Code. Tentative Draft No. 4* (Philadelphia, 1955), p. 233.

36. John Williams, *Warnings to the Unclean* (Boston, 1699), pp. 22, 19–20, 8. Williams (1664–1729) was a Harvard graduate and the minister of Deerfield.

37. See H. B. Parkes, "New England in the 1730's," *New England Quarterly,* 3 (1930), 408.

38. Webb, *Justice of Peace,* p. 189.

39. See Solomon Stoddard, *The Way for a People* (Boston, 1703), p. 21.

40. See Radzinowicz, *English Criminal Law,* II, 2–8; also Dudley W. R. Bahlmann, *The Moral Revolution of 1688* (New Haven, Conn., 1957), pp. 1–66.

41. Radzinowicz, *English Criminal Law,* II, 14–18.

42. Cotton Mather, *Bonifacius. An Essay upon the Good* (1710), ed. David Levin (Cambridge, 1966), pp. 133 and 132–137; also Mather, *Methods and Motives for Societies to Suppress Disorders* (Boston, 1703).

43. See *Diary of Cotton Mather* for scattered references.

44. Suggestive evidence for Virginia appears in the following: *Baroness von Riedesel and the Amer-ican Revolution: Journal and Correspondence of a Tour of Duty, 1776–1783,* ed. Marvin L. Brown, Jr., and Marta Huth (Chapel Hill, N.C., 1965), p. 86 (1779); *The Journal of John Woolman,* ed. Janet Whitney (Chicago, 1950), p. 52 (1757); John Davis, *Travels of Four Years and a Half in the United States of America During 1798, 1799, 1800, 1801 and 1802,* ed. A. J. Morrison (New York, 1909), pp. 400, 413–424; *The Journal of Nicholas Cresswell, 1774–1777* (New York, 1924), pp. 164–165; *Journal and Letters of Philip Vickers Fithian, 1773–1774: A Plantation Tutor of the Old Dominion,* ed. Hunter D. Farish. (New York, 1957), pp. 86, 185–188. See also Lorenzo J. Green, *The Negro in Colonial New England* (New York, 1942), pp. 204–210. The best treatment of interracial sexual activity is in Winthrop D. Jordan, *White Over Black: American Attitudes Toward the Negro, 1550–1812* (Chapel Hill, N.C., 1968), pp. 136–178.

45. Thomas Bacon, ed., *Laws of Maryland at Large, 1637–1763* (Annapolis, Md., 1765), 1715, chap. xliv, sects. 26–28; James T. Mitchel and Henry Flanders, eds., *The Statutes at Large of Pennsylvania from 1682 to 1801* (Harrisburg, Pa., 1896–1915), IV, 63.

46. Hening, *Statutes-at-Large of Virginia,* II, 170 (1662), III, 87 (1691), 138 (1696), 452–453 (1705), V, 360–361 (1753).

47. For Virginia, see *Quebec to Carolina in 1785–1786. Being the Travel Diary and Observations of Robert Hunter, Jr., a Young Merchant of London,* eds. Louis B. Wright and Marion Tinling (San Marino, Calif., 1943), p. 231; and *Journal of Philip V. Fithian,* pp. 105, 130, 134, 211.

48. Adams, *Diary,* III, 260–261.

49. *Journal of Cresswell,* pp. 26, 169–170, 175–176. Cresswell was a young Englishman in his early twenties who provided other evidence of being fairly religious.

50. The young couple was employed as a housekeeper and overseer near Fredericksburg. *The Journal of John Harrower: An Indentured Servant in the Colony of Virginia, 1773–1776,* ed. E. M. Riley (New York, 1963), pp. 137, 142–144.

51. For a similar situation in eighteenth-century England, see Radzinowicz, *English Criminal Law,* II, pp. 270–284; see the general discussion in David H. Flaherty, *Privacy in Colonial New England* (University Press of Virginia, Charlottesville, 1971), chap. vii.

52. Henry Hartwell, James Blain, and Edward Chilton, *The Present State of Virginia and the College,* ed. Hunter D. Farish (Williamsburg, 1940), pp. 66–67. For a similar comment on the Congregational ministry in New England, see Cotton Mather, *A Faithful Monitor* (Boston, 1704), p. 38.

53. Brydon, *Virginia's Mother Church, I,* 379, also 363–364, 375.

54. See Ronald A. Marchant, *The Church Under the Law: Justice, Administration and Discipline in the Diocese of York, 1560–1640* (Cambridge, Eng., 1969), pp. 32–33, 180, 181–184.

55. Hening, *Statutes-at-Large of Virginia, I,* 240 (1643), 310 (1646).

56. Samuel R. Gardiner, ed., *The Constitutional Documents of the Puritan Revolution, 1625–1660* (3rd ed. rev., Oxford, 1958), p. 143. See a discussion of similar criticisms of the oath required of the Massachusetts tythingmen in Mather, *A Faithful Monitor,* pp. 52–53.

57. Webb, *Justice of Peace,* p. 78. The usual moral offenses such as drunkenness or swearing only required one witness.

58. See Flaherty, *Privacy in Colonial New England,* chap. vii.

59. See the warnings of divine wrath conveyed in Samuel Danforth, *The Cry of Sodom Enquired Into* (Cambridge, 1674), and Williams, *Warnings to the Unclean.*

3

"Things Fearful to Name": Sodomy and Buggery in Seventeenth-Century New England

Robert F. Oaks

In recent years, historians have begun to study the long neglected story of human sexuality. The previous neglect of a subject that affects virtually every individual stemmed both from a reluctance to discuss such a sensitive topic and from the difficulties involved in research. Several demographic studies of 17th-century New England recently have begun to probe such questions as the incidence of adultery, divorce, and pre-marital sex, but as yet there is very little information on variant sexual activity such as homosexuality and bestiality.[1]

Research into these areas is more difficult because one of the major sources for the historian of heterosexual activity—birth records—is obviously absent. The most important source for variant sexual activity in colonial New England is court records. This evidence should be used cautiously since it provides information only about people caught in specific acts. One could argue that court records for this period no more reflect the true nature of homosexuality and bestiality in Puritan society than the records of the New York Police Department do of homosexuality in late 20th-century New York City. Nevertheless, these records do show that this type of activity existed in colonial New England and also suggest that some of the few speculations that historians have made are inaccurate. It is not true, for instance, as Edmund Morgan claimed many years ago, that "Sodomy [was] usually punished with death."[2] Nor do the records of Plymouth substantiate Geoffrey May's claim that "between one-fifth and one-fourth [of all sex offenses] were for various homosexual practices."[3] On the other hand, these records do reveal Puritan attitudes toward variant sexual activity and suggest that even extreme attempts to suppress it could not eliminate it.[4]

There was some confusion over terminology in describing variant sex crimes in colonial America. The two terms used most often—buggery and sodomy—sometimes meant different things to different people. Usually, the Puritan colonies used the term sodomy to refer to homosexuality and buggery to refer to bestiality. But occasionally, buggery also meant homosexuality, sodomy referred to bestiality, and, on one occasion, Massachusetts authorities tried without much success to stretch the definition of sodomy to apply to heterosexual child molestation.[5]

Both crimes were capital offenses in all the New England colonies. Homosexuality had been capital in England since the days of Henry VIII, but the Puritan colonies, where laws regulating moral behavior were often severe, patterned their laws not on the English statutes, but on the Old Testament. The one exception was Rhode Island, where the law drew on the New Testament.[6] Plymouth, the first colony specifically to make sodomy and buggery punishable by death (1636), included these crimes with other capital offenses, such as murder, rape, treason, witchcraft, and arson.[7] The law only applied to men, however. Lesbianism usually did not come under the definition of sodomy. John Cotton wanted to include lesbianism as a capital crime in a proposed legal code he drew up for Massachusetts in 1636, but his code was not accepted. Only in New Haven after 1655, when the colony did accept Cotton's code, was female homosexuality a capital crime, and even that exception ended when Connecticut incorporated the colony ten years later.[8]

Yet despite the harsh penalties for sodomy and buggery, Puritan leaders often refused to apply them, especially for homosexual activity. As with other types of crimes, the courts often employed the concept of remission of sentences for many sex crimes. Remission may have resulted from an enlightened attempt to move away from the traditional concept of punishment for retribution, it may have reflected economic realities in an area where labor was scarce, or it may have stemmed from a reluctance to apply capital punishment to crimes feared to be rather common. It is significant that Puritan authorities, despite the penalties on the books, apparently regarded homosexuality—though not bestiality—as not much worse than many "ordinary" sex crimes. Adultery, for example, was also a capital offense, but the death penalty was rarely inflicted in New England for that crime either.[9] This reluctance to punish illicit sexual activity of all types grew stronger in the latter decades of the 17th century.

The first recorded incident of homosexuality in New England occurred in 1629, when the ship *Talbot* arrived in Massachusetts. During the voyage, "5 beastly Sodomiticall boyes . . . confessed their wickedness not to be named." Unwilling to deal with anything so distasteful, Massachusetts authorities sent the boys back to England, arguing that since the crime occurred on the high seas, the Bay Colony had no jurisdiction.[10]

The colony of Plymouth seemed to have more homosexuality than other areas of New England, though this may simply indicate a greater willingness to prosecute such crimes, or, perhaps, less opportunity for privacy. There may have been problems with homosexuality in Plymouth as early as the mid-1620s. The well-known story of Thomas Morton of Merrymount could have homosexual overtones. William Bradford's description of the "great licentiousness" of Morton and his men hints that such activity may have taken place:

And after they had got some goods into their hands, and got much by trading with the Indians, they spent it as vainly in quaffing and drinking, both wine and strong waters in great excess. . . . They set up a maypole, drinking and dancing about it many days together, inviting the Indian women for their consorts, dancing and frisking together like so many fairies, or furies, rather; and worse practices. As if they had anew revived and celebrated the feasts of the Roman goddess Flora, or the beastly practices of the mad Bacchanalians.[11]

Morton does not specify their "worse practices," but it is not unreasonable to assume that some of those Englishmen voluntarily living in isolation from all women except a few Indians would have practiced homosexuality. For some, it may have been situational, stemming from limited opportunities for heterosexual activity; but for others, homosexuality may have been the preference, as it undoubtedly was for English pirates in the West Indies later in the century.[12]

Several years later, in 1636, Plymouth held the first trial for homosexuality in New England. John Alexander and Thomas Roberts were "found guilty of lude behavior and uncleane carriage one [with] another, by often spendinge their seede one upon another." The evidence was conclusive, since the court had a witness and confessions from the accused. Furthermore, Alexander was "notoriously guilty that way," and had sought "to allure others thereunto." This was a clear-cut case, and, it would seem, an obvious time to apply the death penalty, adopted by the colony only a few months earlier. But instead, the court issued a more lenient sentence. Alexander was whipped, burned in the shoulder with a hot iron, and banished from the colony. Roberts, a servant, was whipped, returned to his master to serve out his time, and forbidden from ever owning land in the colony. Apparently there was some dispute over this last restriction, because the phrase "except hee manefest better desert" was inserted in the records, then crossed out.[13]

The leniency extended to the two men is perhaps surprising. Alexander's banishment suggests that the court was not worried about a labor shortage. Nor would a death sentence be out of line with penalties in other areas of English rule. In the mid-1620s, Virginia executed Richard Cornish for sodomy. Though there is some evidence that the charges may have been trumped up to rid the colony of a troublesome individual, the fact that sodomy was even chosen as an excuse for execution indicates that the 17th-century Englishman had few qualms about imposing death as punishment for that crime.[14] And in England, in 1631, the Earl of Castlehaven was found guilty and executed for crimes "so heinous and so horrible that a Christian man ought scarce to name them." Not only did Castlehaven abet the rape of his wife by one of his servants, but he also committed sodomy with several servants. This latter act brought the death sentence. Here, too, there was some remission when the Earl appealed directly to Charles I for mercy, but not nearly to the same degree granted by Plymouth to Alexander and Roberts. The King commuted the Earl's sentence from hanging to the more humane beheading, and then postponed the execution for a month to give Castlehaven "time for repentence."[15]

The Roberts and Alexander case also suggests that Plymouth officials prosecuted with some reluctance. They "often" engaged in such conduct, and Alexander was "notoriously guilty that way." If Alexander was so notorious, why had he not been punished before? Perhaps the magistrates were willing to overlook homosexuality unless it became too obvious, an attitude not unlike that of 20th-century America. It is even possible that the death penalty was an attempt to discourage widespread activity. The fact that it was not applied to such an obvious case only a few months after it went on the books suggests that it was meant only as a warning, and no one seriously thought of using it.

Another Plymouth sodomy case, in 1642, resulted in even more lenient treatment. The court found Edward Michell guilty of "lude and sodomiticall practices" with Edward Preston. Michell was also playing around with Lydia Hatch, and Preston attempted sodomy with one John Keene, but was turned down. To complicate matters ever further, Lydia was caught in bed with her brother Jonathan. The sentences imposed for these various activities are particularly interesting since homosexuality in this case received approximately the same punishment as illicit heterosexuality. Lydia Hatch was publicly whipped. Michell and Preston were each whipped twice, once in Plymouth and again in Barnstable. John Keene, because he resisted Preston's advances and reported the incident, was allowed to watch while Michell and Preston were whipped, though the record intriguingly states that "in some thing he was faulty" too. Jonathan Hatch, regarded as a vagrant, was whipped and then banished to Salem.[16] These penalties were not only extremely light, but were not much harsher than penalties imposed for the relatively common heterosexual crime of fornication.[17]

Lesbian activity was scarcely punished at all. There were no prescribed penalties on the books, which may explain why there is only one recorded case in New England. In 1649, Mary Hammon and Sarah Norman, both from Yarmouth, were indicted for "leude behavior each with other upon a bed." Mrs. Norman was also accused of "divers Lasivious speeches." Her sentence required that she make a public acknowledgement "of her unchast behavior" and included a warning that such conduct in the future would result in an unspecified harsher punishment. Inexplicably, Mary Hammon was "cleared with admonision." It is difficult to understand how one woman could be guilty and the other innocent, though it is possible that the court was more disturbed by Mrs. Norman's "lasivious speeches" than they were by her "leude behavior."[18]

There was undoubtedly much more homosexual activity than the court records indicate. By the early 1640s, Governor Bradford lamented the great number of sex crimes, not only heterosexual offenses, "But that which is even worse, even sodomy and buggery (things fearful to name) [which] have broke[n] forth in this land oftener than once." Bradford tried to explain what seemed to be a virtual crime wave. He suggested that the Devil was particularly active in those regions that attempted "to preserve holiness and purity." But he had nonreligious explanations as well. Because laws were so strict regarding sex crimes, they produced a lot of frustration "that it may be in this case as it is with waters when their streams are stopped or dammed up. When they get passage they flow with more violence." The dams of sexual wickedness obviously had broken in New England. On the other hand, Bradford suggested, perhaps contradicting himself, there was no more evil activity in Plymouth than elsewhere, "but they are here more discovered and seen and made public by due search, inquisition and due punishment."[19]

In addition to Bradford's suggestion that sex crimes were rampant, the court records hint at homosexual activity in addition to the three obvious cases described above. One of the earliest historians to study homosexuality in New England claimed that the Plymouth records "show that of the prosecutions for all sex offenses, between one-fifth and one-fourth were for various homosexual practices."[20]

This estimate is very exaggerated. While there are numerous references to "uncleanness" or "unclean practices," the majority of them do make it clear that these were definitely heterosexual. A somewhat hasty count of sexual offenses in Plymouth records produced the following results: there were 129 definite heterosexual offenses including fornication, "licivious going in company of young men," kissing a married woman, adultery, prostitution, and rape; there were 3 definite homosexual offenses; 2 definite buggery cases; one accusation each for sodomy and buggery; and only 15 unspecified cases that might have been either homosexual or heterosexual. Out of a total of 151 sex offenses, then, there were at the most 19 cases of homosexuality, and probably fewer than that. These figures, however, should not in any sense be interpreted as reflecting the percentage of homosexual activity in Plymouth. It was undoubtedly easier, even in such a close knit society, to escape detection for homosexual activity than for heterosexual activity. The most common crime, by far, was fornication, and it was usually detected when pregnancy resulted, a risk obviously absent for homosexuals.

Some of the possible homosexual cases in the Plymouth records do allow interesting speculation. Most suggestive is the case of Richard Berry and Teage Joanes. In 1649, Berry accused Joanes of sodomy, and both were ordered to attend the next court for trial. Berry also claimed that Joanes committed "unclean practisses" with Sarah Norman, the woman involved in the lesbian case. In the intervening six months between the accusation and the trial, however, Berry changed his mind and testified that he had lied, for which he was sentenced "to be whipte at the poste." If Berry's original intention had been merely to smear Joanes, it is difficult to understand why he would do it in such a way as to implicate himself. It is possible that the two men were lovers. Perhaps they had quarrelled, leading to the accusation, but later reconciled. Berry then decided to suffer the penalty for lying rather than have Joanes suffer the penalty for sodomy. Further evidence for this interpretation stems from a court order three years later when Joanes and Berry "and others with them" were required to "part theire uncivell liveing together." Ten years later, one Richard Beare of Marshfield, a "grossly scandalouse person . . . formerly convicted of filthy, obsceane practises," was disenfranchised. It is possible that this "Beare" is an alternate spelling of Richard Berry.[21] Berry did have a wife, by the way, a rather unsavory woman named Alice. She was accused of several crimes herself. Once she milked someone's cow, another time she stole a "neckcloth," and on another occasion some bacon and eggs.[22]

There are several other cases of "disorderly liveing" or "lude carriage" that suggest the possibility of homosexual activity, but the evidence is far from conclusive. In 1637, for instance, Abraham Pottle, Walter Deuell, Webb Adey, and Thomas Roberts, accused of "disorderly liveing," were required "to give an account how they live." Adey, in particular, got into trouble on several other occasions. He "profaned the Lord's Day" several times by working, for which he was whipped. By 1642, still practicing "his licentious and disorderly manner of liveing," Adey went to jail.[23]

In another case, one John Dunford, "for his slaunders, clamors, lude & evell carriage," was banished from Plymouth. The records are silent as to the exact nature of his "evell carriage," but the rather unusual and severe punishment, especially in light of John Alexander's banishment two years earlier, may suggest homosexual activity.[24] The same may be said of William Latham, fined 40s for entertaining John Phillips in his house, contrary to the court's order.[25] John Emerson was also fined for "entertaining other mens servants," though the sex of the servants is unmentioned.[26] Anthony Bessie was indicted for "liveing alone disorderly, and afterwards for takeing in an inmate [boarder] without order."[27] James Cole was acquitted of the charge of "entertaining townsmen in his house."[28] But Edward Holman was fined for entertaining another man's servant, John Wade, and for taking Wade to Duxbury in his boat.[29]

Other possible homosexual cases include Tristram Hull's, indicated for unspecified "unclean practises." The charge, however, did not keep Hull from being chosen constable of Yarmouth five years later.[30] There was also John Bumpas, whipped for "idle and lasivius behavior."[31] A final possible homosexual case involves Hester Rickard. Convicted of "laciviouse and unaturall practices" in 1661, she was ordered to sit in the stocks, wearing a paper on her hat describing her crime in capital letters. It is likely, however, that her "unnatural practice" was adultery (she was married). On the same day, Joseph Dunham was sentenced to sit in the stocks with a paper on his hat for "divers laciviouse carriages." Dunham was also fined 200 pounds. Though the records do not specifically connect the two, the timing suggests that their cases were related.[32]

The one execution for homosexuality in New England occurred in the colony of New Haven in 1646, when William Plaine of Guilford was convicted of "unclean practices." Though a married man, Plaine reportedly committed sodomy with two men in England before coming to America. Once in Guilford, "he corrupted a great part of the youth . . . by masturbations, which he had committed and provoked others to the like above a hundred times." To make matters worse, this "monster in human shape," as John Winthrop called him, expressed atheistic opinions. Plaine received the death penalty, though it was probably his corruption of youth and his "frustrating the ordinance of marriage" that weighed more heavily on the magistrate than the sodomy.[33]

Though the Puritans nearly always meant homosexuality when they used the term sodomy, one time when it was not used in that context is the exception that proves the rule, while shedding additional light on the practical legal setting for homosexuality itself. In 1641, Massachusetts authorities were horrified to learn that for the previous two years, three men had regularly molested two young girls, beginning when the elder was only seven.[34] The revelations produced outrage and calls for the death penalty, but no one knew exactly how to define the crime. Since the girls apparently consented to the treatment, could it be considered rape? Even if it were rape, at that time there was no specific law against it in Massachusetts, and "there was no express law in the word of God" for a sentence of death. So the authorities tried to stretch the definition of the capital crime of sodomy to fit this case. But this created several legal problems inherent in all accusations for sodomy. English precedent for sodomy and buggery convictions generally required proof of actual penetration. The accused men confessed to molestation, but denied penetration. The magistrates had only the girls' testimony to go on, leading to yet other legal restrictions that provided no man could be compelled to testify against himself, and that two witnesses were needed to any crime that resulted in a death sentence.[35]

In an attempt to solve these problems, the magistrates wrote for advice to other New England colonies, soliciting written opinions from ministers, the nearest equivalent to legal experts.[36] The majority of the respondents concluded that evidence of actual penetration was necessary for the crime to be sodomy. This made the other questions all the more important: could the accused be forced to testify against himself, and, if not, were two witnesses always necessary for a capital conviction? There was disagreement on the former question, though nearly everyone ruled out torture as a means of exacting a confession. As to the number of witnesses, the ministers generally held out for two, except where there was a confession by the accused or "concurrent and concluding circumstances."[37]

Because of the confusion, when the General Court met in May, 1642, they were divided on the sentence. Several magistrates did want the death penalty, but, after much dispute, they finally agreed on a lighter sentence only because the "sin was not capital by any express law of God." The attempt to define it as sodomy had simply not worked. So instead of death, the three were sentenced to severe whippings, confinement to Boston, and in the case of one of them, mutilation of his nostrils and imprisonment.[38]

This whole scandal and the difficulties involved in applying capital punishment are directly related to the whole question of homosexuality. The disagreement over the necessity for penetration, self-accusation, and the number of witnesses applied in those cases as well. A new statutory rape law did nothing to eliminate the legal difficulties in obtaining sodomy convictions. Perhaps the almost rigorous standards of evidence dissuaded authorities from trying to obtain the death penalty for ordinary sodomy cases, falling back instead on more lenient sentences which were possible when the evidence was not totally conclusive.

But if the Puritans were willing to bend over backwards to apply scrupulous legal guarantees to cases involving homosexuality and child molestation—making the imposition of the death penalty practically impossible—they were often willing to forgo these guarantees when prosecuting for buggery. Sodomy and buggery were usually linked together both in the Bible and in Puritan legal codes, but despite the connection between the two crimes, the penalties imposed in 17th-century New England were often quite different. There was little reluctance to impose the death penalty for buggery even though the legal problems were often identical with those inherent in sodomy. Before speculating as to why this discrepancy existed, it might be helpful to describe specific cases and the penalties imposed.

In the same year as the discovery of the mistreatment of the young girls, one William Hackett (or Hatchet) "was found in buggery with a cow, upon the Lord's day." A woman absent from church because of some illness, "espied him in the very act." When Hackett, a boy of about 18 or 20 years of age, came before the magistrates, he confessed to attempted buggery "and some entrance, but denied the completing of the fact." Many of the same problems came up in this case as in the child molestation case. There was only one witness, and the evidence of penetration was sketchy at best, since the boy denied completing the act. But eventually the court agreed "that his confession of some entrance was sufficient testimony with the woman," and the majority of the magistrates sentenced him to death. Governor Richard Bellingham, who still doubted some of the evidence, refused to pronounce the sentence, but Deputy Governor John Endecott had no such qualms and sentenced the boy to die. After the sentencing, the boy, described as "ignorant and blockish," finally confessed "completing this foul fact, and attempting the like before, with other wickedness." On the day of the execution, the cow was first slain in front of the boy, and then after a prayer by the Rev. Mr. John Wilson of the Boston Church, Hackett, "with a trembling body," was hanged.[39]

A few months later, New Haven executed George Spencer on even flimsier evidence. A sow, previously owned by a man for whom Spencer had worked as a servant, gave birth to a deformed fetus, "a prodigious monster." Unfortunately, some people saw a resemblance between the fetus and poor George Spencer. It seems that Spencer had "butt one eye for use, the other hath (as itt is called) a pearle in itt, is whitish & deformed," like that of the fetus. Furthermore, Spencer was notorious for "a prophane, lying, scoffing and lewd speritt."[40]

Spencer, when examined, first said that he did not think that he had committed buggery with the sow in question. Then he denied it outright, but he was sent to prison because of the "strong possibilities." Spencer continued to deny guilt in prison until visited by one of the magistrates, who reminded him that confessing sins would bring mercy. Spencer then confessed to the crime, though later he claimed he did so merely to please the magistrate. On another occasion, when several other magistrates visited him, Spencer again confessed to that crime as well as several others, such as lying, scoffing at the colony's laws, and profaning the Lord's Day ("calling itt the ladyes day"), though he denied other "acts of filthynes, [homosexual?] either with Indians or English." When brought to trial, Spencer denied all that he had formerly confessed, but the court was "abundantly satisfied in the evidence," even though there were no witnesses and Spencer refused to confess under oath. Despite these legal problems, Spencer, according to the law of Leviticus 20:15, was put to death.[41]

Perhaps the most famous New England buggery trial was that of Thomas Granger, a 16- or 17-year-old youth in Plymouth. In 1642, Granger was indicted for buggery "with a mare, a cow, two goats, five sheep, two calves and a turkey." Somebody saw Granger committing buggery with the mare. Unfortunately, Governor Bradford, who recorded the incident in his history of Plymouth, decided to "forbear particulars." Nevertheless, upon examination, Granger "confessed the fact with that beast at that time, [and] sundry times before and at several times with all the rest of the forenamed in his indictment." The court had some difficulty determining which sheep were involved, so they staged a lineup for Granger, where "he declared which they were they and which were not." The court then sentenced Granger to death. The animals were "killed before this face, according to the law, Leviticus xx.15; and then he himself was executed."[42]

With some relief, Bradford reported that both Granger and another man who "had made some sodomitical attempts upon another"—probably Edward Michell or Edward Preston—had learned these things in England. But the Governor warned that these cases showed "how one wicked person may infect many," and cautioned families to choose their servants wisely.[43]

A few months later, in Massachusetts, the Court of Assistants found Teagu Ocrimi guilty of "a foule, & divilish attempt to bugger a cow of Mr. Makepeaces." Fortunately for Ocrimi, his attempt did not succeed. The court ordered him "to be carried to the place of execution & there to stand with an halter about his necke, & to be severely whipped."[44]

And in the same colony in 1646, Robert Miller went to jail, after being accused of buggery. The witnesses disagreed, however, and when the weather turned cold, Miller was released on bond, and ordered to appear at the next court. There is no further mention of Miller, however, so perhaps the charges were dropped for insufficient evidence.[45]

Perhaps the most interesting buggery case occurred in New Haven in 1647. Again, it involved a sow who bore a deformed fetus and a man with the thoroughly improbable name of Thomas Hogg. The fetus "had a faire & white skinne & head, as Thomas Hogg is." Hogg, a servant for the woman who owned the sow, denied guilt. But the case grew stronger when the court learned that on more than one occasion Hogg had been guilty of indecent exposure: "he said his breeches were rent, when indead his sperit was rent." Hogg claimed that "his belly was broake . . . & he wore a steele trusse, & so it might happen his members might be seene," though Goodie Camp testified that she had given him a needle and thread "to mend his breeches." After imprisoning Hogg for the crimes of bestiality and exposure, the court decided to seek additional evidence. The governor and deputy governor accompanied Hogg to the barnyard and ordered him to fondle ("scratt") the sow in question. The official records tell us that "immedyatly there appeared a working of lust in the sow, insomuch that she powred out seede before them." The magistrates then ordered him to fondle another sow, "but that was not moved at all." If that was not evidence enough, "Lucretia, the governors neagar woeman," testified that she had seen Hogg "act filthiness with his hands by the fier side." Other witnesses testified that he had at various times stolen a dumpling and some cheese. The court decided to consider the buggery charge later on, but in the meantime, for his "filthynesse, lyeing & pilfering," Hogg was severely whipped and sent to prison "with a meane dyet & hard labour, that his lusts may not bee fedd." For some reason, the records do not indicate any further consideration of the bestiality charge. Apparently the charge was dropped, because Hogg was alive and out of jail the following year, when the court warned him for not showing up for watch.[46]

In 1662, another case in New Haven, by then incorporated into Connecticut, suggests the difficulties involved in detecting buggery. In that year, a 60-year-old man named Potter was executed for bestiality, even though "this Wretch, had been for now Twenty years, a member of the Church in that Place, and kept up among the Holy People of God there, a Reputation for Serious Christianity." This pillar of the community (or as Cotton Mather preferred, this "Pillar of Salt"), engaged in such practices on and off for 50 years, since age 10, with a wide variety of animals. The fact that he could do this without detection for half a century suggests that even in a close knit society some discreet individuals could indulge whatever sexual passions they had. Ten years before his execution, Potter's wife discovered him "Confounding himself with a *Bitch,*" but he managed to convince her to keep silent. But when his son "saw him hideously conversing with a *Sow,*" the story came to light. Apparently the shocked son reported his father. Before his execution, "A *Cow,* Two *Heifers,* Three *Sheep,* and Two *Sowes,* with all of which he had committed his Brutalness," were killed while Potter watched.[47]

These cases indicate that the Puritans were less hesitant to punish buggery with death than they were sodomy. Again, since they usually linked the two crimes, the differences in the severity of punishment is puzzling. It is possible that the Puritans suspected that homosexuality was so widespread that a strict application of the law would lead to very unpleasant consequences. Edmund Morgan suggests that this is the reason why the full penalties were generally not applied for heterosexual sex crimes.[48] Bestiality, on the other hand, may have been less common in the 17th century (as in the 20th century), and thus easier to control. Then again, one might speculate that the opposite was the case. In the mid-20th century, Kinsey researchers found that the incidence of bestiality was highest in farming communities— similar to 17th-century New England. Kinsey reported that 40 to 50% of all farm boys had some sort of animal contact. Perhaps, then, Puritan leaders suspected that bestiality was a much more widespread phenomenon than homosexuality and imposed harsher sentences in order to suppress the far more serious of the two crimes.[49]

There is another possibility. The harsh punishments for buggery may reflect a general 17th century revulsion with animal contacts. The cases mentioned above provide some clues for such an interpretation. The two pig fetus cases indicate that the Puritans believed it was possible for a man to impregnate an animal, an obvious impossibility in sodomy. This possibility may have made buggery even more heinous. The Puritans were not far removed from the middle ages, when reports of man-like creatures were common. Even more relevant were contemporary accounts written by Englishmen visiting Africa, where, they believed, there was a close connection, including sexual intercourse, between Africans and apes.[50] Even more than homosexuality, bestiality dehumanized man. The horror with which the 17th-century Englishman regarded buggery helped them to rationalize racism toward blacks. In New England, it explains why a son would report his own father to the authorities, and why even the man's wife apparently had considered it a few years earlier. The horror may also explain why New Englanders were willing to dispense with some of the rules of evidence to obtain the death penalty for buggery.

But attitudes toward buggery apparently began to soften as the century wore on. The subject still cropped up occasionally in the court records, but convictions declined. In 1666, William Honywell, jailed in Plymouth on suspicion of buggery, was released for insufficient evidence.[51] The same was true in Massachusetts in 1676 and 1677, when juries found insufficient evidence to convict Jack, a black servant, of buggery with a cow and John Lawrence of buggery with a mare.[52]

The last execution for buggery by the Massachusetts Court of Assistants was that of Benjamin Goad in 1673. This youth, accused of buggery with a mare "in the highway or field" in broad daylight, apparently confessed at first, but then denied it at his trial. The jury, confused by the legal technicalities, decided that if Goad's confession when first arrested plus the testimony of one witness were sufficient for conviction, then he was guilty. But if his denial under oath during the trial took precedence, then Goad was guilty only of attempted buggery. The magistrates then declared that Goad was indeed "Capitolly Guilty." The mare was "knockt on ye head," and then Goad was hanged.[53]

This case provides evidence of changing attitudes, since the execution created some controversy. An increasing tolerance for illicit sexual activity of all kinds in the latter decades of the 17th century apparently produced a corresponding decline in the willingness of many citizens to accept strict enforcement of the moral code.[54] The Rev. Samuel Danforth felt compelled to preach and publish a sermon defending Goad's execution. Danforth admitted that some people objected to, "making such a *Youth,* a childe of Religious Parents, and that in his tender years, such a Dreadful Example of Divine Vengeance." But while others pitied Goad's youth, Danforth pitied "the holy Law of God." Remember, Danforth told his flock, "Goad gave himself to Self-pollution, and other Sodomitical wickedness. He often attempted Buggery with several Beasts, before God left him to commit it . . . and he continued in the frequent practice thereof for several months.[55]

But the tide was running against those who held Danforth's views. In Plymouth in 1681, Thomas Saddeler was arraigned for buggery with a mare. Though he denied it, the jury found him guilty, but of the lesser charge "of vile, abominable, and presumptuous attempts to buggery with a mare." His punishment was rather severe, but it was not capital as it probably would have been earlier in the century. Saddeler was whipped, forced to sit on the gallows with a rope around his neck, branded in the forehead with the letter "P" (for pollution), and banished from the colony.[56]

Saddeler's is the last buggery case in any of the published records of New England. Just as prosecutions for sodomy ended 30 years earlier, buggery too disappeared from the records. There may be additional cases in the records of countless local courts and these sources must be searched before we will have a more accurate picture of variant sexual activity in colonial America, but for now it seems reasonable to conclude that sexual behavior, of whatever kind, gradually became more a matter of personal conscience and less a concern for the courts. It may be true, as Edmund Morgan suggested, that the "Puritans became inured to sexual offenses, because there were so many."[57] The decline of religious fervor toward the end of the century, the inability of earlier repression—actual or threatened— to stop illicit sex, and the increasing secularization of the state—resulting in less concern for enforcing moral law—combined to make prosecutions for variant sexual activity a thing of the past.[58] Not even the Puritans could prevent men and women from practicing many forms of sexual activity officially regarded as sinful. Perhaps nothing is more symbolic of the failure of the "citty upon a hill" than the history of variant sexual activity in 17th-century New England.

Notes

1. See particularly John Demos, *A Little Commonwealth: Family Life in Plymouth Colony* (New York, 1970): Demos, "Families in Colonial Bristol, Rhode Island," *William and Mary Quarterly,* 3d Ser., XXV (1969), 40–57; Philip J. Greven, Jr., *Four Generations: Population, Land, and Family in Colonial Andover, Massachusetts* (Ithaca and London, 1970); Kenneth A. Lockridge, *A New England Town: The First Hundred Years* (New York, 1970); Robert Higgs and H. Louis Stettler, III, "Colonial New England Demography: A Sampling Approach," *Wm and Mary Qtly.,* 3d Ser., XXVII (1970), 282–294.

2. Edmund S. Morgan, "The Puritans and Sex," *New England Quarterly,* XV (1942), 603.

3. Geoffrey May, *Social Control of Sex Expression* (New York, 1931), 247.

4. Two recent pioneering works on the history of homosexuality are Vern L. Bullough, *Sexual Variance in Society and History* (New York, 1976); and Johnathan Katz, *Gay American History: Lesbians and Gay Men in the U.S.A.* (New York, 1976).

5. Louis Crompton, "Homosexuals and the Death Penalty in Colonial America," *Journal of Homosexuality,* I (1976), 277–278; Katz, *Gay American History,* 24.

6. Crompton, "Homosexuals and the Death Penalty," 277–281; David H. Flaherty, "Law and the Enforcement of Morals in Early America," in Donald Fleming and Bernard Bailyn, eds., *Perspectives in American History,* V (1971): *Law in American History,* 213.

7. *Records of the Colony of New Plymouth in New England,* ed. Nathaniel B. Shurtleff and David Pulsifer (Boston, 1855–1861), XI, 12.

8. Katz, *Gay American History,* 20, 22: Crompton, "Homosexuals and the Death Penalty," 278–279.

9. For more on the concept of remission, see George L. Haskins, *Law and Authority in Early Massachusetts: A Study in Tradition and Design* (New York, 1960), 204–205; and Jules Zanger, "Crime and Punishment in Early Massachusetts," *Wm. and Mary Qtly.,* 3d Ser., XXII (1965), 473–474. For the death penalty and adultery, see Flaherty, "Law and Morals in Early America," 213–214.

10. *Records of the Governor and Company of the Massachusetts Bay in New England,* ed. Nathaniel B. Shurtleff (Boston, 1853–1854), I, 52, 54; "Francis Higginson's Journal," in Stuart Mitchell, ed., *The Founding of Massachusetts* (Boston, 1930), 71.

11. William Bradford, *Of Plymouth Plantation 1620–1647,* ed. Samuel Eliot Morison (New York, 1970), 204–206.

12. See B.R. Burg, "Pirate Communities in the Seventeenth Century: A Case Study of Homosexual Society," forthcoming in the *Journal of Homosexuality.* Professor Burg kindly provided me with a manuscript copy of his article.

13. *Records of Plymouth,* I, 64.

14. Crompton, "Homosexuals and the Death Penalty," 290–292; Katz, *Gay American History,* 16–19.

15. Caroline Bingham, "Seventeenth-Century Attitudes Toward Deviant Sex," *Journal of Interdisciplinary History,* I (1971), 447–472. Dutch New Netherland also executed two individuals for sodomy in 1646 and 1658. In 1646, the guilty party (a black man) was sentenced to be choked to death and then burned. In the second case, the man was tied in a sack and thrown into a river to drown; Katz, *Gay American History,* 22–23, 570n.

16. *Records of Plymouth,* II, 35–36.

17. See Demos, *A Little Commonwealth,* 157–158, 158n.

18. *Records of Plymouth,* II, 137, 163.

19. Bradford, *Of Plymouth Plantation,* 316–317.

20. May, *Social Control of Sex Expression,* 247.

21. *Records of Plymouth,* II, 146, 148; III, 37, 177.

22. Ibid., III, 28, 36, 75, 82.

23. Ibid., I, 68 to 92; II, 36, 42.

24. Ibid., I, 128.

25. Ibid., I, 87.

26. Ibid., I, 118.

27. Ibid.

28. Ibid., III, 17.

29. Ibid., III, 126.

30. Ibid., II, 36, 115.

31. Ibid., II, 170.

32. Ibid., III, 210.

33. John Winthrop, *The History of New England from 1630 to 1649,* ed. James Savage (Boston, 1853), II, 324; Katz, *Gay American History,* 22.

34. *Records of Massachusetts Bay,* II, 12–13; Winthrop, *History of New England,* II, 54–58.

35. Ibid.; Bullough, *Sexual Variance,* 437.

36. Winthrop, *History of New England,* II, 54–58; Bradford, *Of Plymouth Plantation,* Appendix X, 404–413.

37. Winthrop, *History of New England,* II, 54–58.

38. Ibid.; *Records of Massachusetts Bay,* II, 12–13. On the same day the court handed down these sentences, they adopted several laws to eliminate some, though not all, of the confusion. Developing the concept of statutory rape, the court decreed that any man having "carnall copulation" with any "woman child under ten years ould" would be put to death, regardless of whether or not the girl consented. Rape of a married or engaged woman also carried the death penalty. Rape of an unmarried woman over ten years old could be punished by death, but the judges were given the discretion of applying a lesser penalty. And finally, a man who committed "fornication with any single woman," with her consent, could be punished by forcing them to marry, a fine, corporal punishment or any or all of these at the discretion of the judge. *Records of Massachusetts Bay,* II, 21–22.

39. Winthrop, *History of New England,* II, 58–60; *Records of Massachusetts Bay,* I, 334.

40. *Records of the Colony and Plantation of New Haven, from 1638 to 1649,* ed. Charles J. Hoadly (Hartford, 1857), 62–69.

41. Ibid.; Winthrop, *History of New England,* II, 73.

42. Bradford, *Of Plymouth Plantation,* 320–321; *Records of Plymouth,* II, 44.

43. Bradford, *Of Plymouth Plantation,* 321.

44. *Records of the Court of Assistants of the Colony of Massachusetts Bay, 1630–1692* (Boston, 1901–1928), II, 121.

45. *Records of Massachusetts,* I, 79.

46. *Records of New Haven,* 295–296.

47. [Cotton Mather], *Pillars of Salt: An History of Some Criminals Executed in this Land, for Capital Crimes, With Some of their Dying Speches* . . . (Boston, 1699), 63–66. Evans No. 877.

48. Morgan, "The Puritans and Sex," 602.

49. See Alfred C. Kinsey, Wardell B. Pomeroy, and Clyde E. Martin, *Sexual Behavior in the Human Male* (Philadelphia and London, 1948), 623, 669–670.

50. Winthrop D. Jordan, *White Over Black: American Attitudes Toward the Negro, 1550–1812* (Chapel Hill, 1968), 28–32.

51. *Records of Plymouth,* IV, 116.

52. *Records of the Court of Assistants,* I, 74, 87.

53. Ibid., I, 10–11.

54. Flaherty, "Law and Morals in Early America," 229.

55. [Samuel Danforth], *The Cry of Sodom Enquired Into; Upon Occasion of the Arraignment and Condemnation of Benjamin Goad, For His Prodigious Villany* . . . (Cambridge, 1674), Evans No. 186.

56. *Records of Plymouth,* VI, 74–75.

57. Morgan, "The Puritans and Sex," 595.

58. Flaherty, "Law and Morals in Early America," 228–233, 244.

4

"To Ravish and Carnally Know": Rape in Eighteenth-Century Massachusetts

Barbara S. Lindemann

In the last ten years, the number of reported rapes in the United States has risen faster than the official count of any other major crime committed, and this fact, together with feminist efforts to publicize rape as the quintessential expression of male dominance over women, has generated much debate. Most of the common explanations for rape assume that its frequency will change along with changes in certain historical conditions: the strength of patriarchy, the presence of conquering armies, the repressive nature of sexual mores, the degree of prosperity, and the existence of active feminist movements. Yet almost no historical studies of rape exist.[1] This article contributes to what little is known about rape in the past by examining rape prosecutions in eighteenth-century Massachusetts.

By the 1690s, Massachusetts law clearly defined rape in accordance with common law. In the language of all formal indictments of the eighteenth century, "to ravish" a woman was to gain "carnal knowledge of any woman above the age of ten years against her will and of a woman child under the age of 10 years with or against her will."[2] Conviction for this offense brought a mandatory death sentence and, like other equally serious crimes, required the testimony of two witnesses, or of one witness plus evidence that would be equivalent to the testimony of a second witness. When the number of capital offenses was reduced from fourteen to seven in 1780, rape remained on the list, along with willful murder, sodomy, burglary, robbery, arson, and treason against the commonwealth.[3]

Capital cases in eighteenth-century Massachusetts were tried in the Superior Court of Judicature, established in 1692–93 and renamed the Supreme Judicial Court in 1780.[4] Between 1698 and 1797, the court heard forty-three indictments of rape or attempted rape, representing a total of forty separate cases involving thirty-six defendants.[5] The sparse existing records reveal prosecution patterns, the age and/or marital status of most of the victims, the social standing of the accused, and details of a few of the cases—but not enough information to determine under what circumstances rape most commonly occurred. Yet an examination of the court's disposition of rape cases does disclose significant patterns.

Official court summaries record in set language the basic facts of each case: the defendant's name, occupation, and place of residence; the crime of which he or she is accused; and, in rape cases, the victim's name, marital status, place of residence, and occasionally age, if a teenager or younger. Many of the documents presented to the court in the course of trials have been preserved along with the official court records in the Suffolk County Courthouse. Unfortunately, the files are far from complete, and only a few remain for the recorded rape cases.

For most cases, all we know of the crime comes from a summary similar to the following, which describes what will be termed "attempted rape" throughout this article:

Samuel Corey, of Lancaster, in the County of Worcester, Labourer, on the thirteenth day of January, in the Year of our Lord seventeen hundred and eighty four, at Lancaster aforesaid, with force and arms [a standard legal phrase that does not necessarily mean he was armed], in and upon Hannah Grant, wife of Thomas Grant of said Lancaster, Yeoman, in the peace of God and of this Commonwealth, then and there being, did make an assault, and her the said Hannah, then and there did beat, throw down, and evilly intreat, with an intent her the said Hannah, against her Will, then and there feloniously to Ravish and carnally know, and other wrongs to the said Hannah then and there did, to the great damage of said Hannah, and against the peace of the Commonwealth aforesaid.[6]

Depositions by witnesses could be found for only five cases, all from the first half of the century. In four of the five, most of the testimony addressed the question of the victim's consent, an issue that arises inevitably from the common law definition of rape as carnal knowledge of a woman against her will. The victim of the case in which consent was not in question was the wife of cordwainer who accused an American Indian laborer of attempted rape in 1723. The defense witnesses emphasized the good character of the defendant and questioned the victim's credibility. The victim, Rebeccah Tripp, charged that her next-door neighbor Simon Tripp tried to rape her while she slept. Alone in the house with her children, her husband being out of town, she first attempted to stop the attacker by screaming; when this failed, she struck him and cried out again, rousing her son George. The intruder then crawled out of the house into the lean-to, where she recognized him.

Four witnesses testified to Simon Tripp's good character, and another commented shortly, "This Indian called Simon Tripp is of as good cretit [*sic*] as she that talk of him." One witness asserted that Rebeccah had originally given different versions of the story: first she claimed that the devil had been in the house, then a thief, and finally someone she did not know. The jury found Simon Tripp guilty and sentenced him to twenty-five stripes, a £50 bond, costs of prosecution, and two sureties of £25 each for good behavior until the next court term.[7]

Although Rebeccah Tripp was suspected of falsely accusing her neighbor, the jury credited her testimony, perhaps because, as Lyle Koehler asserts, "rape was considered so serious that a woman would not lie about it."[8] Or perhaps jury members were reluctant to give the word of an Indian laborer more credit than the testimony of an Englishwoman. The penalty was the most severe handed down to those found guilty of attempted rape in the first half of the century.

Convictions were not obtained in the two most fully documented cases in which the victim was apparently not able to convince the jury of her resistance to a sexual encounter with a man of equal social standing. In Lynn on May 10, 1698, in the presence of four witnesses and her husband, Mary Hawthorne accused Moses Hudson, a husbandman, of abusing and forcibly lying with her ten days earlier. Hudson did not deny her charges, but assured her husband that he would not repeat the offense if the rape went unreported. When the case reached the Superior Court a year and a half later, six witnesses gave depositions. Ebenezer Hawthorne, present when the victim accused Hudson, testified that the defendant admitted that God had forsaken him, the devil had possessed him, and that "he did commit that sin with her." Another quoted Mary's statement to the accused on May 10: " 'You know I used all the arguments that could be and told you what an awful sin it was and how can you be so wicked and you said no body sees us and I told you God saw us which is greater than all.' Moses did not answer or deny what she charged him with in my hearing. On the same day Hudson told me that Mary Hawthorne came to him and asked him for tobacco and to smoke it and he did smoke with her. And I asked if it was so for I hope God had given you more grace than to do so and he said God had left him and afterwards I heard the said Hawthorne's wife tell him why did you say I smoked with you and he said if I did say so I said that which was not true."[9] Still another witness asserted that he had gone to Mary Hawthorne after hearing of the assault and ravishing and asked her if she had done her duty as a woman ought in such distress. She answered yes, she could see John Potter at work in his father's field, and she called out but could not make him or anyone else hear.

The grand jury members may have refused to indict because some doubt was left in their minds. Perhaps the victim had invited the rape by requesting to smoke with the defendant. Perhaps she had not done all she could to resist the rape. Or the jury may have been convinced by the testimony of one witness who suggested that penetration had never occurred. Lediah Favinton reported that sometime in early May, when asked what ailed her, Mary Hawthorne replied that Moses Hudson had laid violent hands on her, forced her, and "raged of his lust; and with my struggling and striving and jostling hindered him that he did not satisfy his lust in my Boddy; but I thinks he thought he had."[10] Without penetration, the offense could not legally be classified as rape.

Consent was clearly a central issue in a Middlesex County case tried thirty years later in which the grand jury found enough evidence to bring an indictment, but the jury refused to convict. Abigail Kindall charged that on an evening when her husband was out of town, Thomas Procter entered her house "without leave" and waited until her four small children were asleep. He then went to her bed and pulled off the bedclothes, "which wonderfully surprised and put her in great fear." She argued with him and called out to wake the children, all to no avail. He "got upon her" and ravished her, and then told her he believed he had got her with child. Since it was commonly believed in this period that a woman could not conceive from a rape,[11] it is surprising that Kindall included this last detail in her deposition. Procter may have been telling her he had not forced her. She, pressed by the magistrate to tell all (and in fact forced to take an oath when she went to tell her story to the magistrate), may have wanted to prove that penetration had occurred.

Procter denied Kindall's charges but admitted that he could have been there that night, as he often passed by her house on his way home from work. His presence at the time of the alleged rape was verified by Kindall's seven-year-old son, who reported that Procter had entered the house without permission, asking Kindall if her husband was at home and if he would return that night. When she replied that she could not tell, Procter sat by the bed and smoked until the child fell asleep. John Doan, the final deponent whose account remains, testified that Kindall told him that Procter took a chair and sat down by the bed and "talked idly there as if he would have come to bed with her: but she said she did not believe it, but when he did come he did what he did do, so quick that she had no opportunity to resist him." Doan suggested that perhaps she had been distracted and mistaken about what Procter had done; she admitted this was possible. Was this then a flirtation that went beyond Abigail Kindall's intentions? Or was it a situation in which a man took advantage of his friend's wife in her husband's absence? Or was it an affair in which a wife later charged her lover with rape in order to protect herself against an accusation of adultery? It may have been all three. The jury entertained enough doubt that it declared Procter innocent of the charge.

Even in a case involving a five-year-old victim—one in which consent could not be a legal issue—the defendant accused of assault with intent to ravish tried to establish that the girl had been a willing partner. The charge against Emmanuel Lewis, a laborer of Boston, was that he did "assault, hurt, grieve and wound [her] . . . in the private parts so that her life was greatly despaired of." In his interrogation, recorded by the justice of the peace, Lewis asserted that on March 18, 1733, his employer of about eighteen months had left him alone with her young grandchild. "The child put its hand into his Breeches and asked the Examinant to lye with it. . . . he took the child into his lap and laid its face upon his breast, denied that he attempted to have carnal knowledge of it that the Child did not cry when he lay with it, but asked him to do it more—That the Child pulled up its Coats— put his yard to its Body but nothing further." The jury found him guilty, and the judges sentenced him to be tied to a cart and carried to the gallows, where he would be whipped twenty stripes.[12]

A conviction was probably obtained fairly easily in a fourth case from Plymouth, 1756, where the victim resisted and nine witnesses testified. A cooper was punished by twenty lashes and a month's imprisonment for pulling fifteen-year-old Mary Seller into his shop. She testified that he pinned her down and covered her head, tore off her petticoats and other clothes, and attempted to lie with her, but her shouts brought rescuers to her aid. The testimony of the other witnesses does not survive.[13]

Few as they are, these cases for which details remain are revealing. Patriarchal law defined rape narrowly. The rules of evidence were such that a conviction was

Table 1
Rape Prosecutions in Massachusetts, 1698–1797

	Rapes and Attempted Rapes*	Population†	Rate per 100,000 Population
1698–1704	1	55,941	1.78
1705–14	1	62,390	1.60
1715–24	1	91,008	1.09
1725–34	4	114,116	3.50
1735–44	2	151,613	1.31
1745–54	0	188,000	.00
1755–64	5	222,600	2.24
1765–74	8	266,565	3.00
1775–84	6	317,760	1.88
1785–97	12‡	378,787	3.16

Sources: Records of the Superior Court of Judicature and the Supreme Judicial Court, New Suffolk County Courthouse, Boston, 1698–1797; U.S. Bureau of the Census, *Historical Statistics of the United States, Colonial Times to 1970,* 2 vols. (Washington, D.C.: Government Printing Office, 1975), 1:29; 2:1168.

Note: Records include Maine to 1790.
*The distribution of cases per decade is about the same when counted for 1700–1709, 1710–19, etc.: 1698, 1; 1700–1709, 1; 1710–19, 0; 1720–29, 2; 1730–39, 4; 1740–49, 1; 1750–59, 3; 1760–69, 7; 1770–79, 5; 1780–89, 8; 1790–97, 8.
†Population figures are from mid-decade (1700, 1710, 1720, etc.).
‡Two assaults occurred in 1796, none in 1795 or 1797.

possible only when a victim could convince a male jury that the defendant was fully aware of her refusal and resistance. Any indication that the victim was willing to socialize alone with her attacker (by smoking with him, for example) or that she put up little resistance could be taken as consent, even if she believed the contrary. In the absence of visible and serious injuries, two witnesses had to testify to the crime; if the victim had been unable to rouse help, witnesses were unlikely. Mary Hawthorne had witnesses only to her alleged attacker's confession of guilt; a conviction was not obtained. Abigail Kindall accused a man who seemed to be a trusted friend. She was "surprised" and fearful. He denied he had raped her, and the jury apparently believed him. The rules of evidence were weighted for the defendant.[14]

The most striking finding from the eighteenth century is that so few cases reached the high court: only one per decade before 1729 out of a population that grew from 55,941 in 1700 to 114,116 in 1730 (see Table 1). Although the absolute number of rape prosecutions increased at the end of the century, it did not increase in proportion to the population. Thus the decade rate per 100,000 between 1725 and 1734 was 3.5, and the thirteen-year average between 1785 and 1797 was 3.16, the two highest rates in the century. The decade rate per 100,000 fluctuated between a low of no prosecutions in the decade 1745–54 to a high 3.5 in 1725–34.[15] With so few cases, it is difficult to attach much significance to these small fluctuations.

What is significant is the small number of rape prosecutions and the consistently low prosecution rate, with minor fluctuations, throughout the hundred-year period.

A look at recent rape rates demonstrates how low comparable rates were in eighteenth-century Massachusetts. Since 1960, the rate of rape prosecutions per 100,000 has almost quadrupled, rising from 3.75 in the year 1960, to 7.29 in 1970, to 13.45 in 1979. Since the recent increase has been so great, it is useful to compare the decade average for both the 1960s and the 1970s to the decade average found for the eighteenth century.[16] From 1960 to 1969, an average of 47.7 rape cases were prosecuted per 100,000 population; this rate more than doubled in the following decade, climbing to 100.2 for all the years 1970–79. In contrast, the highest average for any decade in eighteenth-century Massachusetts was 3.5 cases per 100,000 population. How much of this difference can be explained by a more efficient criminal justice system and how much by modern women's greater willingness to report rape?

There is no way to know how many rapes or attempted rapes actually occurred in the eighteenth century or how many occur today. Nor can we know what proportion of the cases reported to magistrates two hundred years ago ever came to trial. One eighteenth-century observer guessed that as much as 90 percent of crime went unreported in England in 1790; no doubt this percentage was even higher for acts of rape, a crime generally considered to be less frequently reported than other offenses.[17] Estimates of the current figure for unreported rape vary widely from 55 percent to 95 percent.[18] Thus if we say that 98 percent of rape went unreported in the eighteenth century and 50 percent of rape goes unreported today, we can attribute a maximum of 48 percent of the difference in prosecution rates to differences in reporting rates. This means that the 1960s rate is six times higher, and the 1970s rate fourteen times higher, than that in the eighteenth century.

Can the remaining difference be explained by the existence of a modern police force and a criminal justice system more effective in bringing miscreants to trial? An examination of the criminal justice system in eighteenth-century Massachusetts suggests that it was not six to fourteen times less effective than the current system.

A rape charge would come to the attention of the authorities in a variety of ways. Most likely a victim first brought her complaint to the local justice of the peace, a man of high social standing, who summoned witnesses and the accused, tried to extract a confession from the suspect through close questioning, heard testimony from witnesses, and then decided whether to hold the accused in jail or on bail for a hearing before the grand jury. A complaint could also be taken to or initiated by local grand jurymen, citizens who represented their town on the grand jury for one or two years and who were sworn to watch for breaches of the law and to bring presentments against offenders before this body, which met several times a year at the county courts. Victims thus had ready access to the justice system.[19]

Furthermore, the probability of apprehending the accused was likely greater than it is now. Today 53 percent of reported rapes are committed by strangers to the victim, and 30 percent by people with whom they are slightly acquainted. In eighteenth-century Massachusetts, communities were small enough that most inhabitants knew each other by name. Boston in 1790, for example, had reached a population of only 15,000. In inland towns, strangers quickly became known. Thus the chances of being raped by a stranger were not great, and the suspect was likely to be apprehended.[20]

It is harder to assess the likelihood that the local officials would bring an indictment to the Superior Court. Today many cases are dropped or settled by plea bargaining, either because the victim is unwilling to testify or because the district attorney decides that there is insufficient evidence to obtain a conviction. Strict rules of evidence govern a rape trial; jurors cannot be informed of a defendant's past arrests or convictions, and in most states the victim is questioned closely to determine not only her veracity but also her moral probity. Aware of such difficulties, a prosecutor often hesitates to bring charges unless the case against the accused is strong.

Eighteenth-century justices of the peace and grand jurymen weighed different questions but may have been equally cautious in bringing indictments. They would, in the first place, be acquainted already with those involved in the case—victim, witnesses, and accused alike—and therefore take into account their reputations and social standing. They would be more concerned with the truth of the charge than with the amount of evidence needed to ensure a jury conviction. Rules of evidence in trials were not strict. Confessions and hearsay evidence were freely admitted, the prosecution did not have to produce witnesses for cross-examination, and the accused could not refuse to answer questions that might incriminate him.[21] Conviction for a capital offense demanded at least two witnesses, but in practice judges interpreted this requirement loosely.[22] Lyle Koehler concluded from his examination of extensive seventeenth-century trial materials that the victim was generally believed, since the Puritans thought that the accused—but never the victim—was likely to lie about so serious an offense. The victim's word alone was enough to convict a man of attempted rape, and in lieu of testimony from a second witness, evidence from a jury of midwives that a virgin's hymen had been broken, or that the vaginal area was bruised or lacerated, was sufficient to convict the accused rapist. Furthermore, Koehler found few cases (8 of 79) in which the victim was accused of inviting the attack, and in those few, the rapist was found guilty and given a harsh punishment.[23] If the justice of the peace were convinced of the accused's guilt, he was therefore likely to send the case to the grand jury.

The capital nature of the crime did make local officials reluctant to press charges. This fact does not, however, account for the low prosecution rate in the eighteenth century, since the figures included both rape and attempted rape cases. Only twelve of the forty cases brought before the Superior Court charged rape, and three of these were reduced to an accusation of attempted rape; the remaining twenty-eight cases involved the lesser offense. It is likely that justices of the peace and grand juries brought indictments for attempted rape even when a forcible rape accusation had been brought before them; juries were far more apt to convict an accused of this lesser charge (see Table 2).

Unless one is willing to say that the level of prosecution bears no relation to the level of actual commission of the crime, the conclusion is inescapable that the number of rape prosecutions was so much smaller in eighteenth-century Massa-

Table 2
Disposal of Rape and Attempted Rape Indictments, 1698–1797

	Guilty	Not Guilty	No Presentment
Rape:			
1698–1764	2	2	1
1765–79	3	4*	
1780-97	—	—	—
Attempted rape:			
1698–1764	9	—	—
1765–79	5*	1	—
1780–97	10	6	—

Sources: Records of the Superior Court of Judicature and the Supreme Judicial Court, New Suffolk County Courthouse, Boston, 1698–1797.

*Includes three defendants first tried and acquitted of rape, and subsequently tried and convicted of attempted rape.

chusetts than it is today because many fewer rapes were committed in proportion to the population.[24]

The other striking aspect of these figures from the eighteenth century is that the rate of rape prosecutions remained surprisingly constant even though Massachusetts underwent significant demographic, economic, and social changes in this hundred-year period. Massachusetts grew in population seven-fold during this time, due to a healthy natural increase and migration from abroad. Boston, its major port city and center of New England's thriving overseas trade and shipbuilding industry, expanded from 6,000 residents in 1690 to 24,000 in 1800, becoming denser and more complex socially and occupationally.

The colony also was hard hit by the major European wars; periods of relative prosperity were punctuated by temporary war-induced booms ending in decades of depression and inflation. Five separate wars each gave a temporary boost to trade and agriculture, but left behind economic recession, currency inflation, and greater numbers of poor, including many widows. Yet these economic cycles had no effect on the rape prosecution rate. The numbers of the poor who needed public relief multiplied with each war and increased steadily throughout the century. However, the increase in the numbers of rootless poor had no impact on the rate of rape prosecutions.

Curiously, the presence of large numbers of British and American troops in and around Boston between 1768 and 1776 also did not affect the rate of rape prosecutions. In the years immediately before the American Revolution, Boston had one of the largest troop concentrations on the continent, and yet not a single rape case from that seaport town was brought before the courts in that period. One thousand British troops arrived in Boston in September of 1768 under the vigorous protest of the residents. Living among a population of 15,000, they camped on Boston Common and were housed in the Court House, Faneuil Hall, rented warehouses, manufactories, and other empty buildings. The soldiers were idle, bored, and lonely, and under harsh military discipline. The citizens among whom they lived were generally hostile, often taunting and hazing them. Any offense committed against civilians—assault, theft, or inciting slaves to attack masters—brought a soldier to trial in colonial courts. Petty theft, robbery, and prostitution increased in Boston. Bostonian propagandists reported alleged incidents of sexual assault and attempted rape against local women.[25] None of these cases reached the Superior Court of Judicature, however. Relations between troops and townspeople were so tense that half the troops were removed in 1769, and after the Boston Massacre of 1770 the rest were housed in Castle William in Boston harbor.[26]

As hostilities between Great Britain and its American colonies intensified, however, troop levels in Boston rose again; by December 1774, 4,000 soldiers filled this city of 16,000, encamped on the Boston Common among an ever more hostile citizenry. When the British withdrew from Boston in March 1776, they numbered 9,000 men and officers and almost 1,000 women and children.[27] Meanwhile, from spring 1775 until March 1776, American forces formed an arc around Boston stretching from Cambridge south to Dorchester. Their numbers fluctuated between a low of around 7,000 to a high of about 17,000. In March 1776 the American forces left for New York, marking the end of the military phase of the revolution in Massachusetts. Yet the rate of rape prosecutions was no different in this difficult period than in those preceding or following.[28]

Changes in the sexual behavior of unmarried couples also did not have any impact on the number of rape prosecutions. Premarital pregnancies, which reflect the rate of extramarital heterosexual activity, increased gradually throughout the century. Approximately 10 percent of firstborn children were conceived before marriage in the late seventeenth century; by the 1780s this figure rose to a high of 30 percent. Daniel Scott Smith and Michael Hindus think that premarital pregnancies increased during periods of social stress, when ''there was more ambiguity and uncertainty in the parent-child relationship, when the social supports of morality were weakened or not appropriate to the current realities of coming of age, and when there emerged a segment of the population outside the mainstream of the culture.''[29] Unable to provide their marriageable children with land, fathers were losing control over their offspring; no new system of social and sexual control had yet replaced the decaying communitarian and patriarchal system. Consequently, more and more people were engaging in sexual activity before marriage. Yet the rate of rape prosecutions neither declined nor increased.

Thus neither wars, troop movements, economic fluctuations, increases in the numbers of rootless poor, geographical expansion, population growth, nor changes in sexual mores affected rape rates in eighteenth-century Massachusetts. Although these rates did not change during the century, the pattern of prosecution did alter during two periods at the end of the century. Between 1765 and 1779, when a little over half of the century's rape cases were heard, juries, as in earlier decades, were somewhat more likely to bring in a not guilty than a guilty plea. However, in four of these seven rape cases, the grand jury brought in two indictments, and when the petit jury failed to convict three of the accused rapists, the defendant was brought to trial again and found guilty of attempted rape (see table 2). Strikingly, after 1779, the grand jury brought no charges of rape to court, the typical penalty for those convicted of attempted rape was increased to thirty lashes plus one or two of the other punishments listed above, and jurors demonstrated a much greater reluctance to convict those accused of attempted rape than had jurors in earlier decades.

Three times in the 1760s—in Suffolk, Worcester, and Bristol counties—the grand jury brought an indictment for rape, and the petit jury delivered a verdict of not guilty. The accused was then tried a second time on a charge of intended rape, found guilty, and given a quite heavy sentence (twenty to thirty lashes in a public place, a jail term, and an hour standing on the gallows with a rope looped around his neck and over the crosspiece). In the Boston case of 1765, the victim was described as a ten-year-old virgin and the defendant, a wigmaker. The defendant in the 1768 Worcester case was a tailor and his victim, the wife of a trader. During the same court term in Worcester a black servant was tried for rape and sentenced to death. The next year in Bristol a yeoman was acquitted of rape at the very end of the court session. The court did not meet again at Bristol until 1770, when this man was found guilty of the same deed on a reduced charge of attempted rape, filed the previous year by the grand jury that had unsuccessfully indicted him for the more serious offense.[30] In sum, of the four defendants tried for rape in the 1760s, three were found guilty of the lesser charge of attempted rape, and one was sentenced to death. Not only was there a clear recognition among the citizens who sat on grand juries in eastern counties of Massachusetts that juries were reluctant to convict in rape cases; there was also a determination that accused rapists should not go unpunished.[31]

These changes did not happen all at once. Another decade passed before efforts to get a rape conviction stopped entirely. Of the three laborers charged with rape in the 1770s, one was acquitted and two were sentenced to death. For one of the convicted defendants the grand jury had prepared two presentments, one charging the accused with attempted rape and the other with rape. This time the petit jury found the accused guilty of the rape charge, and the attempted rape indictment did not have to be presented.[32] That grand juries prepared two indictments in four rape cases suggests that they recognized the growing unpopularity of capital punishment, a trend reflected in the legislature's move in 1780 to cut the number of capital crimes in half.[33]

Juries exhibited a similar kind of reluctance to convict on charges of attempted rape in the 1780s and 1790s. In five cases, two of them involving the same defendant, the jury found the accused guilty of assault, but not guilty of the formal charge of rape. Three of these assault convictions—in the three counties of Essex, Suffolk, and Lincoln—brought considerably lighter sentences than those handed down for attempted rape. In the Essex case the indictment charged that the defendant, a cordwainer, "tore all the clothes . . . from off [his victim's] body except her shift and deprived her of them."[34]

The other two of the five cases in which an acquittal of intended rape led to an indictment and conviction for a lesser offense involved the same man but different victims. Stephen Burroughs apparently had either seduced or assaulted three young girls, and although the court was determined to punish him, the jury refused to go along with a charge of attempted rape. On April 19, 1791, Burroughs first appeared in court accused of attempted rape of one Molly Bacon, described as under the age of fifteen. When the jury acquitted him, the charge became more specific, and he was brought to trial for "open gross lewdness and lascivious behavior to one Molly Bacon, singlewoman and spinster, by opening her apparel then and there on her body, and by exploring the naked bodies of him the said Stephen and her the said Molly together—Therby exciting her the said Molly to open acts of lewdness and incontinency."[35] The jury found him guilty, and the justices sentenced him to a whipping of thirty lashes and one hour in the pillory.

An unrelated case was tried, and then Burroughs was again brought before the bar on a charge of attempted rape of Lucy Bacon, "infant under the age of thirteen" and probably Molly Bacon's sister. A different jury once again found him not guilty, and the case was dropped. The court was not yet finished with him, however, as he was immediately after charged with "open gross lewdness and lascivious behavior to one Alice Putney, singlewoman and spinster." After hearing a description of Burroughs's behavior similar to that quoted above, the jury sentenced him to one hour on the pillory, thirty stripes with the lash, and a three-month jail term. The last entry for that court day was an indictment against one Stephen Burroughs for an attempted rape of Alice Putney, with the note that the "Attorney General saith that he will prosecute the said Burroughs no further on this indictment."[36] Clearly the attorney general had seen the futility of convincing Burroughs on a charge of intended rape.

The full significance of the Stephen Burroughs case is not so clear. The indictment certainly describes behavior that could not technically be defined as an assault with intent to ravish, since the victims seem to have been enticed or seduced, rather than forced, and were over ten years old. The grand jury hit upon the catchall category of "lewd and lascivious behavior," which had been used throughout the colonial period to punish people for sexual misbehavior of various sorts.[37] And yet the girls involved were apparently not similarly charged, as they would have been if the jury members had thought they had consented to the sexual activity. Perhaps public feeling was changing about the age at which a girl should be considered a victim of statutory rape, although the law still defined it as ten and under. The jury, feeling the girls had been victimized, but considering that Burroughs had not raped them according to the legal definition, had to fall back on the best charge available to them. The justices thought that his offenses were as serious as attempted rape and sentenced him accordingly.

These cases in which prosecutors and juries tried to redefine the original charge may be unusual, isolated cases that could be easily accounted for by missing court transcripts or lack of information about the local circumstances of the alleged crime and trial. More likely, however, they are related to the changing sexual mores at the end of the century and are a part of a wide pattern of changes in criminal prosecution. At the same time that premarital sexual activity was increasing, fewer people were being brought before the courts for fornication (as long as pregnancy was not involved) or for such offenses as breaking the sabbath.[38] Although, as mentioned above, increased premarital sexual activity did not affect the relative number of rape cases brought to court, it may well have affected the disposition of cases that came to trial, particularly since criminal courts increasingly ignored illicit sexual activity, except for a few offenses such as prostitution. In this atmosphere, men who brought accused rapists before the bar and who sat on juries would likely reevaluate older assumptions and argue with previously accepted answers to such questions as, How serious is the offense? Who is hurt the most by it? Are there any conditions that might exonerate a rapist of blame? To what extent should a victim's testimony be believed? Until the larger society reached a new consensus about the crime of rape, a process that would take several decades at least, jury decisions would be unpredictable.

More deeply rooted aspects of the culture may explain the consistently low rape rates throughout the century, and these aspects may have changed enough by the end of this period to affect the disposition of cases but not the incidence of the reported crime. In the first place, law, customs, and social practice in eighteenth-century Massachusetts recognized the authority of men in the family, the church, the state, the economy, and the political system. Men wrote the laws and enforced them, effectively prescribing the limits of male sexual behavior. Women seem universally to have accepted as proper and necessary their subordination to men and even, until the last decades of the century, internalized society's estimation of female inferiority.[39] Since women were taught from childhood to defer to men, many instances of coerced sexual relations were probably not perceived as rape— even by the victim, and certainly not by the assailant or the neighbors.[40] Thus the only cases that would be reported and prosecuted were those in which the community acknowledged that the attacker had no right to the woman sexually. Rape by a husband was a contradiction in terms. Rape of a servant by a master would be difficult to prosecute and was probably not reported. If a young man raped a single woman of the same or lower social standing, the issue of consent would make his crime difficult to prove unless there was clear evidence of her resistance.

The cases of rape most likely to come to the attention of the authorities would be those in which the assailant was of a lower social order than the victim, or in which the victim was a married woman who forcefully resisted. Support for this interpretation is found in the higher conviction rate of assailants of married women and of minors. The corresponding rate was surprisingly low in the six cases involving single women: only one of five defendants was found guilty by a jury, and a sixth case was not prosecuted. Of the fifteen cases in which the victim was married or widowed, thirteen defendants were found guilty (including the cases discussed above for which file material was available). Of the thirteen cases involving victims under twenty-one, all the defendants were found guilty as charged or guilty of a lesser offense (see Table 3). The overall conviction rate in these two categories was thus high—82 percent. The number of cases involving single adult women is so low that it is risky to attach too much significance to this prosecution rate. It may simply be that evidence was weak in these six cases for reasons unrelated to the age and marital status of the victim. Nevertheless, the pattern is highly

Table 3
Disposal of Rape and Attempted Rape Indictments, by Victim's Age and Marital Status

	Guilty	Not Guilty
Girls 10 and under	6	1*
Girls 11–21	6	1†
Single women	1	5‡
Married women	10	6⸴
Widows	1	1ǁ

Sources: Records of the Superior Court of Judicature and the Supreme Judicial Court, New Suffolk County Courthouse, Boston, 1698–1797.

*Defendant found not guilty of rape, but guilty of attempted rape; counted in both columns.
†Defendant found not guilty of rape, but guilty of lewdness; counted in not guilty column.
‡One defendant charged with attempted rape, but not prosecuted; counted in not guilty column.
⸴One defendant found not guilty of rape, but guilty of attempted rape; counted in both columns. One defendant found not guilty of attempted rape, but guilty of assault; counted in not guilty column.
ǁDefendant found not guilty of attempted rape, but guilty of assault; counted in guilty column.

suggestive and supports Susan Brownmiller's theory that rape was considered an offense not against a woman so much as against her father or husband.[41]

Analyzing the conviction patterns according to the defendants' social standing indicates that rape was more likely to be punished when the accused was at the bottom of the social order. All of the defendants but one—a man identified simply as "esquire"—were from the middle or lower social orders. Laborers constituted the largest single group (twelve); three, all black, were servants; two were mariners; and one was an "infant," no doubt a teenager, whose social standing was not indicated. A large number, eleven artisans and six "yeomen," were from the middle orders. Twelve of the indictments were for rape and the rest for attempted rape. Of the five found guilty and sentenced to death, two were black servants, one was an Indian laborer, and two were white laborers. The two other non-white defendants were found guilty of attempted rape and given harsh sentences. In 1708 a black servant was fined £5, whipped twenty stripes, and ordered to be sold overseas, to be jailed if he ever returned. An Indian laborer, Simon Tripp, was found guilty in 1723 of assault with intent to rape. Of those accused of rape who were not brought to trial, or were acquitted or convicted of a lesser offense, five were farmers or artisans and only two were laborers. Farmers and artisans were thus not as likely to be tried for rape nor as likely to be convicted when tried.

Therefore, one reason so few cases appeared in the Superior Court of Judicature is that few assaults were perceived as rape. In a patriarchal and explicitly hierarchical culture, rapes committed by men of the upper or middle orders never came to public attention, much less to the courts. Because of their positions of prestige and authority, respectable men of the community could force their attention on servants or single girls, finding a grudging acquiescence. Not even the victims would recognize such relations as rape. When men of the lower order raped women of a higher social standing, they threatened the prerogatives of other men, using physical force as their primary means of obtaining compliance. Their actions most clearly were condemned by society and forbidden by the laws of rape, and they were brought before the courts.

This interpretation sees rape as an expression of male control over women, regulated by law in a way that serves the men who hold political power more than it protects women. Rape is as well a *sexual* assertion of authority, and its practice is affected by the cultural definition of normal sexual relations. The patriarchal setting of Massachusetts minimized the number of cases that came before the courts. At the same time, the cultural expectations about sexual behavior probably minimized the occurrence of rape. Extramarital sexual activity by men and women alike was severely condemned and frequently punished. Ministers enjoined women not to flaunt their sexual attractiveness. Men were not extolled for the sexual conquest of many women; on the contrary, they were condemned if not prosecuted. Women were understood to be as interested in sex as men. Thus neither in marriage nor in courtship would a man believe that a woman really meant yes when she said no. The rape prototype of female enticement, coy female resistance, and ultimate male conquest was not built into the pattern of normal sexual relations.[42]

Finally, family and community structure effectively upheld sexual mores and minimized the opportunity for rape. Communities were small throughout the century; residents knew all the other residents and were related to many of them. Strangers were rare enough to be curiosities and quickly known. Even the bustling port city of Boston held only 24,000 inhabitants by 1800, still small enough that most residents could know each other by face, by family, and by reputation. Most women lived under the authority, or "protection," of a male: father, husband, or master. Consequently, the opportunities for rape as defined by law and custom— of a woman who resisted by a man who had no right to her sexually—were limited.

The right of the community to watch over a wide range of personal behavior and exact conformity to law and custom was generally accepted. Although the early Puritan efforts to punish sin in every area of private and public life had failed by the end of the century, county courts continued, albeit decreasingly, to punish behavior that later would be viewed as private and thus out of reach of the criminal justice system: adultery, fornication, illegitimacy, and profanity. Social pressures were even more important than laws in setting limits on individual sexual behavior. "The force of public opinion, the prevailing concept of conventional behavior, the threat of becoming a subject of gossip, the difficulties of shielding from neighbors such unconventional conditions as pregnancy out of wedlock, and continued acceptance of the sinfulness of immorality, all served to uphold the moral law much more effectively than secular laws and law enforcement."[43] Doubtless some of the cases then punished as fornication would today be considered rape. At the same time, the condemnation of all extramarital sex probably reduced the incidence of rape even by today's definition. The culture discouraged rape, and the community structure minimized opportunities for it to occur.

Geographical expansion did not change the character of New England village life. Population growth and increases in the number of wandering poor were not yet great enough to transform the face-to-face quality of community relations. The decline in paternal control over land distribution at the end of the century had not yet led to the dispersal of younger generations many hundreds of miles to the west, beyond the reach of parental supervision. As long as the conditions that discouraged rape remained—small close-knit communities that discouraged free sexual expression by men outside of wedlock and in which few women lived alone—rape rates were kept low, unaffected by population growth, westward expansion, wars, and economic reversals.

Notes

1. The first five chapters of Susan Brownmiller's *Against Our Will: Men, Women, and Rape* (New York: Simon & Schuster, 1975) rely on historical materials. Theodore Ferdinand's analysis of Boston rape arrest records from 1849 to 1951 indicates a gradually climbing rate, with fluctuations during wars and changing economic cycles ("The Criminal Patterns of Boston since 1849," *American Journal of Sociology* 73 [July 1967]: 84–99). His work and a section in Lyle Koehler's *A Search for Power: The "Weaker" Sex in Seventeenth-Century New England* (Urbana: University of Illinois Press, 1980) are the best historical studies to date. Edward Shorter's speculation about the historical conditions that contribute to rape ("On Writing the History of Rape," *Signs: Journal of Women in Culture and Society* 3, no. 2 [Winter 1977]: 471–82) does not hold up under close examination (see Heidi I. Hartmann and Ellen Ross, "Comment on 'On Writing the History of Rape,' " *Signs* 3, no. 4 [Summer 1978]: 931–35).

2. As defined by Sir Matthew Hale, *Pleas of the Crown,* 1:626, quoted in H. A. Snelling, "What Is Rape?" in *Rape Victimology,* ed. Leroy G. Schultz (Springfield, Ill.: Charles C. Thomas, 1975), p. 146. See also Cyril J. Smith, "History of Rape and Rape Laws," *Women Lawyers Journal* 60 (Fall 1974): 189–90.

3. Edwin Powers, *Crime and Punishment in Early Massachusetts* (Boston: Beacon Press, 1966), pp. 279, 307, 309.

4. The official court records of the Superior Court of Judicature and the Supreme Judicial Court are complete for the years 1698 to 1797. Court records after 1797 are today scattered throughout the state and in Maine in the counties where the court met in circuit sessions. I was aided in the earliest stages of this research by N. E. H. Hull, who generously gave me a list of all rapes recorded in the Superior Court of Judicature from 1698 to 1773. The analysis of those cases is entirely my own.

5. On three occasions a grand jury presented two indictments of an individual for one alleged crime, leading to two separate petit jury trials. Each of these indictments has been counted as one case, not two, giving a total of forty cases of rape. However, when a defendant was accused of two different crimes, both were counted. Thus those forty cases involved thirty-six defendants.

6. Superior Court of Judicature Records, 1784, p. 130, New Suffolk County Courthouse, Boston (hereafter cited as Sup. Ct. Recs.).

7. Ibid., 1723, p. 140, file 17129.

8. Koehler (n. 1 above), p. 96.

9. Sup. Ct. Recs., 1699, p. 291, file 4022.

10. Ibid.

11. July 29, 1729, Sup. Ct. Recs., 1725–30, p. 236, file 23157; Koehler (n. 1 above), p. 100.

12. August 13, 1734, Sup. Ct. Recs., 1733–36, p. 119, file 37793.

13. "Murphy Indicted," July 20, 1756, Sup. Ct. Recs., 1755–56, p. 274, file 75839.

14. I am here much indebted to the fine article by Catharine A. MacKinnon, "Feminism, Marxism, Method, and the State: Toward Feminist Jurisprudence," *Signs* 8, no. 4 (Summer 1983): 635–58.

15. I computed the decade average per 100,000 population by dividing the total number of rapes for the decade by the population figure midpoint in that period and then multiplying the result by 100,000.

I used the same method for recent decade averages. Computing figures from mid-decade to mid-decade for the eighteenth century left an awkward number of years at either end of the series, but simplified the computation of averages using the estimated population figures available for 1700, 1710, etc. Using the even decades (1700–1709, 1710–19) would not substantially change my conclusions (see Table 1).

16. These averages are computed using data from the entire United States, which probably yield a higher figure than data from Massachusetts alone. However, since contemporary statistics are for forcible rape only, and exclude statutory rape (intercourse, consenting or not, with an underage female, defined as under eighteen in most states), they are more conservative than eighteenth-century figures, which include both crimes. This downward bias compensates for the bias involved in using national statistics. According to the U.S. Department of Justice count of offenses known to the police, 56 percent of known rape cases were "cleared by arrest or exceptional means" in 1979, 65 percent in 1970 (Federal Bureau of Investigation, *Uniform Crime Report of the U.S.* [Washington, D.C.: Government Printing Office, 1979], p. 14; ibid., 1970, p. 12). I have used the more conservative figure of 56 percent in computing prosecution rates. Brownmiller (n. 1 above) states that 76 percent of arrested offenders in 1973 were prosecuted (p. 175). Michael J. Hindelang and Bruce J. Davis ("Forcible Rape in the U.S.: A Statistical Profile," in *Forcible Rape,* ed. Duncan Chappel et al. [New York: Columbia University Press, 1977], p. 106) cite a California study that showed a 70 percent prosecution rate between 1969 and 1971. I again used the more conservative figure to conclude that 39 percent of rapes known to the police were prosecuted. The decade average was computed as described above (U.S. Department of Justice, Law Enforcement Assistance Administration, *National Criminal Justice Information and Statistics* [Washington, D.C.: Government Printing Office, 1979], p. 402; and U.S. Bureau of the Census, *Historical Statistics of the U.S., Colonial Times to 1970,* 2 vols. [Washington, D.C.: Government Printing Office, 1975], 1:8, 413).

17. J. M. Beattie ("Toward a Study of Crime in Eighteenth Century England: A Note on Indictments," in *The Triumph of Culture: Eighteenth Century Perspectives,* ed. Paul Fritz and David Williams [Toronto: A. M. Hakkert, 1972], p. 103) quotes the eighteenth-century source and believes it plausible in light of modern estimates.

18. Brownmiller (n. 1 above), p. 175; Hindelang and Davis (n. 16 above), pp. 97–98.

19. David Flaherty, *Privacy in Colonial New England* (Charlottesville: University Press of Virginia, 1972), pp. 201–5, 227–32.

20. Today the "clearance rate" is higher in rural areas (65 percent in 1979) than in urban areas (48 percent in 1979) (*Uniform Crime Report* [n. 16 above], 1979, p. 14; Brownmiller [n. 1 above], p. 351). Koehler (n. 1 above), p. 98, found that in 85.3 percent of the seventeenth-century New England rape cases where he could identify both rapist and victim, the rapist was a neighbor or a member of the household of the victim. Koehler does not say, however, for how many of his cases he has such information.

21. George L. Haskins, *Law and Authority in Early Massachusetts* (New York: Macmillan Publishing Co., 1968), pp. 49–50.

22. Powers (n. 3 above), pp. 91, 279.

23. Koehler (n. 1 above), pp. 96–97.

24. Analyzing somewhat incomplete Massachusetts court records for an eighty-year period in the seventeenth century, Catharine Baker found only fourteen cases of rape and two cases of assault with intent to rape brought before the Court of Assistants, the highest provincial court where felony cases were tried. This amounts to one rape or attempted rape prosecution recorded every five years among a population that grew from about 900 people in 1630 to 56,000 in 1700 (Catharine Baker, "Sexual Assault in Seventeenth Century Massachusetts" [unpublished seminar paper, Brandeis University, 1974]; see also her unpublished shortened version of this paper, "Rape in Seventeenth Century Massachusetts" [paper presented at the Third Berkshire Conference on Women's History, Bryn Mawr College, 1976]). Koehler found a higher number—seventy-eight cases—in all of New England in an eighty-year period, apparently because he included cases of sexual assault other than rape and attempted rape (U.S. Bureau of the Census [n. 16 above], 2:1168; Koehler [n. 1 above], p. 95).

25. Page Smith, *A New Age Now Begins* (New York: McGraw-Hill Book Co., 1976), pp. 304–8; Brownmiller (n. 1 above), pp. 115–17.

26. Smith, pp. 345, 455.

27. Ibid., pp. 455 ff., 654 ff.

28. Henry Steele Commager and Richard B. Morris, eds., *Spirit of '76,* 2 vols. (Indianapolis: Bobbs-Merrill Co., 1958), 1:116, 138, 139; Smith (n. 25 above), pp. 575, 581. Courts were closed during much of the Revolutionary War (John Murrin, "Anglicizing an American Colony: The Transformation of Provincial Massachusetts" [Ph.D. diss., Yale University, 1966], pp. 222, 225). Nevertheless, rape cases *did* come before the Superior Court in those years at a rate only somewhat lower than the decade before or after. Rape atrocities were committed by Hessian and British soldiers against American women in other states, but no cases from Massachusetts came to the attention of the authorities (Mary Beth Norton, *Liberty's Daughters* [Boston: Little, Brown, & Co., 1980], pp. 202–4; Brownmiller [n. 1 above], pp. 115–21).

29. Daniel Scott Smith and Michael Hindus, "Premarital Pregnancy in America: An Overview and Interpretation," *Journal of Interdisciplinary History* 5, no. 4 (1975): 537–71, quote on 559.

30. "John Ward Indicted," March 11, 1766, Sup. Ct. Recs., 1766–67, pp. 1, 2, files 100811, 100815; "Samuel Quinn Indicted," November 3, 1768, ibid., 1767–68, p. 259, files 152337, 152338; "Arthur Indicted," November 3, 1768, ibid., 1767–68, p. 261, file 152339; "Bliss Indicted," October 1, 1769, ibid., 1769, p. 171, and "Bliss Indicted," October 9, 1770, ibid., 1770, p. 212, files 90508, 145469, 14554.

31. After 1730, Massachusetts conviction rates for infanticide and for adult murder dropped, much earlier than did those for rape convictions (see Peter C. Hoffer and N. E. H. Hull, *Murdering Mothers: Infanticide in England and New England, 1558–1803* [New York: New York University Press, 1981], p. 77).

32. "Bryan Sheehan Indicted," Sup. Ct. Resc., 1771, p. 206, files 90741, 132119. It is, of course, possible that double presentments by grand juries before and after that period simply were not preserved.

33. Powers (n. 3 above), pp. 308–9. The patterns for the following fifty years indicate the importance of a similar study for the nineteenth century. Michael Hindus (*Prison and Plantation: Crime, Justice, and Authority in Massachusetts and South Carolina* [Chapel Hill: University of North Carolina Press, 1980], p. 103) found seven Massachusetts rape cases between 1801 and 1830; of these, all the defendants were found guilty, six executed, and one pardoned. The number of prosecutions jumped to sixteen in the twenty-year period before 1852, at which time rape was struck from the list of capital offenses in response to renewed agitation against capital punishment. Only two of these cases resulted in "full conviction" (ibid., p. 95). Hindus sees an important correlation between a low conviction rate and public feeling against the death penalty; the correlation between the number of prosecutions and sentiment against capital punishment is not similarly clear.

34. "Newhall Indicted," Salem, Essex, November 7, 1786, Sup. Ct. Recs., June–November 1786, p. 467, file 133633; "Durfee Indicted," Boston, Suffolk, August 28, 1787, ibid., 1787, p. 220, files 104765, 104791; "Cooper Indicted," Pownalborough, Lincoln, July 11, 1797, ibid., 1797, p. 215, files 141398, 141400.

35. "Burroughs Indicted," Worcester, Worcester, April 19, 1791, ibid., 1791, pp. 129, 130, files 155603, 155604, and p. 130, files 155602, 155605.

36. Ibid.

37. Powers (n. 3 above), p. 412.

38. William Nelson maintains that agreement about ethical values was breaking down in Massachusetts between 1760 and 1830, an early sign of profound social and economic changes that led to major modifications of criminal law in the first half of the nineteenth century. Beginning in the 1780s, the courts became increasingly reluctant to prosecute cases involving private morality, such as fornication and illegitimacy, and spent more and more time on those involving property. In distinguishing what we now term private from public morality, the courts stopped enforcing a particular standard of sexual or family conduct (William Nelson, *The Americanization of the Common Law* [Cambridge, Mass.: Harvard University Press, 1975], p. 4). Michael Hindus contends that these changes began before 1780 and were not fully accomplished by 1830. By the second half of the eighteenth century prosecutions for sexual offenses reflected not moral disapproval but economic and class interests: the magistrates wanted to ensure that illegitimate babies would not become public charges and thus prosecuted poor, unwed mothers ([n. 33 above], pp. 49–50, 63–70).

39. See Norton (n. 28 above), esp. pp. 110–24.

40. See MacKinnon's fine analysis (n. 14 above) of patriarchal law governing rape. Koehler (n. 1 above) explains rape and attempted rape in seventeenth-century New England as an aspect of the complete control that men had over women. Noting that individual motivations for rape will always vary, he searched the court testimony of twenty-six rapists for the "cultural tendencies which collectively might predispose" them to the crime. Men raped women for the same reasons that they insisted on complete female inferiority and subordination: a "profound inability to acknowledge that women had any basic 'rights,' including the right to accept or reject [sexual] overtures" (p. 93). Clearly the victims who took their attackers to court did not perceive the situation this way; more significantly, had these "cultural tendencies" been hegemonic, as Koehler implies, courts would never have heard rape cases.

41. Brownmiller (n. 1 above), pp. 16–30.

42. See Norton (n. 28 above), pp. 51–56, on the importance attached to female virginity before marriage in the revolutionary period.

43. David Flaherty, "Law and the Enforcement of Morals in Early America," *Perspectives in American History* 5 (1971): 203–53, esp. 245.

The Urban Geography of Commercial Sex: Prostitution in New York City, 1790–1860

Timothy J. Gilfoyle

To many nineteenth-century Americans, New York City was the sexual opprobrium of the nation. Prostitution, Dr. William Sanger despondently observed in 1858, "boldly strides through our most thronged and elegant thoroughfares.... It is in your squares and in your suburban retreats and summer resorts; it is in your theatres, your opera, your hotels, ... slowly but steadily extending the poison."[1] Sanger's avid indictment was hardly unprecedented. In the 1830s, the lawyer George Templeton Strong complained that the city's prostitutes were so numerous and visible that New York was infested with a "whorearchy."[2] These observers were simply commenting upon a tradition of commercialized carnality that distinguished Manhattan as early as the seventeenth century and that remained strong into the 1980s. From its earliest days when prostitutes were found promenading along the Battery to the recent closing of Plato's Retreat on charges of prostitution and "unsafe sex," Gotham has always been considered the most sinful of America's large cities.

Despite the preoccupation (some might say obsession) with nineteenth-century vice by clerics, reformers, and police officials and the more recent analyses of social historians, the geographical evolution of prostitution in New York has never been the subject of sustained inquiry. Where exactly did the nineteenth-century male go in search of such illicit sex? Did the city systematically segregate the sex trade from the presumably more legitimate forms of pecuniary gain? How and why did red-light districts move? Most scholars have examined prostitution sociologically and usually in the period following the Civil War.[3] Antebellum investigations have concentrated on antiprostitution reform movements and the rise of prostitution in conjunction with the changing labor market in New York. Only a few accounts explain prostitution in terms of its spatial development and its role in neighborhood formation.[4] This essay attempts to define and explain why the specific physical and spatial pattern of prostitution—its moral geography—changed and evolved in New York's most significant period of growth, from 1790 to 1860.

Geographically, prostitution in New York passed through three distinct phases in this period.[5] From 1790 to 1820, commercial sex was confined to three specific areas. Then from 1820 to 1850, prostitution "suburbanized," spreading throughout most neighborhoods in the city, while several new zones of concentration appeared with substantial amounts of prostitution. Although these concentrated areas of vice were significant, the combination of segregation and dispersal was unique. Finally, between 1850 and 1920, prostitution was once again segregated in specific parts of the city. This physical pattern was unusual because, unlike most other urban activities, prostitution was more segregated from 1790 to 1820 than in the early industrial city thereafter.[6] Instead of being confined to poor, undesirable parts of the city, some prostitutes followed the middle class and the wealthy in their movement uptown, lived in "respectable" neighborhoods, and were attached to institutions such as the hotel and theater that serviced the growing middle class.

Colonial New York was preeminently a seaport, and prostitution flourished in the streets and taverns close to the docks. New York, remarked John Watt in the 1760s, was "the worst School for Youth of any of his Majesty's Dominions, Ignorance, Vanity, Dress, and Dissipation, being the reigning Characteristics of their insipid Lives."[7] For much of the eighteenth century, "courtesans" promenaded along the Battery after nightfall. On the eve of the Revolution, over 500 "ladies of pleasure [kept] lodgings contiguous within the consecrated liberties of St. Paul's [Chapel]." A few blocks north, at the entrance to King's College (later Columbia University), Robert M'Robert claimed that dozens of prostitutes provided "a temptation to the youth that have occasion to pass so often that way." The often-quoted traveller Hector St. John de Crevecoeur repeated similar concerns when he saw the "dissipations and pleasures" near the College. After Isaac Bangs visited the area in 1776, he "thought nothing could exceed (the prostitutes) for impudence and immodesty." The more he became acquainted with them, he concluded, "the more they excelled in their Brutality." A final haunt was at the foot of Broad Street in the temporary houses replacing those destroyed in the fire of 1776. Nicknamed "Canvass-town" and "Topsail Town" after the material used as roofs, the buildings "afforded cheap and convenient lodgings for the frail sisterhood, who plied their trade most briskly in the vicinity of the shipping and the barracks."[8]

By the turn of the nineteenth century, prostitution in New York was concentrated along specific streets (Map 1). The Frenchman Moreau de St. Mery derogatorily remarked in 1794 that "whole sections of the streets are given over to streetwalkers for the plying of their profession." Women "of every color can be found in the streets, particularly after ten o'clock at night, soliciting men and proudly flaunting their licentiousness in the most shameless manner." After 1800, residents and early neighborhood associations deplored the proliferating houses of ill-fame on East George Street, as well as "certain houses in George and Charlotte Streets frequented at unreasonable hours by idle Negroes and other dissolute persons." The district attorney verified that prostitution was increasingly found on certain streets. Between 1790 and 1809, New York's chief prosecutor indicted 195 establishments for prostitution, two-thirds (sixty-five percent) of them near the East River docks (hereafter East Dock), and an astonishing twenty-six percent located on East George and George streets.[9]

Map 1
Major Areas of Prostitution, 1790–1819

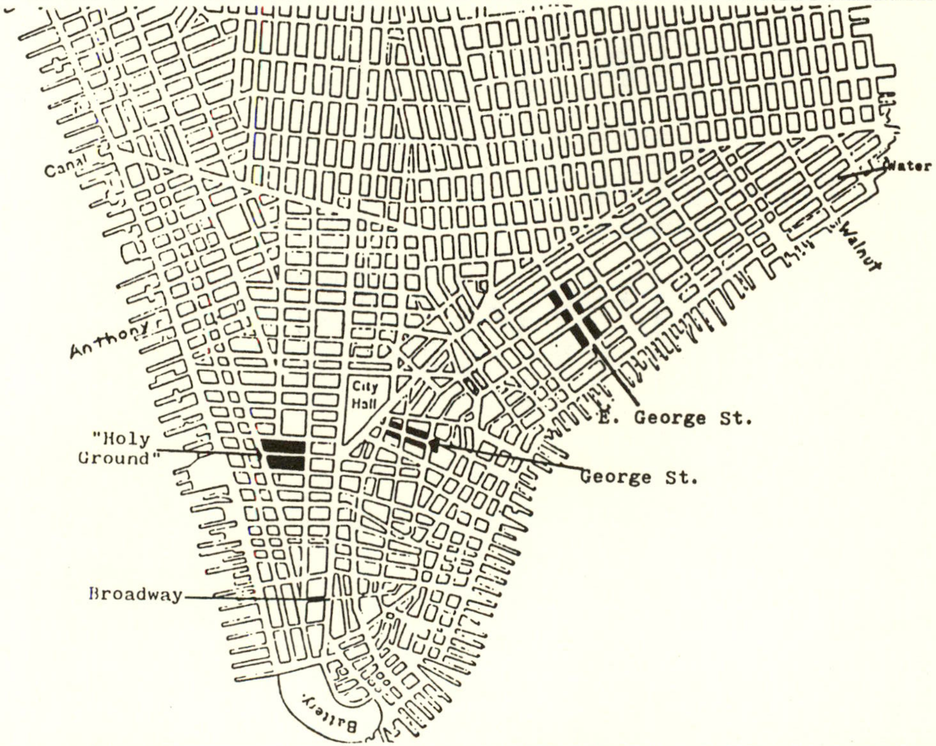

Another district of deviance was the irreligious "Holy Ground" behind St. Paul's Chapel. In the two blocks along Church, Vessey, and Barclay streets, the city's most expensive "houses of debauchery" prospered on land owned by the Episcopal Church and adjacent to Columbia College. More than a score of residents complained to the Common Council in 1802 about the "idle and disorderly loose women" on Barclay Street who behaved "in such a manner as [was] too indecent to relate." As the city's northernmost passage between the East and Hudson rivers, Barclay Street was "a thoroughfare of considerable import for sailors and people of that class from the ship yards and who frequently . . . behave with great incivillity [sic]."[10]

Prior to 1820, then, prostitution was confined and well ordered. Vice in preindustrial New York was concentrated in three specific, delineated areas. Two were in the heart of the growing metropolis and the other on its outermost fringe.[11] George Street was in a north-central location, just off the City Common (later City Hall Park), two short blocks from the Park Theatre and four blocks from the East River wharves. Nearby, the exclusive prostitution in the "Holy Ground" was only a block from the Hudson River. In contrast to these centrally located districts, East George Street was on the outer, northeast fringe of the city in the midst of a neighborhood devoted to the shipping, dock, and marine industries. An 1812 report on immorality acknowledged that "droves of youth" indeed resorted to the outskirts of the city to commit their depredations.[12]

Compared with its later evolution, prostitution was an orderly, controlled urban enterprise, restricted to a few blocks, and physically linked to the city's waterfront commerce. In this segregated, concentrated world of illicit sexuality, prostitution was a private, isolated affair. Little streetwalking occurred outside the informal, spatially defined areas of prostitution. For the most part, the visible activities and solicitation of prostitutes and their clients took place inside the brothel and saloon, or on a small, remote street away from the glaring public eye. Spatially, commercial sex was autonomous, secluded, and limited to fringe areas of the city. In such an environment, prostitutes did not compete with their neighbors for urban turf.

After 1820, prostitution moved from the waterfront to the residential neighborhood. The expansion of vice produced a spatial revolution as these entrepreneurs of sex moved into previously untouched and unavailable neighborhoods. A new sexual tableau emerged as the geography of prostitution broke its earlier physical confines and followed a vigorous citywide growth that paralleled the expansion of New York's built-up area. For the first time, prostitutes competed with ordinary residents for the use and control of certain streets and public areas. As various forms of urban space—houses, streets, parks—were suddenly in short supply, people had to compete for them. The Committee for Suppressing Immorality complained in 1812 that "the vast number of Brothels, and houses of Seduction now kept in the City [were] alarming." By midcentury, a consensus of observers despairingly admitted that the "most unlicensed debauch is witnessed in every hold and corner of the city—in the great thoroughfares, in the public institutions of the metropolis—even in the temple dedicated to Almighty God."[13] Its unprecedented

Map 2
Houses of Prostitution, 1830–1839

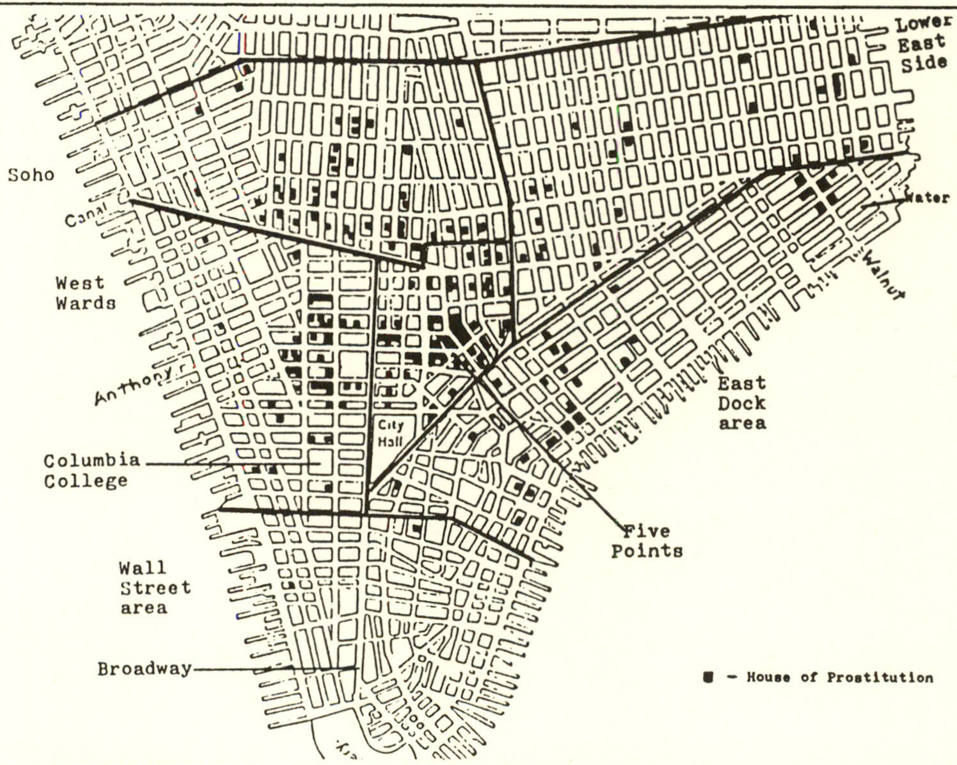

Lower East Side

Water

Walnut

East Dock area

Five Points

Soho

Canal

West Wards

Anthony

City Hall

Columbia College

Wall Street area

Broadway

■ – House of Prostitution

proliferation made prostitution an integrated public activity, dramatically altering the social fabric of Gotham.

Areas of the city previously unaffected were suddenly confronted with the ubiquitous and sleazy vitality of prostitution. The conspicuous growth of commercial sex was so spasmodic and threatening to the emerging middle-class "cult of domesticity" that many residents clamored for government intervention. Gotham's physical expansion simply did not match its population growth. "The public show of extravagance, audacity, and licentiousness of the women of the town, demands the corrective interposition of the magistrates," insisted one newspaper in 1820. Citizens were so "scandalized and public opinion [so] outraged," that police officers for the first time were ordered to report all prostitutes found on Broadway and the city's other major arteries.[14] For the next century, the competition between practitioners of deviant sexuality and their opponents was a landmark of urban life. As New York grew, so did commercialized sex.

The prodigious physical dispersal of prostitution after 1820 can be illustrated several ways. First, "bawdy houses" were found in all of the city's major neighborhoods. In the 1820s, prostitutes were living at the northern edge of the city on 13th Street, and two decades later on West 20th and 21st streets.[15] At the opposite end of the city, streetwalking on the Battery, the oldest and southernmost portion of Manhattan, continued (Map 2).[16] By the 1820s, the East Dock area, Five Points, and West Wards each had from twenty-six percent to thirty percent of the city's prostitution (Table 1). Five Points contained the most brothels, but its concentration of vice was unimpressive compared with the East Dock area from 1790 to 1820, or Soho after 1850. The only known underground guidebook from the period, *Prostitution Exposed, or a Moral Reform Directory,* detailed the spread of prostitution throughout Manhattan. Authored by the pseudonymous pornographer "Butt Ender" in 1839, *Prostitution Exposed* revealed that Five Points, the West Wards, and the Lower East Side, respectively, contained thirty-one percent, twenty-five percent, and twenty percent of the city's best-known and most alluring brothels.[17] No single area enjoyed a monopoly on the expensive and well-frequented habitats of sex.

Block-by-block persistence of the "social evil" was a third example of prostitution's dispersal. Blocks with documented houses of prostitution in at least three of the four decades from 1820 to 1860 were in Soho, the West Wards, Five Points, Corlears Hook, and Water Street (Map 3). Prostitutes did not confine themselves to a few specific areas and move when neighborhood opposition grew too intense, but persisted and anchored themselves in most city neighborhoods. Finally, houses of prostitution followed a citywide pattern of decreasing physical density during the antebellum period.

A comparison of the total number of city blocks with blocks having prostitution in the three decades from 1820 to 1849 reveals that the ratio of addresses to blocks declined from 2.28-1 in the 1820s to 1.95-1 in the 1830s. Although the ratio increased to 2.20-1 by midcentury, it remained below the level of the 1820s (Table 2).[18] The low ratio of houses to blocks indicates a decreasing density rate and an increasing dispersion of the "whorearchy" throughout the city, just the opposite

Map 3
Blocks with Prostitution in Three or More Decades, 1820–1859

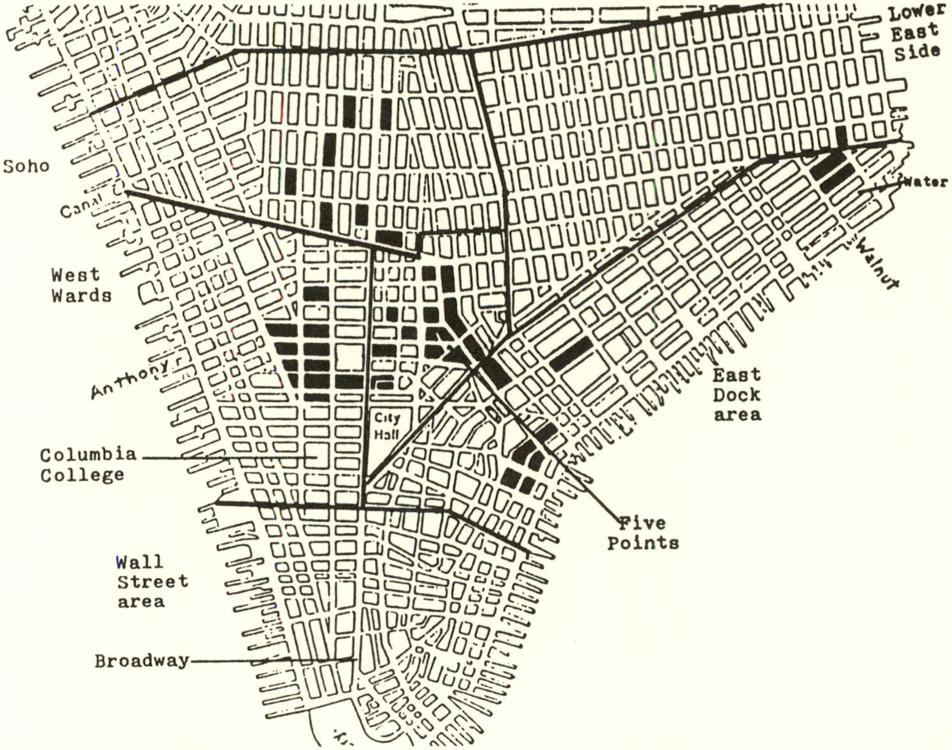

Lower
East
Side

Water

Walnut

East
Dock
area

Five
Points

City
Hall

Soho

Canal

West
Wards

Anthony

Columbia
College

Wall
Street
area

Broadway

Table 1
Location of Houses of Prostitution by Neighborhood, 1790–1869 (by percentage)

Years	Number of Addresses	East Dock	Five Points	West Wards	Wall Street	Soho	Other
1790–1809	182	65	6	21	7	0	.5
1810–1819	245	55	15	22	5	0	4
1820–1829	253	30	30	26	2	8	4
1830–1839	271	17	35	20	0	16	11
1840–1849	207	19	36	28	4	11	3
1850–1859	366	8	32	12	2	41	7
1860–1869	99	10	12	8	5	45	19

Sources: New York District Attorney indictment papers, Court of General Sessions, 1790–1869; New York Police Court papers, 1820–1860; **National Police Gazette**, 1845–1880; Stephen Allen papers, Court Minutes, 1819, and Tavern Complaints, 1822; Butt Ender, **Prostitution Exposed; or a Moral Reform Directory** (New York, 1839); Free Lovyer (sic), **Directory of the Seraglios in New York, Philadelphia, Boston, and all the Principle Cities of the Union** (New York, 1857 and 1859); Charles DeKock, **Guide to the Harems, or Directory to the Laides of Fashion in New York and Various Other Cities** (New York, 1855); William H. Bell (policeman) Diary, 1850–1851; House of Refuge papers; **Sun**; **Herald**; **Tribune**.

Note: Addresses are based on whether a single location was cited one or more times for prostitution violations by an source. If the same address was cited more than once or by another source, it was counted only one time. Percentages have been rounded.

of a city with carefully marked and functionally segregated red-light districts. Compared with medieval German cities with zones lasting centuries, Paris with brothels in the same area since the Middle Ages, San Francisco with its more than seventy-five-year-old Tenderloin, or even American frontier towns with brothels on the edge of the settlement, the moral geography of prostitution in antebellum New York was ill-defined and constantly changing.[19] Whether north or south, new neighborhood or old, prostitutes openly lived and candidly worked in all parts of antebellum New York.

The moral geography of New York that emerged from 1820 to 1850, however, was spatially more complicated and uneven than this description of suburbanized, physically dispersed prostitution. A closer examination of the neighborhoods of vice reveal a variety of nuances in their spatial and geographical patterns. While the tentacles of commercial sex extended over the whole body of New York, they held a tighter grip on certain parts. Some neighborhoods became strongholds of prostitution. Indeed, a hierarchy of prostitution zones appeared with four different forms of concentration: (1) a large cluster, (2) a ribbon development, (3) small clusters, and (4) fluctuating zones of streetwalking prostitutes (Map 4). Where prostitutes congregated, lived, and worked in large numbers, the spatial pattern of their settlement fell into one of these categories.

The primary zone was the large cluster development centered around Paradise Square in Five Points, the most notorious slum in the Western Hemisphere. Five Points offered the most congenial environment for every form of social deviance.

Map 4
Blocks with Multiple Houses of Prostitution, 1820–1829

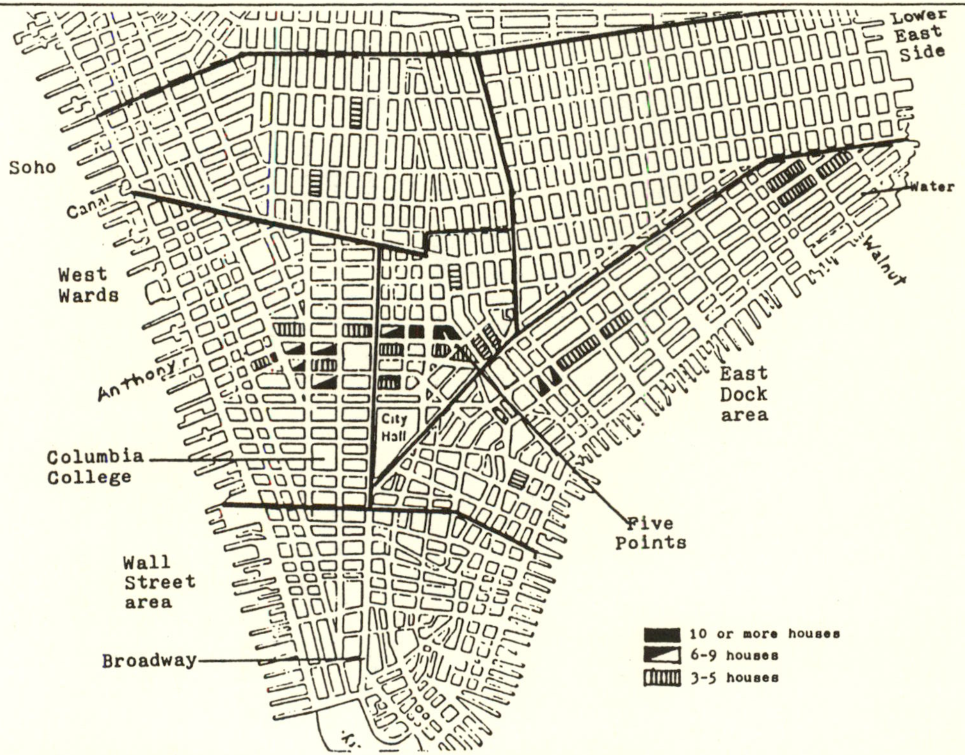

Lower East Side

Water

Walnut

East Dock area

Five Points

10 or more houses
6-9 houses
3-5 houses

City Hall

Soho

Canal

West Wards

Anthony

Columbia College

Wall Street area

Broadway

Table 2
Physical Concentration of Prostitution, 1820–1859

Years	No. of Plotable Addresses	No. of Blocks	Ratio
1820–1829	210	92	2.28:1
1830–1839	253	130	1.95:1
1840–1849	198	90	2.20:1
1850–1859	323	130	2.48:1

Sources: See Table 1.

If "ever immorality and licentiousness were presented in more disgusting forms," proclaimed the *Sun,* "we confess we have never yet beheld them."[20] From 1830 to 1839, twenty-seven of the forty-three blocks (sixty-three percent) surrounding Paradise Square housed prostitutes at least one time. Sexual favors were especially abundant on the blockfront bounded by Anthony, Leonard, Orange, and Centre streets. In each of the four decades from 1820 to 1860, there were at least seventeen domiciles of sex reported on this single block. And at least one adjoining block contained ten or more similar establishments. Finally, all institutionalized forms of prostitution were found in Five Points: brothels, saloons, theaters, dance halls, hotels, and cheap lodging houses.

A secondary zone was the long ribbon development in the West Wards extending along Church and Chapel streets, continuing north where Chapel became Laurens Street and was nicknamed "Rotton Row." This neighborhood, despite having some of the most expensive brothels, never achieved the sexual density and concentration of Five Points. On the eastern side of Manhattan, two small tertiary zones of illicit carnality thrived. Clustered around the wild, lively, and dangerous saloons and cheap boardinghouses on Water and Cherry streets in the Fourth Ward and Walnut Street in Corlears Hook, these areas also lacked the amount and scale of prostitution of Five Points. Finally, those areas of public streetwalking, infrequently mentioned and less physically defined as more institutionalized forms of sex, were fluctuating zones of prostitution that changed in location and intensity throughout the period. At least four such areas existed from 1820 to 1850. Broadway from City Hall Park to beyond Canal was notorious for the variety and beauty of its streetwalkers. Working in conjunction with the brothels and hotels in the West Wards, Five Points, and Soho, women collected in groups of five or six on numerous corners along New York's most famous avenue. During the 1830s, the "Female Rialto" at the foot of Rivington Street and "Slamm's Row" along Delancey Street were major zones of streetwalkers. Finally, the Battery remained a consistent nighttime resort for ladies of the night.[21]

After 1850, the moral geography of New York underwent a spatial reorganization. The deconcentrated structure of prostitution gave way to the emergence of a new primary center, Soho (Map 5). With forty percent of the prostitution, Soho became the first large-scale, truly exclusive red-light district in New York's history, and the leading brothel guides emphasized its importance. Charles DeKock's *Guide*

Map 5
Blocks with Multiple Houses of Prostitution, 1850–1859

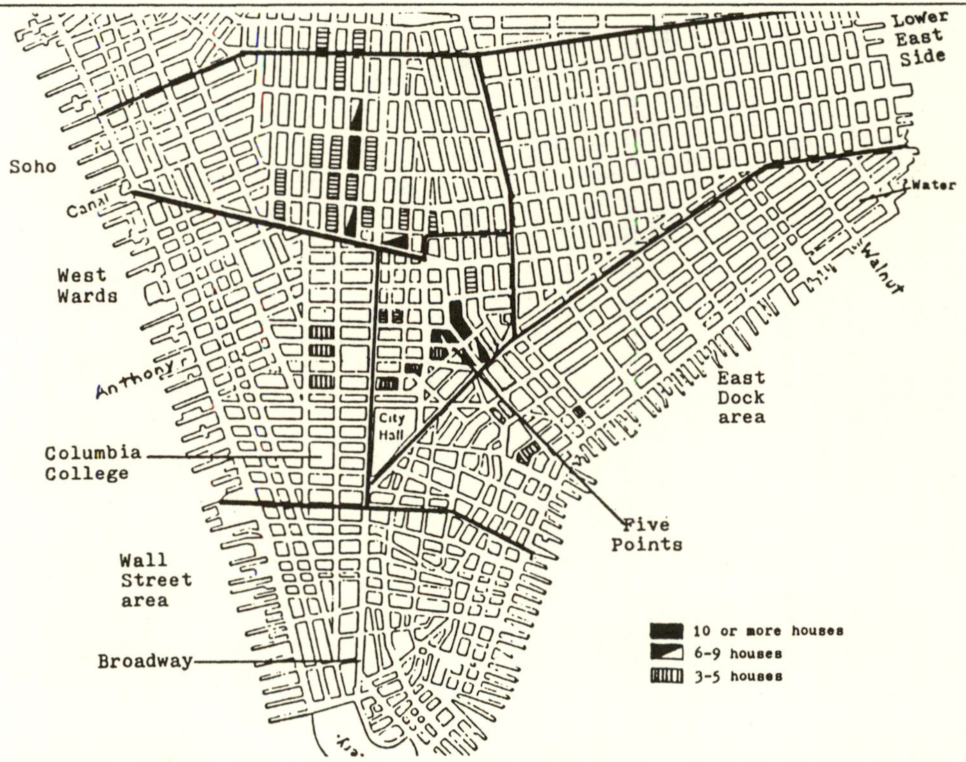

Lower East Side
Water
Walnut
East Dock area
Five Points
City Hall

Soho
West Wards
Canal
Anthony
Columbia College
Wall Street area
Broadway

■ 10 or more houses
▨ 6-9 houses
▥ 3-5 houses

to the Harems located sixty-one of the best-known brothels and houses of assignation in Soho, seventy-five percent of the city's total, while the *Directory of the Seraglios* in New York put seventy-four of the 102 leading houses of carnality there. Only a few houses were listed in Five Points. Furthermore, other tertiary zones of concentration declined in importance. The West Wards had less than a quarter of the leading brothels in the city, while Corlears Hook was not even mentioned.[22]

Why did the moral geography of New York follow this unique pattern? First, rapid population growth left New York unprepared to deal with myriad social problems, prostitution being only one of them. Between 1800 and 1820, the city's population increased 205 percent, passing the 100,000 mark. In the next thirty years, the populace ballooned a staggering 417 percent as New York became the first American city to pass the half-million figure. A large portion of this population was young, single, and foreign born. J. D. B. DeBow reported that there was "among the immigrants a larger proportion of females of the productive age than among the natives." And by no means did men and women arrive in equal numbers. In 1844–1845, four males arrived in New York for every three females. By 1851–1852, that proportion had increased to three to two. Among the whole populace, especially women between twenty and thirty in age, a similar imbalance occurred. In 1840, for every 100 males, there were 127 females. By 1860, the ratio was nearly the same, 100 to 125.[23] Demographically, the rise of prostitution was a product of new sources of supply and demand.

While a surplus of males in the city provided a ready clientele for prostitutes, gender discrimination in the "free market" gave young women few opportunities for economic advancement. Prostitution was, in large part, based on the impoverishment of the working-class female population. In 1833, the *New York Sun* admitted that low pay was

a grievance of the very first magnitude, and pregnant with the most mighty ills of society. . . . This unjust arrangement of remuneration for services performed diminishes the importance of women in society—renders them helpless and dependent—destroys in the lower walks of life much of the inducements to marriage—and of course in the same degree increases the temptation to licentiousness.[24]

More important, however, was the continual stream of transient males in and out of the city. In 1835, approximately 22,000 crewmen aboard ships entered Manhattan. By 1860, the number tripled. From 1840 to 1855, sixty-eight percent of the 3,298,000 immigrants arriving in the United States came via New York City. And by the 1880s, James MacCabe estimated that there were more than 70,000 "strangers from distant parts of the country temporarily sojourning in New York at all periods of the year."[25] Prostitutes gravitated toward this variable population. From 1820 to 1860, the most significant proportions of houses of prostitution were located in the vicinity of three institutions accommodating this mobile group: the hotel, the theater, and the transit station. Paradise Square in Five Points, for example, was ideally located. Its center on Anthony Street was virtually equidistant from the working-class saloons and theaters on the Bowery and the middle- and upper-class clientele frequenting Broadway's hotels and restaurants.[26] West of Broadway were the major ferry terminuses on the Hudson River at Canal, Barclay, and Cortlandt streets. Only one or two blocks from Broadway, the houses on Church and Chapel streets also enjoyed the advantage of being directly behind the first major hotels ever constructed in New York. During the 1830s, at least thirty-four houses of prostitution (thirteen percent) were within 2.5 blocks of a hotel. By the next decade the figure nearly tripled to ninety-six (forty-six percent). Some, such as Mary Benson's brothel at 100 Church Street, were reputed to be the favorite resort of patrons from the Astor House and American Hotel.[27] Finally, the tertiary zones clustered around Water and Walnut streets were at major ferry nodes along the East River. From 1840 to 1849, alone, eighty-two percent of all the prostitution found along the East River was within 2.5 blocks of a ferry station.[28]

As the leading urban leisure institution, theaters also attracted prostitutes who openly plied their trade in the infamous "third tier." When morally sanitized theaters banned blatant sexuality by mid-century, prostitutes simply moved their business to the adjacent streets. During the 1820s, only eleven percent of the houses of prostitution in the city were within 2.5 blocks of a theater. But in the next two decades the numbers rose to thirty-three percent and forty-two percent, respectively. Some brothels specifically catered to theaters. Sarah McGindy's and Mrs. Newman's brothel in Theater Alley behind Park Row serviced performers and patrons alike in the neighboring Park Theater. Sarah Brady's establishment on Church Street and Mrs. Bowen's on Leonard Street each advertised its proximity to the National Theater.[29]

A final factor influencing the way prostitutes used and controlled urban space was the state and the law enforcement power of the municipality. Because New York did not adopt a professional police force until 1845, law enforcement entailed few preventive responsibilities and tended to be reactive. Only when residents complained about noise and disorderly conduct did the watch suppress prostitution. This lenient approach continued even after the creation of a professional force. Compared with its predecessor in London, New York's police force was amateurish, decentralized, and undisciplined, and it operated before 1860 in an environment of legal toleration of prostitution.[30]

These trends intensified after 1850, and partly explain why prostitution became more segregated. From 1850 to 1859, seventy-nine percent of the prostitution that stayed in the Fifth Ward was located within 2.5 blocks of a major hotel. Farther north in Soho, a similar tendency emerged, as seventy-three percent of its brothels were equally close to the large "monster" hotels appearing on Broadway after 1850. Theaters, with fifty-four percent of all the city's brothels within 2.5 blocks, remained a major force in determining the moral geography of Gotham. Even reformers in Five Points blamed the theater for aiding the spread of prostitution. "Struggling on into early womanhood, with a fearfully precocious development of passion, but without one sentiment of decency or shame to screen and protect her, . . . we can only hope to neutralize the attraction of the bar-room or the theater by rendering more attractive the domestic hearth."[31] This geographical reorganization was further spurred by industrial expansion south of Canal Street, forcing the primary and secondary zones of concentration north to Soho as real estate values escalated. Finally, evangelical reformers became more of a presence in Five Points after 1850. In 1854, the Five Points House of Industry was established in the very heart of the neighborhood. Land purchases by these reformers removed sympathetic landlords who previously catered to prostitutes.[32]

The movement of prostitutes into the emerging, newly settled residential neighborhoods of New York and their locational attachment to institutions servicing the middle class indicates that just as the class structure of antebellum New York was redefined by industrialization, so was prostitution. By the 1860s, James MacCabe admitted that the leading first-class houses of prostitution—fully furnished, renting for $1,000 per month, often unknown to their immediate neighbors—were in the best city neighborhoods.[33] When the middle classes abandoned downtown, prostitutes followed them. Increasingly, it appears that the class structure among prostitutes mirrored the clients they serviced, many of whom were wealthy or middle class. While most prostitutes stayed in the city's slums, significant numbers moved uptown. Commercial vice was no longer segregated in riverfront districts; it was found in the enclaves and retreats of middle-class neighborhoods.

The moral geography of New York was convulsively rearranged from 1790 to 1860. After enjoying a period of concentration and isolation in the early nineteenth century, sexual chaos followed in the second quarter of the century. Unlike older European cities or even American cities later in the century, clearly marked red-light districts did not develop in New York. By 1830, resident and visitor alike needed only a ten- or fifteen-minute walk from their domicile before confronting a prostitute or "house of ill-fame." Linked to leading economic and leisure-time institutions, the vulgar reality of prostitution was integrated into the public life of the city. From the ramshackle rookeries of Five Points to the exclusive mansions on Park Place, New Yorkers shared their immediate residential space with the female merchants of commercialized sex. Dr. Sanger's observation connecting it with the most refined theaters, operas, and hotels was no hyperbole. Prostitution, for a short time, transcended the emerging spatial divisions of the city and was a daily fact of life experienced by all classes. Many deplored this new urban vision, but its vivid truth proclaimed antebellum New York "a wide-open town" of illicit revelry and public sexuality.

Notes

1. William W. Sanger, *The History of Prostitution* (New York, 1858, reprint 1937), 29, 593–599.

2. Allan Nevins and Thomas Milton Halsey, eds., *The Diary of George Templeton Strong,* 5 vols. (New York, 1952), I, 260.

3. Ruth Rosen, *The Lost Sisterhood: Prostitution in America, 1900–18* (Baltimore, 1982); Mark Thomas Connelly, *The Response to Prostitution in the Progressive Era* (Chapel Hill, 1980); Marion S. Goldman, *Gold Diggers and Silver Miners: Prostitution and Social Life on the Comstock Lode* (Ann Arbor, Michigan, 1981); Anne Katherine M. Butler, "The Tarnished Frontier: Prostitution in the Trans-Mississippi West, 1865–90" (Ph.D. dissertation, University of Maryland, 1979); Yuji Ichioka, "Ame-yuki-san: Japanese Prostitutes in Nineteenth-Century America," *Amerasia Journal* 4 (1977), 1–17;

James R. McGovern, " 'Sporting Life on the Line': Prostitution in Progressive Era Pensacola," *Florida Historical Quarterly* 54 (1975), 131–41; Al Rose, *Storyville, New Orleans* (University, AL, 1974); Judith R. Walkowitz, *Prostitution and Victorian Society: Women, Class, and the State* (Cambridge, England, 1980).

4. Mary Christine Stansell, "Women of the Laboring Poor in New York City, 1820–1860" (Ph.D. dissertation, Yale University, 1979); Larry H. Whiteaker, "Moral Reform and Prostitution in New York City, 1830–1860" (Ph.D. dissertation, Princeton University, 1977); Carroll Smith-Rosenberg, "Beauty, the Beast, and the Militant Woman: A Case Study in Sex Roles and Social Stress in Jacksonian America," *American Quarterly* 23 (1971), 562–584. Spatial examinations include Richard Symanski, *The Immoral Landscape: Female Prostitution in Western Societies* (Toronto, 1981); Neil Larry Shumsky and Larry M. Springer, "San Francisco's Zone of Prostitution, 1880–1934," *Journal of Historical Geography* 7 (1981), 71–89; and John C. Schneider, "Public Order and the Geography of the City: Crime, Violence, and the Police in Detroit, 1845–75," *Journal of Urban History* 4 (1978), 183–203.

5. To trace the spatial evolution of prostitution, I plotted addresses of houses of prostitution from 1790 to 1870. The addresses were in the following: New York City District Attorney Indictment papers, Court of General Sessions; and the New York City Police Court papers, New York City Municipal Archives and Records Center (hereafter referred to as DA papers and PC papers, respectively); *National Police Gazette,* 1845–1880; Stephen Allen papers, Court Minutes, 1819, and Tavern Complaints, 1822, New York Historical Society (NYHS hereafter); Butt Ender, *Prostitution Exposed; or a Moral Reform Directory* (New York, 1839); and Charles DeKock, *Guide to the Harems, or Directory to the Ladies of Fashion in New York and Various Other Cities* (New York, 1855), both in possession of Prof. Leo Hershkowitz, Queens College, City University of New York; Free Lovyer (sic), *Directory of the Seraglios in New York, Philadelphia, Boston, and all the Principle Cities of the Union* (New York, 1857 and 1859); William H. Bell (policeman), Diary, 1850–1851, NYHS; House of Refuge papers, New York State Library; *Sun; Herald; Tribune.* The wide variety of sources allowed me to examine prostitution over a long period of time and not just when it was suppressed with frequent arrests. Using police and court records, I included only places and names accused of the specific disorderly conduct charge of prostitution (frequently written as "whorring"). Other disorderly charges—quarreling, disturbing the peace, operating an unlicensed saloon—were ignored. Although some of these establishments were, quite likely, haunts for prostitutes, the lack of certainty led me to reject their inclusion. In addition, not all houses of prostitution appeared in the police and court records. The following maps and tables, therefore, are a cautious measure and probably *underestimate* the amount of prostitution in New York. This is further substantiated in *McDowall's Journal,* May 1833, which listed 59 streets with houses of prostitution, 19 of which never appeared in any other records for that decade; and in several municipal reports which listed more than 300 houses of prostitution in 1845. See *Documents of the Board of Aldermen* (New York, 1846), XII, 384 (document 21), 542 (document 33).

6. The development and evolution of functional segregation and the more clearly spatially defined city has been a favored topic among urban historians. See David Ward, "The Emergence of Central Immigrant Ghettoes in American Cities, 1840–1920," *Annals of the Association of American Geographers* 58 (1968), 343–359; Olivier Zunz, *The Changing Face of Inequality: Urbanization, Industrial Development, and Immigrants in Detroit, 1880–1920* (Chicago, 1982), 15–177; Elizabeth Blackmar, "Rewalking the 'Walking City': Housing and Property Relations in New York City, 1780–1840," *Radical History Review* 21 (1979), 131–148; John C. Schneider, *Detroit and the Problem of Order, 1830–80* (Lincoln, NB, 1980); Sam Bass Warner, Jr., *The Private City: Philadelphia in Three Periods of Its Growth* (Philadelphia, 1968) 11–17, 50–61, 169–200.

7. Quoted in Carl Bridenbaugh, *Cities in Revolt* (New York, 1977), 318.

8. William A. Duer, *Reminiscences of an Old New Yorker* (New York, 1867), 10; I.N. Phelps Stokes, *The Iconography of Manhattan Island, 1498–1910,* 5 vols. (New York, 1912), IV, 581, 862; V, 1194, 1204, 1343; Edward Bangs, ed., *Journal of Lt. Isaac Bangs, 1776* (Cambridge, Mass., 1890), 29. For the de Crevecoeur quote, see *Magazine of American History* 2 (1878), 749.

9. *Moreau de St. Mèry's American Journey, 1793–1798,* translated and edited by Kenneth and Anna M. Roberts (Garden City, NY, 1947), 156, 173. For petitions, see *Minutes of the Common Council of the City of New York, 1784–1831,* 30 vols. (New York, 1917) (hereafter MCC), III, 393 (November 21, 1803); V, 192 (July 11, 1808), 266 (September 19, 1808). George Street, later renamed Spruce

Street, was the dividing line between the Second and Fourth wards. East George Street was in the Seventh Ward and later renamed Market Street. Charlotte Street was a block east and renamed Pike Street. Another fifteen percent of the indictments were in the Seventh Ward, many of which were probably on or in the vicinity of East George Street.

10. *Moreau de St. Mèry,* 156; Stokes, *Iconography,* IV, 862; Petition of 23 residents to Common Council, September 21, 1802, Common Council papers, box 30, New York City Municipal Archives and Records Center (hereafter NYCMA); MCC, V, 603 (July 10, 1809). In order to illustrate and measure the physical movement of prostitution over time, I divided the city into neighborhoods based upon their ward numbers and physical separation by major thoroughfares. Since neighborhoods and their perceived boundaries change, this is an admittedly imperfect method. Nevertheless, it is the best means of breaking down the physical city into constant parts and then measuring geographical change over time. The neighborhoods and their boundaries are: Wall Street area—south of Fulton Street (First Ward and parts of the Second and Fourth wards); West wards—north of Fulton Street, west of Broadway to Hudson River, south of Canal Street (most of the Third and all of the Fifth wards); East Dock area—north of Fulton Street, east of Chatham Street, Park Row, and East Broadway to East River, south of Canal and Grand streets (most of the Fourth and Seventh wards); Five Points—area bounded by Broadway, Canal Street, Centre Street, Hester Street, Bowery, Chatham Street, Park Row (all of the Sixth and part of the Fourteenth wards); Soho—area bounded by Canal Street, Centre Street, Hester Street, Bowery, Houston Street, Hudson River (all of the Eighth and most of the Fourteenth wards); Lower East Side—Bowery, Houston Street, East River, Grand Street, and East Broadway (all of the Tenth and Thirteenth and part of the Eleventh wards).

11. By 1808, the physical development along Broadway had reached as far north as Anthony Street and the vicinity of the Collect Pond. Further east, the city spread as far as Grand Street on the Bowery and Montgomery Street in the Seventh Ward. In fact, only small parts of the Fifth, Sixth, and Seventh wards remained undeveloped. Only the filling of swampland and the Collect slowed their conversion to completely developed real estate. The best description of New York's physical development can be found in U.S. Department of the Interior, Census Office, *Tenth Census of the U.S., 1880, Report on the Social Statistics of Cities,* comp. by George Waring, Jr., 2 vols. (Washington, DC, 1886), XVIII, map facing 555; and James Grant Wilson, Memorial History of New York City (New York, 1893), III, 208.

12. Locating specific and near-specific addresses was accomplished by matching block numbers with street addresses using the following: Tax Assessment maps, Third Ward (1859); *Record of Assessments, Fifth Ward* (1853), (1819, 1821, 1832, 1834, 1837, 1839, 1859), Third Ward (1939), Eighth Ward (1830), NYCMA; George W. and Walter S. Bromley, *Atlas of City of New York* (Philadelphia, 1899); *Longworth's American Almanac, New York Register, and City Directory* (New York, 1828 and 1834) have tables for locating street numbers.

13. *MCC,* VII, 72 (March 18, 1812); *Fireman's Own,* October 6, 1849, in Charles P. Daly papers, New York Public Library, scrapbook 21, page 69.

14. *Niles' Register,* October 14, 1820.

15. Wilson, *Memorial History of New York City,* III, 208; and Census Office, *Report on the Social Statistics of Cities,* XVIII, 564–565. For maps illustrating a decade-by-decade breakdown of the location of prostitution, see Timothy Gilfoyle, "Prostitution and the Commercialization of Sex in New York City, 1790–1920" (Ph.D. dissertation, Columbia University, in progress), chapter 2.

16. PC papers, box 7451, *Prudden v. Murray,* August 5, 1838; *The Rake,* July 9, 1842, copy in DA papers, *People v. Meighan,* August 8, 1842.

17. Butt Ender, *Prostitution Exposed,* cited 75 addresses. The breakdown by neighborhood was: Five Points—23, West Wards—19, Lower East Side—15, Soho—12, East Dock—5, Wall Street—1.

18. Because of the lack of specific addresses, it is impossible to compute similar ratios from 1790 to 1819. The high percentage in the East Dock area and especially on George and East George streets would seem to indicate, however, that there were higher concentration ratios during this period. Significantly, in the decade 1850–1859, the concentration jumped to 2.46:1, statistical evidence that a new exclusive red-light district in Soho just west of Broadway was beginning to appear.

19. Symanski, *Immoral Landscape,* 38; Robert Dykstra, *The Cattle Towns* (New York, 1968), 260.

20. *Sun,* May 29, 1834.

21. *Tribune,* March 14, 1855; Butt Ender, *Prostitution Exposed.* "Slamm's Row" was between Norfolk at Essex streets. For the Battery, see note 16.

22. The Water Street area, however, was the exception to this trend, remaining the leading center of waterfront vice throughout the century. See DeKock, *Guide to the Harems;* Free Lovyer (sic), *Directory of the Seraglios.*

23. J. D. B. DeBow, *Statistical View of the U.S.: A Compendium of the Seventh Census* (Washington, DC, 1854), 121–23. On male-female ratios, see Franklin B. Hough, *Statistics on the Population of the City and County of New York* (New York, 1866); and Stansell, "Women of the Laboring Poor," 88. Among whites, the sex ratios were:

	Male	Female	Male (20–30)	Female (20–30)
1830	100	106	100	100
1840	100	108	100	127
1850	100	102	100	108
1860	100	105	100	125

24. *Sun,* March 14, 1833. On female labor in New York, see Stansell, "Women of the Laboring Poor."

25. James D. MacCabe, *New York by Sunlight and Gaslight* (Philadelphia, 1882), 53. On the number of crewman, see Robert Albion, *The Rise of New York Port, 1815–1860* (New York, 1939), 398; on immigration, see Edward K. Spann, *The New Metropolis: New York, 1840–1857* (New York, 1981), 24.

26. The center of block 166 was approximately 825 feet from Chatham Square, 1100 feet from the Bowery, and 975 feet from Broadway.

27. Butt Ender, *Prostitution Exposed.*

28. Ferry terminuses are found on W. Hooker, *Plan of the City of New York* (New York, 1817); and D. H. Burr, *Map of the City of New York* (New York, 1837), Columbia University Map Collection. On the problem of pimps recruiting innocent girls at steamboat and ferry stations, see *Advocate of Moral Reform,* October 2, 1848.

29. Butt Ender, *Prostitution Exposed.* On the "third tier," see Claudia D. Johnson, "That Guilty Third Tier: Prostitution in Nineteenth Century American Theaters," in Daniel Walker Howe, ed., *Victorian America* (Philadelphia, 1976), 111–120. The locations of nineteenth century theaters are in Mary C. Henderson, *The City and the Theater: New York Playhouses from Bowling Green to Times Square* (Clifton, NJ, 1973); and George W. and Walter S. Bromley, *Atlas of the City of New York* (Philadelphia, 1899). Prostitution was also spatially linked to the saloon. The vast numerical expansion of saloons, however, makes similar geographical comparison with houses of prostitution less meaningful than with hotels, theaters, and ferry stations. In 1827, for example, the municipality issued 2305 tavern and excise licenses in the lower eight wards of the city, a plentiful 5.4 saloons on each city block. The Fourth and Sixth wards each had impressive averages of more than seven liquor establishments per block. With such a large and dense quantity of saloons in each ward, most houses of prostitution were likely to be located within one or two blocks. Statistics on excise licenses from 1821 to 1837 are in Documents of the Board of Aldermen (New York, 1837), III, 593. The number of blocks is based upon William Hooker, *Map of the City of New York* (New York, 1831).

30. Wilbur R. Miller, *Cops and Bobbies: Police Authority in New York and London, 1830–70* (Chicago, 1973), 16, 44, 102–103.

31. Five Points House of Industry, *Monthly Record,* May, 1858.

32. Miller, *Cops and Bobbies,* 204; Carroll Smith-Rosenberg, *Religion and the Rise of the American City: The New York City Mission Movement, 1812–70* (Ithaca, 1971), chapter 8.

33. MacCabe, *Secrets,* 208–209, 285–288.

PRUDERY AND PASSION: VICTORIAN AMERICA

6

Introduction

Sexual deviance is what society says it is. The point was well illustrated in the stigmatized behavior of America in the nineteenth century. Abnormality was classified simply as sexual conduct in which intent was other than procreation. Enforcement continued to involve "elevation of norms to the sacred." Increasingly, however, the main force against deviance was community or peer pressure. A new prudery was afoot in the land, in substantial degree, a product of an attempt by a rising middle class to demonstrate respectability in a period when proper definition of it was unclear. One result was that excesses begot excesses. A consequence was an arguable level of "sexual repression." Major contours of that debate are roughly as follows. One tact is to assert that alleged "repression" is better understood as enhanced regulation over public discourse because many more aspects of societal life were sexualized. A second is to challenge the assumed close correlation between apparent sexual etiquette, which was proscriptive, and actual social behavior. A third is to suggest that whatever the nature of repression, it was never uniform, depending rather on variables such as gender, ethnic/racial factors, social class, and even geography. At any rate, a rigid measure of "proper form" developed in matters related to sexuality as well as other social conduct that was measured against, in the words of one character in an eighteenth-century English stage drama, "What will Mrs. Grundy say?"

Yet definition of sexual deviance was not based merely on the word of Mrs. Grundy. It was premised also on an understanding of human physiology as well as interaction between it and nineteenth-century social mores. Basically, that physiological view involved two conventional assumptions about the body. A first was that the somatic well-being of the mind or intellect depended on the material body for energy and power. Operating properly, the mind could stimulate the body's resources, bringing increase in blood flow to the brain and enhancing its creativity or effectiveness. Too little or too much flow, however, could have highly negative consequences. The second assumption stated that the body was at any given time a closed or all-inclusive energy system. Because it was an economic unit, an increase in vital power in one part of the body meant other parts were, at least, diminished. Placed in the context of sexuality, this meant a great concern over male sperm loss because it would obliterate all energies in the body system, at least for some period of time. Sexual activity could be carried out only at the expense of nonsexual and higher uses, i.e., creativity, spiritual excellence, worldly success. One was inevitably accomplished at the expense of the other. Carried to its logical extreme, celibacy would be the social ideal. Biblical injunction to "go forth and multiply" modified this conclusion by giving sanction, indeed imperative, to sexual activity for purposes of procreation, but that only. The injunction meant that all sexual practice other than for procreative purposes was defined as deviant and stigmatized. This included all forms of birth control. All contraceptive devices, condoms to intravaginal forms, obtained social condemnation.

While there was acknowledgment in the previous two centuries that sexual desire existed in men and women, the dictates of nineteenth-century prudery *sought* to deny that desire (with uneasy levels of acceptance) at least in women. Women were held to be immune from "sensuality" and possessed a "natural frigidity." On the other hand, and more covertly, the fact that the essential nature of females was so involved in their sexual organs, suggested a sexual boundlessness quite frightening to the society of the period. Put in terms of physiological theory, women were not only dangerous to the well-being of men but to the advance of civilization itself. Women were sperm absorbers. Common conjecture among some historians has been that male-enforced demonstration of "sexlessness" in women of nineteenth-century America was an effort to deny female desire. In this situation female display of sexuality or indications that the existence of desire implied health problems meant "something was wrong." In a most interesting and provocative essay elsewhere, G. J. Barker-Benfield has argued that male ill-ease about the potential of female sexuality in the later nineteenth century encouraged the growth of gynecological surgery as a response to those anxieties (*The Spermatic Economy. . . .* , 1972: See Bibliography Cit.). Whatever the case here and for purposes of this introductory statement, the point is that women must be prohibited not only from indulging their own brands of deviance (female masturbation, for example, or increased heterosexual desire), but must also not be allowed complicity or co-conspiratorial participation in stigmatized behavior by males. This section contains five chapters that speak to application of the "deviant" label to aspects of male and female human sexuality in nineteenth-century America.

As might be expected, among the worst expressions of male sexual deviance in that century were masturbation and homosexual activity. Both were ejaculatory waste and perversion at the extreme. In the first chapter of this section, Vern L. Bullough and Martha Voght concern themselves with the confusion that existed between these sexual practices in nineteenth-century America. During the previous two centuries, sexuality was openly dealt with and discussed. Almost all forms of deviance fell under the label "sodomy." This at various times included anal sex, bestiality, masturbation, oral genital contacts, and even some forms of birth control. In the nineteenth century this catchall label gave way to another, "crimes against nature" or "crimes that could not be named." Few Americans had any real ideas of what practices were included. Given force by Biblical injunction of "wicked-ness," which the phrases came to connote, they were applied to all sexual practices or people (sodomists) who were considered sexually evil.

Among the practices that fell clearly under these phrases during most of the nineteenth century was homosexuality, which was classified also under terms "onanism" or masturbation. "Onanism" like "sodomy" had Biblical origin and force. It was defined loosely as the "spilling of seed" without the purpose or possibility of impregnation. Only by recognizing that "onanism" or masturbation were umbrella terms, which included homosexuality, is it possible to understand the public horror evoked by their use. These practices portended debilitation of mental and physical capabilities and illness. Moreover, masturbation was com-monly connected directly to homosexuality because the practice of the former led inevitably to the latter. It was asserted also that pederasts were "diseased" indi-viduals whose problem stemmed from youthful masturbation. Finally, assumption was that the "solitary vice" or "secret sin" led men to separate from women and dispose them against normal marriage just as did homosexual acts. The equation between masturbation and homosexuality continued, according to Bullough and Voght, in varying degrees into the twentieth century.

Prostitution was in origin an ancient form of sexual deviance, but one regarded very differently at times across the American past. For at least the first fifty years of the nineteenth century it was understood as a personal moral infraction on the part of both prostitutes and clients and one for which they bore individual respon-sibility. In the latter part of the century the public mood was such to increasingly see causation in social circumstance. The extreme of which, in the period of so-called Progressive reform, was what can be labelled "sociological morality," briefly put, "I am depraved because I am deprived." Moreover, across much of the nineteenth century there were two major responses to prostitution as deviant behavior. One was essentially a personal, moral, and religious vision, which op-posed prostitution stringently and concluded that its eradication was an obtainable ideal. The second was ostensibly one of resignation—the conclusion that prosti-tution was inevitable in society. It should be dealt with, therefore, as a sanitary issue and criminal concern. This vision led toward segregation and legal regulation of the practice. The former vision was at least abstractly the dominant one. Yet every major urban center had its "red-light" district, which was apparently allowed and tolerated by socially respectable and influential segments of these communities. Neil L. Shumsky seeks to explain this "tacit acceptance" in his analysis of the period 1870–1910 provided in this section.

While antiprostitution statutes were "on the books" in most cities, they were simply laxly enforced, if at all, in certain "segregated" geographical locations of those centers. Shumsky argues this was the case because the presence of these "red-light" districts provided at least two social benefits to the "respectable citi-zenry." They expressed a socio/economic class bias in allowing a form of behavioral control over the bestial rampant sexual appetites by social inferiors, the working-class poor, or immigrants. Such districts would not stop prostitution but would discourage its "scattering" into respectable neighborhoods—for these areas were almost always located in marginal parts of cities. They would also protect "respectable" women from the rampant sexual urges of the fringe population. Secondly, "red-light" districts helped to establish the boundaries of acceptable behavior. There were those who went and those who did not, the latter being the measure of respectability. Deviant actors provided a behavioral contrast, allowing those "who did not" a greater sense of their own territorial identity. This contrast capability was provided also at a very crucial point in time. This was a period in which American sexuality was being sharply circumscribed and strictly "deployed" into the family setting. Patronization of prostitutes was a violation of marital "mutuality." In brief, "red-light" districts in the period 1870–1910 played a primary role in the establishment and maintenance of acceptable behavioral norms.

Not unlike prostitution, sexual assault is a continuing concern in the present volume. Central to the sexual script of Victorian America was the idealization of female virtue. Impurity in women was a threat to the delicate moral and sexual balance of the period. A prescribed natural frigidity and lack of desire put limitations on their respectable sexuality even in marriage. Indeed societal affirmation of that purity was intended to serve as a symbolic regulator or control of male lust. But there were fissures in this structure, the dark lurking fear of female's potential sexual boundlessness, if only as residue of an earlier age. In part this explains the fact that even women forced into sexual intercourse against their will were somehow still stained by the event. In such "falls from grace" victims were in danger of blame for the act of the perpetrator. As noted previously, behavioral warning to females about future contact was quite likely one message invoked by the "unwritten law." Elizabeth Pleck speaks to the whole issue of sexual assault in the third chapter of this section. If at first glance the strategies employed in "crimes against women" by nineteenth-century feminists appear simplistic, Pleck points out that they must be understood in proper historical context. They were up against and seeking the attention of a society that was at best indifferent, at worst hostile to any public discussion of sexual crimes perpetrated on women.

Feminists' concerns here were broad. They included support services for victims, condemnation of rape, incest, battery, pornography, and lobbying efforts to overcome legislatively perceived sources of ill fortune. Some advocates ascribed greater weight to one cause over another but all held in common relief of longstanding injustices to their gender. The front was broad. On the one hand stood liberal feminists, epitomized by Elizabeth Cady Stanton and Susan B. Anthony. They entered this realm of women's welfare through the avenue of the temperance crusade in the 1850s. The main focus of their concern, sexual violence in marriage, was the then radical remedy of divorce. Punishment for rape was also simple. It should be a capital offense. Another position was that of conservative feminists, a la Lucy Stone and husband Henry Blackwell. They saw issues of the marriage state and divorce as peripheral to greater control of their lives by women through suffrage. This would assure proper statutory protection for women against sexual violence. Here, too, rape would call for the death penalty. Two other significant voices on the issue of "crimes against women" were Women's Christian Temperance Union (WCTU) and the Chicago-based, The Protective Agency for Women and Children. The former originated with a sole interest in temperance then broadened its concerns. While alcohol might remain the primary social villain in the plight of women, sexual violence and male licentiousness were also targets. The latter seemed more interested in strategies than final solutions. Both the WCTU and the Chicago agency urged legal aid and judicial remedies. For reasons which Pleck elaborates upon, feminist interest in "crimes against women" declined in the last decade of the nineteenth century.

A next concern in this section is with female same-sex relationships. The concept of male homosexuality was a historical creation. In development it required a necessary distinction between homosexual behavior and homosexual identities. As understood until circa the last two decades of the nineteenth century, the former was viewed as a potentiality for sin in all human beings, unless legally circumscribed and judicially punished. The latter, understood as disease (yet also criminality) was conceived as an individual condition of being that included stereotyped characteristics such as effeminacy and promiscuity. With the crucial period of reconceptualization of homosexuality, that phenomenon took on for the first time a social purpose for the larger culture. It would provide a clear-cut boundary between permissible and nonpermissible expression of sexuality. It fostered and facilitated segregation of such deviant actors. Among actors it also encouraged development of social structure, that is, a conscious homosexual community. The matter of female same-sex intimacy, while it played into this scenario, had its own particular contours. For one thing, recognition of lesbianism had to overcome the Victorian notion of heterosexual bias and of female passionlessness. The two combined to assure the popular mind that if women would not readily respond to male advances, they would certainly not make other women their sexual object choice and or would not feel desire for other women. Moreover, close bonds between women were quite respectable in Victorian America, even perhaps encouraged by default, amidst extensive constraints on cross-gender relationships. In a crucial period approximating the turn of the century, the understood nature of those "above suspicion" relationships changed radically. They underwent "morbidification," as Lillian Faderman explains in the fourth chapter of this section, with profound consequences for female same-sex relationships.

Attitudes toward love between women in contemporary America are very different from what they were *during much* of the previous century. The latter allowed a broader spectrum for expression of love and affection. That intense and intimate relationships were not deemed improper was suggested strongly by the fact that whereas men were prosecuted for homosexual behavior throughout almost all the western world, women were generally ignored by law. By the opening years of the twentieth century and the emergence of the *condition* of homosexuality, certain sexual theorists concluded that female intimate same-sex relationships invited, if not assured, a syndrome of ills. Moreover, certain sexologists, in seeking to protect homosexuals form persecution by attributing their sexual proclivities to a congenital base, seemed invariably to cast homosexual relations in a distasteful and violent light. Congenital homosexuality thus became inextricably linked with morbidity in popular perception. Before the women's movement of the 1960s, when earlier lesbian novels were published—be they accepting or condemning of such relationships—they shared in common the theme that such relationships inevitably led to negative ends. Twentieth-century fashion gave stern warning against and acted to deter even adolescent same-sex "crushes" because of the "morbid" way in which they would be perceived. Of recent decades, the lesbian-feminists movement as one segment of the larger woman's movement opened the way in fiction and otherwise for a more positive and optimistic view of female same-sex relationships. The central ingredient here is the Lesbian-Feminist assertion that lesbianism is a political choice and has nothing to do with congenital propensities as once asserted. Women are fully capable of both heterosexual and homosexual arousal. In a basically heterosexual culture, females simply move easily to a heterosexual commitment. Once this is in place they tend to "screen out" same-sex attractions. Faderman adroitly describes the transition.

The final chapter of this section is concerned with one form of "conventional deviance," namely premarital pregnancy and social response to such behavior. The behavior warrants examination in this section because it well illustrates the mercurial potential inherent in the social construction of deviance and social variables that affect response to it. In the eighteenth century no substantial long-term liabilities were attached to premarital sex or pregnancies obtained in that state, at least if the end result was marriage. While out-of-wedlock births continued to be matters of moral concern in that century, bastardy tended to become primarily an economic issue. If the newborn did not become the responsibility of the community, then neither the mother nor the child suffered sustained social scars. But by the later nineteenth century, America had lost its tolerance for premarital sex whatever its outcome, especially if pregnancy was involved. The level of social stigma in the case of illicit pregnancy was elevated dramatically. It meant for affected females enormous trauma and emotional consequence: embarrassment, guilt, sense of betrayal, and great fear about the future. For the family of the young woman, it meant shame and perhaps anger at such a symbolic affront to patriarchal authority. A characteristic of social response to out-of-wedlock pregnancy changed from a matter of concern, primarily by private charitable organizations, to the domain of professional social service personnel and municipal public agencies. In the late nineteenth century rescue and recovery efforts were largely in the hands of middle-class women operating in the context of evangelicalism and social purity. Under the impact of Progressivism, this activity passed to others, formally trained and specialized for these tasks.

Cleveland, Ohio, and its environs were no different than most urban centers in these regards. Marian J. Morton explores the matter of response to out-of-wedlock pregnancy at that location in her chapter titled, "Seduced and Abandoned in an American City: Cleveland and Its Fallen Women, 1869–1936." The specter of "seduced and abandoned" women haunted Cleveland's reformers in the late nineteenth century. However exaggerated by Victorian sensibility and rhetoric, their fears about "fallen women" were grounded in very real economic and sexual vulnerability in that city and others as well. In this regard, Cleveland's middle-class women were quite alert to the dangers and temptations of their city. Their charity organizations operating in the evangelical style of nineteenth-century benevolence sought to rescue bodies *and* souls. Gradually, and influenced by Progressive social thought, the array of these organizations took on professional coordination. Gradually, also, in two decades of the twentieth century the constituency of their efforts changed in two respects: age and ethnicity. The former moved downward from what it had been. In the latter case, number of foreign born and especially Cleveland's blacks moved upward substantially. The "Great Depression" in the 1930s did not alter, in any significant way, characteristics of clients, but it did help to diminish zeal for reclamation of that clientele. Social service organizations were hit hard; many went heavily into the "red" and/or collapsed. In general, the number of women seeking help from the several agencies of the city declined. Professionalization of agency personnel continued, a corollary of which was use of techniques not welcomed by clients. Age and racial characteristics of unwed mothers noted previously meant that clients no longer fit the traditional model of reclaimable women who had "fallen from grace." The increasing view of them was sexually promiscuous burdens on the tax payers. Yet, and overall, the frightened pregnant women who sought help remained essentially the same people as they had been at the conclusion of the Civil War: too often poor, too often abandoned, too easily exploited, too dependent on others.

7

Homosexuality and Its Confusion with the "Secret Sin" in Pre-Freudian America

Vern L. Bullough and Martha Voght

Anyone doing research into attitudes toward sex is faced with the problem of ferreting out the terms which have been used in the past to describe various kinds of sexual activities. For those attempting to investigate what any particular society regarded as 'deviant sex' the problem is compounded both by changes in the meaning of terms and by the lack of any precise definition of what is meant unless there are examples to serve as illustrations. This paper is concerned with American medical conceptions of masturbation and homosexuality in the nineteenth century based on a few such examples and the effect the confusion of the two had in creating a general fear of sex. This particular confusion seems to be primarily a nineteenth-century phenomenon although even before that time definitions were not very rigorous.

In the seventeenth and eighteenth centuries Americans were fairly open in their discussions of sex but even then there was a lack of scientific precision in their descriptions of sexual activities and almost all types of deviant sexual behavior were classed as sodomy. From surviving sermons and extant law cases it appears that sodomy at times included not only anal intercourse but bestiality, mutual masturbation, oral genital contacts, and even some forms of birth control.[1] By the nineteenth century, however, sodomy had lost much of its sexual connotation for most Americans. Instead of legal references to sodomy, Americans, following the English common law, adopted the terms 'crime against nature' or the 'crime which could not be named,' and it is not at all clear that most Americans knew just exactly what these acts constituted. The fullest legal explanation of what was meant derives from Sir Edward Coke's (1552–1634) exposition of English common law.[2] Later commentators, rather than spell out what constituted such acts, cite him, as well as Biblical and statutory references on the subject without ever defining what is meant. Perhaps typical of later attitudes is that of Sir William Blackstone who wrote:

I will not act so disagreeable a part, to my readers as well as myself, as to dwell any longer upon a subject the very mention of which is a disgrace to human nature. It will be more eligible to imitate in this respect the delicacy of our English law, which treats it, in its very indictments, as a crime not fit to be named.[3]

Inevitably enforcement was not particularly effective and all of the convictions for the 'crime against nature' we have been able to trace down in nineteenth-century America involved adults and minors or humans and animals, not consenting adults. Further difficulties existed in enforcement because common law tradition held that solicitation to commit a sex act was neither a criminal act nor a misdemeanor. Generally also the law held that both participants in an illegal act were guilty and this meant that one person involved in an illegal sex act could not testify against another without being found guilty himself or herself.

If the law was ambiguous on the subject of sodomy, and more or less unenforced, sodomy itself remained a sin to Bible-reading Americans although they were not clear just exactly what it meant. The result was to classify as sodomists those people who were regarded as evil. Frontier Alabama, for example, had a town named Sodom, not because of the sexual activities of the inhabitants but because their neighbors regarded them as murderers, bandits, vandals, and general hell-raisers.[4] Youngstown, Ohio, still has a Sodom-Hutchins Road which in the past led to a town of Sodom, one of a group of towns named after Biblical sites and not necessarily implying sexual irregularity, only an evil place.

Reformers and purists also used the term to classify things they did not like as evil. Anthony Comstock, for one, repeatedly referred to sodomists without ever really understanding what might be implied. Comstock also indicates another difficulty of attempting to find key words which might describe sexual activity and how easy it is to be misled unless there is an explanation of what is meant. This is illustrated by Comstock's hostility to 'long-haired men and short-haired women,' which might be taken as a reference to homosexuality, but in his mind such people were free lovers who lusted after the opposite sex without legal restrictions, who defended books which he considered to be obscene, who advocated birth control, and who in general opposed the Comstock definition of purity.[5]

Medical writers followed general social usage and used terms as ambiguously as their lay brethren. Although medical journals were somewhat freer from the prudery of lay society, medical practitioners blurred sexual definitions and discarded older and blunter terminology. The result was the same kind of confusion that existed in society at large. This appears most obvious in the discussion of homosexuality, a field which so far has received very little attention. In fact almost no scholarly investigation has been concerned with nineteenth-century American sexual practices in general.[6]

During most of the nineteenth century homosexuality was often classified under the term *onanism* or *masturbation*. The term *onanism*, like *sodomy*, had a Biblical origin but unlike *sodomy* its association with sexual activity was clearly spelled out. Since the sin of Onan (apparently *coitus interruptus*) was interpreted as the spilling of his seed without possibility of procreation, almost all forms of sexual activity not resulting in pregnancy could be classed with Onan's sin, and it became a convenient medical handle partly because its Biblical sanction made it less likely to offend sensibilities. Inevitably, however, classifying all 'deviant' sex practices as onanism caused confusion.

There have been several studies on the growing concern over masturbation in the nineteenth century,[7] but masturbation was a catchall term, and without understanding the implication of homosexuality which it carried, it is difficult to understand why our ancestors regarded it with such horror. This horror was undoubtedly accentuated because medical concern with onanism was a comparatively new phenomenon, and was regarded by many physicians as a new scientific discovery. Probably the most influential force in bringing sexual activity to medical attention was the Lausanne physician S. A. Tissot (1718–97) who taught that all sexual activity was dangerous because it caused blood to rush to the brain which in turn starved the nerves (making them more susceptible to damage) and thereby increasing the likelihood of insanity. In his classic work, *L'Onanisme* (1760),[8] he argued that the worst kind of sexual activity was the solitary orgasm since it could be indulged in so conveniently and at such a tender age that excess was inevitable. Moreover, since onanism was a Biblical sin, the realization of guilt which such an act entailed opened the nervous system to further damages. Tissot also illustrates the ambiguity which came to dominate American medical thinking since his description of female masturbation would today be labeled as homosexual activity because he did not describe a solitary orgasm but a mutual one. Since such confusion existed from the beginning of medical thinking about masturbation there is little wonder that homosexual activity was incorporated into the sin of Onan. Tissot's ideas seem to have been more suggested by religious pamphleteering on the subject than any real scientific research,[9] but his influence on the medical profession was profound. In this respect nineteenth-century medicine departed from most earlier medical writers who, when they discussed sex, did so in terms of moderation rather than the kind of prohibitions put forth by Tissot.

Tissot's teaching that excessive sexual activity caused insanity led a great many American investigators to emphasize the danger of sex. Benjamin Rush listed masturbation as one of the inciting causes of mental disease. In addition he felt the overuse of the sexual power might lead to 'seminal weakness, impotence, dysury, tabes dorsalis, pulmonary consumption, dyspepsia, dimness of sight, vertigo, epilepsy, hypochondriasis, loss of memory, manalgia, fatuity, and death.' Rush, however, retained enough of his classic medical training to include some positive aspects of sex and felt that abnormal restraint was also dangerous since it produced 'tremors, a flushing of the face, sighing, nocturnal pollutions, hysteria, hypochondriasis, and in women the furor uterinus.'[10]

Increasingly, however, American physicians emphasized the special dangers of sexual activity that did not result in procreation. Such activity was supposed to debilitate the patient's physical and mental capacities causing him easily to succumb to grave physical and mental illness. As evidence for such assertions, physicians offered their observations that large numbers of patients in mental institutions masturbated, and from this they concluded that it was such practices that originally had caused them to become ill. Inevitably when physicians could find no other cause for insanity, they looked to masturbation, and numerous tracts were written warning young men and women of its perils. Thomas L. Nicholas, a nineteenth-century hydropathic practitioner, felt that though some people might be hereditarily predisposed toward insanity, the risk was increased by exhaustion from masturbation, disappointment in love, grief, and disorder of the passions.[11] Some physicians, even though they might have believed in the dangers of masturbation, hesitated to speak about the subject because it was so unmentionable. In this they were following English examples and William Acton, for example, complained that many medical writers found the topic so unmentionable that the field was dominated by quacks. He wrote to correct this but in the process gave his support to the whole concept of masturbatory insanity.[12]

In the United States Alfred Hitchcock, writing in the *Boston Medical and Surgical Journal* in 1842, felt called upon to chastise his fellow physicians for their reticence on sexual subjects and urged them to be more candid in putting the blame for much of the illness of Americans on onanism. It was medical silence on the matter, he wrote, that encouraged 'wasted lives' as young people engaged in the practice without knowledge of its horrible results. He reported that he himself had observed several fatal cases, including one of a twenty-three-year-old man who died after six years of habitual masturbation.[13] Henceforth in most medical writings insanity, illness, and masturbation came to be increasingly linked together. The famed Abraham Jacobi, considered the founder of pediatrics in the United States, was only reflecting current prejudice when he blamed infantile paralysis and infantile rheumatism on masturbation.[14] Those few holdouts who hesitated to accept such linkages were severely criticized by Allen W. Hagenbach, who had studied some 800 male 'insane' at Cook County Hospital in Chicago. Hagenbach wrote that although there might have been some overexaggeration of the effects of masturbation, it was still difficult to overrate them. Unfortunately, he added, some medical practitioners in order 'to counteract the exaggerated statements of charlatans and popular works designed to excite the fears for a mercenary end, go to the opposite extreme of regarding the practice as harmless.' To support his thesis he offered several case studies. One in which he reported masturbation as an 'exciting cause of insanity' involved a young man who started the practice at fifteen, even though 'aware of the injurious results.' He said the youth eventually 'attempted suicide to put an end to his mental suffering. He died in a state of complete dementia. As is frequently the case, his delusions were self accusatory in character.' To the modern reader what appears from this description is a severe anxiety state involving the peculiar norms of the day, but Dr. Hagenbach was a man with a passion against masturbation. His blindness to anything but his own preconceived notions is evident from his statement that the penis of the typical masturbator was 'enormously enlarged' when elsewhere in his own study he reports that after measuring the genitalia of twenty-six insane masturbators he found only five with enlarged penises, eighteen that could be regarded as normal, and three with 'atrophied' appendages, whatever that might mean. Hagenbach was one of those who used masturbation to include almost any kind of behavior that did not specifically involve heterosexual intercourse. One of his cases, for example, an 'insane masturbator' unwilling to make 'any efforts at reform,' was described as an effeminate young man who carried a fan and did needlework. He added that 'the corrupted sexual feelings, such as forming morbid attachments for persons of his (own) sex, are quite marked, and it became necessary to remove several patients to different wards to separate him from the object of his regards.' All of this was due to the fact that the youth had begun to masturbate at age fourteen.[15] Obviously once a youth began to masturbate he was started on the inevitable path to homosexuality. Others adopted the same conclusions.

Joseph W. Howe, a physician writing in 1889, for example, flatly stated that pederasts were diseased individuals whose problems stemmed from youthful onanism.[16] Another physician, James Foster Scott, published a book as late as 1899 in which he classified all kinds of acts as masturbation including withdrawal, coitus in *os,* coitus *interfemora,* pederasty, bestiality, mutual masturbation, and 'self pollution.' It was masturbation which led men to separate 'further and further from women,' and 'to be put into a peculiarly unnatural relation to them.' This in turn resulted in an indisposition to marriage and encouraged sexual adventures with others of the same sex. As far as females alone were concerned, Scott held any kind of withdrawal was mutual masturbation and that any child conceived during such perverted coition would have a malformed sexual instinct.[17]

There are other references in the medical literature to the same beliefs,[18] although not all medical discussion of masturbation had case studies that enable us to document the equation of homosexuality and masturbation. From medical literature it crossed over into the popular literature. John Ware, a Massachusetts physician, in his *Hints to Young Men on the True Relations of the Sexes* (1879), told his readers that masturbation caused an inability to form a 'legitimate and permanent union with one of the other sex,' which probably came as close to discussing homosexuality as one could get at that time without actually mentioning it.[19] The reference, however, is ambiguous and some have interpreted it as referring to prostitution. Masturbation was believed by some authorities to be a learned activity, traceable to bad companions at school. A Dr. X. Bourgeois, in *The Passions in Their Relations to Health and Diseases,* held that though masturbation had several causes, including disease, use of aphrodisiac foods, and occupations requiring prolonged sitting, its chief cause was the 'sensual education' in the boarding schools.[20] Underneath such careful language was a recognition that homosexuality did exist in such institutions although only occasionally was it reported in medical journals. A boy's corrective institution in Baltimore, for example, had an epidemic of gonorrhea in 1886 spread by rectal intercourse and this fact was included in the account in *The Medical News.*[21] William Hammond also published an incident of school sex in 1883 where one of his patients had become the passive partner in a homosexual affair.[22]

When the sex lives of girls and women were discussed, even fewer distinctions were drawn between masturbation and homosexuality than was the case with males. Mary Wood-Allen, a physician writing for a popular audience in 1898, ascribed insanity and ruined complexions to masturbation and warned girls against 'sentimental friendships' with other women, perhaps a ladylike way of describing homosexual relations.[23] Other authors made no such division in their descriptions of female sexual practices. As late as the period of the First World War, a revised edition of a book by the homeopathic physician, the late Henry Guernsey, called sexual contacts between young women 'mutual masturbation,'[24] while Irving Steinhardt, a New York physician, said that female masturbation was harmful enough 'but when practised between girls, it is a most pernicious habit, which should be vigorously fought against.'[25]

In fact it was widely believed that masturbation was more frequent among young girls than young boys, although as early as 1876 Oskar Berger, a German physician, had concluded that 99% of the men and women had masturbated, and that the other 1% concealed the truth. Accepting the possibility of these statistics, a popular sex manual of the 1890s, *Light on Dark Corners,* claimed that though masturbation was not responsible for a hundredth part of the trouble it was supposed to cause, it had many harmful results including skin disease, indigestion, and circulation problems. Acne and various kinds of neurasthenia were held to be particularly obvious results although the authors felt called upon to caution their readers that no one could tell a masturbator simply by looking him or her in the face. As far as other sexual disorders and 'perversions' were concerned, the book recognized their existence but did not discuss them. For treatment of these unnamed perversions the authors recommended bodily and mental rest, a change of environment. Drugs such as bromides and camphor were also regarded as helpful, but the real treatment would have to be physical or suggestive. 'Sex perversions are, after all, diseases of the will, and must not be thought of or treated from a moral or religious standpoint. The will power, the ability to overcome the abnormal desires can and must be developed through power of suggestion, right living, and inspirational occupation.'[26]

The correlation of homosexuality with masturbation continued well into the twentieth century and even the great G. Stanley Hall, the sponsor of Freud in America and an important force in psychology, believed that onanism was in part caused by 'seduction of younger by older boys' and wrote that it was regarded by some as a major cause of 'one or more of the morbid forms of sex perversion.'[27] Hall repeated the fears of nineteenth-century physicians about masturbation and believed that it was encouraged by many things including springtime, a warm climate, improper clothes, rich food, indigestion, mental overwork, nervousness, defective cleanliness, prolonged sitting or standing, monotonous walking, sitting crosslegged, spanking, late rising, petting and indulgence, corsets, straining of the memory, erotic reading, pictures, play solitude, perfumes, overeating, fondling, rocking chairs, pockets, feather beds, horseback riding, and bicycles.[28]

Not all American physicians accepted the equation of homosexuality and masturbation, and eventually a few began to publish their doubts, probably encouraged in this by the investigation of German researchers. One of the first tentative attempts to separate homosexuals from onanists appeared in American medical journals in 1882 and 1883. Dr. G. Alder Blumer advanced the concept of 'perverted sexual instinct' first proposed by C. Westphal of Berlin when reporting the case of a feminine-appearing male who abhorred women but denied sexual contacts with men. Blumer concluded that the man was probably insane in some fashion, possibly epileptic, but refrained from lumping him with the 'insane masturbators.'[29]

Shortly after publication of Blumer's article in 1882 a New York physician, J. C. Shaw, was approached by a homosexual for treatment. Dr. Shaw searched the literature for similar cases but found none mentioned by American medical journals. He did find two similar cases reported in France, one each in England and Italy, and several in Germany. To acquaint his fellow physicians with this 'perverted sexual instinct' as a distinct medical problem, separate and apart from other sexual irregularities, he summarized some of the cases reported in European medical journals.[30] From these beginnings the American medical profession gradually became aware of the differences in sexual behavior, and eventually recognized that not all deviations from what was considered 'normal' could be classed as onanism. Many then immediately set out on a massive hunt for all kinds of 'perversion,' losing sight in the process of what a wide range of activities were included within what would later be defined as the norms of sexual behavior.

The medical damage, however, had been done, and it took a long time for the public, and even many of the profession itself, to catch up with new concepts about sexual behavior. Unfortunately physicians had come to be regarded as experts not only as diagnosing sexual difficulties but in advocating cures, and here also medical practitioners made some serious blunders. One of the logical extensions of the belief that masturbation caused insanity was to attempt to cure insanity by castration. By the 1850s and 60s American medical journals had reported several cases of successful treatment of insanity by this surgery. Some physicians, however, opposed such a drastic solution. Studies at an Ohio mental hospital where castration was widely used, for example, showed that in some cases the insane improved, but there were more where no recovery occurred and some patients had even become more difficult to handle.[31] Castration, clitoridectomy, circumcision, blistering of the thighs, vulva, or prepuce, and harsh corporal punishment, nonetheless, continued to be advocated by some physicians throughout the nineteenth century as cures for masturbation and other 'perversions.'

The whole question of the nineteenth-century concern with masturbation has received some scholarly attention. Rene A. Spitz argued, for example, that it served as a convenient cover to express one's antisexuality while secretly practicing it. That is adult males could rage at 'white heat' about the widespread habit, the most difficult sexual act to observe, because it did not touch upon their own sexual activities with prostitutes, mistresses, and various forms of sadistic and masochistic behavior. Proof for this he found in the fact that the harsh punishments for masturbation were directed primarily at children, women, and the insane, those least able to resist society, and also least able to express themselves. Thus, according to Spitz, overconcern with masturbation was an effort of guilt-ridden sensual men to rid others of this species of crime.[32] E. H. Hare questioned this explanation and pointed out that the milder forms of treatment had only been dropped when they failed to prove effective, and there was no need to hunt for any deeper explanations for harsher treatment. Hare, nonetheless, believed that the concern with masturbation may have reflected an actual increase in its practice. He claimed that the earlier centuries were concerned with sodomy and bestiality, not masturbation, because the moral strictures of Puritanism emphasized the sins of Sodom and the fear of venereal disease.[33] In the process of arguing for an increase in masturbation, however, he has to ignore the massive concern with masturbation in the medieval penitentials and later religious writings.

Neither of these explanations seems satisfactory to us. Rather the problem seems to be that one term, such as *sodomy* or *onanism,* originally descriptive of some specific form of sexual conduct, came to be used to describe all forms of deviant activity. In nineteenth-century America, due to inhibitions about open discussion of sexual behavior, confusion over earlier legal references, and poor medical observation, *onanism* or *masturbation* became the catchall term. Often, in fact, physicians did not bother to do any observation of their own but merely repeated what others had said without any effort to document it. J. Milne Chapman, an Edinburgh physician who published an article on masturbation in an American medical journal, is perhaps an extreme example of this since after stating that masturbation was the cause of all female disease he concluded that masturbation was 'disgusting' and any study of it 'distasteful.'[34]

Many physicians were probably conscious that there were various forms of 'deviant' sex behavior and if it were only permissible to refer to such activities under the rubric of onanism, they did so. Unfortunately, in the process they added to the anxieties which nineteenth-century Americans felt about sex in general and 'deviant' sex in particular. As justification for this carelessness, it should be pointed out that most physicians probably believed that sex was debilitating and could only be justified by procreation. Medical journals provide too many examples of bodily problems caused by excessive sexual demands and many of these seem quite ludicrous to us today. One physician, for example, after observing two cases of diarrhea in 'vigorous men' both of whom had recently married, blamed their disorder on excessive sexual demands of their wives who were 'a little loose in their characters.'[35]

A nineteenth-century sex manual by Mrs. Elizabeth Osgood Goodrich Willard, a nonphysician, indicates how medical notions passed into general belief and indicates better than anything else we can cite how the whole notion of sex, particularly 'deviant sex,' came to be regarded with such horror. Mrs. Willard, following Tissot, explained that sex caused a person to waste his or her strength and she compared regular sexual activity to a man piling up bricks and then throwing them down, or to a man beating the wind with his fist. 'A sexual orgasm,' she wrote, 'is much more debilitating to the system than a whole day's work.'

It is this constant abuse of the sexual organs, producing constant failures and the most loathsome diseases; it is this ridiculous farce of a strong man putting forth all the nervous energy of his system, till he is perfectly prostrated by the effort, without one worthy motive, purpose or end; it is this which has so disgraced the act of impregnation. When human beings are generated under such conditions, it is no wonder they go through life as criminals, without a single good purpose or deed, and where all sense of shame is not lost, hanging their heads as if ashamed of their existence.

She then added

We must stop this waste through the sexual organs, if we would have health and strength of body. Just as sure as that the excessive abuse of the sexual organs destroy their power and use, producing inflammation, disease and corruption, just so sure is it that a less amount of abuse in the same relative proportion, injures the parental function of the organs, and impairs the health and strength of the whole system. Abnormal action is abuse.[36]

In effect everything except heterosexual intercourse undertaken as part of pro-creation was abuse, and abuse in much of the nineteenth century was equated with onanism. Inevitably *masturbation* became the term which American physicians used, even when they were aware of the variety of human sexual activities. As American physicians became conscious of continental investigations and as discussion of sexual 'perversions' under terms other than onanism appeared in the medical literature, the sexual attitudes we normally call Victorian began to disappear. Unfortunately though physicians finally began to have a better understanding of sex, the misconceptions under which they labored became the dominant theme of American sex manuals until fairly late into the twentieth century. Scholars interested in specific forms of sexual activities in the nineteenth century have to understand the ambiguity and prejudices with which physicians approached the whole subject of sex and with this knowledge it becomes understandable why the best sources for finding attitudes toward homosexuality are under the rubric of masturbation. The very overtones of this discussion still dominate many discussions of homosexuality today.

Notes

1. We deal with this subject at great length in a book tentatively entitled *History and sex,* which will be published by the University of California Press. As far as legal enforcement is concerned there is an article in press by the senior author on "The law and homosexuality: The American experience to 1900." The ambiguity appears from almost the first prosecutions of the law. See, for example, George Lee Haskins, *Law and authority in early Massachusetts* (New York, 1960); Edmund S. Morgan, "The Puritans and sex," *New England Quarterly,* 1942, 15, 600ff.; Geoffrey May, *Social control of sex expression* (New York, 1931); Henry B. Parkes, "Sexual morality and the great awakening," *New England Quarterly,* 1930, 3, 133–135; Parkes, "Morals and law enforcement in colonial New England," *New England Quarterly,* 1932, 5, 151ff. Emil Oberholzer, *Delinquent saints* (New York, 1956), does not deal significantly with the topic of homosexuality but is helpful. The early sermons on the subject concentrated on bestiality, Samuel Danforth, *The cry of Sodom enquired into* (Cambridge, 1674) and Cotton Mather, *Magnalia Christi Americana* (Hartford, 1820), II, 349. For Virginia see the *Minutes of the council and general court of colonial Virginia* (Richmond, 1924), pp. 85, 93; and William Waller Hening, *The statutes at large* (New York, 1823), I, 438. There are many others.

2. Edward Coke, *Institutes of the laws of England* (reprinted London, 1797), III, chap. x, "of buggery or sodomy," 58–59.

3. William Blackstone, *Commentaries on the laws of England,* new ed. with notes by John Frederick Archbold (London, 1811), IV, 215.

4. C. F. Arwedson, *The United States and Canada in 1832, 1833, and 1834* (London, 1834), 2 vols., II, 7.

5. Anthony Comstock, *Frauds Exposed* (New York, 1880), and *Traps for the young* (New York, 1883).

6. The best work on the subject is Sidney Ditzion, *Marriage, morals and sex in America* (New York, 1953). There are also several unpublished Ph.D. dissertations dealing with some aspects of sexual purity including David Pivar, "The new abolitionism: the quest for social purity" (University of Pennsylvania, 1965); Graham J. Barker-Benfield, "The horrors of the half known life: aspects of the exploitation of women by men" (University of California, Los Angeles, 1968), Stephen Nissenbaum, "Careful Love: Sylvester Graham and the emergence of Victorian sexual theory in America 1830–40" (University of Wisconsin, 1968). None, however, deal with homosexuality.

7. A good brief summary of the development can be found in Alex Comfort, *The anxiety makers* (New York, 1969). See also E. H. Hare, "Masturbatory insanity: the history of an idea," *J. mental sci.,* 1962, 108, 1–25; and R. H. MacDonald, "The frightful consequences of onanism," *J. hist. ideas,* 1967, 28, 423–431. There is also considerable discussion in Norman E. Himes, *Medical history of contraception* (Baltimore, 1936).

8. It went through many editions and translations. We consulted Samuel A. Tissot, *L'onanisme, dissertatione sur les maladies produites par la masturbation,* 4th ed. (Lausanne, 1769).

9. For the source of some of his ideas see Comfort (n. 7), pp. 70–74, and MacDonald (n. 7), pp. 423–426.

10. Benjamin Rush, *Medical inquiries and observations upon the diseases of the mind* (Philadelphia, 1812), p. 347.

11. Norman Dain, *Concepts of insanity in the United States, 1789–1865* (New Brunswick, N.J., 1964), p. 160.

12. See Steven Marcus, "Mr. Acton of Queen Anne Street, or, the wisdom of our ancestors," *Partisan review,* 1964, 31, 201–230.

13. Alfred Hitchcock, "Insanity and death from masturbation," *Boston Medical and Surgical Journal,* 1842, 26, 283–286.

14. A. Jacobi, "On masturbation and hysteria in young children," *American Journal of Obstetrics* 1876, 8, 595–596, 9, 218–238.

15. Allen W. Hagenbach, "Masturbation as a cause of insanity," *Journal of Nervous and Mental Disorders,* 1879, 6, 603–612.

16. Joseph W. Howe, *Excessive venery, masturbation and continence* (New York, 1889), pp. 113–115.

17. James Foster Scott, *The sexual instinct* (New York, 1899), pp. 419–427.

18. One of the best collections of pamphlets and books on the subject is in the College of Physicians, Philadelphia. I am indebted to them for copies of their catalogue and for help in microfilming part of their collection. This article only skims the surface of the material to be found there.

19. John Ware, *Hints to young men on the true relations of the sexes* (Boston, 1879). The original edition was first published in 1850.

20. Dr. X. Bourgeois, *The passions in their relations to health and diseases,* tr. from the French by Howard F. Damon (Boston, 1873), p. 109.

21. Randolph Winslow, "Report of an epidemic of gonorrhea contracted from rectal coition," *Med. Newsletter,* 1886, 49, 180–182.

22. William Hammond, *Sexual impotence in the male* (New York, 1883), p. 56.

23. Mary Wood-Allen, *What a young woman ought to know* (Philadelphia, 1898), pp. 148, 173–176.

24. Henry N. Guernsey, *Plain talks on avoided subjects* (Philadelphia, 1915), p. 82.

25. Irving D. Steinhardt, *Ten sex talks to girls* (Philadelphia, 1914), p. 57.

26. B. G. Jeffries and J. L. Nichols, *Light on dark corners* (1894, reprinted New York, 1967), pp. 149–155, 173–174.

27. G. Stanley Hall, *Adolescence* (New York, 1904), 2 vols., I, 435, 445.

28. Hall (n. 27), p. 437.

29. G. Alder Blumer, "A case of perverted sexual instinct," *American Journal of Insanity,* 1882, 39, 22–35.

30. J. C. Shaw and G. N. Ferris, "Perverted sexual instinct," *Journal of Nervous and Mental Disorder,* 1883, 10, 185–204.

31. J. H. Marshall, "Insanity cured by castration," *Medical and Surgical Reporter,* 1865, 13, 363–

364; H. J. Bigelow, "Castration as a means of cure for satyriasis," *Boston Medical and Surgical Journal,* 1859–60, 61, 165–166.

32. Rene A. Spitz, "Authority and masturbation," *The Psychoanalytic Quarterly,* 1952, 21, 490–527.

33. Hare (n. 6), pp. 1–25.

34. J. Milne Chapman, "On masturbation as an etiological factor in the production of gynic diseases," *American Journal of Obstetrics,* 1883, 16, 449–458, 578–598.

35. H. F. Vickery, "Sexual excess a cause of diarrhea," *Boston Medical and Surgery Journal,* 1890, 122, 287.

36. Mrs. Elizabeth Osgood Goodrich Willard, *Sexology as the philosophy of life* (Chicago, 1867), pp. 306–308.

8

Tacit Acceptance: Respectable Americans and Segregated Prostitution, 1870–1910
Neil L. Shumsky

During the latter half of the nineteenth century and early years of the twentieth, American cities experimented with the informal legalization of prostitution. While laws against prostitution, solicitation, and pandering remained on the books, they were selectively enforced. Women who confined their activities to certain ''segregated'' or ''tolerated'' districts were generally left alone and allowed to practice their profession. By 1900, nearly every large American city, and many smaller ones, too, possessed a recognized and well-known red-light district where prostitution flourished. San Francisco's Barbary Coast, New Orleans' Storyville, Chicago's Levee, and New York's Tenderloin may not have been household words, but few citizens of the metropolis remained unaware of such regions, their residents, and the forbidden pleasures obtainable there. Even the most naive knew about the local district.

Historians, sociologists, and contemporary observers have offered many explanations for the existence of these districts. Taking an economic view, some have suggested that prostitutes themselves chose to cluster in areas that were advantageous for business and where the greatest number of potential clients might be found. Others have argued that concentration resulted from conscious decisions by policemen and other municipal officials who believed that prostitution could not be abolished and that they could oversee it better if it was confined to a single section of town. Still others have emphasized public health considerations and claim that concern about venereal disease produced a desire to regulate prostitution and provide frequent health examinations of the women, examinations which could be more easily offered if prostitutes were limited to a particular district.

All of these explanations have merit and point to correlates of the red light district in almost every American city of the late nineteenth and early twentieth centuries. And yet, each of them, collectively and individually, fails to explain the ''tacit acceptance'' of respectable American urbanites for a separate zone of prostitution. None of the explanations accounts for the almost universal willingness to sanction the existence of urban prostitution so long as prostitutes confined their activities to a distinct area, usually located on the fringe of the Central Business District. Americans considered prostitution to be evil, animal, and unhealthy—but also inevitable. They tolerated it as long as they also believed that it could be segregated and restricted to a certain segment of the social order. At the same time, they saw social benefits to be derived from the existence of a separate red light district. It served, in their eyes, as a means of controlling the lower and working classes and of protecting respectable women from the supposedly rampant sexuality of immigrant men. Such a district helped establish the boundaries of proper behavior; those who accepted the sexual norms of proper society avoided the district while those who rejected propriety frequented it.

In order to develop this analysis, it is necessary to distinguish carefully between the historical study of prostitution and the historical study of the red light district. In recent years, social historians have begun to study prostitution as an indication of such important problems as social values, gender politics, reform, and class relations in a number of Western societies including the United States, England, Spain, France and Italy. However, with a few exceptions, their interest has been in prostitution generally and not in the specific phenomenon of the red light district.[1] Obviously, the two subjects are closely related. There could not be red light districts, as we generally define them, without the prior existence of prostitution; but, there can be, is, and has been, prostitution without the existence of red light districts. The red light district is a distinctive social and geographic form which sometimes characterizes prostitution and was especially prevalent in American cities during the late nineteenth and early twentieth centuries. The question of why American urban prostitution took this particular form at that particular time is a question different from, but no less important than, why prostitution existed in these cities at all.

Put in the simplest terms, the red light district was a kind of ghetto, but instead of being an ethnic ghetto, it was an economic and social ghetto meant to segregate a certain group of people. Respectable Americans accepted the red light district as long as it did not spill over into their own space. Within the red light district, thus, lived all those people whose economic livelihood depended on prostitution—not just the women themselves but also the parasites who attached themselves to prostitutes and took advantage of their activities, pimps and madames to be sure, but also merchants who profited from the fact that prostitutes were frequently not allowed to leave the segregated district and therefore had to shop locally. There were clothiers who dealt in the distinctive raiment which marked the prostitute and singled her out from other women, furniture dealers who felt justified in charging whatever the market would bear, crooked doctors who promised cures for venereal disease in an age when no such cures existed, and unscrupulous laundrymen who made tidy sums from washing large quantities of used sheets and towels.[2] But the red light district frequently did not have exclusive use of its space. It overlapped with two other important urban regions, the downtown entertainment district and Chinatown. Located in and among the cribs and parlor houses, French restaurants and hot-sheet hotels, were dance-halls, variety shows, theatres and gambling dens. Respectable restaurants and cabarets adjoined brothels and low dives. By the turn of the century, "slumming" had become a popular form of middle-class entertainment as respectable citizens sought cheap, but socially-acceptable, visual thrills. An evening on the Barbary Coast, in Storyville, or at the Levee was one of the great entertainments offered by San Francisco, New Orleans, or Chicago.[3]

These thrills of the forbidden and the erotic were frequently combined with those of the distant and the exotic because the entertainment and red light districts also overlapped with Chinatown in many large American cities. One recent study has, in fact, argued that "the Chinatown of the late 19th and early 20th centuries should be considered as a segment of the much larger red light district."[4] According to Gunther Barth, this conjunction of Chinatown, the entertainment district, and the red light district can be understood as part of the functioning of the "safety valves of the control system." Within these parts of town, Chinese immigrants were "liberated . . . briefly from the shackles of work which debt bondage placed on their shoulders." In particular, "the visit to a gambling hall, a brothel, or an opium den added precious hours of freedom" to the lives of indentured emigrants. In Chinatown, "they saw themselves momentarily admitted to that life of leisure which in part had motivated them to leave their native village in search of a fortune overseas."[5]

Prostitution was especially important in Chinatowns because of the gender ratios for Chinese immigrants to the United States in the nineteenth century. With the inordinately high ratio of men to women, Chinese men had the option of celibacy or patronizing prostitutes (given the contemporary attitude toward inter-racial sex), and the great tongs, or secret societies, quickly began to import girls for sexual purposes. These associations soon controlled prostitution in the Chinatowns and became rich from the business.[6]

However, the Chinatown red light district had other than Chinese clients. White men seem to have been regular patrons, and "there seems no doubt that the dollars of white visitors enabled American Chinatowns to support many more bordellos, opium dens, and gambling halls than would have been possible solely on the basis of Chinese patronage." Chinatown prostitutes of all races seem to have had certain advantages in attracting white customers. These women, in general, sold their services more cheaply than their sisters outside this area. Moreover, white customers seem to have felt freer about asking Chinese women to perform certain acts which they would not have mentioned to white prostitutes. Finally, Chinatown provided its customers with a level of anonymity and security from apprehension not guaranteed elsewhere in the city. Whether men patronized white or Chinese prostitutes, they knew that Chinatown's underworld would provide protection from the city's police and that a complex security system allowed customers to avoid arrest if raids did occur.[7] This desire of white men for illegal sexual services helps explain why Chinese immigrants, who were disadvantaged in the general labor force, "had a motive to find compensatory livelihoods in illegal industries."[8] Taken together with Chinatown's internal demand for prostitution, the relationship between Chinatown and the red light district becomes much easier to understand.

The geographic overlap of the red light district with Chinatown was obviously one of the distinctive features which differentiated the late nineteenth-century

American urban red light district from that of earlier Western cities. Another major difference was the general location of the zone of prostitution at the end of the century. Prior to this time, red light districts had frequently been located on the outskirts of cities, often beyond the city's walls. During the thirteenth century, the prostitutes of Paris were confined to certain streets outside the city's fortifications. During the Middle Ages, London, too, restricted prostitutes to a section just outside the city walls.[9] But, in American cities, the red light district was usually located in the heart of the city, frequently adjoining the Central Business District. This location created a fascinating paradox. On the one hand, by segregating all prostitutes and confining them to a single district, the city seemed to make prostitution *in*visible. Simply by staying out of this section, one could avoid taking cognizance of the business or its practitioners. But, by locating the district at its very center, the city emphasized its existence and heightened its visibility. In some cities, citizens almost had to avoid the red light district consciously, thus intensifying their awareness of its existence. By allowing the red light district to occupy such visible locations, American cities contradicted what has always been suggested as one of the major reasons for segregating prostitution, making it less noticeable.[10]

The explanation of this paradox lies in understanding the very existence of the red light district in American cities and recognizing why American urbanites tacitly accepted the district until the great crusade of the World War I era virtually wiped the district off the map. Perhaps the most obvious explanation argues that prostitutes found it economically advantageous to cluster in areas attractive and accessible to their clients. By gathering together, women could offer their patrons a range of alternative partners, and a man could shop for an appealing bedmate. Therefore, prostitutes generally congregated on the fringe of the central business district, in or near the downtown entertainment section where restaurants, cafes, dancehalls, and theatres drew men looking for amusement. Such an area also benefited from its usual location near major concentrations of hotels and boarding-houses, thereby providing access to both prospective clients and accommodations.[11]

This argument explains why prostitutes themselves might have preferred to assemble in a particular district, but it assumes that these women could freely choose their location. In fact, they could not. Municipal officials, especially the police, endlessly debated the acceptable location for prostitution, and prostitutes reacted quickly to any change in official policy by relocating.[12] Therefore, the role of the police must also be considered when accounting for the existence of the red light district. Generally-speaking, nineteenth-century police departments across the country confined prostitution to certain locations. For example, the General Superintendent of Chicago's Police Department issued a set of "Rules Governing the Regulation of Vice." Rule 10 explicitly stated that "no house of ill-fame shall be permitted outside of certain restricted districts," nor could any be established within two blocks of a school, church, hospital, public institution, or street car line. The following year, San Francisco's Board of Health, in conjunction with the Police Department, required all prostitutes to "confine themselves to . . . named streets and boundaries."[13]

John Warren, a New York City officer for 30 years, reflected a common view among police when he described prostitution as "a crime against the state" which "cannot be wholly eradicated." For the good of society, however, it had to be regulated by law, and this could be done most effectively if the practice was confined to specific districts. Several other New York police told the 1875 Assembly Committee on Crime "that as houses of ill-repute could not be suppressed, they should be licensed." J. Thomas Hollinberger, a District of Columbia Police Captain, testified before the Illinois Vice Commission that he favored segregation because repression could not be accomplished.[14] The police also had another motive for advocating segregation: they believed it would make their own job easier. Criminals, they thought, would flock to the crime-ridden ambiance of the red light district where cops could scoop them up with the aid of hookers acting as stool pigeons.[15]

The segregated district could not have survived without police involvement, but the fact that the police advocated segregation is not alone a sufficient explanation for its persistence. The basic problem is why the urban populace (or that part of it with power and influence) permitted the police to tolerate an activity clearly in violation of the law. None of the literature about the disappearance of the red light district suggests that the police, on their own initiative, voluntarily changed their minds and attempted to suppress prostitution. Every account of the early twentieth-century crusade against prostitution argues that the public, or some segment of it, turned against the system of segregation and forced its abandonment.

If we accept the argument that "the public" turned off the red light after 1910, we need to know why they let it burn brightly before then. Moreover, many contemporaries recognized the implicit acceptance of the system. In 1880, a New York policeman charged with neglect of duty for not suppressing brothels on his beat claimed that he had done his best but was hindered by the apathy, and even the opposition, of citizens, magistrates, and others. The Syracuse Vice Commission later claimed that the appalling conditions in that city at least partly resulted from the "indifference" and "tacit acquiescence" of the citizenry. The Charleston Vice Commission concluded that the local district reflected a "lack of united effort in demanding a change in the intolerable conditions as they now exist."[16]

Another explanation claims that American cities tolerated segregated red light districts between about 1870 and 1910, at least in part, for health reasons. During the late nineteenth century, most Americans blamed the spread of venereal disease on prostitutes who infected their patrons. Those who also believed prostitution ineradicable suggested solving the public health problem by instituting a system of medical regulation and examination. Only uninfected prostitutes would be allowed to practice their profession. Usually, this system also involved physical segregation in order to keep better track of the women and ensure their compliance with the regulations.[17]

Throughout the period, but especially in the 1870s, many Americans, and especially doctors, toyed with the idea of actually legalizing prostitution and requiring medical inspection of prostitutes. In 1867, the New York City Board of Health called for the registration of all prostitutes as a means of controlling disease, and in 1876 a city grand jury argued that legalization would stop the spread of disease.

In 1874, a physician introduced a bill in the Pennsylvania legislature calling for the registration and medical inspection of all prostitutes. Three years later the Medical and Chirurgical Faculty of Maryland appointed a Committee of Five to memorialize the new legislature on the need for the medical regulation of prostitutes. On two occasions, the proponents of medical regulation actually carried the day, and systems of registration and examination were instituted in St. Louis in 1871 and San Francisco in 1911.[18]

Clearly then, a large number of Americans advocated segregating prostitutes for public health reasons. Despite 40 years of agitation, however, only two cities experimented with systems of inspection, and one of those depended largely on the support of vice interests themselves. The red light district generally existed without medical inspection, not as a reason for ensuring it.

Certainly the tendency toward "natural" segregation, together with police attitudes and public health concerns, all played a major part in the emergence and survival of the districts, but fell short of providing a completely satisfactory explanation for the phenomenon. That segregated prostitution endured in the face of constant and vociferous opposition (especially from churches and political reformers, among others), suggests a degree of acceptance by at least some segment of the population whose influence vastly outstripped the combined impact of marketing convenience, police attitudes, and public health theory. Unfortunately, there is almost no direct documentary evidence to show who countenanced the system and why. Unlike the early twentieth-century reformers who labored to extinguish the red light district, no one actively crusaded to preserve it, and no large group lobbied publicly for segregation. While there are isolated documents, quotations, and references, those who approved segregation left behind them no mountain of reports, studies, and papers. We have only the record of tacit acceptance, showing the "indisputable fact that a considerable percentage of the general adult population, both male and female . . . believe[d] that segregation [was] the one and only practical method of handling the social evil."[19]

However, it does seem likely that the comfortable classes of American cities generally tolerated the existence of the segregated district. As we have already seen, police departments, physicians, and municipal agencies frequently advocated the segregation of prostitutes. In addition, on three occasions, American cities formally instituted systems of legalized prostitution, and, each time, primary sponsorship seems to have had respectable origins. In 1871, St. Louis began registering prostitutes and examining them for venereal disease. The experiment lasted for four years, and, although it originated with a group of people "whose identity . . . is now lost in the past," John Burnham believes the plan was "backed by well-intentioned, respectable citizens (including a number of leading physicians)." Indeed, the most active public supporter of the measure was Mayor Joseph Brown, "an upstanding real estate and traction magnate."[20]

Nearly 30 years later, New Orleans made it "unlawful for any prostitute or woman notoriously abandoned to lewdness, to occupy, inhabit, live or sleep in any house, room or closet" outside of particular boundaries. Alderman Sidney Story (hence "Storyville"), "a respectable citizen and businessman," drafted the ordinance and based it on his study of European conditions. In his work, he had the assistance of Thomas McCaleb Hyman, "a prominent New Orleans attorney . . . who did the legal research."[21]

Finally, in 1911, San Francisco began its own system of regulation and medical inspection. After the Fire of 1906, many citizens became concerned about the scattering of prostitutes throughout the city. The Civic League of San Francisco, an omnibus organization composed of about 90 neighborhood clubs and associations, took up the problem and asked its Committee on Education and Public Morals to study the situation jointly with its Committee on Public Health, Pure Food, and Tenement House Legislation. In 1907, after an extensive investigation, the two committees issued a report calling for the establishment of a segregated district and compulsory medical examination of all the prostitutes in the city.[22]

In addition to the experiences of St. Louis, New Orleans, and San Francisco, the European situation strongly suggests that respectable citizens generally accepted the segregation and regulation of prostitutes. This is, of course, not to say that the American and European conditions were identical. Nonetheless, we cannot disregard similarities which seem to reinforce the general pattern. In England, middle-class reformers sponsored the Contagious Disease Acts and especially favored their extension. In Italy, the urban middle class feared rural immigrants as a threat to property and political and economic stability. Administrators therefore sought to "prevent unpleasant contact between the bourgeoisie and the dangerous classes." One mechanism was by regulating prostitution.[23]

Arguing that respectable Europeans and Americans tacitly accepted the existence of segregated prostitution suggests a fascinating situation. During the last three decades of the nineteenth century, at precisely the time the red light district was flourishing, middle-class Americans and Europeans were confining their own sexuality to marriage. Perhaps the leading proponent of the historical interpretation that sexuality was being limited to marriage, Michel Foucault, has forcefully argued that during the eighteenth and nineteenth centuries sexuality became subject to social regulation and control. "The deployment of sexuality," as he calls it, "first developed on the fringes of familial institutions" and "gradually became focused on the family." The family became "reorganized" and "intensified" as "parents and relatives became the agents of a deployment of sexuality." Keith Thomas foreshadowed Foucault's argument in his study of the double standard and its decline in the nineteenth century. Thomas suggested that middle-class respectability and the heightened emphasis upon family life were major sources of attack upon the double standard, and he found that "a large body of middle-class opinion . . . has regarded illicit sexual activity outside marriage as equally unacceptable for men and women alike." Recently, Jeffrey Weeks, Michael Mitterauer and Reinhard Sieder have extended and developed these arguments. Weeks has shown that by 1800 sexual activity was "enshrined as a central element" in families. The idea of sexuality limited to marriage was "integrated into the bourgeois familial ideology of the nineteenth century." Mitterauer and Sieder's study of the European family has demonstrated that "middle-class standards . . . involved the confinement of sex within marriage'' and that ''a growing discrimination against pre- and ex-tramarital [sexual] relationships'' also developed among the middle class.[24]

Although Foucault, Thomas, Weeks, Mitterauer and Sieder all examined sexuality, marriage, and the family among the European bourgeoisie, other historians have recently made similar arguments about the American experience. Carroll Smith-Rosenberg has shown that a new ideology limited intercourse to marriage. Ellen K. Rothman has demonstrated that intercourse ceased to be an acceptable form of premarital sex for respectable American men and women during the second quarter of the nineteenth century. ''Coitus was placed on its own continuum . . . as an altogether separate terrain, accessible only to married people.'' Finally, Robert Griswold's study of family and divorce in California has shown that, contrary to popular belief, middle-class men were not ''allowed'' to visit prostitutes. ''To have permitted such adultery would violate the mutuality of the marriage bond and render meaningless the insistence that men and women adhere to the same sexual standard.'' Griswold cites numerous cases of men divorced for consorting with prostitutes and concludes that ''men were subject to the same standards of marital fidelity as women.''[25]

Thus, *two* problems require explanation. Why did the tolerated red light district spring up? Why did it become most important during the very era that so many Americans were becoming committed to the notion of marital fidelity and exclusive sexuality within marriage? The answers to both of these questions emerge by asking yet another. How was the new ideology spread and reinforced? By what mechanism did it come to be established and accepted? Although these historians of marriage and the family have devoted much attention and effort to explaining *why* the new system occurred, they have not spelled out *how* it occurred. It is in regard to this issue that the meaning and purpose of the red light district emerge, for it was a distinct part of the new deployment of sexuality. It elucidated for respectable Americans what the new standard had become for them—sexuality confined to marriage. Its existence helped disclose clearly and unmistakably the difference between acceptable and unacceptable behavior.

According to Kai Erikson, every group of people maintains boundaries. ''Its members tend to confine themselves to a particular radius of activity and to regard any conduct which drifts outside that radius as somehow inappropriate or immoral.'' His theory also contains an implicit definition of a deviant—''a person whose activities have moved outside the margins of the group.'' Therefore, ''deviant persons often supply an important service to society by patrolling the outer edges of group space and by providing a contrast which gives the rest of the community some sense of their own territorial identity.'' Erikson also argues that every society has its own way of deploying deviants and deviance; and he identified three which appear frequently: special days on which rule violation is tolerated, special societies in which deviant behavior is considered normal for adolescents, and special clubs whose business it is to infringe ordinary group rules. Finally, Erikson posits a particular kind of deployment pattern characteristic of American society—''deviant behavior as the special property of a particular class of people who were more or less frozen into deviant attitudes.'' Americans have ''generally thought it best to handle the problem by locking these people into fairly permanent deviant roles."[26]

In American cities between roughly 1870 and 1910, the segregated red light district served as another form of boundary maintenance—literally as well as figuratively. Nearly every advocate of segregation emphasized the need to avoid contaminating respectable neighborhoods and to separate moral from immoral behavior, just as traditional public health proponents had fought for the quarantine of biological plagues. The argument appeared repeatedly in New York City during the 1870s and 1880s. Letters and editorials in the *Times* questioned the desirability of police raids on disorderly houses and suggested that the major result would be to drive prostitutes into neighborhoods currently free from the nuisance. One study of Chicago's police department suggested that prostitution "be hammered and kept down" but not to the "extent of scattering it all over the city" and into the residential portions. The foreman of San Francisco's grand jury of 1913 wrote Mayor Rolph that repression would not end prostitution, but simply scatter it into respectable neighborhoods. The district gave people a choice; they could either go there or avoid it.

And this was the point. The existence of the district allowed people to declare themselves openly—to accept or reject the new standard of morality. A New York City grand jury of 1876 advocated segregation because "patronage . . . would be limited to those who are not ashamed or afraid to be seen" in the district. After a police raid in 1883, a group of citizens protested. They preferred prostitutes to be confined to an area "known and avoided by all the respectable people" rather than be in places where one's presence was no sign of shame. One doctor summed it up most fittingly. If a cesspool existed, "let it remain a cesspool." Avoid spreading its contamination everywhere. "Isolate it." People who wanted prostitutes "would go to them. Those who wished to avoid them could do so. They were well known for what they were."[27] The red light district clearly demonstrated the difference between acceptable and unacceptable behavior and thereby set boundaries for respectability.

The toleration of prostitution in a special, segregated district leads to yet another important question—where was this region to be located? The proponents never answered the question directly; they said only that it should be kept isolated from respectable neighborhoods. But even though they failed to define the difference between respectable and unrespectable overtly, it is possible to understand the distinction from the actual locations of the districts. The red light district was universally restricted to poor or marginal neighborhoods of American cities.[28]

By permitting prostitution in these areas of cities, but not in their own, respectable Americans not only developed the boundaries of proper behavior but also elaborated their own self-conception. Those citizens were distinguishing themselves from groups which had different sexual habits. As a result, prostitution was tolerable in *their* parts of the city. In other words, perceived sexual practices and ideology had become a major aspect of respectability. Jeffrey Weeks has similarly argued that in Victorian England the "prime task" of the new attitudes toward marriage and sexuality was "to articulate the class feelings and experiences of the bourgeoisie itself.'' During this era, the new ideology of the family ''became a vital organizing factor in the development of middle-classness, and in the creation of a differentiated class identity.'' The domestic idea, with its attendant sexual fidelity, became ''an expression of class confidence, both against the immoral aristocracy, and against the masses, apparently denied the joys of family life and prone to sexual immodesty and vice, 'fit only for sleep or sensual indulgence.' '' Taking it one step further, Weeks has shown that the family not only exalted sexuality, ''via the indispensable marriage bond,'' but also ''severely regulated it. The paradox was that the more ideology stressed the role of sex within conjugality, the more it was necessary to describe and regulate those forms of sexuality which were without it.''[29]

The tolerated red light district, existing near marginal neighborhoods, thus served to set boundaries and help define respectability. But it also existed to regulate the sexuality of less-comfortable Americans who presumably had not adopted or could not express the new standards of behavior. Just as in Europe, respectable Americans sought to control the sexuality of others, and the tolerated red light district was an important mechanism for doing so.[30] This idea can best be illustrated with another argument frequently presented by the champions of the segregated district. Over and over again, they claimed that without the district, respectable women would not be safe. Some who made the argument phrased it delicately. William Sanger said that the segregated district prevented virtuous women from being annoyed and insulted. James Rolph, the mayor of San Francisco, wrote that because of the system any woman could ''walk all the streets of San Francisco, at any hour, day or night, without insult or embarrassment.'' Others were less cautious in expressing their concerns; they believed the district necessary because of the '' 'passions of men who otherwise would be tempted to seduce young ladies.' '' A. E. Boynton, President pro tem of the California Senate, opposed closing San Francisco's Barbary Coast because that action would lead to the ''debauching of girls of good families . . . most of whom would preserve their virginity'' otherwise. Finally, some openly expressed their real anxieties. One member of the Wisconsin Vice Commission believed in segregated prostitution because ''the old Adam in man, . . . if denied gratification in one direction, would be certain to seek it in some other, probably more dangerous direction.'' As one physician told the American Medical Association in 1874, ''if prostitution were abolished, crime of the most heinous and revolting character would be of incessant occurrence, and no virtuous woman would be secure from the assaults of the libertine.'' The Bridgeport Vice Commission said it without mincing words. ''Vice is one of the weaknesses of men; it cannot be extirpated; if repressed unduly at one point, it will break out more violently and bafflingly elsewhere; a segregated district is really a protection to the morality of the womanhood of the city, for without it rape would be common.''[31]

This fear of rape and seduction leads one to wonder the perceived source of the danger. Some proponents of segregation feared a general ''licentiousness among men'' and attributed the danger to the ''many men whose passions were so violent and so ill-regulated that they would attain their gratification at any risk.''[32] But others had a more restricted view of the problem and associated the danger with marginal members of society. One Wisconsin banker justified the district because of the number of sailors and lumberjacks in his town. The sheriff of Sheboygan said he kept the lights on because his town had six hundred Greeks, three or four hundred Lithuanians, and as many Austrians. Closing down the district would make the city worse than it already was. Julius Rosenstirn, the chief advocate of segregation in San Francisco, denied that laws could restrain the "mariner returning from the voyage, the miner, the woodsman, and the cowboy." Granville Price discovered that Galveston's city fathers allowed the district on into the 1930's and believed it necessary because of certain elements in the population—seamen and dock laborers, soldiers, college students, salesmen, mechanics, waiters, clerks, soda jerkers and bootleggers. Finally, the statistics of the New York City Dispensary in 1937 conveyed an "idea of the vice and disease which exist among and infect the large class who populate the overcrowded tenement districts of the city." The numbers seemed "to suggest almost promiscuous intercourse."[33]

The comfortable classes believed that large numbers of less well-to-do people had different sexual standards and feared that without the segregated district these different mores would lead to attacks on "respectable" women. In this attitude, they reflected a general belief that the poor and the immigrants were vicious, licentious, and animalistic. Witnesses before Congressional committees throughout the 1870s, 1880s and 1890s made this point regularly and told lurid anecdotes— presumably illustrative of immigrant and working-class depravity. Henry J. Deily, representing the American Defense Association, told the House Committee on Immigration about a school teacher in Pennsylvania who had had to quit his job "because of the vile habits and practices of the Polish and Hungarian children." It was "utterly impossible to instill any sense of decency or decorum into their sex, the example of their parents and associates being too strong." The children had "no greater sense of shame or morality than a dumb brute." Adelbert Dewey, former editor of the *Journal of United Labor,* told the same committee about a building in Detroit inhabited by a "colony of Huns." Five rooms, each ten feet square, housed 127 people. In one room, five families were "sleeping in one common bed." Children "reared with such surroundings" would never make "respectable, law-abiding citizens," and Dewey especially warned his listeners who had "wives, mothers, sisters, and daughters." Did they "want to see such customs perpetuated?" Did they even "want to see it tolerated?"

In 1886, Secretary of State Bayard, concerned about the "quality" of immigrants to the United States, sent a circular letter to all American consuls in Europe and asked for information about marriage and divorce, natural and illegitimate children. The responses clearly reveal a belief that lower-class Europeans had a less refined set of sexual values. George W. Roosevelt wrote from Nantes that illegitimacy was "rarely known outside the working classes." From Dusseldorf, D.J. Partello reported an "excellent" standard of morality among the upper classes "but the contrary . . . case among the lower." Albert Woodstock, consul at Catania, found the morals of all classes "deplorable" from an American point of view, while Henry C. Crouch found that the Milanese had "a freer and broader conception of the marital relation than prevailed in the United States."[34] These beliefs produced a broadening of the groups forbidden to enter the United States. Until 1891, law had prohibited criminals, paupers, the insane, and the Chinese from immigrating. The Immigration Act of 1891 added to these classes "persons suffering from loathesome or dangerous and contagious diseases" (the widely-used euphemism for venereal disease) and "persons convicted of a felony or other infamous crime or misdemeanor involving moral turpitude."[35] Violations of proper behavior presumably originated outside the United States.

Because of their presumed immorality, some groups seemed like a threat to respectable women. They also seemed threatening because so many of them were unmarried. To Julius Rosenstirn, laws "making the sexual act of unmarried individuals a punishable crime, while sanctifying it with a license" made no sense. The fierce call of the jungle could not be restrained, but since marriage was "impossible for the great majority of laboring men," he advocated regulated prostitution. The Medical Board of New York's Bellevue Hospital claimed that the expenses of living were a great obstacle and that a constantly increasing number of men could not afford wives. One San Francisco workingman himself wrote that he had come to San Francisco from England and been unable to marry. He was "a strong, robust, virile man" who, because of poverty, had turned in "bitter loneliness to the companionship and the caresses of the harlot."[36]

This, then, became a major concern to respectable Americans in the latter half of the nineteenth century. What should be done about what they perceived to be the rampant, uncontrolled, and uncontrollable sexuality of groups like workingmen and immigrants? They could not afford to marry, but, it was feared, if some outlet was not provided for their sexual urges, they would run amuck and attack respectable women on the streets. Obviously, because of their animality, celibacy was not an option. Because of contemporary medical belief, masturbation could not be advocated. And because of social, sexual, and religious strictures, homosexuality was not even considered. The only remaining option, if the wives, mothers, daughters, and sisters of respectable Americans were to be protected, was to provide an arena for the deployment and control of other men's sexuality. In 1874, Samuel D. Gross spoke to the American Medical Association and made this point clearly by quoting Sir William Jenner. "A large portion of the male population . . . are, at the age when the passions are the strongest, precluded by the necessity of their position from marriage. Under such conditions, either prostitution, seduction, or masturbation will be the prevailing vice. If by law public prostitution could be put down, the two latter of the three vices would undermine the health and lower the moral nature of the masses far more than does the present prevalence of the social evil. The inverse relation in the prevalence of masturbation, illegitimate children, and prostitution cannot be too strongly impressed on the public mind."[37]

Thus, accepting the existence of the red light district was part of the community politics of the era. American cities were becoming divided between the haves and the have-nots. There was a shifting balance of power with a disproportionate share of the resources—social, political, and economic—going to some segments of the population. Those who gained from the new distribution of resources wanted to entrench themselves further by controlling their adversaries. At the same time, they wanted to keep peace within the community and isolate themselves from the contagion of infection. One way of doing so was by providing their rivals with a separate space within which to act, a space within which to watch over, regulate, and subdue the lower, working, and immigrant classes.

The irony and the social biases inherent in the system did not escape the opponents of segregation. In 1874, Dr. J. Marion Sims addressed the American Medical Association on the subject of venereal disease and said that some scheme had to be created to prevent its importation from abroad. He proposed that a quarantine officer examine every sailor and steerage class passenger entering the country and remand syphillitics to hospitals. Aaron M. Powell, a leading advocate of repression, attacked Sims for "unjustly discriminating against the poor." If, as Sims also argued, prostitution was necessary to protect society in general and respectable women in particular, Powell sardonically observed that no home was "too sacred to furnish its offerings." If a victim class of women was inevitable, if somebody's daughters had to be despoiled, it was a Christian duty to be self-sacrificing, and the most Christian women of the community should offer themselves on the altar.[38]

Respectable women did not rush out to satisfy Powell's injunction, and Americans tolerated segregated districts for well over half a century. In this regard, they resembled their counterparts in both England and Italy where more formal systems of regulation were adopted. Judith Walkowitz has shown that in England the Contagious Disease Acts "broke new ground as domestic social measures, creating supervision of the lives of the poor." In Italy, according to Mary Gibson, the regulation of prostitution "represented an attempt by the state to extend its control over one section of the lower classes and isolate these contaminating agents as much as possible from the rest of society."[39]

Perhaps because of a lower level of class consciousness, perhaps because of a greater tradition of individual freedom, Americans never adopted a national system of regulating and segregating prostitutes, as did England, Italy, and several other European countries. But they did share with their European counterparts certain ideas about family, marriage, sexuality and the working class. In the United States, these ideas took form in the segregated districts of late nineteenth-century cities. The district helped set proper boundaries for sexual expression, reinforce the definition of respectability, and control the sexual behavior of marginal citizens. In doing so, the district became an important element in the establishment of acceptable behavioral norms.

Notes

1. For a few exceptions to this generalization, see Richard Symanski, *The Immoral Landscape: Female Prostitution in Western Society* (Toronto, 1981); Neil Larry Shumsky and Larry M. Springer, "San Francisco's Zone of Prostitution, 1880–1934," *Journal of Historical Geography* 7 (1981): 71–89; Ivan Light, "From Vice District to Tourist Attraction: the Moral Career of American Chinatowns, 1880–1940," *Pacific Historical Review* 43 (1974): 367–394; Ivan Light, "The Ethnic Vice Industry, 1880–1944," *American Sociological Review* 42 (1977): 464–479.

2. Al Rose, *Storyville, New Orleans: Being an Authentic, Illustrated Account of the Notorious Red-Light District* (University of Alabama, 1974): 29–30; Sanborn Map Company, *San Francisco* (San Francisco, 1899).

3. Rose, *Storyville;* Sanborn Map Company, *San Francisco;* Herbert Asbury, *The Barbary Coast* (New York, 1933): 278–298; Light, "Ethnic Vice Industry": Light, "From Vice District to Tourist Attraction."

4. Leonard U. Blumberg, Thomas E. Shipley, Jr., and Stephen F. Barsky, *Liquor and Poverty, Skid Row as a Human Condition* (New Brunswick, NJ, 1978): 212, 221.

5. Gunther Barth, *Bitter Strength, a History of the Chinese in the United States* (Cambridge, MA, 1964): 109–110, 126–129.

6. United States Bureau of the Census, *Historical Statistics of the United States, Colonial Times to 1957* (Washington, D.C., 1960); Light, "From Vice District to Tourist Attraction"; 372–373; Barth, *Bitter Strength,* 102, 107; Thomas W. Chinn, ed., *A History of the Chinese in California* (San Francisco, 1969), 67–68.

7. Light, "From Vice District to Tourist Attraction": 370–374.

8. Light, "The Ethnic Vice Industry": 468–469.

9. Symanski, *Immoral Landscape,* 21–22; Vern and Bonnie Bullough, *Prostitution, an Illustrated Social History* (New York, 1978): 119.

10. For a somewhat different interpretation of the visibility issue, see Symanski, *Immoral Landscape,* 2–5.

11. David R. Johnson, *Policing the Urban Underworld* (Philadelphia, 1979): 6, 152; Granville Price, *A Sociological Study of a Segregated District* (M.A. Thesis, University of Texas, Austin, 1930), 60; Walter C. Reckless, "The Distribution of Commercialized Vice in the City: A Sociological Analysis," in George A. Theodorson, ed., *Studies in Human Ecology* (New York, 1961): 52; Walter C. Reckless, *Vice in Chicago* (Chicago, 1933): 164; Syracuse, New York. Committee of Eighteen, *The Social Evil in Syracuse* (Syracuse, 1913), 15.

12. Shumsky and Springer, "San Francisco's Zone of Prostitution": 71–89.

13. Chicago. Vice Commission, *The Social Evil in Chicago* (Chicago, 1911): 329, see also 33, 110; San Francisco. Department of Public Health, *Annual Report . . . 1911* (San Francisco, 1911): 3.

14. John H. Warren, Jr., *Thirty Years' Battle With Crime . . .* (New York, 1970): 39, 44; New York *Times,* Dec. 5, 1875; Illinois. Senate. Vice Committee, *Report* (np, 1911): 356; see also, New York *Times,* May 26, 1880; John F. Decker, *Prostitution: Regulation and Control* (Littleton, CO, 1979): 61; Robert M. Fogelson, *Big-City Police* (Cambridge, MA, 1977): 32, 70; Reckless, *Vice in Chicago,* 5; James F. Richardson, *The New York Police* (New York, 1970): 186; Robert E. Riegel, "Changing American Attitudes toward Prostitution (1800–1920)," *Journal of the History of Ideas* 29 (1968): 445; Samuel Walker, *A Critical History of Police Reform* (Lexington, MA, 1977): 98–99.

15. Thomas Byrnes, *1886 Professional Criminals of America* (New York, 1969): xvi; Mark Haller, "Historical Roots of Police Behavior: Chicago, 1890–1925," *Law and Society* 10 (1976); Reckless, *Vice in Chicago,* 235, 272.

16. New York *Times,* Feb. 5, 1880; Syracuse. Committee of Eighteen, *Social Evil,* II; Chicago. Vice Commission, *Social Evil,* 144; Raymond B. Fosdick, "Prostitution and the Police," *Social Hygiene* 2 (1916): 15; Charleston, South Carolina. Law and Order League, *Special Report* (Charleston, 1913): 20. See also, New York *Times,* March 5, 1874; Johnson, *Policing the Urban Underworld,* 147.

17. David J. Pivar, *Purity Crusade* (Westport, CT, 1973), 52–62; Aaron M. Powell, *State Regulation of Vice Regulation Efforts in America. The Geneva Congress* (New York, 1978): 48–49, 86; William M. Sanger, *The History of Prostitution* (New York, 1937): 693.

18. New York *Times,* Feb. 8, 1867; June 3, 1876; Powell, *State Regulation of Vice;* William L. Barrett, *Prostitution in its Relation to the Public Health* (St. Louis, 1873); Pivar, *Purity Crusade,* 51–60; John C. Burnham, "Medical Inspection of Prostitutes in America in the Nineteenth Century: the St. Louis Experiment and Its Sequel," *Bulletin of the History of Medicine* XLV (1971): 203–218; John C. Burnham, "The Social Evil Ordinance: A Social Experiment in Nineteenth-Century St. Louis," *Bulletin of the Missouri Historical Society* 27 (1971): 203–217; Neil Larry Shumsky, "The Municipal Clinic of San Francisco," *Bulletin of the History of Medicine* 52 (1979): 542–559; Neil Larry Shumsky, "Vice Responds to Reform; San Francisco, 1910–1914," *Journal of Urban History* 7 (1980): 31–47.

19. Portland, Oregon. Vice Commission, *Report . . . to the Mayor and City Council . . .* (Portland, 1913), 207.

20. Burnham, "The Social Evil Ordinance," 204, 209.

21. Rose, *Storyville*, 193, 38.

22. George Flink, "Report of the Chairman of the Committee on Education and Public Morals of the Civic League," Red Plague Committee Papers (Commonwealth Club of California, San Francisco); Julius Rosenstirn, "The Municipal Clinic of San Francisco," *Transactions of the Fifteenth International Congress on Hygiene and Demography* IV (Washington, 1913): 93–115; Julius Rosenstirn, *The Municipal Clinic of San Francisco* (New York, 1913); Julius Rosenstirn, *Our Nation's Health Endangered by Poisonous Infection through the Social Malady, the Protective Work of the Municipal Clinic of San Francisco and Its Fight for Existence* (San Francisco, 1913).

23. Judith R. Walkowitz, *Prostitution and Victorian Society* (Cambridge, Eng., 1982), Chapter 4; Mary S. Gibson, *Urban Prostitution in Italy, 1860–1915; An Experiment in Social Control,* (Ph.D. Thesis, Indiana University, 1979): 28–29.

24. Michel Foucault, *The History of Sexuality* (New York, 1978), I, 110; Keith Thomas, "The Double Standard," *Journal of the History of Ideas,* XX (1959): 203–204; Jeffrey Weeks, *Sex, Politics, and Society* (London, 1981): 24–26; Michael Mitterauer and Reinhard Sieder, *The European Family* (Oxford, 1982): 129, 133.

25. Carroll Smith-Rosenberg, "Sex as Symbol in Victorian America: An Ethnohistorical Analysis of Jacksonian America," in John Demos and Sarane Spence Boocock, *Turning Points: Historical and Sociological Essays on the Family* (Chicago, 1978): S224; Ellen K. Rothman, "Sex and Self-Control: Middle-Class Courtship in America, 1770–1870," *Journal of Social History* 15 (1982): 415; Robert L. Griswold, *Family and Divorce in California, 1850–1890* (Albany, 1982): 76, 117–118.

26. Kai Erikson, *Wayward Puritans, A Study in the Sociology of Deviance* (New York, 1966): 10, 11, 27–28, 196.

27. New York *Times,* April 1, 5, 1874; June 3, 1876; Nov. 26, 1883; May 25, Dec. 8, 1892; Alexander R. Piper, *Report of an Investigation of the Discipline and Administration of the Police Department of the City of Chicago* (Chicago, 1904): 15; William H. Ford to James Rolph, Jr., Feb. 28, 1913, James Rolph, Jr. Papers (California Historical Society Library, San Francisco); W. E. Whitehead, "The Social Evil," *Pacific Medical Journal* 5 (1871–72): 56–57. See also Cyrus Willoughby Waterman, *Prostitution and Its Repression in New York City, 1900–1931* (New York, 1968): 13; Reckless, "The Distribution of Commercialized Vice," in Theodorson, ed., *Studies in Human Ecology,* 50–52; William Burgess, *The World's Social Evil* (Chicago, 1914): 269; Kay Ann Holmes, "Reflections by Gaslight: Prostitution in Another Age," *Issues in Criminology* 7 (1972): 84. Marion S. Goldman has also used Erikson's theory of deviance to explain nineteenth-century treatment of prostitutes. Her interpretation focuses on the way in which "respectable" women were distinguished from prostitutes and how the categorization of the "prostitute" helped define proper behavior for other women. She thus relies on Erikson's theory of creating deviant roles as a deployment strategy. Marion S. Goldman, *Gold Diggers and Silver Miners. Prostitution and Social Life on the Comstock Lode* (Ann Arbor, 1981), esp. Chapter 7. This argument is unquestionably correct and is supported by the work of both Judith Walkowitz and Ruth Rosen. Walkowitz has found that in England, at the same time, working-class prostitutes became "a specially identified professional class." Walkowitz, *Prostitution and Victorian Society,* 210. Rosen notes that singling out "degraded" women served as an object lesson and a threat to others. "The specter of the whore was always before them as a reminder of what they might become or how they might be treated if they failed to live up to the angel image." Ruth Rosen, *The Lost Sisterhood* (Baltimore, 1982), 6. Rosen's edition of the letters of Maimie Pinzer abounds with examples of prostitutes being labelled and differentiated from other women as a means of boundary-setting. Ruth Rosen and Sue Davidson, eds. *The Maimie Papers* (np, 1977): 10–11, 23, 273–274, 296, 328, 373. It is my contention that the toleration of the segregated red light district had functions in addition to defining and setting boundaries to women's proper sexual behavior. See also, Warren, *Thirty Years' Battle,* 145; and Reckless, *Vice in Chicago,* 54–55 on the "outcaste" nature of prostitutes.

28. Symanski, *Immoral Landscape,* 125–147; Rosen, *Lost Sisterhood,* 78; Wisconsin. Legislature. Committee on White Slave Traffic and Kindred Subjects, *Report and Recommendations . . .* (Madison, 1914): 26; Leonard U. Blumberg, Thomas E. Shipley, Jr., and Stephen F. Barsky, *Liquor and Poverty, Skid Row as a Human Condition* (New Brunswick, NJ, 1978): 212, 221.

29. Weeks, *Sex, Politics, and Society,* 28, 31; see also, 23, 32–33.

30. See Walkowitz, *Prostitution and Victorian Society,* 88 and Gibson, *Prostitution,* 31 for discussions of European middle-class attempts to control working-class sexuality.

31. Sanger, *History of Prostitution,* 652–653; James Rolph to J.C. Westenberg, Aug. 7, 1913, James Rolph, Jr. Papers; New Orleans *Mascot,* June, 1892 (quoted in Rose, *Storyville,* 37); A.E. Boynton to Miss L.H. Wall, March 24, 1913, San Francisco League of Women Voters Papers (California Historical Society Library, San Francisco); Wisconsin. Committee on White Slave Traffic, *Report,* 185; S.D. Gross, *Syphilis in its Relation to the National Health . . .* (Philadelphia, 1874): 38; Rosen, *Lost Sisterhood,* 5.

32. Edmund Andrews, *Prostitution and Its Sanitary Management* (St. Louis, 1871): 21; Sanger, *History of Prostitution,* 647.

33. Wisconsin. Committee on White Slave Traffic, *Report,* 27, 149, also 116; Rosenstirn, *Our Nation's Health,* 17; Fred Franklin to Paul Smith, June 1, 1917, Paul Smith Papers (Special Collections, UCLA Library, Los Angeles); Price, Segregated District, 17, also 3, 16, 25; Sanger, *History of Prostitution,* 680. These ideas about working-class sexuality are still prevalent today. In her study of contraception, Lee Rainwater claims that the lower classes are usually assumed to be much more permissive about sexual behavior than the upper classes. "One popular middle-class stereotype of the lower-class person is that he is highly sexed. Middle-class people cherish a fantasy of the lower class as impulsive and freely self-indulgent because they are not hemmed in by prudery and constriction." Lee Rainwater, *And the Poor Get Children* (Chicago, 1960), ix, 98.

34. United States Congress. House of Representatives. 49th Cong. 2nd Sess. Executive Document 157. *Emigration and Immigration. Reports of the Consular Officers of the United States* (Washington, 1887), 45, 84, 177, 256, 274, 282, 328; United States Congress, House of Representatives. 51st Cong. 2nd Sess. Report No. 3472. *Immigration Investigation* (Washington, 1891), ii, 237, 436, 589, 604, 970; United States Congress. House of Representatives. 52nd Cong. 1st Sess. Executive Document 235. *Letter from the Secretary of the Treasury Transmitting a Report of the Commissioners of Immigration Upon the Causes Which Incite Immigration to the United States* (Washington, 1892): 1, 125. In his book on the repression of the red light district, Howard Woolston commented that "hordes" of immigrants brought with them views on sex "prevalent in their particular countries and in the social strata from which they came." Howard B. Woolston, *Prostitution in the United States* (New York, 1921), 17. Charles Rosenberg has argued that "public health advocates assumed that sexual license was characteristic of slum life and, like drink, one of those traits which kept the poor poor." Charles Rosenberg, "Sexuality, Class and Role in 19th-Century America," *American Quarterly* 25 (1973): 144. Finally, Brian Harrison refers to the "widespread assumption [in England] that working people were generally more promiscuous than other classes." Brian Harrison, "Underneath the Victorians," *Victorian Studies,* X (1967): 252.

35. 26 *Stats* 1084.

36. Rosenstirn, *Our Nation's Health,* 10–11; Sanger, *History of Prostitution,* 669; E. Teesdale, *Rev. Paul Smith Answered by E. Teesdale,* Unidentified Pamphlet, Paul Smith Papers.

37. Gross, *Syphilis,* 38.

38. Powell, *State Regulation of Vice,* 14–18.

39. Walkowitz, *Prostitution and Victorian Society,* 88; Gibson, *Prostitution,* 31.

9

Feminist Responses to "Crimes against Women," 1868–1896
Elizabeth Pleck

American feminists have long responded to "crimes against women" by providing local support services for victims, lobbying for legislative reform, and exposing the social origins of women's oppression. In one generation, for example, women initiated the following activities:

> A separatist women's religious group established a commune in rural Texas for battered wives and wives of alcoholics.
> The San Diego women's movement opened a shelter for battered wives.
> Chicago feminists provided legal aid for victims of incest, rape, and wife beating; appeared in court along with rape victims to encourage them to testify; and lobbied the state legislature to pass stiffer criminal penalties against rapists and perpetrators of incest.

At the same time, women activists across the nation demanded compensation for battered wives. Some lobbied for the passage of new laws, while others drew attention to the courtroom trials of women victims. Concerned about the relationship between sex and violence, women writers and organizers denounced pornography and male sadomasochism, and began to concern themselves with the lives of prostitutes. A well-known novelist caused a sensation when she published a book charging a famous male novelist with incest. Believing that all women are enslaved by the fear of rape, a leader of the women's movement called for self-defense training for women and stiffer penalties for convicted rapists. A feminist intellectual published her treatise on "crimes against women," in which she denounced the Christian religion and the state as sources of women's degradation. More conservative women hoped that the passage of a national constitutional amendment would offer the ultimate remedy for the problem of wife beating.

This catalog of feminist interest, which appears so contemporary, represents instead the activities of American women's organizations between 1868 and 1896. This range of responses to what nineteenth-century feminists termed "crimes against women" disproves the assumption that the earlier women's movement, preoccupied with the suffrage question, ignored concerns such as violence against women. This essay explores the origins and decline of nineteenth-century feminist responses to crimes against women by analyzing the beliefs and actions of four sets of reformers and organizations: liberal feminists Susan B. Anthony and Elizabeth Cady Stanton; conservative feminists Lucy Stone and Henry Blackwell; the Women's Christian Temperance Union (WCTU); and Chicago's Protective Agency for Women and Children. These reformers—some primarily intellectuals, others mainly activists—differed in the degree to which they gave sustained attention to crimes against women, but their shared goal was increased protection for women and stiffer criminal penalties for male offenders. All identified the roots of such crimes in the nature of the family, male sexuality, and intemperance.

Some assigned greater weight to one cause over another, however, and some feminists were more vigorous in their critique of the family. To understand their responses, it is crucial to keep in mind that these reformers perceived crimes against women through the rhetoric and social thought of an earlier age. It is tempting to criticize them for overemphasizing women's victimization, eliding types of victimization that were quite distinct, or oversimplifying and even confusing the issue in their arguments. Indeed, their understanding of the issue was at times simplistic, and they often advocated severe punishments, although not with as much vehemence or meanness of spirit as the male reformers of their day. But these limitations must be understood in historical context: nineteenth-century feminists were trying to gain the attention of a society at best indifferent and at worst hostile to any public discussion of violence against women. Their rhetorical excesses and mistakes serve as warnings for the women's movement today, but their courage and concern for the suffering of other women also serve as examples of commitment in the face of social conservatism and public indifference.

Liberal Feminists

Elizabeth Cady Stanton, Susan B. Anthony, and their less well-known colleague Matilda Joslyn Gage first became interested in crimes against women in the 1850s as a result of their involvement in the women's temperance crusade. They demanded that wives of drunkards, who were often beaten, should have the right to divorce their husbands on grounds of cruelty or habitual drunkenness. For the next nine years they campaigned unsuccessfully to reform New York's divorce law. Both Stanton and Anthony knew many women victims, and Anthony had aided one New York woman who fled with her daughter from an abusive husband.[1] The Civil War and then the postbellum campaign for woman's suffrage preempted this early interest. Between 1868 and 1870, however, Stanton and Anthony actively wrote, spoke, and demonstrated on behalf of women who were victims of violence or sexual exploitation. They championed the cause of Hester Vaughn, a servant accused of infanticide; called for the conviction of Albert McFarland, a wife beater who murdered his ex-wife's fiancé; and demanded the death penalty for rape.[2]

Although Stanton believed that rape and wife beating occurred mainly among the poor and "refined sensualism" was common mainly among wealthy men,[3] those implicated in these cases were not poor and immigrant men, but men of property and education. McFarland was a New York lawyer, and Vaughn's seducer was her wealthy Philadelphia employer. Stanton aided an abused ex-wife of a Massachusetts senator, and before the Civil War she spoke out about many cases of "aggravated cruelty" among the Dutch aristocracy in New York.[4] Feminists charged that the law had treated these men too leniently; they cried out against the double standard by which Hester Vaughn was sentenced to death for infanticide, "which could not be proved against her . . . while he who betrayed her walks this green earth in freedom."[5]

Just after the end of the Civil War, when Stanton and Anthony became involved in these cases, Victorian silence about this double standard was beginning to give way to public discussion of health, sexuality, prostitution, and marriage. Advocates of free love wanted to bring out into the open "the secret sexual practices" of moral hypocrites, and Stanton sought to expose the secrecy upon which traditional marriage rested.[6] At the same time, the popular press contributed to the heady atmosphere by feeding its audience a steady diet of stories involving sensational divorces, scandalous courtroom trials, and brutal family crimes. Indeed, the few criminal statistics available on husband-wife murder suggest that domestic violence may have been increasing as part of a general crime wave attributed to postwar economic and social tensions.[7] The increase in violent crimes, however, did not lead to the discovery of female victimization, since Stanton and Anthony had been pointing out instances of it as early as the 1850s. But the combination of a more open cultural atmosphere, sensationalized press reports, and fears of a crime wave may have made the public more willing to listen to their arguments and may have abetted the perception that such "outrages" were increasing.

As former abolitionists, Stanton and Anthony frequently relied on the analogy with slavery when they discussed crimes against women. Denied personal liberty, a wife was subjected to the authority of a master, whose commands she was forced to obey. They referred to married women who had to flee their abusive husbands as "fugitive wives" running to Indiana and Connecticut divorce mills "like slaves to their Canada, from marriages worse than plantation slavery."[8] Stanton and Anthony's concern was not only for married women, but for the treatment of women in general. They never devised a single term to describe the forms of woman's victimization, but relied instead on the repetition of specific examples: "the prosecutions in our courts for breach of promise, divorce, adultery, bigamy, seduction, rape; the newspaper reports every day of every year of scandal and outrages, of wife murders and paramour shootings, or abortions and infanticide."[9] The single common denominator in these crimes was not so much male violence as male sexual privilege and aggression.

What these feminists were interested in, then, was "social purity." Social purity reformers advocated a single standard of sexual morality, and, since the 1860s, British feminists had waged political campaigns based on these beliefs. Led by Josephine Butler, these women fought to repeal the Contagious Diseases Acts that required the medical inspection of prostitutes. Social purity activists opposed the acts in part because they facilitated men's use of prostitutes by reducing the risk of venereal disease, and in part because they identified with the plight of prostitutes forced to undergo inspection. After the defeat of the acts, advocates of social purity pressed for the complete abolition of prostitution. Reformers in the United States also fought the medical regulation of prostitution when the idea was introduced in the 1860s and 1870s. Many of the American social purity activists were advocates of temperance and woman's suffrage as well; Stanton and Anthony, for example, successfully opposed inspection laws when they were introduced in the New York State legislature.[10]

Stanton and Anthony were also influenced by two works published in 1869 that incorporated social purity ideas: John Stuart Mill's *Subjection of Women* and Harriet Beecher Stowe's *Lady Byron Vindicated.*[11] Mill characterized sexual intercourse as merely an "animal function"—as the worst form of degradation when an unwilling wife became the object of her husband's animalism. Mill was as fond of the analogy between slavery and marriage as were Stanton and Anthony. He did not deny that many marriages operated tolerably under a system of absolutism on one side and loving submission on the other, but he believed that as long as husbands possessed unlimited power in marriage, brutal men could commit violence against their wives and children. Mill, like Stanton and Anthony, rejected the ideal of family stability, and favored divorce for wives on grounds of cruelty.

Mill's *Subjection of Women* also helped inspire Harriet Beecher Stowe to publish *Lady Byron Vindicated,* a denunciation of the English romantic poet for having committed incest with his half-sister. Stowe, an old friend of Lady Byron, defended the estranged wife of the poet against an attack by her husband's mistress, whose memoirs had been published that year. Lady Byron had confided to Stowe that her husband had fathered a child by his half-sister before they were married, and that the affair continued after she married him. Stowe implied that Lady Byron also had been beaten by her husband when he was drunk. Public reaction ran against Stowe for defaming Lord Byron and for discussing in print a subject that was not to be mentioned in polite society. But Elizabeth Cady Stanton compared the book favorably with John Stuart Mill's *Subjection of Women:* "Our present civilization is marked with as hideous outrages on the mothers of the race, in marriage, and out of it, as has ever blackened the pages of history at any period of the world."[12] She added "incest in high places" to the other outrages she described before a women's rights convention in 1870.[13]

Although Stanton and Anthony directly credited many of their ideas to the writings of Mill and Stowe, they were more circumspect about the influence of their colleague Matilda Joslyn Gage. Active in the women's rights movement since the 1850s, Gage became president of the National Woman Suffrage Association in 1879. She published her major work, *Woman, Church and State,* in 1891.[14] In it she traced the historical origins of state and legal oppression of women in West European and American history, and linked these dual sources of oppression with diverse forms of women's victimization, from wife beating to polygamy and witchcraft. When canon law gained ascendancy over civil law, she argued, many of the punishments for crimes against women were eliminated. Canon law also embedded in the law a view of a woman as the property of her husband, a view that was later incorporated in common law. Gage had worked out this argument by the time the first volume of the *History of Woman Suffrage,* which she coauthored with Stanton and Anthony, appeared in 1881. The volume included Gage's essay "Woman, Church and State," in which she also exposed the legal and religious sources of women's oppression. Likewise, Stanton argued that "men abuse wives, taught by law and gospel that they own them as property."[15] It is difficult to say whether this idea originated with Stanton or with Gage.

Stanton and Anthony never hewed entirely to Gage's analysis, but often combined it with arguments about social purity. Indeed the "hideous outrage" of marital rape (always referred to through euphemism) appeared to confirm both perspectives. Because the wife was her husband's property, he had the right to sexual intercourse with her at his pleasure. They also combined their belief in social purity with a call for temperance. Thus, in an address before a social purity convention, Anthony singled out the "twin vices" of "drunkenness and licentiousness" committed by "the bloated drunkard" and "the diseased libertine" (a reference to the communication of venereal disease to wives by their husbands).[16]

Their solution to the problem of women's slavery in marriage was to reform the institution of marriage or to emancipate the wife through divorce. Stanton argued that she was not seeking to destroy the family, but to create a marriage of equals, based on companionship and spiritual union as well as physical attraction and concern for children. No marriage could be equal, however, until the wife had the right of "voluntary motherhood," the right to refuse her husband intercourse. For the wife trapped in a "discordant marriage," Stanton advocated full divorce with the right of remarriage, and held that the mother should be given special consideration in the award of child custody. For Stanton, marriage was not a sacrament but rather a contractual relationship that either party should be free to dissolve.

After 1870, Stanton and Anthony held no further dramatic protest meetings against crimes against women. In their journal, *The Revolution,* stories of infanticide and of sons murdering their mothers were buried amidst reports of the fight for suffrage. Stanton continued to advocate divorce, but she was less specific about the reasons for it. Her 1870 speech on "Marriage and Divorce" mentioned that abuse of children and wives arose out of man's ownership of women as property. Five years later, her standard public lecture still called for liberalized divorce and even decried male domination in the family, but did not mention the abuse of wives or children.[17]

Stanton's self-censorship can be explained in several ways. For one, she had lost suffragist support as a result of her impassioned attack on marriage, stemming from the McFarland-Richardson trial in 1869. In addition, the passage in 1873 of the Comstock Law, which banned dissemination through the mails of birth control information and pornography, helped to end open discussion of such topics as rape and incest. Radical ideas about labor or homesteads for ex-slaves were generally subdued by a conservative climate, while many liberal divorce laws dating from the antebellum period were removed from the statute books. Then came the Beecher-Tilton scandal, brought about by Victoria Woodhull's exposure of Henry Ward Beecher's adultery with one of his female parishioners. Stanton and Anthony, friends of both the accused and his accuser, were tarnished by their association with known advocates of free love and presumed adulterers. On the lecture circuit, they responded to the hisses and boos of their audiences by muting their rhetoric so as not to alienate their listeners further.

Stanton and Anthony had never regarded women's victimization as a separate issue, but rather as a means of dramatizing the need for voluntary motherhood, woman's right to divorce, temperance, and social purity. They used instances of wife beating and incest, for example, to strengthen their claim for a woman's right to divorce, but they believed that the solution, divorce, was more important than the problem, domestic violence. They had risked violating cultural standards of propriety by attacking the family and advocating divorce, but after being associated with several sex scandals they could no longer afford to do so. Nineteenth-century feminists could either do battle against specific domestic outrages without attacking the institution of the family (as did the advocates of temperance), or they could attack the family and champion divorce while remaining vague about the circumstances that required it (as did Stanton and Anthony); they could not do both.

Conservative Feminists

As leaders of the American Woman Suffrage Association, Lucy Stone and her husband Henry Blackwell have been regarded as the conservatives of the nineteenth-century women's movement. They viewed the question of marriage and divorce as peripheral to the suffrage movement; divorce, they argued, was not a woman's issue. They even helped pass a resolution at a national suffrage convention "that the ballot for woman means stability for the marriage relation, stability for the home, and stability for our republican government."[18] Stone's reputation as a conservative also arose because of the split in suffrage ranks regarding acceptance of the Fourteenth Amendment. Stone and Blackwell, who worked to include woman's suffrage as part of the amendment, were willing to accept the enfranchisement of only black men, whereas Stanton and Anthony opposed the introduction of male-only suffrage into the U.S. Constitution. Lucy Stone held conservative views on other issues as well. She did not favor general strikes, and she was unsympathetic when labor unrest led to violence. She and her husband also maintained a dignified silence about Harriet Beecher Stowe's denunciation of Lord Byron, and she found the involvement of Stanton and Anthony with the Beecher-Tilton scandal and their association with Victoria Woodhull an embarrassment.

Before Stone and Blackwell became editors of the *Woman's Journal* in 1872, the journal featured articles that called divorce for women "an escape out of tyranny into freedom." Under their editorship, such articles quickly disappeared. During those first years they seemed deliberately to avoid controversial issues in order to concentrate on women's rights. In 1876, however, Stone announced her intention of publishing a weekly catalog of crimes against women. As justification she cited the appearance of newspaper reports that indicated an increasing incidence of "crimes against women." Such reports compelled her to overlook "standards of propriety" in detailing torture, maiming, and brutality against women.[19] Beneath the headline of "crimes against women," readers of the *Woman's Journal* found stories of wife murder, rape, incest, and wife beating; a mutual suicide agreed upon in a love pact; physical assaults by boys against girls; and even crimes committed by women, such as infanticide or crimes of passion where women had responded to seduction, rape, or male violence.

Although Stone and Blackwell were regarded as the conservatives of the women's rights movement, their analysis of crimes against women was virtually identical with that of Stanton and Anthony. They, too, believed that abuse of wives grew out of a husband's ownership of his wife as a form of property—"domestic tyranny," as they sometimes called it. They believed in social purity, and Stone campaigned for the punishment of male pimps and procurers rather than prostitutes. Indeed, Henry Blackwell argued that "the most oppressed and abused class of women in society" was not the assaulted wife, who could still cling to a mantle of respectability, but instead that class of woman "which associates with men outside of the legal sanctions of marriage" (i.e., prostitutes).[20] They also railed against the "hydra-headed monster" of intemperance and of male licentiousness, and gave special attention to the status of married women, although they recognized that crimes against women were committed whether the victims were "living in or out of the marriage relation."[21] And though they knew that wife beating occurred in every class and ethnic group, they held that "a large majority of such crimes" occurred among immigrants, because women were held in low regard in the countries from which the immigrants came.[22]

The most marked difference between Stanton and Anthony, on one hand, and Stone and Blackwell, on the other, was in the solutions they emphasized. In 1879 Stone introduced a bill in the Massachusetts legislature to protect the assaulted wife whose husband had been convicted of criminally assaulting her.[23] The proposed bill gave an assaulted wife the right to apply at a neighborhood police court for a legal separation, an order requiring her husband to pay support for her and her children, and the award of custody over her children. Three times she introduced this legislation—in 1879, 1883, and 1891—and three times it failed.

The idea for this bill came from the prominent English suffragist Frances Power Cobbe, who had sent Stone a copy of the protection bill she helped pass in Parliament. Cobbe's article, "Wife Torture in England," published in the *Contemporary Review* in 1879, had shocked the English public with tales of atrocities and helped attract popular support for her bill. More sophisticated than most Americans, Cobbe acknowledged that the assaulted wife was not always innocent or defenseless; sometimes she fought back or even initiated violence. She herself learned about this issue when members of Parliament unsuccessfully attempted to pass a law requiring the flogging of convicted wife beaters. Cobbe opposed the legislation because she believed that a husband who had been beaten would retaliate against his wife. She favored a protection bill as a more suitable alternative, especially for working-class women, among whom assaults "were tenfold as numerous and twenty times more cruel" than among women in "the upper ranks of society."[24] Divorce was an alternative, but many women could not afford it and even if they did secure one, they would still confront the problem of economic survival for themselves and their children. Therefore, Cobbe persuaded several prominent liberals to sponsor her bill, and in 1879, it sailed through the House of Commons without much opposition.

When Lucy Stone received a copy of Cobbe's article and the protection bill she published both in the *Woman's Journal,* pointing out that wife beating occurred in every country and was increasing in the United States. She supplied statistics from the Boston police that indicated there were 500 arrests of wife beaters every year.

To remedy this situation, Stone and Blackwell introduced a protection bill that they believed offered distinct advantages. It granted the assaulted wife both custody of her children and economic support. By locating jurisdiction of these cases in neighborhood police courts, where decisions favoring the plaintiff were the rule, the bill almost ensured judgments in favor of the wife. But Massachusetts legislators raised several objections to the bill. Support orders, they claimed, were unenforceable because abusive husbands would flee the state. They also argued that assaulted wives would not make use of the law, and that legal separations granted by mundane police courts would become excessively easy to obtain. Ironically, Lucy Stone, the ardent opponent of divorce, was now accused of encouraging the dissolution of marriages.

After her protection bill had failed for the second time, Stone began to favor the punishment of wife beaters rather than the protection of their victims. She had long believed that criminals were punished too leniently; she favored capital punishment for rapists and believed that out of "maudlin sympathy" assailants of women received especially light sentences.[25] The rhetoric of extreme punishment was then in vogue, and some women in the social purity movement and the WCTU were advocating castration of rapists.[26] Influenced by English ideas, Maryland in 1882 became the first state to pass a bill to punish wife beaters with flogging at the whipping post. A similar bill was introduced in the Massachusetts legislature in 1885. Unlike male reformers who sought to introduce extreme punishments in the criminal law, Stone threw her support behind the bill because she believed a fine or imprisonment would merely deprive the wife beater's family of economic support. But the bill lost by a wide margin.[27] After this defeat, Stone tried one more time to pass her protection bill, but does not appear to have continued other legislative efforts.[28]

The failure to achieve passage of either bill only strengthened Stone and Blackwell's belief that women would never be protected from brutality until they were considered equals under the law. Because women were unable to vote, they argued, penalties for wife beating were mild. Would battered wives "ever be adequately protected," Lucy Stone wondered, "until women would help make the laws?"[29] Enacting laws to ensure equality between the sexes would help to remove prejudice against women. Even the former wife beater would no longer regard his wife as his property, since he would realize the general esteem in which women were held.[30]

Stone and Blackwell contended that assaulted wives, recognizing they were protected under the law, would be more willing to complain to the police and press their cases in the courts. Judges, who had come to fear the wrath of the female electorate, would sentence wife beaters to long prison terms and governors would refuse to pardon wife murderers.[31]

Stone and Blackwell's arguments about the causes of crimes against women were virtually identical with those of Stanton and Anthony. Nonetheless, they attached the label "crimes against women" to a range of previously nameless acts, and they initiated legislation on behalf of assaulted wives. Stone and Blackwell differed from Stanton and Anthony primarily in their attitude toward divorce. In our own times, the battered women's movement is often sympathetic to and even encourages divorce and criticizes the mental health field for counseling women to remain in unhappy and violent marriages. It might seem, then, that the greater the tolerance for divorce, the more vigorous the efforts on behalf of assaulted wives. But in the late nineteenth century, it was extremely controversial to advocate divorce. Precisely because Stone opposed divorce, she could raise the issue of crimes against women without giving the appearance of threatening family stability. She did so primarily to demonstrate that solutions other than divorce—protective legislation and suffrage—would more truly aid assaulted wives.

The Women's Christian Temperance Union

The WCTU began as an organization solely interested in the question of temperance. After Frances Willard became president of the organization in 1879, the WCTU began to insist that drunkenness was not only the cause but also the effect of a variety of social problems. As the largest women's organization of its day, the WCTU favored a variety of social reforms from the introduction of police matrons to prison reform, to the eight-hour working day, and the kindergarten. Temperance workers also successfully campaigned for the passage of state laws designed to benefit abused wives of drunkards.

Because each spouse was immune to a tort brought by the other, wives did not have the legal right to sue an abusive husband for damages. Therefore, the WCTU championed special legislation that gave the drunkard's wife the highly unusual right to sue for damages. The laws did not hold the drunkard, a creature of his appetites, entirely responsible for his actions; rather, they held that the rum seller who had encouraged the man to drink should pay for the consequences of his customer's actions.

In 1873, the New York and Arkansas legislatures passed the first of these laws. In all, twenty states from Maine to New Mexico enacted such legislation, the last of them in 1891. The injured party could sue the saloonkeeper or the owner of the saloon for damages caused from injury inflicted by an intoxicated person. In some states, only the wife could sue for damages, although in others, several injured parties, including a husband, child, parent, or employer, were given the right to sue. In order to be awarded damages, the law generally required the wife to notify the saloonkeeper in advance that he should refuse to serve her husband.

Only a few drunkards' wives could afford to hire a lawyer to sue for damages, but in the few cases that reached the courts, wives generally won their suits and were awarded damages.[32] Ann J. Wilson of Genesee, Michigan, had informed the town saloonkeeper not to serve her husband. On the night in question, her husband had been served enough to make him drunk early in the evening and then served a second time later that night. When her husband finally came home, he attacked her in front of their children and struck her on the head with a chair. She was awarded damages, although the amount of the award was not stated.[33] Courts also upheld other legal transactions that favored the assaulted wife. One Illinois husband who pleaded with his wife not to separate from him signed a note promising to pay her six hundred dollars if he became drunk or abused her. He did, and she sued him for divorce. The Illinois Supreme Court upheld the validity of his promissory note.[34]

The WCTU also promoted the establishment of model facilities for dependent, neglected, and abused children. When there was no other society to protect children from cruelty, they ran their own. In the 1890s, the San Diego Union, an organization comprised of WCTU members from a range of social backgrounds, founded a home for dependent women and children. Although their major interest was in providing a home for neglected and abused children and orphans, they also took in the children's poverty-stricken mothers, some of whom had been assaulted by their husbands. The San Diego Union also ran a day-care facility for the children of working mothers and a kindergarten. Their shelter continued well into the twentieth century.[35]

In all of these efforts, the WCTU marched forward under the banner of Christianity, motherhood, and the protection of innocent women and children. But they could not bring themselves to favor divorce as a solution for the sufferings of the drunkard's family. At first, articles in the *Union Signal,* the official publication of the WCTU, favored divorce only on grounds of adultery, although other articles argued that so long as saloons remained open, drunkenness was an acceptable grounds for divorce. They voiced no opinion on cruelty as a grounds for divorce, although from the general tone of conservatism, it appears that they would have favored a legal separation in cases of abuse rather than a divorce that permitted remarriage. They assumed that the legally separated wife did not require the right of remarriage because she was an asexual being and self-sacrificing mother who would be content to live modestly by respectable wage-earning.[36]

Although WCTU members regarded intemperance as the major cause of social ills, their increasing involvement in social purity campaigns suggests that they regarded male licentiousness if not as a twin evil, then at least as a secondary one. Therefore, they lobbied for legislation on behalf of assaulted wives, and unlike Stone, whose bill had been defeated because legislators perceived it as an attack on traditional marriage, the WCTU succeeded. The WCTU could claim to be alleviating misery, supporting women's traditional role, and protecting the family, rather than securing for women an independent existence.

Instead of attacking the traditional patriarchal family, women in temperance hoped to shore it up by forcing men to realize their responsibilities. They acknowledged that women as well as children were dependents, but they were not critical of female dependency, as were feminists. Instead they called for the protection of dependent women by decent men. Alcohol and lust had turned gentle men into brutes who had to be reformed. Indeed, the WCTU seemed more concerned with uplifting men than with raising the status of women.[37] In sum, they did not believe in a marriage of equals, but in a marriage of respectables in which the protective husband remained the authority.

The Protective Agency for Women and Children

Nineteenth-century Americans established hundreds of societies for the protection of children, but only one, the Protective Agency for Women and Children, founded in Chicago in 1885, protected assaulted wives and rape victims. The first protective agency, organized by men, had opened in New York City in 1868; like those that followed in other eastern cities, it arose within the context of the urban charity movement of the post-Civil War decades. Similarly, the Women's Education and Industrial Union in Boston protected working women by investigating employee fraud, operating a lunchroom for employed women, conducting classes in labor law, and aiding victims of consumer fraud.[38] The Chicago agency carried protective work in a unique, new direction and became the most significant organizational effort to aid female victims of violence in nineteenth-century America.

Although the Chicago Woman's Club, sponsor of the protective agency, began as a literary society, by 1885 it had become deeply interested in a variety of reforms—lobbying the state legislature to pass compulsory school attendance laws and to abolish child labor; aiding in the establishment of a juvenile court; and demanding, with the WCTU, that city jails hire police matrons.[39] Edith Harbart of the Cook County Suffrage Association suggested that the club establish a separate department devoted to the protection of women and children. She believed that the club, which included so many wives of Chicago's elite men, would lend respectability to a protective agency. The Woman's Club agreed, and at the opening meeting of the Chicago agency, speakers denounced the "debauching" of women clericals and the extremely low age of sexual consent under Illinois law (at that time, only ten years). They called for a society that would hire its own agents, though it would be staffed primarily by women volunteers; its membership would be restricted to women.

The formal organization and daily operation of the agency were remarkable in other respects. Half of the officers were required to be members of the Woman's Club and the other half were from diverse city and suburban women's organizations. Most of the women were wealthy, with the possible exception of the representatives from the Swedish and Bohemian women's clubs. The governing board of the agency consisted of delegates from fifteen associations of women in Chicago including the WCTU, the Chicago Woman's Club, the Cook County Woman's Suffrage Association, and several social purity organizations. The agency established an office to offer legal aid, where women handled cases of sexual molestation, incest, rape, sexual harassment, wife beating, and consumer fraud. Other agencies referred women who were seeking legal assistance to them, and they in turn cooperated with these agencies. In a typical case, the protective agency handled the legal proceedings for a Russian immigrant who had been raped by her father. It cooperated with the Illinois Humane Society in terminating the father's right to custody and helped place the girl in an orphan asylum.[40]

The Chicago protective agency also sought out women believed to be rape victims, based on the reports of interested parties. Instead of waiting for the victim to come to their office, women went to her home, inquired as to the validity of her story, and asked her if she had enough money to hire her own lawyer. If she did not, they hired one for her and tried to provide her with a place to live and a job. These methods drew criticism from detractors who told the agency "that to go out in the highways and byways of life, and lift up those who are downtrodden, under the feet of wicked men, [was] very dirty business."[41] Agency members also appeared in court on behalf of rape victims, both because they believed that the presence of respectable women helped create a moral atmosphere and in order to encourage the victim to testify in a courtroom dominated by men. Rape victims, they believed, felt ashamed to testify and did not want to subject themselves to cross-examination, especially about their sexual history. But, the women claimed, "the shame and scandal of these crimes lies in the fact, not the telling of it." They went on to attack the double standard according to which a rape victim had to demonstrate to a jury "an unblemished reputation."[42]

The agency activists did not often discuss the ultimate solution to crimes against women. They did write of the economic dependency and exploitation of women and children, and they assumed that some mothers and older children would have to support themselves. But they seemed more interested in methods than in solutions; they believed in educating women about their legal and social status and viewed the sisterhood of women as a means of bringing about change. True virtue in marriage, child rearing, and personal relations was their ultimate goal.

The Chicago agency justified its work by arguing that women were the natural protectors of other women and children. Single females and working women were in special need of protection because they were removed from their families and forced to fend for themselves in a world of men, while girls were especially vulnerable because they were sexually pure, young, and innocent. It was women's responsibility to protect these innocents from the "human brutes," or rapists, who preyed upon them. The protective agency defended itself against the charge that it was helping to break up the family by claiming that the marriages it helped to terminate were not "true marriages" but instead "a falsity and a sham" because of the violence, cruelty, or immorality that occurred within them.[43] In fact, however, helping abused women to gain separations enlarged the experience and deepened the feminist consciousness of agency members. By the third year of their work, they began to question the nature of marriage: "We come to ponder much more on these great questions—the sexual and financial relations of men and women, and often wonder what is wrong."[44] Within a few years they began to connect the victimization of women with the general inequality between the sexes.[45]

Eleven years after its founding, the protective agency merged with a larger, well-funded, and predominantly male organization, the Bureau of Justice, which furnished legal aid to indigent clients. In the agreement of consolidation, however, the women asked for and received sole jurisdiction over the cases affecting women and children, since they believed it "a self-evident truth that women can do better work for the wronged of their own sex than men can do."[46] As a result of the merger, their case load grew rapidly. They began to provide those assaulted wives with children legal aid to secure divorces, rather than just legal separations.[47] In 1905 the agency merged a second time, to form the Legal Aid Society of Chicago. The reason for this merger appears to have been the same as in the first—joining with a larger, better-funded organization that would provide the agency a necessary guarantee of autonomy.[48] The protective agency still maintained its separate identity and was represented on the Board of Legal Aid. By 1912, however, reports of its work disappeared from the annual report of Chicago Legal Aid. Among other ominous signs of change was the replacement of their old motto, "woman's work for women," with "men's and women's work for the wronged and helpless." By the 1920s, Chicago Legal Aid's official policy was to discourage divorce and urge reconciliation whenever possible. It is not known whether the organization continued to aid rape victims.

Reexamining the history of the protective agency reveals the problems that women reformers encountered when they worked on behalf of women victims. First, efforts on behalf of assaulted wives led reformers to consider "the most embarrassing of all questions which come before us"—the issue of divorce.[49] They began cautiously by securing only legal separations for women. Later they began to help women secure divorces, but only on the grounds of extreme cruelty or drunkenness. The charge that aiding assaulted wives led to the breakup of the family had helped defeat Stone's protection bill. Opposition to divorce grew after a government report in the 1880s demonstrated that divorce was more common in the United States than in any other Western country. National magazines decried the prevalence of divorce, and even societies for the prevention of cruelty to children had to defend themselves against new charges that they were breaking up the family. Thus, women reformers tended to favor reforms that would force men to assume family responsibilities, such as child support and desertion laws, rather than those that would separate the family.

A second obstacle to the Chicago agency's work was the cultural attitude toward any discussion of rape, incest, or sexual molestation. The agency was forced to admit that "for obvious reasons, these cases cannot be told to the public."[50] The modesty of a virtuous woman was compromised by having to consider sordid incidents, and the virtue of the victim was further damaged by revealing the facts in her case. The agency was continually forced to challenge beliefs that the victim had provoked an attack or was of "blemished reputation." Ironically, because the prostitute's reputation had already been blemished, she could more readily become an object of pity and attention.

Why was the Chicago protective agency the only one of its kind when there were hundreds of societies established for the prevention of cruelty to animals and to children? Lucy Stone noted that there was more concern for beaten horses and dogs than for bruised and beaten wives.[51] She called for a society to prevent cruelty to wives, but she never organized one, and the protective agency in Chicago was the closest approximation of this goal in the nineteenth century. In fact, over the last three hundred years, concern for children (regardless of gender) has been much greater than for adult women, and the protective work on behalf of women that existed in the nineteenth century focused on intemperance and prostitution. Historians Linda Gordon and Ellen DuBois have recently argued that in the nineteenth century interest in social purity, and especially in prostitution, substituted for interest in crimes against women, especially rape.[52] They are quite correct that prostitution was the dominant metaphor for woman's victimization. But concern for social purity stimulated interest in crimes against women. It was not that crimes against women went unrecognized but rather that interest in the issue could not be sustained.

The Decline of Women's Interest

By the 1890s the feminist response to crimes against women began to diminish. Older leaders of the women's movement who had been interested in the issue died, while younger women and black women of all ages found it an unappealing, somewhat dated cause. Black suffragists, for example, who formed their own woman's clubs in this decade, associated crimes against women with the lynching of black males for alleged rape of white women.[53] They believed concern for the protection of women to be largely a subterfuge for racism. In the North the suffrage movement began to attract college-educated social reformers who were less interested in denouncing and punishing the brutishness of men than in eradicating the social conditions believed to cause crime. In addition, concern about crimes against women had flourished during the nadir of the suffrage movement, but as their movement gained momentum, suffragists began to shed the more controversial, less popular issues.

In contrast, English suffragists continued to debate divorce reform for assaulted wives as late as 1911. The English had been the first to respond to domestic violence, and English reformers from Mill to Cobbe had linked protection for assaulted wives with divorce reform. Furthermore, English suffragists continued to cling to social purity ideas with a vehemence that had disappeared elsewhere.[54]

In the United States the response to crimes against women had depended as much on the social purity and temperance campaigns as it had on the movement for women's rights. The transformation of these movements by the 1890s diminished interest in what had always been a peripheral issue. The entire premise of social purity rested upon the protection of female sexual virtue from ruin. With the transition in sexual mores that occurred in the late nineteenth and early twentieth centuries, otherwise respectable women were giving away what had once been so zealously protected. As the value of female virtue began to decline, so did the elaborate lengths that were taken to defend it. Nonetheless, Progressive era reformers revived interest in prostitution not as an issue of social purity or individual sin, but rather as a social problem exacerbated by the anonymity of the modern metropolis. Instead of punishing male customers of prostitutes, these reformers concentrated on protecting health and hygiene. Their solution was to eliminate the cities' red-light districts. Even the temperance campaign, one of the last bastions of traditional moral categories, began to abandon its early rhetoric in favor of pamphlets concerning the effect of alcohol on health or the relation between saloons and prostitution. The monstrous drunkard became the pitiable alcoholic, who either suffered from a curable medical disease or, in more severe cases, was a genetic misfit. Control over such men passed to another set of reformers, the professional case workers and psychiatrists.

The earlier response to crimes against women had been moralistic, sexually prudish, and punitive in its attitude toward criminals. But these characteristics were not so much embarrassing excesses of belief as qualities essential to articulating women's position and waging a variety of reform campaigns. With the disappearance of rhetoric about "evil beasts" and social purity, the emotional outrage necessary to generate a public campaign was gone. Only after another eighty years would feminists renew their sisterhood with victims of crimes against women, to refute once again popular stereotypes and to challenge the conspiracy of silence.

Notes

The author has benefited from the criticisms of this paper by Estelle Freedman, Linda Gordon, and Sonia Michel.

1. Ida Husted Harper, *The Life and Work of Susan B. Anthony,* 2 vols. (Indianapolis: Hollenbeck, 1898), 1:204.

2. Ellen DuBois, *Feminism and Suffrage: The Emergence of an Independent Women's Movement in America, 1848–1869* (Ithaca, N.Y.: Cornell University Press, 1978), pp. 145–147.

3. Lois W. Banner, *Elizabeth Cady Stanton: A Radical for Woman's Rights* (Boston: Little, Brown & Co., 1980), p. 73.

4. Elizabeth Cady Stanton, *Eighty Years and More: Reminiscences, 1815–1897* (1898; reprint ed., New York: Schocken Books, 1981), p. 215.

5. *The Revolution* (New York) (January 14, 1869), pp. 24–25, reprinted in Ellen Carol DuBois, ed., *Elizabeth Cady Stanton, Susan B. Anthony: Correspondence, Writings, Speeches* (New York: Schocken Books, 1981), p. 123.

6. William Leach notes this post–Civil War change in atmosphere but not the distinct chill in the air that resulted from the discovery of the Beecher-Tilton affair. William Leach, *True Love and Perfect Union: The Feminist Reform of Sex and Society* (New York: Basic Books, 1980), pp. 118–119.

7. Edwin Powell's figures for police arrests in Buffalo show that murder and assault rates increased dramatically at the end of the Civil War. These increases could not have been due only to an increased willingness of police to make arrests, since the arrest rate for violent crimes grew twice as fast as the total arrest rate. See Edwin H. Powell, "Crime as a Function of Anomie," *Journal of Criminal Law, Criminology, and Police Science* 57, no. 2 (June 1956): 161–171. Similarly, the rate of major crime in Boston grew by 21 percent between 1867 and 1874, even though the number of police in Boston increased only 10 percent. See Theodore N. Ferdinand, "The Criminal Patterns of Boston since 1849," *American Journal of Sociology* 73, no. 1 (July 1967): 84–99. Only a small proportion of incidents of family violence ever appear in police records, though murder between spouses is well recorded. In Philadelphia the rate of husband-wife murders increased dramatically from 1 per 1 million persons between 1839 and 1845 to 4.1 per 1 million between 1874 and 1880, then vacillated slightly before declining at the end of the century. Manuscript Docket Books, Court of Quarter Sessions, Philadelphia, City Archives of Philadelphia.

8. Paulina Wright Davis, *A History of the National Woman's Rights Movement* (New York: Journeymen Printers Cooperative, 1871), p. 66.

9. Susan B. Anthony, "Social Purity," in Aileen S. Kraditor, ed., *Up from the Pedestal: Selected Writings in the History of Feminism* (Chicago: Quadrangle Books, 1970), p. 160.

10. David Pivar, *Purity Crusade: Sexual Morality and Social Control, 1868–1900* (Westport, Conn.: Greenwood Press, 1973), p. 51.

11. John Stuart Mill, "The Subjection of Women," reprinted in *Essays on Sex Equality: John Stuart Mill and Harriet Taylor Mill,* ed. Alice S. Rossi (Chicago: University of Chicago Press, 1970); and Harriet Beecher Stowe, *Lady Byron Vindicated: A History of the Byron Controversy* (Boston: Fields, Osgood & Co., 1870).

12. Leach (n. 6 above), pp. 118–119.

13. Davis (n. 8 above), p. 68.

14. Matilda Joslyn Gage, *Woman, Church and State* (1891; reprint ed., Watertown, Mass.: Persephone Press, 1981).

15. Davis (n. 8 above), p. 72.

16. Anthony, p. 159; and Elizabeth Cady Stanton, "Speech to the McFarland-Richardson Protest Meeting,' May, 1869," in DuBois, ed. (n. 5 above), p. 127.

17. Contrast the speech she gave at the annual convention of the National Woman Suffrage Association in 1870 with her favorite speech for the lecture circuit, "Home Life." See Judith Papachristou, *Women Together* (New York: Alfred A. Knopf, 1976), p. 62; Elizabeth Cady Stanton, "Home Life," in DuBois, ed. (n. 5 above), pp. 131–138.

18. *Woman's Journal* (Boston) (December 3, 1870).

19. Ibid. (January 28, 1877).

20. Ibid.

21. Ibid.

22. Ibid. (May 15, 1875).

23. Wife beating had been a crime under Massachusetts law since the colonial period—as early as 1641. Any remaining doubt about the legal status of wife beating was resolved in 1871, when the Massachusetts Supreme Court ruled it a misdemeanor. The law held several advantages for women. A wife who left her husband because he beat her could apply for both a protection order requiring him to vacate her premises and forbidding him from forcing her to return, and an order requiring him to support her and her children. If a wife or her child was injured by a drunken husband, she could sue the saloonkeeper for damages. Finally, a husband convicted of assaulting his wife was required to post a bond for up to two years. Yet there were difficulties as well. A wife had to swear out a complaint against her husband, and, in some jurisdictions, police were instructed not to arrest a man unless they saw him commit a violent act. Then, too, if a husband claimed to have reformed and he demanded his wife's return, she was legally required to go back to him. Most important, the protection and maintenance orders required a lawyer to press the case before the state supreme court, and lawyers' fees were an expense only a few women could afford. On Massachusetts law regarding wife assault, see *Acts and Resolves Passed by the General Court of Massachusetts, 1874* (Boston: Wright & Potter, 1874), pp. 132–133; George A. O. Ernst, *The Legal Status of Married Women in Massachusetts* (Boston: Massachusetts Woman Suffrage Association, 1895), pp. 23, 24. *Massachusetts Laws, Statutes, Acts and Resolves Passed by the General Court of Massachusetts in the Year of 1879* (Boston: Rand, Avery & Co., 1879), p. 444.

24. Frances Power Cobbe, "Wife Torture in England," *Contemporary Review* (April 1878), p. 57.

25. *Woman's Journal* (January 29, 1876) and (June 11, 1881).

26. Simeon E. Baldwin, "Whipping and Castration as Punishments for Crime," *Yale Law Journal* 8, no. 9 (June 1899): 381.

27. When this bill lost, its sponsor substituted another one to punish wife beaters with a three- to ten-year prison term. It also lost. See *Documents Printed by the Order of the House of Representatives of the Commonwealth of Massachusetts, 1884* (Boston: Wright & Potter, 1884).

28. Henry Blackwell opposed legislation designed to punish wife beaters at the whipping post. See *Woman's Journal* (February 11, 1905). Similarly, Matilda Gage viewed flogging as a "retributive punishment common among barbarians." She argued that the "remedy for crimes against women . . . does not lie in the punishment of offenders, but in different sentiments in regard to woman in both church and state" (Gage [n. 14 above], p. 145).

29. *Woman's Journal* (April 8, 1892).

30. Ibid. (January 11, 1879) and (January 18, 1879).

31. Ibid. (January 18, 1879).

32. Henry Campbell Black, *A Treatise on the Laws Regulating the Manufacture and Sale of Intoxicating Liquors* (St. Paul, Minn., West Publishing, 1892), pp. 277–377.

33. Wilson v. Booth, 57 Mich. 249.

34. *Woman's Journal* (April 19, 1877).

35. Ruth Bordin told me about the existence of this organization, which is described in her book, *Women and Temperance: The Quest for Power and Liberty, 1873–1900* (Philadelphia: Temple University Press, 1981), p. 103.

36. Barbara Leslie Epstein, *The Politics of Domesticity: Women, Evangelism, and Temperance in Nineteenth-Century America* (Middletown, Conn.: Wesleyan University Press, 1980), p. 134; Bordin, p. 14.

37. Janet Giele discovered that this concern with men's reform was present in many of the *Union Signal* articles—far more than in the *Woman's Journal*. But the *Union Signal* articles also expressed more hope for the ultimate redemption of men. See Janet Giele, "Social Change in the Feminine Role: A Comparison of Woman's Suffrage and Woman's Temperance, 1870–1920" (Ph.D. diss., Radcliffe College, 1961).

38. Annie Nathan Meyer, *Woman's Work in America* (New York: Henry Holt & Co., 1981), p. 289.

39. Dorothy Edward Powers, "The Chicago Woman's Club" (M.A. thesis, University of Chicago, 1939).

40. Unpublished Case Record, Illinois Humane Society (December 5, 1900), University of Illinois at Chicago Circle Archives.

41. "First Annual Report of the Protective Agency for Women and Children, 1887," p. 13, Chicago Historical Society. Mari Jo Buhle first alerted me to the existence of this organization.

42. Ibid., p. 11.

43. Ibid., p. 10.

44. "Third Annual Report of the Protective Agency for Women and Children, 1889," p. 10, Chicago Historical Society.

45. "Sixth Annual Report of the Protective Agency for Women and Children, 1892," p. 10, Chicago Historical Society.

46. "Eleventh Annual Report of the Protective Agency for Women and Children, 1897," p. 14, Chicago Historical Society.

47. Reginald Heber Smith and John S. Bradway, *Growth of Legal-Aid Work in the United States,* Bulletin no. 67 (Washington, D.C.: U.S. Department of Labor, 1936), pp. 201, 207.

48. Legal Aid in Chicago appears to have been the only legal aid society to have emerged out of a woman's protective agency.

49. "First Annual Report" (n. 41 above), p. 10.

50. Ibid., p. 14.

51. *Woman's Journal* (January 18, 1879). Even this obvious analogy was lost on many suffragists. The Boston Woman's Educational and Industrial Union offered quite a different one: "We form a Society for the Prevention of Cruelty to Children, and shall we forget the needless torture of women who must stand all day whether there is work to do or not?" Quoted in Karen J. Blair, *The Clubwoman as Feminist: True Womanhood Redefined, 1868–1914* (New York: Holmes & Meier, 1980), p. 46.

52. Linda Gordon and Ellen DuBois, "Seeking Ecstasy on a Battlefield: Danger and Pleasure in Nineteenth Century Feminist Sexual Thought" (University of Massachusetts—Boston and State University of New York at Buffalo, Departments of History, April 1982).

53. Ida B. Wells, a black journalist who campaigned against lynching, claimed that most of these charges of rape were untrue, though her treatment of the issue did not fully explain the lynching of black men for beating or murdering their own wives. See Ida B. Wells, *A Red Record: Lynchings in the United States, 1892–1894* (Chicago: n.p., 1895), p. 13.

54. Margaret May, "Violence in the Family: An Historical Perspective," in *Violence and the Family,* ed. J. P. Martin (Chichester, West Sussex: John Wiley & Sons, 1978), pp. 149–150.

10

The Morbidification of Love between Women by Nineteenth-Century Sexologists
Lillian Faderman

Studies such as those by Carroll Smith-Rosenberg (1975) and by William Taylor and Christopher Lasch (1963) of early and mid-19th-century correspondence between women indicate that intense female same-sex emotional relationships were casually accepted at that time. Such relationships were considered within the bounds of legitimate, "normal" behavior according to these studies; they lead the reader to conclude that before the last decades of the 19th century there was virtually no stigma of morbidity or deviance attached to love between women. Much of the fiction that was written during the 19th century and earlier confirms Smith-Rosenberg's and Taylor and Lasch's findings. In Charles Brockden Brown's (1799–1937) *Ormond*, for example, the female narrator, who has just been reunited with a beloved woman friend, exclaims:

The appetite for sleep and for food were confounded and lost amidst the impetuousities of a master passion. To look and to talk to each other afforded enchanting occupation for every moment. I would not part from her side, but ate and slept, walked and mused and read, with my arm locked in hers, and with her breath fanning my cheek. . . . O precious inebriation of the heart! O pre-eminent love! what pleasure of reason or of sense can stand in competition with those attendant upon thee?

At the conclusion of the novel, the two women vow to spend their lives together (that one has a husband is treated as being largely inconsequential), and here the narrator observes:

Henceforth, the stream of our existence was to mix; we were to act and to think in common. . . . Eyes and ears were to be eternally employed upon the conduct of each other; death, when it should come, was not to be deplored, because it was an unavoidable and brief privation to her that should survive.

The two do not doubt that they will be forever united in "that state to which death is a passage."

Such intense love relationships between women were depicted in numerous novels of the subsequent century. In Louisa May Alcott's (1884) *Work: A Story of Experience* the female heroine, Christie, tells Rachel, "I must love somebody, and 'love them hard' as children say; so why can't you come and stay with me?" Christie's devotion to Rachel gives her life

the zest which it had lacked before. Now someone cared for [Christie], and, better still, she could make someone happy. . . . There was nothing in her possession that she did not offer Rachel, from the whole of her heart to the larger half of her little room. . . . [With Rachel, Christie] found happiness in the work that gave her better food than mere daily bread, and never thought of change; for love can make a home for itself anywhere.

Although these fictional relationships are generally not specifically sexual, it must be remembered that neither are heterosexual relationships in novels of this period specifically sexual. But several novels do depict a sensual element (which is sometimes quite direct and sometimes rather coy) in the love between the female characters. For example, in Henry Wadsworth Longfellow's (1849/1965) novel *Kavanagh* Cecilia tells her woman friend, Alice, that she will send a carrier pigeon to Alice's bedroom to act as "a Iachimo in my Imogen's bed-chamber, to spy out its secrets. . . . He will see the book with the leaf turned down, and you asleep, and tell me all about you." In *A Mortal Antipathy* Oliver Wendell Holmes (1892) creates two female characters, Lurida and Euthymia, who have carried on a romantic friendship all through their school days and after graduation. At one point Lurida, who dabbles in art, tells her friend: " 'It is a shame that you will not let your exquisitely molded form be portrayed in marble. . . . ' She was startled to see what an effect her proposal had produced, for Euthymia was not only blushing but there was a flame in her eyes which she had hardly ever seen before." The women in these romantic novels are incapable of sinful behavior, and they are no more tainted or morbid than they are evil or corrupt.

That such relationships were not deemed improper is, as I have suggested elsewhere (Faderman, in press), evidenced by the fact that whereas men were persecuted for homosexual behavior throughout almost all of the Western world, women were generally ignored by the law.[1]

As late as 1896, Dr. Allan Hamilton, writing in the *American Journal of Insanity,* observed that "until within a comparatively recent period the mere insinuation that there could be anything improper in the intimate relations of two women would have drawn upon the head of the maker of such a suggestion a degree of censure of the most pronounced and enduring character." Hamilton went on to describe a "case" of lesbianism that had come to his attention a few years earlier and stated that "at that time her mental perversion was not of a recognized kind." Thus it is probable that the mid-19th-century reader would have been no more shocked in reading of Alice and Cecilia in *Kavanagh* (Longfellow, 1849/1965), that "in a word, they were in love with each other," than would the families of Sarah Butler

Wister and Jeannie Field Musgrove had they read the letters that passed between these women in the 1860s:

[Jeannie to Sarah] Dear darling Sarah! How I love you and how happy I have been! You are the joy of my life. . . . I cannot tell you how much happiness you gave me, nor how constantly it is all in my thoughts. . . . My darling, how I long for the time when I shall see you. . . . I want you to tell me in your next letter, to assure me, that I am your dearest. . . . I do not doubt you, and I am not jealous but I long to hear you say it once more and it seems already a long time since your voice fell on my ear. So just fill a quarter page with caresses and expressions of endearment. . . . Goodbye my dearest, dearest lover—ever your Angelina.

[Sarah to Jeannie] If the day should come when you failed me either through your fault or my own, I would forswear all human friendship, thenceforth. . . . I shall be entirely alone [this coming week]. I can give you no idea how desperately I shall want you. (Smith-Rosenberg, 1975, pp. 4–5)

It is my contention that most 20th-century readers would greet these statements with a very different attitude, not simply because we know more about human sexual behavior in this century but primarily because medical science and psychology for the past 100 years have morbidified intense love relationships between women by inventing a syndrome of ills (which has changed from era to era) that supposedly accompany such affection, and by denying the validity or seriousness of the affection where such ills are clearly not present. My focus in this paper is on the work of Havelock Ellis and that of the predecessor by whom he was the most influenced, Richard von Krafft-Ebing. Both men believed that "true inversion," as Ellis (1897/1901, p. 133) called it, is congenital, that "antipathetic sexual instinct as an anomaly of sexual life (i.e., homosexuality) is only found in individuals who are tainted, as a rule, hereditarily" (Krafft-Ebing, 1882/1925, pp. 444–445).

Congenital Lesbianism

Although the theory of congenital lesbianism has been less widely accepted by psychiatrists and psychologists in the 20th century than those theories of Freud and his disciples who believed that homosexuality is "caused" by environmental factors,[2] nevertheless, Radclyffe Hall's (1928) *The Well of Loneliness,* with its preface by Havelock Ellis and its view of Stephen Gordon, the heroine, as a congenital invert, remains the one lesbian novel known to a wide public. Also, the congenital theory has of late been adopted by many gay militants because they believe (speciously) that it is politically expedient: that is, if homosexuality is an inherited condition, it can in no way be considered immoral; if people are born homosexual, then those not so born cannot "catch" homosexuality; therefore, there is no reason to make laws limiting the rights of homosexuals to teach, serve in the armed forces, and so forth. Significantly, the congenital theory has recently (1975) been used by Sergeant Leonard Matlovich's lawyers to argue that since his homosexuality is inherent it cannot be termed a vice and it cannot be spread to nonhomosexuals; therefore, it constitutes no cause for dismissing him from the air force. It would seem, then, that the congenital theory is far from dead, and we may expect it to be even further revived with the popularization of sociobiology.[3]

In the late 19th and early 20th centuries both Krafft-Ebing and Ellis pleaded, supported by their position that homosexuality was congenital, for the reform of antihomosexual laws (primarily for males, since lesbians were generally ignored by the law). But together with their sympathetic support for the rights of homosexuals, they invariably cast homosexual relationships in a morbid and violent light. Congenital homosexuality thus became inextricably linked with morbidity in popular perception. Ellis (1897/1901), for example, began his discussion of female homosexuals in the 19th century (in the chapter "Sexual Inversion in Women") with the story of Alice Mitchell, whom he called a "typical invert," who "cut [her lover's] throat." This he followed by two other cases of lesbian murder and attempted murder. Next he stated, "Homosexual relationships are also a cause of suicide among women" (p. 120)—with the apparent implication that heterosexual relationships are not. Although Ellis suggested throughout his study that many talented and gifted people have been homosexual and that (ostensibly disagreeing with Krafft-Ebing) homosexuality is not necessarily linked with morbidity, his emphases in all his case histories of women lead the reader to precisely the opposite conclusion.

The first 19th-century scientist to treat female homosexuality in any detail was Karl Westphal, who in 1870 reported in the *Archiv für Psychiatrie* a case of a woman who dressed in men's clothes and was amorously involved with women, and whom he identified as a congenital invert. Krafft-Ebing then expanded on Westphal's study and pointed out that lesbianism was due to "cerebral anomalies," that it was the sign of "an inherited diseased condition of the central nervous system" and a "functional sign of degeneration." This inherited condition he consistently referred to as "taint."[4] Although later writers such as Iwan Bloch, Magnus Hirschfeld, and John Addington Symonds agreed that homosexuality was congenital, they rejected Krafft-Ebing's views that the condition was also pathological. However, Havelock Ellis (and other writers such as Paul Moreaux, B. Tarnowsky, and Cesare Lombroso) largely accepted those views, as I have suggested and will further demonstrate, and it was Ellis' book on sexual inversion that remained for years one of the most influential treatises on homosexuality in English.[5] Hence, it was primarily through the work of Krafft-Ebing and Ellis that the stereotypes of lesbian morbidity were handed down from the late 19th century to the 20th century.

Krafft-Ebing and Ellis specifically distinguished between female homosexual behavior and female homosexuality. The former they saw as being common in particular situations. The latter they invested with a host of morbid symptoms which they deemed "typical" of the "true invert." Krafft-Ebing (1882/1925) recognized that it was not unusual for prepubescent children to engage in homosexual acts which, he believed, sprang from "hypersexuality, precocity, or some external influences" (p. 446). However, he insisted, such acts do not lead to inverted sexuality unless the individual has been born an invert. Krafft-Ebing also recognized a *faut de mieux* homosexuality—that is, the indulgence in homosexual acts in situations in which members of the opposite sex are not available, such as boarding schools, prisons, and garrisons. But in such cases, he contended, there is an immediate return to normal sexual intercourse as soon as the obstacles to it are removed. In this way Krafft-Ebing (1882/1925) emphasized the distinction between "perversity" and "perversion" and concluded that "no case has yet been demonstrated in which perversity has been transformed into perversion—i.e., into an inversion of the sexual instinct" (p. 288). He further insisted that although an "untainted" female may be raised exactly like a male, she will not become homosexual, but rather "*the natural disposition is the determining condition; not education and other accidental circumstances, like seduction*" (italics are Krafft-Ebing's, 1882/1925, pp. 288n–289).[6] A homosexual, then, according to Krafft-Ebing, is, as a rule, not one who engages in homosexual behavior but rather one who is born in an inverted state.

Engaging in homosexual behavior by itself, Havelock Ellis (1897/1901) agreed, has no necessary relationship to true sexual inversion. Girl children may act out the "precocious play of the normal instinct" by mutual sexual touching and kissing; certain employments, such as hotel service, in which the women workers are kept in constant association with each other, day and night, and lace making, in which the women are confined for long hours in close contact to one another in heated rooms, may lead to "homosexual practices." But these practices constitute "a spurious kind of homosexuality" (p. 127). Ellis argued that as soon as such females are given the opportunity to have relationships with men, the "normal instincts" will be brought "into permanent play" (p. 132).

Ellis, like his predecessor, largely ignored the role of social pressure in establishing this "normal instinct," although he occasionally hinted, without bringing the point to its obvious conclusion, that socialization and peer pressure or support might have something to do with what sexual feelings the 19th-century woman ultimately accepted as being appropriate for herself. With regard to the subsequent marriage of women who had regularly fallen in love with their female classmates when they had been students, Ellis observed that once they participated in "practical life" they learned to understand "the real nature of such feelings" and they developed a "subsequent distaste for them" (p. 132). Presumably, the women learned from the outside world that loving another female was considered perversion ("the real nature of such feelings") and thus realized that they must repress those emotions.

Ellis also understood, more or less, that the women's movement (which toward the end of the century was experiencing considerable growth in America, France, Germany, and England) fostered love between women (pp. 147–148). (Ellis claimed here to support women's rights, but as with his support of homosexual rights, he was ambivalent at best. The women's movement, he said, has "involved an increase in feminine criminality and in feminine insanity. . . . In connection with these we can scarcely be surprised to find an increase in homosexuality, which has always been regarded as belonging to an allied, if not the same, group of phenomena.") The movement taught women to be independent of men and to disdain "the old theory which placed women in the moated grange of the home to sigh for a man who never comes," Ellis pointed out. But a corollary of such independence was homosexual behavior: Since women were still restricted in employment opportunities, and working women did not come in frequent contact with men but were segregated with other women, many working feminists, he observed, "find love where they find work." However, Ellis was quick to state in this regard that a woman who has been led to homosexuality through feminism is very likely not a real lesbian, but again only "a spurious imitation," unless she was born with the "germs" of inversion. In such a case, the women's movement might "promote hereditary neurosis."

How, according to Ellis, might one distinguish between the "spurious imitation" of the lesbian and the "true invert"? His case histories established the criteria: One common phenomenon which, he suggested, appears with almost uniform consistency in true inverts is the tendency of these women to have had girlhood crushes on other females. A second phenomenon, which *is* consistent in all his case histories, is congenital taint:

Case XXIX, Miss S.: She belongs to a family in which there is a marked neuropathic element.

Case XL, Miss M.: There is a neurotic element in the family.

Case XLI, Miss B.: Among her brothers and sisters, one is of neurotic temperament and another is inverted.

Case XLII, Miss H.: Among her maternal relatives there is a tendency to eccentricity and to nervous disease.

In insisting on the prevalence of congenital taint among homosexuals, Ellis seems to have ignored the common sense of his supposed collaborator, John Addington Symonds, who pointed out that at that moment in Europe there was probably not a single person who had inherited no neuropathic stain whatsoever (see Note 5 above). Ellis also seems to have ignored his own observation that "normal" girl children frequently indulged in same-sex crushes and erotic play.

A third phenomenon which, according to Ellis, distinguished "the actively inverted woman" from females who have schoolgirl crushes and *faut de mieux* lesbians is "a more or less distinct trace of masculinity" (pp. 133, 140). But, despite this assertion, where Ellis described the physical appearance of the subjects of his case histories, he often admitted that "the general conformation of the body is feminine" or that "her person and manners, though careless, are not conspicuously man-like" (pp. 136, 137). The seeming discrepancy is explained with the statement that such masculinity "may, in the least degree, consist only in the fact that she makes advances to the women to whom she is attracted" (p. 134). He did not deal with the corollary that at least one of the two partners in every homoerotic relationship between "schoolgirls" and between "lace makers" was by this reasoning a true invert.

Although most of his own case histories pointed in another direction, Ellis also repeatedly tried to associate lesbianism with transvestism, from the very beginning of his chapter "Sexual Inversion in Women," when he referred to 16th- and 17th-century women who were executed for dressing in male attire and using dildos. This association is emphasized by his report on the Countess Sarolta V. (which constitutes appendix E of his book), based on a medicolegal account published a few years earlier in Friedreich's *Blätter für Gerichtliche Medicin.* The totally bizarre case of Countess Sarolta is briefly referred to in the "Sexual Inversion in Women" chapter as being *"in most respects so typical"* (p. 140n, emphasis added) of true lesbians. Sarolta came from a family that had always been remarkable for eccentricity. One aunt was hysterical and somnambulistic; another aunt "lay in bed for seven years on account of an imaginary fatal illness," but at the same time gave balls; a third aunt believed that the console in her drawing room was bewitched; and a fourth aunt would not allow her room to be cleaned and would not wash or comb herself for 2 years. Her mother was "nervous and could not bear the moonshine." Her father's family "were generally regarded as rather crackbrained."

Sarolta's father educated her as a boy and his two sons as girls. The sons were dressed in women's clothing until they were 15. The father traveled extensively with Sarolta, insisting usually that she dress as a man. In 1888, at the age of 22 (Ellis observed that until that point her affairs had been typically brief—in conformity with the stereotype he wished to establish—with the exception of one previous relationship that had lasted for *3 years!*) she met a woman who believed her to be a man. The following year they were married. Sarolta deceived her bride's family by stuffing handkerchiefs or gloves into her trouser pocket to produce the appearance of sexual organs and by urinating in a standing position. When she was arrested, because of some financial difficulty with her father-in-law, one of her greatest concerns was having to give up her masculine garments in jail.

Ellis emphasized that Sarolta "recognized the morbidity of her sexual inclinations," that is, her love for other women. And he concluded by reiterating the expert opinion on her case that her "incriminated actions" were "due to her marked and irresistible sexual impulse." Through this incredible case, which he specifically called "typical," Ellis established the mystique of the "true lesbian"—a mystique that was subsequently accepted by many lesbians themselves who became transvestites and "butches" because such behavior demonstrated ipso facto that they were the genuine article, that they must be taken seriously and not be forced into heterosexual patterns. With the advent of the new women's movement in the 1960s, the butch and the female transvestite have largely disappeared, although the number of women who identify themselves as lesbians (and who have *chosen* to become lesbians after making a commitment to feminism) has multiplied, suggesting that one's sexual orientation generally has considerable references to one's immediate society, to "fashion" or to one's views regarding the appropriateness of a particular kind of sexual orientation.

Flame Relationships

Whereas our contemporary climate permits relatively abundant opportunities for two adult women to make a permanent commitment to each other, such was obviously not the case in the Victorian era and earlier. If two young women of marriageable age wished to act on what was, even in Ellis' view, a fairly common attraction to one another,[7] they would have been beset with practical difficulties: How would they support themselves, since so few jobs were open to women? How, in an era when single women did not often leave their communities, would they resist pressure from family and peer group to marry? How, even if they were able to leave their communities, could they manage on the streets in the evening, in restaurants, theaters, anywhere, when it was generally assumed that a good woman seldom goes about unaccompanied? Perhaps one way of overcoming those difficulties was transvestism, which would have permitted two women to live together, one passing as a man. That such a solution was adopted and was successful with any frequency is doubtful. What must have happened much more often is that women commonly enjoyed "intimate attachments," in Ellis' phrase, to other women only until they received a suitable masculine proposal, which resulted in what Ellis saw as "the normal impulse" being brought "into permanent play" (p. 132).

Ellis denied that such premarital intimate attachments between women were lesbian. He did not take into account the social pressures I have outlined above which would guarantee that a woman marry if she could and when she could, usually regardless of the strength of her homoerotic attachment. Although he devoted a section of his work (appendix D) to establishing how entirely common erotic love between young women was in his day, he pointedly invalidated the seriousness of such love relationships by describing them as "school-friendships of girls"—although some of the females included in this study were women in their 20s, and although he admitted that "these friendships are often found among girls who have left school" (p. 254) and thus cannot be considered "school-friendships" at all.

Ellis actually entitled appendix D "The School-Friendships of Girls." The appendix begins with an Italian study by two medical men, Obici and Marchesini, who observed female pupils between the ages of 12 and 20 in Italian normal schools in the late 19th century. They discovered that the "flame" ("rave," "spoon," "crush"—i.e., same-sex infatuation or love among young people) was in every college "regarded as a necessary institution," and that although it was often nongenital, "all the sexual manifestations of college youth circle around it," and "all the gradations of sexual sentiment" were expressed within it (p. 243).

Obici and Marchesini made clear that such a relationship was in no way simple friendship. Its beginning generally had the form of "a regular courtship": The one who was struck first would take frequent walks in the garden when the other was likely to be at her window; she would pause on the stairs to see her beloved pass; she was filled with "a mute adoration made up of glances and sighs"; she would send her beloved flowers, little messages, and finally "long and ardent letters of declaration" (p. 244).

The two doctors had read over 300 love letters which had been "carefully preserved by the receivers." From these letters they concluded that the "flame" generally arose from a "physical sympathy," an admiration for the physical form and style of the beloved. The letters themselves are "full of passion; they appear to be often written during periods of physical excitement and psychic erethism."

Obici and Marchesini specifically enumerated almost a dozen points that distinguished these relationships from ordinary friendships, such as: the frequent exchange of love letters; anxiety to be together, to embrace and kiss; persistent jealousy; exaltation of the beloved's qualities; determination to conquer all obstacles to the manifestation of the love; the pleasure of conquest (p. 245).

In addition to the Obici and Marchesini study, Ellis cited similar research from England and America. His English informant also distinguished between a friendship and—as it was commonly known in English girls' schools and women's colleges—a "rave": The young woman with a rave often had several intimate friends for whom she felt affection without the emotion, pleasurable excitement, and more or less erotic response that characterized a rave. Those who had afterwards been in love with men said that the emotions called forth in both cases were similar (pp. 250–256). The American study of such relationships was carried out at Clark University in Worcester, Massachusetts, by E. G. Lancaster, and published in *Pedagogical Seminary,* July 1897. Lancaster studied over 800 teachers and older pupils with regard to their emotional lives. Although his research questionnaires contained nothing about same-sex love, he reported that a large number of his respondents voluntarily offered information about their homosexual experiences, which led Lancaster to conclude that love of the same sex was very common, especially among young people, that such emotion was not in any way "mere friendship," but rather "the love is strong, real, and passionate" and contains "the same characteristics of intensity and devotion that are ordinarily associated with heterosexual love" (pp. 256–257).

Obici and Marchesini estimated the frequency of flames in normal schools at about 60%—to which a collaborator added the observation that of the remaining 40%, half of them did not indulge "because they are not sufficiently pleasing in appearance or because their characters do not inspire sympathy" (p. 244); that is, as much as 80% of all the females at the normal schools in Obici and Marchesini's study would have liked to or did experience romantic relationships with other females.

Since of these 80% none were specifically known to come from neuropathic families or to be "masculine" in any respect, how did Ellis explain the apparent frequency (i.e., "normality") of this phenomenon of same-sex love? He pointed out that although there is "an unquestionable sexual element in the flame relationship," such a relationship cannot be regarded as an absolute expression of "real congenital perversion of the sex-instinct" (p. 249). That it is a spurious imitation of homosexuality is evidenced not only by the fact that these females eventually slip into a heterosexual life-style but also by the fact that the phenomenon is so widespread. He seems to reason thus: If the majority of females experience this type of same-sex love, it cannot be "abnormal"; real abnormal sexual emotion is, therefore, something else—identifiable by characteristics that the majority of these young women do not ostensibly share. In this way, Ellis rejected as being "spurious imitations" all manifestations of homosexual love that proved it to be entirely common, and he characterized as being indicative of "true inversion" what was identifiable as morbid: a marked neuropathic heredity, a strain of violence, a penchant for transvestism.

His immediate disciples, such as Thoinot, who saw apparent flaws in Ellis' theory, dealt with those flaws not by invalidating the theory, but rather by building on it. For example, how could one explain the phenomenon of a woman who had been married and had children but later became sexually involved with another woman? She suffered from congenital inversion that did not show itself until late in life, that is, "retarded inversion," as Thoinot called it in 1898. (See Karlen, 1971, p. 195. In fact, if Ellis' colleague, the English sex researcher J. A. Hadfield, can be believed, Ellis himself saw flaws in his congenital theory but adhered to it for political purposes alone. Hadfield, 1958, wrote: "Havelock Ellis maintained that homosexuality was of a constitutional type, but he admitted to me in person that he made this statement only because he wanted to emphasize that the individual could not help being what he was.")

Ellis' English contributor to appendix D hinted that raves among females were in some schools so much a "fashion" that "hardly anyone [was] free from it," and any student newly entering the school "would soon fall victim to the fashion." Occasionally there would be a "lull in the general raving," and after an interval it would appear again "in more or less of an epidemic form" (p. 252). Ellis once more did not draw this point to its logical conclusion: It would seem that homosexual passion or lack of it might often be dictated by what one's immediate environment admits as an appropriate passion, in the same way that large-breasted women are "in" with regard to male heterosexual interest in some eras and "out" in other eras. Erotic love has perhaps far less to do with innate instinct and far more to do with "fashion" than most sexual theorists have recognized.

20th-Century Views

The "fashion" in the 20th century, as a result of the psychologists' attention to homosexuality, has generally been to regard same-sex love as morbid and accompanied by the various ills I have enumerated above. Thus the flame or rave usually does not run to "epidemic proportions" as it commonly did in 19th-century girls' schools and women's colleges. Females know today, as a result of the popularization of psychology, that such affectional behavior is generally considered queer and sick. When a female feels a particularly strong attraction to another female, she will undoubtedly try to hide it rather than "moon" openly as her counterpart in a more romantically inclined, less "psychologically knowledgeable" era would have. She is not able to regard herself as having a common emotional/erotic experience. As a result of our growing "sophistication" over the last hundred years, she will be given to understand that her love is morbid. The case of Miss M., which Ellis cited in his chapter "Sexual Inversion in Women," is a prototype in this respect. A year previous, Ellis reported, Miss M. had come across a translation of Krafft-Ebing's book. From that book she learned "that feelings like mine were 'under the ban of society' " and that such feelings were "unnatural and depraved." Before reading Krafft-Ebing she had no notion that her feelings were anything other than a manifestation of love for a particular person (Ellis, 1897/1901, pp. 134–137).[8]

Such "wisdom" is reflected as well in the subsequent fiction. Before the lesbian-feminist movement that began in the late 1960s, almost all of the fiction that dealt with love between women took one of two positions: The woman who loved another female was either a villainous pervert or a pathetic invert. Love between women was no longer romanticized as it had been previous eras: At best, such love was a sorry, doomed thing; at worst it brought in its wake suicide, homicide, and a host of plagues. Clemence Dane's (1917) *Regiment of Women,* a novel about a destructive lesbian teacher in a girls' school, is an early example of the latter. The central character (whose last name is appropriately, Hartill—heart ill) is responsible for the suicide of a 14-year-old student who is infatuated with her (and whom she treats with incredible cruelty), for the seduction and near-ruin of an innocent young woman (who escapes because she is not a pervert like Clare Hartill but rather "as sound and sweet as an apple"), and for the great suffering of numerous other females who have the misfortune to come under her sway. At the conclusion the young woman is snatched from Clare's clutches by a heroic male, who understands that Clare is "abnormal," "perverse," "unpleasant," and generally evil. But the novel ends with the chilling suggestion that Clare will continue to kill and corrupt the innocent: "There were other fish in the sea. . . . That child in the Fourth." After the publication of this novel the schoolgirl crushes that Ellis described as being essentially "harmless" must certainly have been viewed (possibly for the first time?) with considerable alarm.

At the other extreme was Radclyffe Hall's (1928) *The Well of Loneliness,* with its introductory commentary by Havelock Ellis and its central character who is largely a composite of Ellis' case histories. Stephen Gordon, who is bright, generous, sensitive, and loyal ad nauseum, is a congenital invert, a member of the third sex, a man trapped in a woman's body. Despite all her sterling qualities, she suffers because of her stigma throughout the novel, and she is consistently pathetic. At the conclusion she is alone, having given her lover up to a man for the other woman's greater happiness. The book ends with Stephen exhorting God to acknowledge the third sex "before the whole world."

These two novels, which have in common the view that love between women is necessarily doomed to be miserable, were perhaps the prototypes for the fiction of subsequent decades. Novels about love between women that did not take that view were, until the last few years, extremely rare. But more recently, the lesbian-feminist movement has opened the way for fiction such as Marge Piercy's *Small Changes*, (1972), Bertha Harris' *Confessions of Cherubino* (1972), Rita Mae Brown's *Ruby-fruit Jungle* (1973), and Elana Nachman's *Riverfinger Woman* (1974), which once again depicts love between women as being healthy and joyous. In this sense, the recent work has more in common (despite its explicit, "modern" focus on sex) with those novels of the 19th century and earlier that depicted love between women than with 20th-century fiction that showed the influence of the sexual theorists.

Lesbian-feminists have suggested that lesbianism is a political choice—that it has nothing to do with congenital propensities (or with, as Freud believed, early parent-child or sibling relationships), but rather that a woman becomes "woman-identified" and a lesbian when she understands the social and personal inequities between males and females. (See, for example, Abbott & Love, 1973; Johnston, 1973; Shelley, 1971, pp. 476–481.) And, in fact, not a few women in the contemporary feminist movement have, after years of identifying themselves as heterosexuals, chosen to become lesbians, sometimes in anger over what they perceive to be the nature of male-female relationships, sometimes as the result of having first learned through movement doctrine that antilesbianism is an antifeminist weapon and then (more positively) meeting other women whom they can love once the conditioned barriers to same-sex love are removed.

Notes

1. In America the only colonial law that seems to mention sexual relations between women was that passed in 1655 in the New Haven Colony; and even that law, based as it was on the ambiguous biblical injunction, is unclear and may be a reference to a woman practicing fellatio or permitting a man to perform anal intercourse on her: "If any woman change the natural use into that which is against nature, as Rom. I. 26. she shall be liable to . . . punishment." Throughout the 18th and most of the 19th century the law did not acknowledge lesbian relationships. There is some evidence that women in Europe who disguised as men were persecuted and even executed—for example, Catherina Margaretha Lincken in Germany in 1721 (Müller, 1891) and a woman in 16th-century France, described in Montaigne's (1889) *Journal du voyage en Italie en 1850* (cited in Ellis 1897/1901, pp. 118–119). But these women seem to have been condemned not for loving other women but specifically for dressing in male attire and "using illicit inventions [i.e., dildos] to supply the defects of [their] sex" (Montaigne, 1889, p. 11).

2. In "The Psychogenesis of a Case of Female Homosexuality" Freud (1920) explained that his patient had no congenital taint but suffered from penis envy as a result of rivalry with her brother. This caused her to change "into a man" in her thinking, and she "took her mother in place of her father as her love object"; therefore, she became a lesbian.

3. See *Time,* August 1, 1977. John Addington Symonds (1896/1971) presented a much sounder argument in favor of social acceptance of homosexuality. Victorians by the late 19th century were becoming extremely concerned with the facts of the Malthusian theory: Food increased arithmetically; population increased geometrically. If the population continued to grow unchecked at the same rate the Victorians had witnessed, it would be only a matter of time before the food supply ran out. With reference to this alarming problem, Symonds suggested a powerful argument in defence of homosexuality: "In the present state of over-population, it is not to be apprehended that a small minority of men exercising sterile and abnormal sexual inclinations should seriously injure society by limiting the increase of the human race." Or, to put the point in terms that we have learned from 20th-century history, is it better for a society to check overpopulation through forced sterilization and wars waged for the real or imagined need for more *Lebensraum* or through ceasing to discourage what is initially a natural human sexual inclination, through ceasing to attempt to socialize all its members into heterosexuality? If homosexuals today need any defensive argument in favor of homosexuality, Desmond Morris (1967) has presented a very good one. Homosexuals, he says, "provided they are well-adjusted and valuable members of the society outside the reproductive sphere . . . must now be considered as valuable non-contributors to the population explosion" (p. 101).

4. A year before his death, Krafft-Ebing (1901) wrote "Neue Studien auf dem Gebiete der Homosexualität." In this article Krafft-Ebing reversed his lifelong stress on homosexual "degeneracy" and "taint" and conceded that although many deviants had mental disorders and were neuropathic, homosexuality was not a disease but rather a congenital anomaly that was not necessarily incompatible with mental health. But *Psychopathia Sexualis* is, of course, a far better known work than this article.

It is probably safe to guess that many readers who are familiar with his book and the theories promulgated there have no knowledge of the subsequent essay, and its impact on popular notions regarding homosexuals has been minimal.

5. John Addington Symonds, the author of *A Problem in Modern Ethics*, collaborated with Ellis on *Sexual Inversion* but died before the work was published, and his family demanded that his name as coauthor be removed from the text. There are significant differences in the two works regarding the view of homosexuality as pathologically based. Symonds (1896/1971) argued in *A Problem in Modern Ethics* that ancient Greece, where homosexuality was a cultural custom and was even institutionalized, "offers insuperable difficulties to the theorists who treat sexual inversion exclusively from the point of view of neuropathy, tainted heredity, and masturbation" (pp. 36–37). He specifically criticized Krafft-Ebing, suggesting that at that moment in Europe there was probably not a single person who had inherited no neuropathic stain whatsoever. If that be true, Symonds argued, everybody is liable to sexual inversion, and so the principle of heredity becomes purely theoretical (pp. 48–49). Symonds did believe, however, that the true homosexual was a person born with sexual instincts improperly correlated to his/her sexual organs, and that no inherited or latent morbidity is (necessarily) involved. He granted that many homosexuals evince "nervous anomalies," but these, he said, are "not evidence of an originally tainted constitution, but the consequence of the unnatural conditions to which [they have] been exposed from the age of puberty" (p. 74).

6. Krafft-Ebing later in this work recognized, in apparent contradiction, the existence of "lasting acquired antipathetic sexual instinct." One may, he said, permanently acquire this abnormality through *faut de mieux* homosexuality: Where "no restoration occurs, the deep and lasting transformations of the physical personality may occur . . . In this condition of deep and more lasting psycho-sexual transformation, the individual is like unto the (congenital) urning [homosexual] of high grade. The possibility of a restoration of the previous mental and sexual personality seems in such a case, precluded" (p. 297).

7. Ellis said, "it frequently happens" that a young woman may experience "periods of intimate attachment to a friend of her own sex" (p. 132).

8. Miss M., a "true invert," did not indulge in genital sexuality, like most of the "schoolgirls" Ellis described in appendix D. In fact one would be hard put to find significant differences in Ellis' description of Miss M.'s "inverted instinct" and the flame relationships that are cited in appendix D. If anything, she was less specifically sexual in her interests. Miss M. is quoted as saying: "I love few people . . . but in these instances when I have permitted my heart to go out to a friend I have always experienced most exalted feelings, and have been made better by them morally, mentally, and spiritually. Love is with me a religion. The very nature of my affection for my friends precludes the possibility of an element entering into it which is not absolutely sacred."

11

Seduced and Abandoned in an American City: Cleveland and Its Fallen Women, 1869–1936

Marian J. Morton

The spectre of the seduced and abandoned woman haunted Cleveland's reformers in the late nineteenth century.[1] The Cleveland Woman's Christian Association, for example, envisioned such a woman, imperiled by urban life:

In the hustle and activity of the age, the women are following hard after the men. Not satisfied with their quiet country homes, many of them press their way to the cities. What shall be done to care for these women? Be they never so pure, they are liable to fall into disgrace and sin. . . . They do not realize the snare and pitfalls that lie so thickly about them. They do not know that many men go about "like roaring lions seeking whom they devour."[2]

However exaggerated by Victorian sensibilities and rhetoric, these fears for the fallen women were grounded in the very real economic and sexual vulnerability of thousands of women in the growing city. Most of these women have been lost forever to the historian, living and dying in anonymity. Some, however—what small proportion it is impossible to guess—came to the attention of benevolent and reform-minded citizens. Although these women too remain anonymous, their true identities expunged from the registers of institutions and social work agencies, existing records suggest that despite the great economic and social changes that took place in the city from 1869 to 1936, Cleveland's fallen women remained sexually exploited, cast adrift from family, and so poor that they became the objects of a moralistic charity that sought to reform and reclaim them.

Other Americans shared the anxieties of the Cleveland WCA. The long-standing identification of the city with vice and sin was heightened by decades of explosive urban growth following the Civil War and especially by the waves of European immigrants who swelled the urban populations. To many reformers, "the city was an illusive trap set carefully for country virgins."[3] In this setting the fallen woman came to symbolize much that was wrong with urbanizing America: the greater independence of women and the more permissive sexual behavior already percep- tible in the postwar years, the economic exploitation and poverty more visible in the city slums, the collapse of familial and small-town morality, and the decay of orthodox religion in the face of urban anonymity and secularization.[4]

Efforts to rescue these fallen women took many forms in Cleveland and elsewhere. Social purity forces, emulating the antebellum moral reform societies, sought to save prostitutes by stamping out prostitution. Organizations such as the Young Women's Christian Association (YWCA) and the Woman's Christian Temperance Union established residences for young working women where they might be sheltered from vice. For those who already had fallen, the Salvation Army, the National Florence Crittenton Mission, the YWCA, and the local Catholic dioceses opened refuges and maternity homes across the country which, in the evangelical style of nineteenth-century benevolence, tried to rescue both bodies and souls. As part of progressive efforts to systematize and professionalize philanthropy, several cities formed the Inter-City Conference on Illegitimacy; the Cleveland Conference on Illegitimacy shared its goal of preventing unwed motherhood. These attempts, because they were made mostly by middle-class women, have been well documented.[5]

We know less, however, about the fallen women themselves. Historians have been most interested in prostitutes, but although Cleveland reformers certainly worried about prostitution, the seduced and abandoned women described here were for the most part not "painted ladies" or purveyors of the "social evil," but women whose sexual activities were extramarital although not professional. The few existing studies of sexually delinquent women elsewhere suggest that those in Cleveland were not atypical. For example, they resemble the "waifs and the wanton" inmates of the State Industrial School at Lancaster, Massachusetts, the "wayward" women of the Magdalen Asylum of Philadelphia at the turn of the century, and, most closely, the unwed mothers of Boston in 1918.[6] Most important, these women shared poverty, family disruption, and victimization, and offer us another perspective on life in the American city.

The Civil War hastened Cleveland's transformation from a commercial village to an urban metropolis; its population doubled between 1860 and 1870. A wartime boom attracted thousands to the city, many of them immigrants from Western Europe, especially Germany and Ireland, but most from the near-by countryside.[7] The charitable and benevolent associations that served this population were almost entirely church-related and evangelical, predominantly Protestant but with a scattering of Catholic institutions as well. For example, Cleveland's most active relief society, the Bethel House, was originally the Western Seamen's Friends Society, a city mission. In 1884, Bethel House became the organizational basis for Cleveland Associated Charities, the most important dispenser of outdoor relief.

Women flocked to the city too, especially during the war when departing soldiers created job opportunities. The *Cleveland Leader* worried about "the difficulties experienced by young women in employment" and suggested optimistically that "selling jewelry, books, shoes, sewing machines, and dry-goods, and bookkeeping" were jobs that women could manage. Police court records, however, indicate that some women found prostitution more remunerative even though officials frequently arrested keepers and residents of "disorderly houses" and even an occasional patron.[8]

Cleveland's middle-class women, made alert to the dangers of city life by their own missionary and relief activities, were particularly concerned about these urban newcomers. Most active was the Cleveland WCA, an adjunct of the Young Men's Christian Association that shared its evangelical zeal but labored particularly for "women in our midst."[9] The WCA (which became the YWCA in 1893) established, first, a home for "self-dependent"[10] young women and, second, in 1869, the Retreat, the city's first refuge for "women who had lost the glory of their womanhood."[11] In 1873, the Cleveland Catholic Diocese, challenged by the vigorous Protestant proselytising of the Retreat, countered with St. Ann's Maternity Home and Infant Asylum, administered by the Sisters of Charity of St. Augustine. The Salvation Army opened its Rescue Home in 1892, as part of its attempt to minister to and convert Cleveland's poor, and the next year the Cleveland homeopathic medical community established the Maternity Home, which shortly afterward became the Maternity Hospital.

It is to the records of these institutions that we must turn first for informaion about Cleveland's fallen women. The records are not perfect sources. Kept separately by each institution, they most often took the form of annual reports published to encourage generous gifts from their readers, hence stressing their most pitiable cases. Often interpretations of the data were clouded by the class- and ethnic-bound perceptions of the middle-class authors, one generation, for example, stressing "intemperance" as the cause of "down-fall," the next emphasizing "feeble-mindedness." Finally, even when the records have survived and the compilers have done careful computations of the number of inmates, the figures do not represent accurately the number of Cleveland women who "fell," only those who "fell" and came to the attention of the refuges and maternity homes. Almost certainly, women at the top and at the very bottom of the socioeconomic scale escaped notice.

These records do provide us with the era's definition of "fallen," a term almost meaningless in today's sexually permissive climate. To Cleveland women reared within Victorian conventions, however, "fallen" referred to women suspected or guilty of sexual delinquency, especially prostitutes. In actual practice, however, the definition often was expanded to include other kinds of deviance from middle-class norms, including poverty, dependence, transience, illness, and out-of-wedlock pregnancy.

The fallen woman whose portrait emerges from these records was seduced and abandoned by men, loosed from familial restraints, and without economic resources. The refuges and maternity homes sought not only to shelter her body but to save her soul. Prostitutes "willing to leave a house of sin" and be reclaimed were the targets of the missionaries of the Retreat and the Salvation Army Rescue, who visited the city's "vilest slums" and "red-light districts."[12] The Retreat claimed to have rescued two prostitutes in 1875.[13] Such missionary work had its antecedents in the Magdalen and Female Moral Reform societies of the antebellum period, which had in fact made few converts in the brothels.[14] Neither did the Retreat or the Salvation Army Rescue.

It was not those who got paid for their sexual favors who needed refuge and shelter, but those who had given them freely, "ruined" by their indiscretions and then deserted. These were women, as eloquently described by the Retreat, who "from want, or sorrow, or deception, had lost the glory of their womanhood . . . somebody's daughter, perchance more sinned against than sinning."[15] Just such a woman, for example, arrived at the Retreat in 1872 with a baby in her arms; shortly afterward, however, she was married to a doctor, presumably the infant's father, probably as the result of some discreet pressure applied to the indiscreet doctor by the Retreat's board of managers.[16] Accumulated experiences with cases like this one, most of which did not end so happily, led the Retreat board to comment angrily about women "imposed upon—O, the crime of it! by married men, deceived by the sophistry of libidinous lovers. . . . Society excuses the sin in men; in the women never."[17] The same sad story is told in the Salvation Army records, as of the woman who was "deceived; told to come to Cleveland to meet her affianced who had preceded her, presumably to rent rooms, when he promised to marry her. She came; the young man heartlessly deserted her . . . [she] was handed over to us."[18]

The promiscuous behavior of these women was viewed as a moral lapse, fall from God's grace. They would be restored to virtue, therefore, by religious conversion. In the Retreat fallen women were to be converted through Bible classes, daily prayers, and the Christian atmosphere and example of the matron and her pious volunteer helpers. The 1879 "Minutes" noted proudly, "It is believed by the Matron that many of the inmates have really become humble Christians and though rejoicing with trembling, they still hope greatly and give fervent thanks."[19]

Sometimes a woman found her redemption in the Salvation Army's open-handed promises of salvation from sin, as did this girl who had been "Betrayed":

Susie came in deep trouble, expecting to become a mother. The father of the child had deserted her—her pocketbook was empty—her relatives had closed their doors to her. She had been brought up a Catholic, but determined the Army people would be her best friends in trouble. . . . One day she came and asked if her baby could be dedicated to God in the Army way as she would like to see him brought up to God's glory and to be of some service in His Kingdom. . . . She herself has proven so faithful, that she numbers among our soldiers.[20]

Even the seducer himself might be saved, as in this case of "Romance, Ruin, and Rescue," in which a woman had been "betrayed by her sweetheart, a blacksmith in her home town. . . . We learned the name of her betrayer and wrote to the officers of the [Army] corps where he lived. The officer visited him and dealt faithfully with him." The betrayer saw the light and married the mother of his child.[21]

Often, especially if they were pregnant out of wedlock, the inmates of the refuges and maternity homes had been deserted by their own families, as was "Betrayed" Susie. The mother Superior of St. Ann's Hospital in 1904 reported that "the majority [of patients] come to us not only to be fed and cared for, but even to be clothed as well. Often, if the family of the unfortunate girl be in a position to provide for her, it, as frequently in a time of trouble and disgrace, abandons her, and thus she becomes an outcast." Some women had even been deserted by their lawful husbands, she continued.[22] The Maternity Hospital also took in "women who have been deserted by worthless husbands in the hour when some protection was needed."[23] Many of the Retreat and the Rescue inmates, however, stayed only briefly because they were temporarily homeless and needed shelter until they could summon the strength and courage to go elsewhere.

Other women had themselves cast aside the restraints of family life in pursuit of sordid and destructive companions and habits. The Retreat, for example, sheltered scores like the 18-year-old runaway who had been "for several months in scenes of sin and vice" before her mother reclaimed her.[24] Young women also were referred to the Retreat by their own parents who could no longer discipline or safeguard their daughters in an unwholesome urban setting that weakened parental control. Alcohol and drugs were a constant temptation. The Salvation Army Rescue proclaimed that "An Opium Fiend has been delivered from the appetite and is now free, having been saved from many vicious habits."[25]

Maternity homes and refuges, therefore, deliberately sought to create a home and family, for they believed that women out of their familial sphere were easily victimized and that domesticity and maternity had redemptive powers.[26] The matron of the home played the maternal role; the inmates were her children, and together they constituted a family. Even after the women's dismissal from the Rescue, " 'Mother' . . . [kept] track of them and [encouraged] them in their new lives."[27] The Retreat managers described "our Home [as] the 'House Beautiful' of which we read in Bunyan's *Pilgrim's Progress,* a haven between the Hill of Difficulty and the Valley of Temptation. When the girls leave the home, they are better armed for life's difficulties than when they came to us, having been taught, advised, and shown the pathway to right living."[28] Founders and administrators of these homes believed, as did many women reformers and activists of their generation, that a woman's maternal instincts could save both herself and others. Hence, although bearing a child out of wedlock was a sin, it could also be the means to salvation. The Retreat's annual report in 1901 described this process:

One member of the Retreat family who from being a year ago rebellious, untruthful, quarrelsome, and altogether unsatisfactory, is today transformed through the gentle influence of a well-ordered home (her first opportunity to know of such and of the mightier power of mother-love) into a wholesome, reliable woman efficient in the family and hopeful for the future.[29]

However hopeful this young woman may have been, the report also noted that she had to "depend entirely upon her bread-winning powers" unfortunately were not great in Cleveland at the turn of the century, where the largest number of employed women were domestic servants, as they were elsewhere.[30] It is not surprising, therefore, that a disproportionate number of inmates of the refuges and maternity homes appear to have been domestic servants, both before and after their stays.

It is not surprising also that these women were poor, as servants did not earn much money or come from families with financial resources.[31] The evidence of their poverty is both direct and indirect. They often were described, as in the letter from the Mother Superior of St. Ann's, as left penniless by their families or husbands. The Salvation Army Rescue, for example, which probably took the largest share of indigent women, painted this pathetic portrait: "the poor girl (only 18 years of age) was living alone, and she was very poorly clad; no warm clothes at all, just her summer clothing, and poor thing! So sick, she was shivering with cold; she has no fire and no coal."[32] However, as this kind of description was routinely included in the institutions' pleas for financial assistance from the public, these claims of poverty should not necessarily be taken at face value.

The indirect evidence of poverty is more persuasive. Although it is possible that middle-class women came to the refuges for shelter and anonymity, these were charitable institutions that, more often than not, could not collect even modest fees from their clientele and experienced financial difficulties with some regularity.[33] Many women came to the homes for free medical care, and the unmarried mothers who bore their children there were also often ill. The sketchy figures on infant mortality are high, suggesting the inadequate prenatal care associated with poverty. In 1882, the Retreat recorded 4 deaths among 54 infants; of 88 children born in the Rescue Home in 1907, 5 died; of the 505 infants at St. Ann's in 1906—a figure that includes foundlings as well as illegitimate children—179 died, an appalling 35 percent.[34] Poverty is also indicated by the women's confinements in the two hospital facilities, St. Ann's and the Maternity Hospital. Until the 1920s most middle-class women had their babies at home; maternity and lying-in hospitals were the province of poor women who had no homes and upon whom fledgling doctors could learn and practice their professional skills in a convenient setting.[35] The vast majority of St. Ann's patients from 1888 to 1900 (201 out of 249) were charity patients.[36] According to its 1892 by-laws, the Maternity Hospital patients were to be "worthy" women, "worthy" of the charity provided by this benevolent institution.[37]

In the view of the homes' administrators, therefore, fallen women should be saved from poverty as well as from sin, and this salvation was to be achieved through training for honest employment so that women would not be tempted into prostitution or other sexual misconduct for money. All the homes taught women cooking, sewing, laundering, and child-care and, if possible, placed them in domestic service after they were released.[38] Although the illogic, or at least the irony, of placing a woman in a job that had contributed to her "fall" in the first place was obvious, domestic service had certain advantages. It was available, acceptable, and sometimes made it possible for a woman to take her child with her. A woman in financial straits prior to giving birth, however, was not likely to improve her situation much by taking up or resuming domestic service with a child to support in addition to herself.

This pattern, established in the 1870s, of poverty and dependence, family disorganization, and sexual victimization and the middle-class benevolent response to it, persisted into the first decades of the twentieth century as Cleveland and other cities experimented with progressive reformism. The perceptions and treatment of fallen women remained almost unchanged, despite the growing secularization and professionalization of benevolence. In 1910, Cleveland was the sixth-largest city in the country, its prospering economy resting on the manufacture of automobiles, finished iron and steel products, and textiles. Its population, swollen almost 50 percent since 1900, was ethnically diverse; only one-fifth of its citizens were native born of native parentage.[39] This growth and diversity placed great strains on the existing charitable organizations, and in 1913 the Cleveland Federation of Charity and Philanthropy, typifying the progressive desire to combine efficiency and humanitarianism, was formed to systematize the fund-raising and planning for the city's myriad charities. The Federation, renamed the Welfare Federation in 1917, responded vigorously to what it perceived as "the challenges of the city": the sharpening "contrasts between sufficiency and want . . . the noise and monotony of city life," the loss of the "spirit of neighborliness," the spread of disease, "the over-stimulating excitement and the intense city amusement."[40]

Of particular concern to the Federation was "shelter for the unfortunate woman," for "next to the child in helplessness is the weak woman," victim of a double standard that condemns her to "shame and sorrow while the man in most cases escapes censure."[41] This anxiety about female sexual delinquency, as common during the progressive period as it was in the late nineteenth century, was reflected in the lists of inmates in the Cleveland House of Correction; female offenses were almost entirely sexual, including "common prostitution," "street soliciting," and keeping or residing in a "house of ill fame."[42] City officials conducted a highly publicized antivice campaign in 1915 and temporarily closed the red-light district, proclaiming that "the policy of persistent repression of prostitution is now in effect."[43]

Women reformers took their own measures, designed less to repress than to prevent sexual delinquency and exploitation. The YWCA's Stillman Witt Boarding Home and the WCTU's Mary Ingersoll Girls' Club, where women could find respectable and inexpensive lodgings, were expanded. The Women's Protective Association was established in 1916 to provide young women with legal protection and temporary shelter in its Sterling House. The Catholic Women's League founded the Catherine Horstman Training Home for girls referred by the Juvenile Court. In 1912, the National Florence Crittenton Mission opened a home for unwed mothers in Cleveland, part of its large chain of maternity homes.

The proliferation of social agencies prompted the Federation to form a Conference on Illegitimacy, which was to coordinate the policies and practices of agencies dealing with illegitimate children and unwed mothers. These included the maternity homes as well as the probate and juvenile courts and the Cleveland Humane Society, a child-placing agency. The Conference was also a fact-finding body, and its records, particularly the several quantitative studies compiled by its members and the city's Bureau of Vital Statistics, provide further information on the city's fallen women.[44] The Conference's interest, however, was limited to women who were pregnant out of wedlock, not simply sexually delinquent. The refuges and maternity homes had already begun to specialize in obstetrical care, only occasionally providing temporary shelter.[45]

Yet case studies discussed by the Conference reveal the familiar stories of seduction and abandonment. The Florence Crittenton Home, for example, reported on a 17-year-old girl with a one-year-old child who had been at the Home for eleven months; the child's father was the girl's brother-in-law; her mother was a drunkard; the girl wished to leave the Home but had nowhere to leave the baby.[46] The Humane Society received a "neatly and modestly dressed" young woman who had left her small town in Virginia because of her "father's intemperance and general abuse of his family." She had worked first as a domestic servant and then as a marker in a laundry. The father of her child had disappeared after giving her a small sum of money, which was exhausted by the costs of her confinement. She came to the Humane Society to give her baby up for adoption.[47]

Conference quantitative studies always reported a great preponderance of pregnant single women. In 1914, for example, 65 of the 72 women whose marital status was known were unmarried. Only 2 of the 100 men named as fathers married the mothers of their children. Thirteen of the women claimed still to care for these men; only 4 women would take legal steps against them.[48] Yet some women were married, but deserted, divorced, or separated; marriage was no guarantee of support or security.[49]

Conference studies also turned up signs of family disintegration, as in this case.

American girl, 19 years old. Employment sought. Later found to be pregnant. Had given birth to an illegitimate child 18 months previous. Child placed out and later died. Her family had been unable to account for her actions for the past 2½ years. . . . Her older sister also had an illegitimate child. This girl was known to sixteen agencies and had been admitted to three maternity homes as well as other institutions where she defied all suggestions.[50]

As in the late nineteenth century, families were not always disorganized or neglectful, but often simply unable to control their daughters, exposed to new customs and companions. The 1914 report showed that most of the women had become pregnant while living with their families or relatives: "A surprisingly large number of the women in difficulty were living at home at the time of their down-fall. This indicates that something is wrong with parents and home conditions," the report hazarded.[51]

Cleveland's fallen women were still poor, and likely to stay that way. Once again, as study after study revealed, these women overwhelmingly reported themselves as domestic servants. The 1914 study reported, for example, that "a surprisingly large number of the women [37 of the 85 who gave an occupation] were engaged in housework, making it by far the most dangerous occupation, morally." Other occupations listed were factory worker, waitress, clerk, dressmaker, and telephone girl. The average salary was $8.88 a week, although a servant's salary would have been less because it included room and board. This average salary actually declined after the women's release from the maternity homes when they were placed again in domestic service jobs.[52] Two years later the Conference claimed to be "astonished" at the number of unwed mothers apparently engaged in housework, 100 of the 175 being so listed. Some shift in job opportunities was apparent, however, as 17 women worked in factories or shops, and the same number in offices or stores.[53]

The sexual partners of these women seem to have been of roughly comparable social and economic status. According to a 1922 study, one of the few to include information on the fathers of illegitimate children, the largest percentage of these men described themselves as "laborers"; the next significant ranking was factory worker and machinist.[54]

Whatever the men's economic standings, they seldom took financial responsibility for their children, despite the best efforts of the Conference and its members. The Florence Crittenton Home particularly had a policy of pursuing the putative father so that he would marry the woman, or at least provide money for the child.[55] Unwed mothers also received legal assistance from the Humane Society, as in this case:

Bohemian girl, 20 years old, Catholic, living at home. Engaged in office work at $20 a week, applied for assistance when four months pregnant, in securing prosecution of the man involved, stating that he was 22 years old, a Slovak, earning between $150 and $200 a month as a crane electrician. . . . The man involved was arrested and brought [to trial] where he acknowledged paternity and stated his willingness to pay $200 settlement. This was refused, and he was bound over to the Grand Jury, where he was given a sentence to pay $6 a week until the child is 16 years old.[56]

Such legal procedures, however, were expensive and time-consuming, and made anonymity for the women impossible. Even after the passage of a more stringent child support law in 1923, the fathers, when they complied, seem to have paid minimal amounts such as $5 a week.[57]

With little or no financial support from the child's father and probably limited education and job skills, the unwed mother with an infant faced an economic situation like this:

On the question of what work girls with illegitimate children are able to find, [the Salvation Army officer] stated a case of her own experience. A most ignorant and inexperienced girl, an orphan who had not hardly any advantage in life, became a mother at 16 years of age. . . . After the usual stay in the Salvation Army Rescue Home, she secured a position with her baby in a private family where she remained until the baby was more than a year old. After that she boarded the baby in the Home. The child is now six years old. The mother is making $6 a week as a domestic and has a bank account. She has always paid for the baby's board at the Home.[58]

The perpetuation of poverty was revealed in the story of the "unmarried mother who did housework part time and part of the time did sewing outside," and of the woman "who worked in a rag shop and boarded the child with one of the Babies'

Dispensary families. She was firm in her devotion to the child, and when she was sick, borrowed money to pay its board.''[59]

The free care provided by the maternity homes did not protect these indigent women from high maternal and infant mortality rates. The 1914 study, for example, noted that 17 of the 97 illegitimate children in the sample died, a higher mortality figure than the city's 1916 infant mortality rate of 105.4 per 1000 births.[60] In 1921 a Cleveland doctor warned that stillbirths among illegitimate children were double those of legitimate births. Maternal deaths were also much higher; reported illegitimate births were 2 percent of total births, but 4.4 percent of maternal deaths were of unwed mothers. The doctor attributed the infant mortality to the diet of condensed or cows' milk distributed free at dispensaries, and maternal mortality to inadequate pre- and postnatal care. Unwed mothers also had a higher death rate from abortion, which, because illegal, was likely to be either self-induced or administered by ill-equipped amateurs.[61]

These maternity facilities, however, offered more than medical care; all viewed themselves still—perhaps primarily—as reformatory institutions where, as in the nineteenth century, fallen women could be reclaimed to virtue. As the unwed mothers were in large part the same kinds of women they had always been, the homes and hospitals employed almost the same kind of reformatory tactics. The institutions, with the exception of the Maternity Hospital, all had strong denominational links, and in all "the religious element [was] strong."[62]

All still instructed women in cooking, sewing, and other domestic skills and placed them in domestic service jobs when possible. All stressed the desirability of a home-like atmosphere and, at the urging of the Conference, made a six-month confinement period mandatory, during which time the mother's maternal instincts could be fully developed. Every effort was made to keep mother and child together, even after release from the institution and even if this meant continued subsidy by the home or a child-caring agency such as the Humane Society. Social workers warned Conference members of the dire consequences of separating mother and child:

Eleven years ago Bertha was made to give up her illegitimate baby. This was insisted upon by her parents who had what they thought was her interest at heart. . . . A year or so later Bertha married the father of her baby. In a couple of years another baby came to them, but only to live a short time. Last year Bertha wrote a letter to the Humane Society to learn what had become of her first baby and to ask if she might have him for her own. Never since he was torn from her arms, had she been able to go to bed at night without thinking of him. The baby cannot be found. It is quite probable that Bertha will become a nervous wreck, if the aching void that she has carried all these years is not filled.[63]

In two respects these women differed from those of the late nineteenth century: their age and their ethnicity. Case studies described very young girls: a 13-year-old impregnated by a 24-year-old man, for example, or a 14-year-old "colored girl" with an 18-month-old infant.[64] More methodical studies, however, indicate that the average age was about 20, with a maximum age of 34 and a minimum age of 13 in 1914; the median age in 1916 was between 17 and 22.[65] By the 1920s the ages began to drop slightly, a trend that continued. In 1922 more than 25 percent of the women were of school age.[66]

The 1914 study also reported that more than half of the women studied (51 of the 98) were foreign-born, reflecting the city's heterogeneous population.[67] The 1922 report, on the other hand, found a large majority of native-born mothers, but 75 of these 311 were black.[68] By 1923 black unwed mothers accounted for slightly more than 22 percent of all registered illegitimate births, although blacks constituted only 4.3 percent of the city's total population in 1920.[69] These rising figures resulted in the Salvation Army's opening of the Mary B. Talbert Home for black women, who were not routinely admitted to any of the maternity homes except St. Ann's.

This changed ethnic and racial background of unwed mothers was reflected in a rather oblique way by the fascination of the Conference and the social work profession as a whole with "feeble-mindedness" as an explanation for pregnanc_ out of wedlock or any kind of sexual deviancy.[70] Because the backgrounds of these immigrant and black mothers were obviously so different from their own, it was easy for middle-class social workers to regard them as mentally deficient, equating that with sexual nonconformity. Maternity homes were urged to administer IQ tests to their inmates, and a Conference Committee on Feeble-Mindedness reported that "Rescue homes for unwed mothers generally show a larger proportion of feeble-mindedness than the population at large." And, the committee warned, feeble-minded unwed mothers produced feeble-minded illegitimate children.[71] The Conference's insistence on the use of professional social workers suggests the growing conviction that the pious middle-class volunteer of the late nineteenth century no longer had enough in common with fallen women to be effective.

In 1928 Mabel Mattingly, a graduate of the School of Applied Social Sciences of Western Reserve University, published a master's thesis illustrating many of these trends that had developed in the 1920s. The thesis concentrated on 53 mothers who had been able to keep their children, so these women apparently had more resources than most. Yet their story is pathetic and familiar. Their median age was 20, about the same as unwed mothers generally. They were not prostitutes, or even promiscuous; in 95 percent of the cases, pregnancy had occurred only after long-term sexual intimacy.[72] Yet 48 of the 53 women were single, left to cope alone with their pregnancies and infants by men who often were already married.

Most of these unwed mothers had contemplated or unsuccessfully attempted the desperate step of an illegal abortion.[73] Almost half were living with family or relatives, but this had not prevented them from attending public dances and unsavory places of recreation. Half of this group were domestic servants, although only 11.8 percent of employed women in Cleveland were engaged as domestics at this time.[74] Those who had been confined in maternity homes had been trained in domestic service, and some remembered with displeasure the smells of the laundry or caring for numerous babies.[75] Mattingly also noted that in 1926, 28 percent of the recorded illegitimate births were to black women.[76]

The Great Depression did not significantly alter the pattern of characteristics that

Mattingly described, but the zeal for the reclamation of these fallen women began to diminish by the mid-1930s. Like other heavy industry towns, Cleveland felt the slump early and long. Neither private nor public efforts to relieve the city's unemployed and impoverished succeeded. City- and county-sponsored public works programs employed only a fraction of those men out of work and no women. The distribution of surplus foods by private agencies could not begin to feed the hungry. The city itself had not appropriated or distributed funds for direct relief since 1922, leaving this task to Associated Charities and the Jewish Social Service Bureau, whose case workers were swamped, even with the help of scores of volunteers.[77] After 1931 the Welfare Federation's annual fund drives fell far short of their goals—by $500,000 in 1932 and $600,000 in 1933[78]—leaving its participating agencies, especially Associated Charities, to plunge deeper and deeper into debt.[79] Not until 1933 did a public agency, the Cuyahoga County Relief Agency, mandated by the Federal Emergency Relief Act, take over from the private agencies the responsibility for direct relief. By then, 31 percent of Cleveland's work force was jobless.[80]

The Associated Charities had provided jobs for a few women in its Sewing Center, and the federal Civil Works Administration set up the first public works program for women, sewing and distributing garments to families on relief and working in public offices and libraries.[81] Nevertheless, the number of women receiving Mother's Pensions more than doubled between 1928 and 1934, and by 1938 42 percent of all families on relief were headed by women.[82]

Agencies and institutions that served women suffered also. The Women's Protective Association's Sterling House closed for lack of funds. Once wealthy residences like the YWCA's Stillman Witt and the WCTU's Mary G. Ingersoll Club ran deficits, as did the Humane Society and the Catherine Horstman Home.[83] All of the maternity homes, except for Mary B. Talbert, had declining numbers of inmates,[84] and all operated in the red after 1929. By the mid-1930s both the Retreat and the Florence Crittenton Home teetered on the brink of bankruptcy.[85] In response, the Conference on Illegitimacy took a long, hard look at the role of maternity homes in the community and at the kinds of women who used them.

The unwed mothers who came to the Conference's attention during the 1930s were still likely to undergo childbirth without support from the fathers of their children. Women tended to arrive by themselves at the maternity facilities, often in the last stages of labor and in need of emergency care. Few of the fathers seemed interested in visiting the women, although the maternity homes did not encourage such visits unless the man promised to marry the woman or at least acknowledge paternity.[86] By the mid-1930s social workers seldom even pursued or prosecuted the putative fathers either because forced marriages were no longer viewed with favor or because the expense involved was prohibitive, especially when hard times made it less likely that the father would pay anyway.[87]

A 1930 study of cases handled by two child-placing agencies and the Associated Charities indicated that only 15 of the 87 women married after bearing their children, and only 9 of these took their children with them. Three of the fathers received custody, but in one instance the mother had been committed to an institution for the feeble-minded. In only two other cases was financial support secured from the fathers. The vast majority of these women either shouldered the burden of child-care alone, or with some help from their families, or placed their infants up for adoption, a trend that accelerated during the 1930s and was a reversal of the earlier policy of keeping the woman and child together.[88]

Although these unwed mothers could sometimes count on help from their families after their babies were born, families seemed increasingly unwilling or unable to provide support prior to the birth. According to this same study, women pregnant out of wedlock were referred to the child-placing agencies seldom by relatives and most often by maternity facilities such as St. Ann's, the obstetrical dispensaries, or general hospitals, by the Women's Police Bureau and Juvenile Court, or by relief agencies such as Associated Charities or Catholic Charities.[89]

As indicated by the frequent referral from relief agencies, unwed mothers, as before, were poor, their always precarious economic plight worsened by the Depression. A massive report compiled by the Conference in 1936 underscored this poverty. Of those women who were employed in 1935, more than half were domestic servants. Although only 19 listed themselves as unemployed, 80 of the 482 were on relief.[90] Less than half of the city's unwed mothers bore their children in maternity homes; the Cuyahoga County Relief Agency would not pay the costs of confinement there. The proportion of these women who had their children at home or in the charity wards of Cleveland City Hospital increased.[91]

In 1935 almost 30 percent of unwed mothers whose births were registered were black, although blacks constituted only 8 percent of the city's population in 1930.[92] More than 10 percent of all black registered births were illegitimate, as compared with 2.3 percent of white registered births.[93] These blacks were the poorest of the women, and the youngest. The median age for white women was 21, and for black women, 17.[94] Twenty percent of the black women were unemployed; of the 22 who had jobs, 21 were domestics. Almost half of the women on the relief rolls were black, as were more than half of the women whose children were born in Cleveland City Hospital.[95]

The 1936 study had been prompted in large part by the Conference's desire to discover why fewer women entered maternity homes. An obvious explanation was the declining birthrate; regular maternity hospitals also had empty beds.[96] As early as the 1930s, however, there had been criticism of the "strictness and closeness with which a girl is held both during confinement and after."[97] Conference members were even more critical of the policies that the homes felt necessary to achieve their traditional goal of reformation. Homes still kept the women in a cloistered setting, preventing most outside excursions, limited vocational training to domestic work, and insisted whenever possible on the long, expensive confinement.[98] Over the expressed objections of the maternity homes' representatives, the Conference suggested that more flexible and less costly programs, such as the placement of unwed mothers in foster homes, might be preferable to institutional care.[99]

As in the 1910s when the Conference began to stress the professionalization of services and mental testing of unwed mothers, the Conference's shift in policy— the waning enthusiasm for the homes—was a response to changed circumstances and changed perceptions of clientele. The Welfare Federation and the Conference may well have felt that in the face of the economic disaster of the 1930s there were more pressing needs than the reformation of women pregnant out of wedlock, especially as many were black, and especially as the maternity homes did not seem in fact to be reforming or reclaiming their inmates. Although the homes always liked to boast of their successes, they had always recorded occasional failures too. The Retreat board, for example, sadly noted in 1872: "Some [women] have returned to their former lives of sin, tis true, and that is the experience of every such institution [as ours]."[100] And in 1915 the Florence Crittenton Home puzzled "as to what to do with a young woman with a second illegitimate baby who shows no disposition to work or even to be of any service in the household . . . and is back with her original bad companions and seems altogether indifferent."[101] Women who bore a second,—or even a third, illegitimate child after lengthly stays in maternity homes obviously weakened their claims to effect a moral transformation. One of the few case studies from the 1930s, for example, helps to explain the growing reluctance of social workers to refer women to the homes:

This woman of good American stock, a woman of 25 years of age now, is of normal intelligence and healthy. Under proper influences her behavior is socially acceptable. She has been pregnant five times, had two miscarriages, and placed her three children up for adoption. All confinements had been in Cleveland maternity homes. The social agencies had known her . . . [S]he had married the father of her first child, but he had not provided a home, and he was not the father of the other two children. The father of one child was colored, and the father of the other Jewish. While one social agency was attempting to follow her up on two separate cases reported, she was being confined in a maternity home for the second time under a different name. The case work agency never did catch up with her. At Probate Court two separate cases on her children were being investigated when it was discovered she was one and the same mother going by different names.[102]

In 1936 the city's first maternity home, the Retreat, closed its doors; its pleas to the Conference for continued support had been unavailing.[103] The surviving maternity homes sheltered a smaller and smaller proportion of the city's unwed mothers in the decades to come.[104] The Conference of Illegitimacy itself died in 1936. Some of its work was carried on by a committee of the Children's Council of the Welfare Federation, but the Conference's detailed descriptions of fallen women were not duplicated. Later studies of illegitimacy in Cleveland and elsewhere have focused almost exclusively on the race and age of unwed mothers.[105] This narrowed focus had its origins in the 1920s and 1930s, when unwed mothers became increasingly young and increasingly black. The fallen woman who now haunts the American imagination is the black, teen-aged mother of several illegitimate children, all on ADC; she is no longer viewed as a soul reclaimable by pious matrons, but as a sexually promiscuous burden on the taxpayer.

Between the opening and closing of the Retreat, Cleveland experienced dramatic changes. The city's economy shifted from commerce to heavy industry. Its native-born white population gave way to an ethnically and racially diverse citizenry as the city became a giant metropolis. The responsibility for Cleveland's dependent people became less a private and more a public responsibility. Trained professionals took the place of the benevolent ladies who had earlier distributed material relief and spiritual salvation. Yet although her setting may have been very different, Cleveland's fallen woman in the midst of the Great Depression remained much as she had been at the conclusion of the Civil War: too often abandoned, too easily exploited, too often dependent on the charity of those from whose grace she had fallen.

Notes

1. The title is adapted from Wendy Martin, "Seduced and Abandoned in the New World: The Fallen Woman in American Fiction," in Wendy Martin, ed., *The American Sisterhood: Writings of the Feminist Movement from Colonial Times to the Present* (New York, 1972), 257–272.

2. Young Women's Christian Association, Cleveland, Newspaper clipping, 1869, in scrapbook, Container 11, MS 3516, Western Reserve Historical Society. Hereafter this collection will be referred to as YWCA, Cleveland, although the group is called the Woman's Christian Association until 1893.

3. Egal Feldman, "Prostitution, the Alien Woman, and the Progressive Imagination," *American Quarterly* (Summer 1967), 194.

4. Ruth Rosen, *The Lost Sisterhood: Prostitution in America, 1900–1918* (Baltimore, 1982), xiii, 40–46; Mark Thomas Connelly, *The Response to Prostitution in the Progressive Era* (Chapel Hill, NC, 1980), 29–34.

5. On antebellum moral reform, see Barbara Berg, *The Remembered Gate: Origins of American Feminism: The Woman and the City, 1800–1860* (New York, 1978); Carroll Smith-Rosenberg, *Religion and the Rise of the American City: The New York City Mission Movement, 1812–1870* (Ithaca, NY, 1971); Flora L. Northrup, *The Record of a Century, 1834–1934* (New York, 1934); Kathleen D. McCarthy, *Noblesse Oblige: Charity and Cultural Philanthropy in Chicago, 1849–1929* (Chicago, 1982); and on later antiprostitution efforts, David Pivar, *The Purity Crusade, Sexual Morality, and Social Control* (Westport, CT, 1973); Rosen, *The Lost Sisterhood;* Connelly, *The Response to Prostitution.* The Salvation Army refuges are described in Herbert A. Wisbey, Jr., *Soldiers Without Swords: A History of the Salvation Army in the United States* (New York, 1955) and Edward H. McKinley, *Marching to Glory: The History of the Salvation Army in the United States* (New York, 1980); and those of the National Florence Crittenton Mission in Katherine G. Aiken, "The National Florence Crittenton Mission, 1883–1925: A Case Study in Progressive Reform" (Ph.D. dissertation, Washington State University, 1980) and Otto Wilson, *Fifty Years Work with Girls, 1883–1933* (Alexandria, VA, 1933). The Inter-City Conference on Illegitimacy is described briefly in Fred S. Hall, ed., *Social Work Year Book, 1935* (New York, 1935), 596, and often is referred to in the minutes of the Cleveland Conference on Illegitimacy in the collection of the Federation for Community Planning, Cleveland, Ohio, MS 3788, Western Reserve Historical Society.

6. Barbara Brenzel, *Daughters of the State: A Social Portait of the First Reform School for Girls in North America, 1865–1905* (Cambridge, 1983), 107–135; Steven Ruggles, "Fallen Women: The Inmates of the Magdalen Asylum of Philadelphia, 1836–1908," *Journal of Social History* (Summer 1983), 65–82; Percy Gamble Kammerer, *The Unmarried Mother: A Study of Five Hundred Cases* (Boston, 1918).

7. Edmund H. Chapman, *Cleveland: Village to Metropolis: A Case Study of Problems of Urban Development in Nineteenth-Century America* (Cleveland, 1964), 97–150; William Ganson Rose, *Cleveland: The Making of a City* (Cleveland, 1950), 361.

8. Works Progress Administration of Ohio, *Annals of Cleveland, 1818–1935,* vol. 52 (1869) (Cleveland, 1937), 614; vol. 48 (1865), 60, 68, 83.

9. Quoted in Milred Esgar, "Women Involved in the Real World: A History of the Young Women's Christian Association of Cleveland, Ohio" (unpublished typescript, Western Reserve Historical Society), vol. 1, 41.

10. Esgar, "Women," vol., 1, 42.

11. Ibid., p. 41.

12. *The Earnest Worker,* June 1874, 5; *Cleveland Plain Dealer,* clipping, no date, but probably 1893, unpaged.

13. *Earnest Worker,* Novemer 1875, 2.

14. See Berg, *The Remembered Gate,* 177–193; Smith-Rosenberg, *Religion,* 98–113.

15. YWCA, Cleveland, *Annual Report,* 1870, 15, Container 8, Folder 1.

16. Ibid., 1872, 3, Container 8, Folder 2.

17. Ibid., "After Thirty Years" (1899), Container 10, Folder 9.

18. Salvation Army Rescue Home, Cleveland, Ohio, *Annual Report, 1893* (Cleveland, 1893), 7.

19. YWCA, Cleveland, Minutes, March 4, 1879, Container 1.

20. Salvation Army, *Diamonds in the Rough: Annual Report, Salvation Army Rescue Work in Cleveland* (Cleveland, 1905), 6.

21. Salvation Army, *Links of Love: Annual Report, Salvation Army Rescue Work in Cleveland* (Cleveland, 1904), 10.

22. Letter from Sister M. Peter, Superior of St. Ann's to Rev. Ignatius F. Horstman, August 27, 1904, Archives of the Cleveland Catholic Diocese, Cleveland.

23. Maternity Hospital, *Annual Report* (Cleveland, 1909), 17.

24. YWCA, Cleveland, *Annual Report,* 1872, 3, Container 8, Folder 2.

25. Salvation Army Rescue Home, Cleveland, Ohio *Annual Report,* 1893.

26. For another example of this technique, see Barbara Brenzel, "Domestications as Reform: The Socialization of Wayward Girls," *Harvard Educational Review* 50 (Spring 1980).

27. Salvation Army Rescue Home, *Annual Report,* 1893, 4.

28. YWCA, Cleveland, *Annual Report,* 1909, 22, Container 9, Folder 7.

29. Ibid., 1901, 17, Container 12.

30. David M. Katzman, *Seven Days a Week: Women and Domestic Service in Industrializing America* (Urbana, IL, 1981), 44; Rose, *Cleveland,* 608.

31. Katzman, *Seven Days,* 310, gives salary figures for cities comparable to Cleveland.

32. Salvation Army Rescue Home, *Annual Report,* 1893, 5.

33. For example, YWCA, Cleveland, "Minutes," January 3, 1888, Container 1; Florence Crittenton Home, MS 3910, Western Reserve Historical Society, Board of Trustees Minutes, December 15, 1913, Container 1, Folder 11.

34. YWCA, Cleveland, "Minutes," November 7, 1882, Container 1; Salvation Army, *Annual Report of the Salvation Army Home in Cleveland* (Cleveland, 1907), 19; Report of St. Ann's Infant Asylum and Maternity Hospital in Cleveland, Ohio, n.p., Archives of the Cleveland Catholic Diocese.

35. Richard W. Wertz and Dorothy C. Wertz, *Lying-In: A History of Childbirth in America* (New York, 1977), 132–177.

36. St. Ann's Maternity Hospital and Infant Asylum, Report, n.d., n.p., Archives of the Cleveland Catholic Diocese.

37. Maternity Home, Cleveland, Ohio, Constitution and By-Laws, 1892, 1.

38. The regimen in maternity homes resembled that in women's prisons described by Estelle B. Freedman, *Their Sisters' Keepers: Women's Prison Reform in America 1830–1930* (Ann Arbor, 1981), 89–96.

39. Cleveland Federation of Charity and Philanthropy, *The Social Year Book: The Human Problems and Resources of Cleveland* (Cleveland, 1913), 8.

40. Ibid., p. 9.

41. Ibid., p. 34.

42. *Annual Report of the Department of Public Safety, Division of Charities and Corrections and Cemeteries of the City of Cleveland* (Cleveland, 1910), 84–85.

43. Federated Churches of Cleveland, Ohio, *Vice Conditions in Cleveland* (Cleveland, 1916), 2.

44. City of Cleveland, Ohio, Division of Public Health, *Annual Report* (Cleveland, 1925), 118, reported that "birth registration has been a favorite subject for annual lamentations by health officials" at least since 1891; the undercount was estimated as low as 75 percent for some years, but by the late 1920s figures were thought to be about 98 percent accurate. However, if anyone got omitted, women

who bore illegitimate children did. As Daniel Scott Smith has commented, "The most easily counted events in American history tend to be those belonging to people who 'counted' at the time; these are not the people most likely to conceive children out of wedlock," in "The Long Cycle in American Illegitimacy and Prenuptial Bastardy," in Peter Laslett et al., eds., *Bastardy and Its Comparative History* (Cambridge, MA, 1980), 364. A contemporary study of unwed mothers in Boston whose conclusions resemble those of the Conference on Illegitimacy in many ways is Kammerer, *The Unmarried Mother: A Study of Five Hundred Cases* (Boston, 1918); Kammerer points out that "the illegitimacy rate is barely ever accurate, particularly in the United States. A certain group of the population, furthermore, is possessed of sufficient means to enable them to secure abortions which again prevent the registration of their illicit sex intercourse from the pages of birth registration" (p. 2). These records gathered by the Cleveland Conference, therefore, are incomplete, as are the records from the separate institutions, but both sets of records are the best available.

45. This specialization is reflected in the rising proportion of children to women recorded by the Retreat: YWCA, Cleveland, *Annual Report,* 1872, Container 8, Folder 2; *Annual Report,* 1891, 20, Container 8, Folder 4; *Annual Report,* 1912, 39, Container 9, Folder 10. The Salvation Army facility, like others nationally, became known as a "maternity hospital" rather than a rescue in the first decade of this century, as noted in Robert Sandall, *The History of the Salvation Army* (London, 1947), vol. 111, 1883–1953, 199.

46. Federation for Community Planning, Cleveland, Ohio, MS 3788, Western Reserve Historical Society, Conference on Illegitimacy, October 6, 1913, Container 21, Folder 516. Hereafter this collection will be referred to as FCP.

47. *Proceedings of the National Conference of Social Work, 1917* (Chicago, 1917), 285–286.

48. FCP, Conference on Illegitimacy, May 25, 1914, Container 21, Folder 516.

49. Ibid., May 9, 1921, Container 30, Folder 739.

50. Ibid., December 5, 1921, Container 30, Folder 739.

51. Ibid., May 25, 1914, Container 21, Folder 516.

52. Ibid.

53. Ibid., "The Unmarried Mother and Her Child," Container 30, Folder 738.

54. Ibid., "A Study of the Registration of Illegitimate Births for the Year 1922," Container 30, Folder 739.

55. Ibid., January 27, 1916, Container 21, Folder 516.

56. Ibid., December 5, 1921, Container 30, Folder 739.

57. Ibid., February 16, 1925, Container 30, Folder 739.

58. Ibid., April 6, 1914, Container 30, Folder 738.

59. Ibid.

60. Ibid., May 25, 1914, Container 21, Folder 516; City of Cleveland, Ohio, Division of Public Health, *Annual Report,* 26.

61. FCP, Conference on Illegitimacy, "The Illegitimacy Problem from the Medical Standpoint," Container 30, Folder 739.

62. Cleveland Federation of Charity and Philanthropy, *A Social Year Book,* 35.

63. Ibid., "The Unwed Mother as Deserted Wife," Container 30, Folder 738.

64. Ibid., December 8, 1913; May 3, 1915, Container 21, Folder 516.

65. Ibid., May 25, 1914, Container 21, Folder 516; "The Unwed Mother," Container 30, Folder 738.

66. Ibid., "A Study of the Registration of Illegitimate Births," Container 30, Folder 739.

67. Ibid., May 25, 1914, Container 21, Folder 516.

68. Ibid., "A Study of the Registration of Illegitimate Births," Container 30, Folder 739.

69. Ibid., June 21, 1924; Howard Whipple Greene, *Population Characteristics by Census Tracts, Cleveland, Ohio* (Cleveland, 1931), 9.

70. Rosen, *The Lost Sisterhood,* 21–23, discusses the progressive use of IQ tests on prostitutes and the not surprising results that showed these women too as "feeble-minded."

71. FCP, Conference on Illegitimacy, "The Menace of the Feeble-Minded," Container 30, Folder 738.

72. Mabel H. Mattingly, *The Unmarried Mother and Her Child: A Fact-Finding Study of Fifty-Three Cases of Unmarried Mothers Who Kept Their Children* (Cleveland, 1928), 15 and 26.

73. Ibid., p. 26.

74. Ibid., p. 19; Katzman, *Seven Days,* 287.

75. Mattingly, *The Unmarried Mother,* 25.

76. Ibid., p. 7.

77. On Cleveland in the early years of the Depression, see Bing, *Social Work,* 14–26; and Florence T. Waite, *A Warm Friend for the Spirit: A History of the Family Service Association of Cleveland and Its Forebearers, 1830–1952* (Cleveland, 1960), 235–295.

78. FCP, Container 9, F. 178, disclose shortfalls until 1942.

79. Waite, *Warm Friend,* 239.

80. Rose, *Cleveland,* 912.

81. Waite, *Warm Friend,* 257–258; Bing, *Social Work,* 23.

82. Howard Whipple Greene, *Nine Years of Relief, Greater Cleveland, 1928–1937* (Cleveland, 1937), 2; Bing, *Social Work,* 23.

83. FCP, Container 8, Folders 187 and 188, records the deficits of many of the Federation's participating agencies.

84. FCP, Conference on Illegitimacy, November 30, 1936, Container 33, Folder 829. This is a lengthy joint report done by the Conference and a committee of the Federation's Children Council, which shortly thereafter took over the Conference's work.

85. FCP, Container 8, Folders 187 and 188.

86. FCP, Conference on Illegitimacy, January 23, 1943, Microfilm Reel 33.

87. Ibid., May 14, 1934.

88. Ibid., "The Unmarried Family," Container 30, Folder 741.

89. Ibid.

90. Ibid., November 30, 1936, Container 33, Folder 829.

91. Ibid.

92. Ibid.; Greene, *Population Characteristics,* 9.

93. FCP, Conference on Illegitimacy, November 30, 1936, Container 33, Folder 829.

94. Ibid.

95. Ibid.

96. Ibid., October 1, 1936, Container 33, Folder 829.

97. Ibid., "Resume of the Activities of the Cleveland Conference on Illegitimacy, 1930–1931," Microfilm Reel 33.

98. Ibid., May 14, 1934, Microfilm Reel 33.

99. Ibid., Committee on Unmarried Mothers, May 2, 1935, October 21, 1935 and February 5, 1936, Container 33, Folder 829.

100. YWCA, Cleveland, *Annual Report,* 1872, 3, Container 8, Folder 2.

101. FCP, Conference on Illegitimacy, April 19, 1915, Container 30, Folder 738.

102. Ibid., June 3, 1933, Microfilm Reel 33.

103. Ibid., Committee on Unwed Mothers, February 5, 1936, Container 33, Folder 829.

104. FCP, Committee on Unmarried Mothers, "A Study of the Needs of Unmarried Mothers," 1948, Container 33, Folder 829; *Out of Wedlock: Births in the Greater Cleveland Community: Report of the Unmarried Parents Planning Committee of the Welfare Federation, 1971* (Cleveland, 1971), 13.

105. As examples, see ibid,; Smith, "The Long Cycle"; United States Department of Health, Education, and Welfare, *Trends in Illegitimacy in the United States, 1940–1963* (Washington, D.C., 1963).

THE MODERNIZATION OF SEX: AMERICA IN THE TWENTIETH CENTURY

12

Introduction

The social organization of sexuality changed in twentieth-century America from what it had been previously. That change was not abrupt. It was gradual, despite loose usage in the past few decades of the label "Sexual Revolution." Favored candidates for that "revolution" have been several: the first decade of the century, the 1920s, the period of World War II, and belatedly the 1960s. That "revolution" has been defined narrowly as substantial and sustained increase in nonmarital coitus and more broadly as a substantial increase in positive evaluation of sexual expression as an essential part of the human condition. For purposes here, the definition is important; precise dating is unimportant. Two observations, however, might be warranted. One is that change was fickle. It affected different societal groups, locations, and demographic communities in varying degree and not necessarily at the same time. The second is that social changes tend to become "revolutions" only when they have consequence for the middle class and that population is aware of it. At any rate, clearly the more liberal sexual order of the 1970s was very different from what it had been when the century opened.

Social forces responsible for that change are not altogether apparent; but some are. For one thing, the Victorian physiological notion that the body was at any given time a closed energy system passed, along with the corollary imperative that required that semen loss be limited to procreative necessity. For another, the early years of the century witnessed the open recognition *again* of female sexual desire. Not only was it acknowledged, if not altogether applauded, but women were not necessarily understood as passive in initiation of such activity. A third was challenge to the traditional belief in moral absolutes by advances in the physical sciences. Especially significant was the appearance of "sexologists" such as Alfred Kinsey and others. They informed Americans that their actual sexual behavior often contradicted theoretically established norms of conduct. Changes in scientific conclusions were all the more important because the recognized societal base of authority was becoming that of science as opposed to earlier reliance on the "sacred" or religious grounds. Finally, there was the increasing development of effective birth-control methods, which severed the previous connection between sexual intercourse and procreation.

The latter observation points up a matter of some importance—namely that whatever the reality or value of the designation "sexual revolution," its direction of change was essentially heterosexual. Liberal accommodation in American society of other forms of previously stigmatized behavior, while a corollary, indeed probably an inevitable one of heterosexual transitions, cannot be simply understood as a "spin off." In part they were, of course. Social forces at work here are even less clear than those involved in male-female sexual liberality. What seems clear is that a significant amount of strongly stigmatized deviance became less so and became incorporated into "conventional" deviance. Some aspects of the latter passed out of that category altogether, e.g., masturbation. Obviously certain matters noted above also had consequence here. The sexual implication in scientific change that there was no "right" behavior was important, as were more specific events such as social disruption of traditional beliefs, which accompanied World War I and II.

Part III of this volume is addressed, with one exception, to the major issues discussed in previous periodization: prostitution, sexual assault, and same-sex relations—male or female. The first, prostitution, like other forms of deviance is socially constructed stigmatized behavior. Neil Shumsky's chapter, presented earlier in this volume, pointed to a public predisposition in the later nineteenth century toward "tacit acceptance" of it, especially in the form of so-called red-light districts in urban centers. By the early years of the next century, a counter attack to this predilection was mounting. Progressive reformers seized upon prostitution as social scourge to be eradicated as quickly as possible. Never before in American history had guardians of American moral well-being given such zealous attention to commercial vice as they did in the years immediate to United States entry into World War I. The new assault surfaced first in the form of panic over "white slavery." In typical Progressive fashion, the primary instrument of reform was government pressed into service at all levels. The Antebellum weapons of moral suasion and exhortation against sin were cast aside in favor of legislative actions and enforcement by law authorities. In the course of this new movement, the efforts of old purity forces and those of social hygiene reformers became joined. Yet another characteristic of the period was that, as one expression of not uncommon contradictory impulses within Progressivism, this new purity crusade took on a nativism dimension. "Foreigners" became scapegoats for the nation's sexual anxieties. Early illustrations were federal laws in 1903 and 1907. The former sought to punish those who imported women for purposes of prostitution. The latter allowed for deportation of aliens convicted of prostitution. State and local efforts were much more vigorous.

Egal Feldman provides insightful consideration of the issue of the "alien woman" in the Progressive imagination with the first chapter of this section. The plight of this figure was a consequence of three assumptions by Progressives: One was the simple conviction that man and society's behavior could be controlled and regulated effectively. A second seemed to be that prostitution was an urban problem whose precise character depended upon city size. The final assumption was that behind the scenes of urban vice lay the nation's newcomers. A favorite target was southern Italians and Russian Jews, but was not limited to them. Actually there were two antiprostitution campaigns in this regard. One was nativistic with all the ugly xenophobic regalia that it implied. The other was humanitarian, carrying on a heritage from the social gospel movement, the social settlement movement, and other social engineering inclinations within Progressive reform. The latter campaign was shocked by the apparent assumptions of the former, that "immigrant girls" should merely be sent back to their parents diseased and disgraced. Surely America could do better. Government should extend protection to such new arrivals and remove the conditions responsible for their "fall." Alien women should be met at the dock and nurtured carefully thereafter. Significantly, this brand of Progressivism became a particular cause for women. In such fashion was the native-born female placed above the animal passions of American males, and reminded perhaps of the boundaries of respectability. Their commitment was a warning to the bestial male that sexual exploitation of women, all women, was not to be tolerated. When city streets could be made safe and secure for defenseless immigrant girls, all women, indeed men as well, could feel comfortable and safe in the city.

General conservative politics aside, the era of Ronald Reagan ushered in a period of direct popular assault on homosexuals and lesbians as categories of Americans. The spearhead of the increased oppression was, and is, a well-organized, well-financed movement known as the New Right, a coalition of conservative political voices with those of Christian fundamentalism. While the road has never been an easy one for these forms of alternative sexuality, this most recent episode of enhanced homophobia is the third in this century. The first came in the 1920s as one dimension of a reaction against feminism and the perceived distressed state of the traditional family. Efforts to rescue heterosexual marriage, making it more attractive by liberalizing its nature, carried with it a malignant offshoot, which in conjunction with a backlash against feminism, created the first mass-based sustained assault on lesbianism in particular and homosexuality in general. A second homophobic outbreak surfaced circa the 1950s. Not unlike the episode noted above, it was rooted partially in gender organization, which had been badly disrupted by world war. More immediately, the new homophobic zeal surfaced as part of the anticommunist hysteria that characterized McCarthyism. The threat to the American way by lesbians and gays remained a stock theme in the nation's political culture and partisan rhetoric through most of the decade.

One constant issue that helped to organize the political/social strategy among lesbians and homosexuals as well as the larger heterosexual society was that of causation in sexual orientation. Lillian Faderman has taken note of this issue earlier in the volume. So-called Essentialist theory, originating in the late nineteenth century, argues that sexual preference has a congenital or psychological base and therefore is not significantly influenced by time in history or cultural environment. Another position is that of social constructionism, which views sexuality as created by human actors in culturally and historically conditioned ways. In their chapter included in this section, Elizabeth Kennedy and Madeline Davis are immediately concerned with the development of lesbianism in Buffalo, New York. Their primary interest and point of entry into the issue of causation are butch-fem roles. Perspective is that of social constructionism. It is therefore in accord with the overall philosophy of the present volume. Kennedy and Davis use as a case study working-class lesbians in Buffalo circa 1930–1965 with major emphasis on the forties and fifties. The authors seek to document in the period the political and social evolution of this community both in terms of internal dynamics and responses to the changing nature of oppression from outside it. In that city butch-fem roles structured lesbian resistance to intolerance by the larger society as well as relations between one another inside the community. In the case of the former, butch women with their distinctive dress and mannerisms and also butch-fem couples were an overt political statement of lesbian presence in the city. Their aggressive style was a forerunner of and influence on the type of militant consciousness that would later characterize the Gay Liberation Movement. Kennedy and Davis examine the consequence of historical setting and social environment in community development of butch-fem roles. They make clear that lesbian actors came to these roles from a variety of social circumstance. They point out further that within the community there was never in fact a hegemonic view on what properly constituted a definition of true lesbianism. Conclusion from the Buffalo study is that time and cultural milieu far outweighed issues of congenital or psychological causation for understanding butch-fem roles among lesbians of that city.

The meaning of sexual assault and indeed women's sexuality have changed substantially across the national past. Its most dramatic change began to occur in the 1960s, a phenomenon described in the chapter on the subject by Patricia Donat and John D'Emilio provided in this section. But that reconceptualization was far in the future when the twentieth century opened. Currents in psychology at that time encouraged scholarly exploration in causation of sexual aggression. One consequence was to view rape as an act of the perpetrator's disordered mind. The act continued also to be understood primarily as one of passion rather than violence. The responsibility of the rapist for his actions was thereby diminished when such conduct was understood as one of uncontrollable desire. Rape was conceptualized from the perspective of the perpetrator. Discussion of rape centered around the notion of the "sexual psychopath" especially so as the American public developed a popular interest in sex crimes during the 1930s. Estelle Freedman points out, in her examination of that concept during the period 1920–1960 (see Bibliography reference), that this debate did have its up side. It provided a focus for new public discussion of sexual normality and abnormality. In the process, boundaries between the two were renegotiated in a more liberalizing way. A second event of the early twentieth century noted by Freedman was the "resexualization," or rerecognition, of legitimate sexual desire in women. The down side of this phenomenon was to encourage further the Victorian suspicion that females in some way contributed to their own forced sexual exploitation. "Blame the victim" was a prevalent theme through the 1950s.

The issues of rape and sexual assault became major concerns of feminists after the revival of that movement. In their chapter provided in this section, Donat and D'Emilio examine the nature of that discourse as it reconceptualized rape from the perspective of the victim. Feminists argued that such assault was not one of passion but one of violence against women. Rather than an end in itself, rape or the threat thereof was a means to enforce male-mandated female gender roles. It was the cement of patriarchy. This interpretation broadened substantially the scope of concern with the dynamics of sexual assault. New focus was placed on the consequence of female stereotypes in the media, mechanisms of intimidation, and who, beyond the traditional "stranger in the bushes," was the perpetrator of sexual assault. Feminists also began to explore the larger issue of whether American culture was "rape supportive." While there has been some criticism of the reconceptualization, even within feminists' ranks, that perspective has meant a major and permanent change in the public understanding of sexual assault.

Every social history has its great divide and so is the case with homosexuality. One was circa the 1880s, when its social structure began to develop and became visible within urban centers. Closely related chronologically was the recognition of homosexuality as a condition of life and lifestyle, as opposed to merely acts. A second was the experience of gays and lesbians during World War II. The massive mobilization of America for the war forced an otherwise disinclined military and even peacetime industrial establishment to "look the other way" or consciously tolerate homosexuals in their ranks. War-time gains obtained by this community would not be taken away easily in its aftermath. An expression of such will, at least symbolically, was the 1950 formation of the Mattachine Society whose devoted purpose was to "freeing" the nation's "largest minority." It was an event that heralded the homosexual emancipation movement in the United States. A third milestone was the "Stonewall Riots" in New York's Greenwich Village in 1969. Police staged a raid on a gay bar and were met with resistance that might have been modeled on militant civil rights protestors of that decade. Stonewall has been viewed as the beginning of the Gay Liberation movement. Still another historical point of significance was the AIDS crisis, which surfaced in the 1980s.

The AIDS "crisis" was in one sense the newest venereal disease "de jour." The prototype sexual scourge would be syphilis. The former was much more insidious in nature, more stigmatized because of its homosexual origins, and quite different in the meaning of efforts at its management. It would also forge a permanent imprint on perception of the gay community. In the chapter "Gay Villain, Gay Hero . . ." included in this volume, Robert Padgug treats AIDS as an issue of competing ideologies and institution. The disease, like other life-threatening maladies, became a "metaphor," at times conflicting metaphors. Sexuality was central to its social construction because sexuality in general, and homosexuality in particular, appeared to play a paramount role in its etiology and spread. For gay men the AIDS crisis exacerbated already existing discrimination and homophobia. One remarkable matter that developed was, on the other hand, the extent to which the gay community involved itself in the management of AIDS. Indeed, and despite the danger of doing so, the gay community embraced the identification of AIDS with homosexuality, but redefined that association to make self management of the disease central to the integrity of that community. Moreover, the gay-AIDS connection caused significant modification in the lifestyle of the community. Certain homosexual institutions largely devoted to facilitation of stigmatized practice, e.g., public baths, began to disappear under the impetus of the disease. Moreover, as gays began to assert the right to exist as a minority within the majority culture in the 1960s, some sex-related institutions proliferated as expressions of protest. In turn, by the next decade, homosexual identity was responsible for the rapid growth of institutions not directly tied to stigmatized intimacy per se. Gay sexuality or expression thereof, was reconstituted under the impact of AIDS along the line of heterosexual precedent. Steady ''dating'' and more long-term monogamous relationships began to become more prevalent. Finally, the presence of the disease prompted the emergence of two parallel but competing metaphors. One was that of sexual irresponsibility and lack of control as the heart of homosexuality. The second was one of substantial community responsibility on the part of gays in asserting a role in management of the AIDS crisis as well as the capacity to alter sexual behavior as a means to combat the menace. The former pointed toward stigmatized victims and villains. The latter position was that of self-help activism and heroes.

13

Prostitution, the Alien Woman and the Progressive Imagination, 1910–1915

Egal Feldman

In no period of American history did the custodians of American morality direct more serious attention to the eradication of prostitution than they did in the few years preceding World War I.[1] With the passage of the Mann Act in 1910 their efforts also embraced the interests of the national government. Ministers, social workers, men and women of medicine, science and letters all joined in the unusually massive assault. Their united determination to eradicate white slavery reminds one of the previous crusade against black servitude. In both cases its participants first pressed for international and interstate regulation of the traffic. Rescue homes in bleak urban areas suggest memories of the underground railroad; while an abundant literature designed to expose the intricate, sinister workings of the institution leave the impression of another chapter in the writings of abolitionism.[2]

The energetic outburst against sexual immorality, however, grew out of a relatively new presumption; it was predicated upon the conviction that society's and man's behavior can be controlled and regulated; that man and his environment are both perfectible. Edward A. Ross' *Social Control* (1901), or Ellen H. Richards' *Euthenics: the Science of Controllable Environment* (1910), are examples of books which periodically re-enforced such hopes, infusing progressive uplifters with the confidence that success would be theirs.[3] "Whatever one may hold as to ultimate dealings with the subject," remarked the prominent physician Abraham Flexner, in 1914, "it is clear that prostitution is at any rate a modifiable phenomenon." Commissioned in 1912 by the New York Bureau of Social Hygiene to investigate European prostitution, Flexner grew confident that within man's reach was the power, if not to eradicate totally, certainly to minimize the age-old custom of commercialized sexual pleasure. "Civilization," wrote Flexner with a militant optimism so characteristic of his generation,

has stripped for a life-and-death wrestle with tuberculosis, alcohol and other plagues. It is on the verge of a similar struggle with the crasser forms of commercialized vice. Sooner or later, it must fling down the gauntlet to the whole horrible thing. This will be the real contest—a contest that will tax the courage, the self-denial, the faith, the resources of humanity to their utmost.[4]

The Flexner report on vice, published in 1914, drove forward another point, that prostitution was an urban problem whose precise character was largely dependent upon the size of the town.[5] The belief that temptations of modern urban living could easily overwhelm the virtuous was, in fact, a somewhat old but typical notion of the age. "Thrilled by the mere propinquity of city excitements and eager to share" in them, observed the Head Worker, Jane Addams, the young and innocent found it enormously difficult to "keep to the gray and monotonous path of regular work." This particular observation was meant for the benefit of rustic maidens who found themselves in the big metropolis, alone and unattended by family or friends for the first time. "From the point of view of the traffickers in white slaves," Miss Addams noticed, "it is much cheaper and safer to procure country girls . . . because they are much more easily secreted than girls from the city. A country girl entering a vicious life quickly feels the disgrace and soon becomes too broken-spirited and discouraged to make any effort to escape."[6]

Yet it was the condition of the unemployed, friendless immigrant girl that seemed to worry her most. "Loneliness and detachment which the city tends to breed in its inhabitants is easily intensified in such a girl into isolation and a desolating feeling of belonging nowhere," warned Miss Addams. "At such moments a black oppression, the instinctive fear of solitude, will send a lonely girl restlessly to walk the streets even when she is 'too tired to stand,' and where her desire for companionship in itself constitutes a grave danger."[7]

To many Americans, less sensitive, less insightful than Jane Addams, the discovery of a thriving existence of commercialized prostitution in the midst of American cities became the basis for a blanket indictment of urban living. "What forces are there, hidden in American cities, which are dragging them . . . into a state of semibarbarism?" queried a leading popularizer of urban mismanagement and vice in 1907.[8] To many the city emerged as a monster, a veritable house of ill repute. "If I lived in the country and had a young daughter I would go to any length of hardship and privation myself rather than allow her to go into the city to work or to study" was a typical reaction. "The best and the surest way for parents of girls in the country to protect them from the clutches of the 'white slaver' is to keep them in the country."[9] That the city was an illusive trap set carefully for country virgins was a notion strongly endorsed in these years by numerous respected educators, clerics and lawyers.[10] But what is of greater consequence here was the prevalent notion that behind the scenes of urban vice were found the nation's newcomers. Surely it was the foreigner, a good many upright Americans were convinced, who was organizing, supporting and thriving upon the lucrative traffic of prostitution.[11] One might say that there was a nativist assault on prostitution which envisioned well-organized networks of vice connecting European and American cities; export-import syndicates thriving on the trade of loose women, diabolical agencies forever searching for new opportunities in the American metropolis.

Southern Italians and Russian Jews came under special attack by those who dreamed of a purer America. Behind men like Paul Kelly and Jimmie Kelly "and other Italians masquerading under Irish names" were detected the networks of international vice.[12] Serious discussions of procuring and pimping inevitably led to an anti-Semitic rhetoric. "It is an absolute fact that corrupt Jews are now the backbone of the loathsome traffic in New York and Chicago," wrote one irate puritan with dogmatic certainty.[13] It was "the Jewish dealer in women, a product of New York politics, who has vitiated, more than any other single agency, the moral life of the great cities of America in the past ten years," wrote George Kibbe Turner in the respectable and widely read *McClure's Magazine* in 1909. Turner's influential articles, appearing regularly in this popular organ of muckrakers, had for years contained a sharp nativist ring, and his animosity was aimed most directly at New York's Jewry. The traffic in women, wrote Turner, was lodged solidly in the hands of "a large number of criminals," most of whom were "Austrian, Russian, and Hungarian Jews." Well guarded by corrupt Tammany politicians, the lewd enterprise had centered its headquarters in New York City, under the guise of a "Jewish society that goes under the name of the New York Independent Benevolent Association." This organization, explained Turner,

was started in 1896 by a party of dealers who were returning from attendance at the funeral of Sam Engel, a brother of Martin Engel, the Tammany leader of the red-light assembly district. In the usual post-funeral discussion of the frailty of human life, the fact was brought out that the sentiment of the Jews of the East Side against men of their profession barred them generally from societies giving death benefits, and even caused discrimination against them in the purchase of burial-places in the cemetery. A society was quickly incorporated under the laws of New York, and a burial-plot secured and enclosed in Washington cemetery in Brooklyn.[14]

Through the good offices of the Benevolent Association, houses of prostitution in numerous American cities were amply supplied. Focusing less upon any one particular nationality or ethnic group one commentator accused all aliens at once, and warned that

unless we make energetic and successful war upon the red light districts . . . we shall have Oriental brothel slavery thrust upon us . . . with all its unnatural and abnormal practices, established among us by the French traders. Jew traders, too, will people our "levees" with Polish Jewesses and any others who will make money for them. Shall we defend our American civilization, or lower our flag to the most despicable foreigners—French, Irish, Italians, Jews and Mongolians? . . . On both coasts and throughout all our cities, only an awakening of the whole Christian conscience and intelligence can save us from the importation of Parisian and Polish pollution, which is already corrupting the manhood and youth of every large city in the nation.[15]

The link between prostitution and the alien was solidified in the public imagination when confirmed by government investigators. The subject of prostitution served as fodder for the more nativistic passages of the United States Immigration report of

1911 and left the impression, at times, that vice followed immigration as night does day. "A very large proportion of the pimps living in the United States are foreigners," reported the federal investigators, making special note of the fact that "Egyptian, French, Chinese, Belgian, Spanish, Japanese, Greek, Slavic, Hungarian, Italian, and Russian" were the nationalities involved most frequently in the traffic of women. Failing to uncover any evidence of an international "monopolistic corporation whose business it is to import and exploit these unfortunate women," the commissioners were, nevertheless, convinced that there were gentlemen's agreements among foreign procurers, singling out the French and Jews for special attention. "There are large numbers of Jews scattered throughout the United States," they wrote, "who seduce and keep girls. Some of them are engaged in importation, but apparently they prey rather upon young girls whom they find on the street, in the dance halls, and similar places, and whom, by the methods already indicated— love-making and pretenses of marriage—they deceive and ruin." The Italian panderer, they noted, was "vicious and criminal," and was more "feared by their women than are the pimps of other nationalities."[16]

The nativist assault on prostitution proved awkward and somewhat embarrassing to the liberal friends of aliens who were equally swept up by the desire to eradicate commercialized vice. American Jews, for example, were stunned by Turner's revelations, resenting especially his blanket indictment of an entire immigrant group, the Eastern European Jew. Yet subsequent investigations proved that a considerable number of Jews were involved in the business of commercialized vice. The prominent rabbinical figure, Dr. Emil G. Hirsch, preached a special sermon at the Sinai Temple in Chicago on September 25, 1909, when he learned that the President of a neighboring congregation was deeply implicated. "Over on the West Side," thundered Rabbi Hirsch, "the worst thing has occurred that has ever happened to our race. The name of God and Jew has been profaned as never before." In the wake of this revelation, Jews of Chicago, led by Adolf Kraus, President of the local B'nai B'rith Chapter, and Clifford G. Roe, a distinguished attorney, laid plans to combat the scourge of white slavery in their midst.[17]

There were, in fact, two separate campaigns during these years, a nativistic attack on prostitution with all its ugly xenophobic overtones paralleled by an anti-nativist outburst. Whereas the former crusade was irrational, evangelical, uncompromising and completely divorced from the humanitarianism of the early twentieth century, the latter was closely associated with the temper of the social gospel, the social settlement and the more rational humanitarian ambitions of progressivism. The latter's task was more complex, for not only did the anti-nativist assume the responsibility of scientifically searching for the true causes of the disease, but hoped also to clear the fog of prejudice which engulfed the entire issue. In short, he hoped to explain the causes and discover solutions for the problem of prostitution and at the same time to disassociate the reputation of the immigrant from commercialized vice.

Obviously the attack on prostitution was not always polarized between the friends and enemies of aliens. Many of its participants fell somewhere between the two extremes. Nevertheless, in order to appreciate fully the precise nature of the crusade, one should be aware of its emotional extremities.

That the immigrant was a victim as well as a cause was conceded by many. If the tentacles of the "syndicate" stretched across the ocean, the first victim, it was noticed, was usually an innocent unprotected young immigrant. "In other words," explained one investigator, the "watchers for human prey scan the immigrants as they come down the gang plank of a vessel which has just arrived and 'spot' the girls who are unaccompanied by fathers, mothers, brothers or relatives to protect them." Once detected, the victim was approached "by a man who speaks her language." Tempting "promises of an easy time, plenty of money, fine clothes and the usual stock of allurements—or a fake marriage" follow. "In some instances the hunters really marry the victims." If this cultivated approach proved ineffective "intoxication and drugging" were applied to reduce the victim to a state of helplessness and total servitude.

Once a white slave is sold and landed in a house or dive she becomes a prisoner . . . [in] a room having but one door, to which the keeper holds the key. . . . What mockery it is to have in our harbor in New York the Statue of Liberty with outstretched arms welcoming the foreign girl to the land of the free! How she must sneer at it and rebuke the country with such an emblematic monument at its very gate when she finds here a slavery whose chains bind the captive more securely than those in the country from which she has come![18]

This tendency to bewail the innocence of the alien female threatened by the predatory desire of her male counterpart revealed an ambivalent strain in the American attack upon vice. It was also echoed by the United States Immigration Commission's investigations and reports, so frequently referred to by contemporary journalists writing on the subject of white slavery. Attributing the cause of prostitution to the coming of the New Immigration, federal investigators, nevertheless, oozed compassion and concern over the fate of the immigrant female. "The alien woman is ignorant of the language of the country, knows nothing beyond a few blocks of the city where she lives, has usually no money, and no knowledge of the rescue homes and institutions which might help her," they reported in 1910. Even then nativist Turner waxed "melancholy" over the discovery of "little Italian peasant girls, taken from various dens, where they lay, shivering and afraid, under the lighted candles and crucifixes in their bedrooms."[19]

That the immigrant girl was the major casualty of commercialized vice was, in fact, underscored by a number of investigations conducted independently by private agencies during these years. One, launched in Chicago in 1910 by a Church Federation meeting "composed of clergy representing six hundred congregations," requested the Mayor of Chicago to "appoint a commission made up of men and women who command the respect and confidence of the public at large." The Mayor complied, and in March 1910 appointed a Vice Commission consisting of medical and legal experts, Protestant, Catholic and Jewish clergy, leading businessmen and sociologists.[20] The final draft of the Commission's report conceded that "the immigrant woman furnishes a large supply to the demand," but it placed the blame on the lack of protection offered to her by government and private agencies. "Generally virtuous when she comes to this country," it explained, "she is ruined and exploited because there is no adequate protection and assistance given her after she reaches the United States."[21] It was for this reason that Jane Addams and her Hull House staff insisted so strongly upon the need for governmental protective machinery to guard the "foreign girl who speaks no English, who has not the remotest idea in what part of the city her fellow-countrymen live, who does not know the police station or any agency to which she may apply" during the first days following her arrival. It was at this vulnerable juncture, Chicago's social workers warned, that the young immigrant was "as valuable to a white trafficker as a girl imported directly for the trade."[22] Indeed, a New York City investigation in 1913 indicated some surprise that, given the deplorable conditions of immigrant life, the involvement of the alien woman in prostitution was not larger. Conducted by Katharine Bement Davis, Superintendent of the State Reformatory for Women at Bedford Hills, New York, the study was based upon the records of a few thousand prostitutes committed to state reformatories. It was mostly concerned with the relationship of prostitution to the city's heterogeneous population, and concluded that American-born women contributed overwhelmingly more than their proportion to New York prostitution.[23] But even here the immigrant was not handed a total clearance, for the sins of his children devolved upon him. If the foreign-born contributed less than their expected quota, the group that contributed "out of proportion to its percentage in the population" was their American-born daughters. Miss Davis admitted, of course, that there was a reasonable explanation for this.

When we remember that here we have a group in which the fathers and mothers belong to a civilization with speech, tradition and habits different from those of the country in which they are living, the children, native-born Americans with American companions and American schooling, adopt ideals often not of the highest and are very apt, even when quite young, to feel that they know more than their parents.[24]

America's discovery of prostitution and its growing conviction that its roots were European gave rise to a demand, advocated especially by nativists, that immigrant ladies of doubtful behavior be immediately deported; but a number of reformers, friends of aliens, counseled differently. "Certainly the immigration laws might do better than to send a girl back to her parents, diseased and disgraced, because America had failed to safeguard her virtue from the machinations of well-known but unrestrained criminals," warned one of the nation's leading social workers. "Certainly no one will doubt that it is the business of the city itself to extend much more protection to young girls who so thoughtlessly walk upon its streets."[25] Kate Waller Barrett, an authority on the deportation of prostitutes, and a special adviser to the government on matters of immigration, objected also to rash and heartless solutions. In her reports she stressed the social injustice, the misunderstanding that immigrant women were constantly subjected to. "Nothing is more in keeping with the wishes of a man when he has gotten a woman in trouble than to have her deported, and thus put the ocean between them," she argued on one occasion, as only a woman of determined militancy could.[26] A holder of doctoral degrees in medicine and science, President of the National Council of Women, Mrs. Barrett was appointed as Special Agent of the United States Immigration Service in 1914. Her task was to join with European officials in discussions concerning the relationship of the growing European immigration to the United States and the white slave traffic. Her final report of this experience, insisting that the roots of prostitution must be sought in the trans-Atlantic voyage, stressed the necessity for preventive and precautionary measures on board the immigrant steamers. Steamship companies should provide free transportation to woman supervisors, she felt, and urged the separation of sexes in both living and recreation and the prohibition of crew members from visiting the steerage quarters "except as their duties require."[27] Focusing specially upon the case of the deportee, she urged that an international committee be formed to grapple with the problem. "The question of the unattached immigrant woman is comparatively new," she pointed out, quite different from that of the male immigrant with whom America has had years of experience. A woman accused of prostitution must not be flung out of the country upon flimsy evidence, without due process of law.[28]

To remove the conditions responsible for the "fall" of alien women was a task pre–World War I reformers undertook, and they began the moment the unaccompanied female arrived. Chicago's Immigrants' Protective League was founded in part for that reason. Its first Annual Report in 1910 talked ominously of immigrant girls who failed to arrive at their expected destination, whose "ultimate fate . . . could never be discovered." Its agents kept in constant communication with Ellis Island authorities, in part to request lists of names of alien women traveling alone to Chicago and other interior cities. Officials of the League awaited their arrival, and ordered an immediate search for those who did not appear at the time expected.[29] Each year the League published its list of "Girls We Have Been Unable to Locate," and the names of the missing continued to multiply. According to Grace Abbott, Director of the League, a 10 per cent annual rate of disappearance was not unusual during the years of the great migration.[30] Worried kin turned frequently to the League for information, which occasionally confirmed their worst fears. "We learned that she had been called for by a notoriously disreputable man and taken to a rooming house on Washington near Halsted," reported League officials after an investigation of the whereabouts of a young Lithuanian girl in 1913. "Everything pointed to the conclusion that the girl either voluntarily or by deception was leading an immoral life, but neither we nor the agencies to which the case was reported could locate the girl."[31]

Immigrant lodging houses and hotels were for this reason frequently attacked by reformers and scrutinized periodically by government and private agents. The insufficient care exercised by such institutions "in discharging young immigrant women and girls who have been placed in their charge by immigration authorities" was a frequent cause of complaint. That a number of such homes served as recruiting centers for houses of prostitution was established by a number of investigations.[32] The founding of the Clara de Hirsch Home for Immigrant Girls in March 1904 was motivated by such discoveries. Its aim, as expressed by its founders, was "to protect the girl at her very entrance to this country, to afford her temporary shelter, to see to it that she reaches her prospective destination in safety." Immediate priority was extended to those without friends or relatives "or such who are called for by single men or married men without their wives." Once housed, declared a spokesman for the Home in 1912, "we do not permit any girls to leave our premises without making a thorough personal investigation of the prospective living quarters . . . surroundings, the number of lodgers, and rooming facilities," and "are constantly studying new measures and means for the safeguarding of our girls."[33]

For similar reasons private employment agencies, especially those serving newcomers, were eyed suspiciously. That a number were supplying personnel to houses of ill repute was established by Frances Kellor's investigation of employment agencies early in the century. The link between the alien and commercialized vice, explained Kellor, was the "runner," a "suave, attractive young man who can win the confidence of the immigrant girls." He was expected to have an acquaintance with alien tongues and customs, for "his business is to bring them to the office by any means." His character "defies description. There seems to be no meanness to which he will not stoop. . . . If a girl refuses to enter a questionable place it is part of the work of the runner to ruin her and make her more amenable to suggestions."[34] Other investigations during the following years confirmed such findings. One conducted by the Immigrants' Protective League in 1908 revealed considerable collusion, but the "commonest offense," according to Grace Abbott, was ignorance of the character of the places to which the immigrant girl was sent "rather than an active connivance in her ruin."[35] Two years later New York City's Lillian Wald made a respectable audience squirm in their pews by informing them that numerous metropolitan employment agencies "were used as markets for selling girls for prices varying from $3.00 to $50.00 or as procuring places where immoral women and men came and selected their victims."[36] New Jersey's Commission of Immigration reported also at this time that 65 per cent of the agencies investigated "were willing to procure girls to work as servants in alleged disorderly houses and for immoral purposes."[37] The United States Immigration Commission confirmed these findings in 1910 and stamped upon them a national concurrence based upon its own investigations.[38] The link between employment agencies and immigrant prostitution helps explain why progressives urged their total abolition and the creation of free publicly-supported institutions in their stead.

In large part the assault on commercialized vice was led by women themselves, either speaking through their organizations or as isolated individuals. The work of the International Institute for Young Women, launched by the National Young Women's Christian Association in 1910, is an example of a moderate but concerted attack. To guard "those who have sailed their immigrating journey alone" and who have gone "through the hazards of arrival with no protection" was its avowed objective. The majority of newcomers, observed one of its officials, were young, "below thirty years of age and the largest group of all between sixteen and twenty-one!" The International Institute was impressed with the importance of getting "a girl *started right*!" and keeping "her from doing all sorts of things she wouldn't think of doing back home.''[39] The work of Chicago's Immigrants' Protective League and numerous settlement houses pursued the same objectives with considerably less condescension. Especially effective, however, was the program launched by the National Council of Jewish Women. Founded by ninety-five women during the Chicago World's Fair in 1893, the organization dedicated itself ''to the service of faith and humanity through education and philanthropy,'' and elected a scion of a pioneer settler in Chicago, a philanthropist and educator in her own right, Hannah Greenbaum Solomon, as its first president.[40] Within a few years, at the request of the United States Government, the Council became active in immigration affairs and the prevention of the exploitation of alien women became its major concern. Its delegates participated in international white slavery conferences and its workers, whose preventive work at the docks set an example that other organizations would later follow, became permanent fixtures at Ellis Island and other immigration centers.[41] Easily identifiable by their conspicuous badges, able to speak a number of languages, these workers were on a constant lookout for girls traveling alone. Their leaflets and placards, distributed and posted, were also conspicuous at the various ports of entry. ''Beware of those who give you addresses, offer you easy, well-paid work, or even marriage,'' warned one such broadside in three languages. ''There are many evil men and women who have in this way led girls to destruction. Always inquire in regard to these persons of the Council of Jewish Women, which will find out the truth for you and advise you.''[42] ''Bitter experience'' had made such warnings necessary, Marion L. Misch, President of the Council, explained in 1912, especially for the benefit of ''decent people'' who were unable ''to comprehend the moral bias of the white slaver,'' the fiend in human guise who finds ''the steamship piers a prolific hunting-ground.''[43] Once admitted, young immigrant girls were not easily released from the anxious, watchful eye of the Council. For weeks their movements were observed, the nature of their adjustment studied. If prostitution proved a trap, as it did on rare occasions, legal machinery was put in gear to defend the hapless female from the deportation horror. To the National Council of Jewish Women immigration and prostitution were not causal in their relationship. It ''is not a question of immigration,'' explained the Council, ''if an immigrant girl is so unfortunate as to become the victim of some evil man who has traded on her credulity to put her to shame'' but ''a purely local and American and social question, and we must be careful not to confuse the two.''[44]

In the double task of impressing Americans with the need for public protection for the young newcomer, on the one hand, and dispelling the notion that there was a connection between the rise of prostitution and the increase of immigration, on the other, social workers such as Frances A. Kellor, Jane Addams, Grace Abbott and Lillian Wald stand out prominently. Kellor was one of the first to demand that government protection be offered to the female traveler from the moment she commenced her journey to America. ''Has our government any matrons or inspectors who make it impossible for the procurer, who wishes to travel steerage or second cabin for the purpose of meeting her, to accomplish his purpose?'' she queried. ''Is she safeguarded so carefully that members of the ship's crew cannot mislead her?''[45] Jane Addams cautioned immigrant girls against offers of a quick marriage by pleasant-looking strangers, who might well be agents of disreputable houses.[46] Reasons that led to the involvement of immigrant women with vice were many, declared her co-worker, Grace Abbott. Their ignorance of English was in part responsible for their vulnerability. "The more dangerous environment in which they live" was an additional factor. "For it is near an immigrant or colored neighborhood that disreputable dance halls and hotels are usually tolerated." The alien woman also suffers from a hunger for recreation little understood or appreciated by the native-born.[47] In New York City, Lillian Wald, founder of America's first nurses' (Henry Street) settlement in the mid-1890s, met the ugliness head-on. Growing up in a comfortable middle-class environment in Rochester, New York, Miss Wald, like so many other women of her generation, chose a lifetime of service in surroundings of poverty and the struggle of immigrant life. A nurse by training, she preferred to apply her knowledge to the problems of lower Manhattan. "From the very start its poor became her people. She took them to her heart and they gave her quickly their unstinted confidence and trust," Jacob A. Riis, who knew her and the East Side well, wrote in 1913.[48] Like other social and settlement-house workers, she too displayed puritanic zealousness in her desire to protect the alien woman against sexual pitfalls as well as against unsubstantiated charges of prostitution. The vast influx of single women from Eastern Europe did not alarm her, as it did so many others of her generation, for Lillian Wald was certain that the positive value of the European inrush would surely outweigh all sinister nativist forebodings. Nevertheless, she too espoused as necessary a special program of protection and guidance.[49] "The alien is in more danger of moral contamination than the rest of the community," she explained to a convention of social workers in 1908. And, "in the case of the alien girl . . . the danger is increased," especially where she must immediately assume the role of breadwinner. Like Addams, Abbott and Kellor, Lillian Wald sensed the potential danger that grew out of the limited social outlets offered by the American urban environment. The lack of available publicly supported facilities for amusement and recreation, she cautioned, invariably led to a "pitiful dependence . . . upon the casual pick-up." "A definite and inclusive program is demanded by all ethical standards of a moral society. Existing provisions for meeting such needs," she felt, were "too casual and too haphazard."[50]

In part, the conspicuous evidence of women involved in the attack on vice was due to their relative absence from most movements of social reconstruction in the decades before. America had, after all, never before seen a group of women so well educated, so enlightened, yet with nothing to do. The college-bred women of the late nineteenth century were possessed with an overwhelming desire to act, not just aimlessly, but to participate in some meaningful social and moral venture. They believed, as a perceptive student of the career of Jane Addams wrote, that they had "a special position in history and a special duty to posterity." That they were willing to crash head-on with the most sordid aspects of modern America was also in perfect accord with the utilitarian and activist notions of a blustering, masculine society which credited activity above thought, visible accomplishments above ideas. That the preoccupation of long-sleeved spinsters with the reform of sexual perversions did not totally stun the Victorian mentality was in part due to notions which grew out of the same mythology, a mythology that lifted the native-born American woman above the baser animal passions of her male counterpart, attributing to her the custodianship of sexual purity.[51] In another sense, an attack on prostitution was also a means of warning modern industrial and urban America to make way for the New Woman. It was a sharp exhortation that the exploitation exercised by men in factory, lodgings and on the city streets must cease. Surely if modern urban America could be made safe and comfortable for a defenseless immigrant girl, all women and, for that matter, all men too could dwell there in greater comfort and security.

Notes

1. Between 1890 and 1909 the *Readers' Guide to Periodical Literature* lists 36 entries under the subject of "Prostitution"; between the years 1910 and 1914 entries climb sharply to 156 and drop to 41 from 1915 to 1924.

2. The analogy was first presented in Jane Addams, *A New Conscience and an Ancient Evil* (New York, 1912), pp. 4–5; for a review of the literature see Louis Filler, *Crusaders for American Liberalism* (Yellow Springs, Ohio, 1950), pp. 285–295.

3. For an interesting discussion of the influence of Edward A. Ross see Christopher Lasch, *The New Radicalism in America, 1889–1963* (New York, 1965), p. 170; Ellen A. Richards, *Euthenics: the Science of Controllable Environment* (Boston, 1910).

4. Abraham Flexner, *Prostitution in Europe* (New York, 1914), pp. vii, 395–402.

5. Ibid., p. 5.

6. Addams, *New Conscience,* pp. 145, 147, 216.

7. Ibid., p. 89.

8. George Kibbe Turner, "The City of Chicago, A Study of the Great Immoralities," *McClure's Magazine,* XXVIII (April 1907), 575; S. S. McClure, "The Tammanyizing of a Civilization," *McClure's Magazine,* XXXIV (November 1909), 127.

9. Ernest A. Bell, ed., *Fighting the Traffic in Young Girls, or War on the White Slave Trade* (Chicago, 1910), pp, 70–71.

10. See, for example, the long list of contributors to this volume (Bell, *Fighting the Traffic . . .*) on the Title Page.

11. Ibid., pp. 181–182.

12. McClure, *McClure's Magazine,* XXVIII, 117, 124–125, 126–127; Bell, pp. 71–72, 187–188.

13. Turner, "The Daughters of the Poor," *McClure's Magazine,* XXXIV, 57–58.

14. Turner, *McClure's Magazine,* XXXIV, 57–58.

15. Bell, pp. 260–262.

16. United States Immigration Commission, *Abstracts of Reports of the Immigration Commission,* II, 61st Congress 3d Sess. (Washington, D. C., 1911), pp. 342–343.

17. McClure, *McClure's Magazine,* XXVIII, 122–123.

18. Bell, pp. 58–59, 153; Turner, *McClure's Magazine,* XXXIV, 46, 54.

19. Turner, *McClure's Magazine,* XXXIV, 58; *Abstracts of Reports of the Immigration Commission,* II, 342.

20. The Vice Commission of Chicago, *The Social Evil in Chicago* (Chicago, 1911), pp. 1–5.

21. Ibid., p. 40.

22. Addams, *A New Conscience,* pp. 26, 40.

23. George J. Kneeland, *Commercialized Prostitution in New York City* (New York, 1913), pp. 163–167, 198–199.

24. Ibid., pp. 167–168, 200–204.

25. Addams, *A New Conscience,* pp. 34–35.

26. Frank B. Lenz, ed., *Immigration—Some New Phases of the Problem* (San Francisco, 1915), p. 10.

27. United States Department of Labor, Bureau of Immigration, *Annual Report of the Commissioner General of Immigration to the Secretary of Labor, 1914* (Washington, D. C., 1915), pp. 14, 363, 380–382.

28. Ibid, pp. 384–386.

29. Edith Abbott, *Immigration: Select Documents and Case Records* (Chicago, 1924), pp. 608–612; Immigrants' Protective League, *Fourth Annual Report of the Immigrants' Protective League for the Year Ending January 1st, 1913* (Chicago, 1913), p. 13.

30. Ibid., *Annual Report, 1909–1910*, pp. 4, 13–15, 18; Grace Abbott, *The Immigrant and the Community* (New York, 1917), p. 13.

31. Immigrants' Protective League, *Fourth Annual Report*, 1913, p. 13.

32. *Abstracts of Reports of the Immigration Commission*, II, 319–321; United States Immigration Commission, *Reports of the Immigration Commission*, "Immigrant Homes and Aid Societies," 61st Congress, 3rd Sess. (Washington, D. C., 1911), pp. 140–142; Bell, pp. 176, 186.

33. Rose Sommerfeld, "The Clara de Hirsch Home for Working Girls," *American Citizen*, I (November 1912), 253–254.

34. Frances A. Kellor, *Out of Work: A Study of Employment Agencies: Their Treatment of the Unemployed, and Their Influence upon Homes and Business* (New York, 1904), pp. 80–82.

35. Grace Abbott, "The Chicago Employment Agency and the Immigrant Worker," *American Journal of Sociology*, XIV (November 1908), 289, 291–292.

36. Speech made by Lillian Wald on Dec. 4, 1910, Lillian Wald Papers, New York Public Library, New York City.

37. "Report and Recommendations of the New Jersey Immigration Commission," *Survey*, XXXI (March 14, 1914), 738.

38. *Reports of the Immigration Commission*, "Immigrant Homes and Aid Societies," pp. 142–143.

39. Elizabeth Wilson, *Fifty Years of Association Work Among Young Women, 1866–1916* (New York, National Board of the YWCA, 1916), p. 301; William P. Shriver, *Immigrant Forces: Factors in the New Democracy* (New York, Missionary Education Movement of the U. S. & Canada, 1913), p. 139; Edith Terry Bremer, "Foreign Community and Immigration Work of the National Young Women's Christian Association," *Immigrants in America Review*, I (January 1916), 76–78.

40. Mildred G. Welt, "The National Council of Jewish Women," *American Jewish Year Book*, XXXVI (1944–45), 56, 63–64.

41. *American Jewish Year Book*, XXXVI, 65–66.

42. United States Immigration Commission, *Reports of the Immigration Commission*, "Statements and Recommendations Submitted by Societies and Organizations Interested in the Subject of Immigration," 61st Congress, 3d. Sess. (Washington, D. C., 1911), pp. 33–34, 36, 47.

43. Marion L. Misch, "The Americanization of the Immigrant Girl," *American Citizen*, I (July 1912), 31.

44. *American Citizen*, I, 45–46.

45. Frances A. Kellor, "The Protection of Immigrant Women," *Atlantic Monthly*, CI (February 1908), 249–250.

46. Addams, *A New Conscience*, pp. 38–40.

47. Grace Abbott, *The Immigrant and the Community*, pp. 71–75.

48. R. L. Duffus, *Lillian Wald: Neighbor and Crusader* (New York, 1938), pp. 4–5; Jacob A. Riis, "Personals," *Survey*, XXX (July 26, 1913), 551–552.

49. Lillian D. Wald, "The Immigrant Girl," *Proceedings of the National Conference of Charities and Corrections*, June 1909, pp. 261, 264.

50. Ibid., p. 264.

51. Jill Conway, "Jane Addams: an American Heroine," *Daedalus*, XCIII (Spring 1964), 761–762, 773; for a somewhat different, but provocative, explanation see Christopher Lasch, *The New Radicalism*, pp. 56–57, 64–67.

14

The Reproduction of Butch-Fem Roles: A Social Constructionist Approach

Elizabeth Lapovsky Kennedy and Madeline D. Davis

All commentators on twentieth-century lesbian life have noted the prominence of butch-fem roles.[1] Their presence was unmistakable in prefeminist communities where the butch projected the male image of her particular time period—at least in dress and mannerism—and the fem, the female image; and all members were usually one or the other. The tenacity of butch-fem roles underlines the appeal of an essentialist theory, which assumes that sexuality and gender transcend time and culture and reflect biological or psychological givens. However, our study of the Buffalo lesbian community's culture, social organization, and consciousness reveals significant changes within this seeming continuity. Our approach views sexuality as socially constructed, that is, created by human actors in culturally and historically conditioned ways. In this essay we argue that social constructionism provides a necessary dimension for understanding how butch-fem roles have operated in the community and in the development of individual identity.[2]

Essentialist approaches to butch-fem roles, as well as to homosexuality in general, have a long tradition.[3] The nineteenth-century medical literature considered the "invert," the man or woman whose character and mannerisms appeared to imitate those of the "opposite sex," as congenitally flawed. These researchers had little commentary on cases of more "normal" appearing behavior—passivity in women, aggressiveness in men—in which the desired object was nevertheless of the same sex. By the early 1900s psychologists and sexologists, led by Sigmund Freud, began to explore homosexuality in terms of childhood trauma and parental insufficiency.[4] This approach never fully supplanted theories of congenital causation but nevertheless was extremely powerful as a new kind of essentialism, which viewed homosexuality as a psychological disorder caused by abnormal personality development.[5] Over the years essentialism has at times been adopted by the lesbian and gay community and used as a basis from which to argue for tolerance and acceptance. Radclyffe Hall's *The Well of Loneliness* is an apt example; the novel pleads for the acceptance of Stephen, an unmistakably masculine lesbian, who cannot help being who she is.[6] The essentialist tradition still has a powerful influence on contemporary thinking about sexuality. For instance, the dominant ideology of our society considers the distinction between men and women as fixed and ultimately based in biology. Similarly, it categorizes lesbians and gay men as distinct kinds of people.[7] Such ideas unquestionably lurk in the background of popular thinking about butch-fem roles as well.

The relatively new social constructionist approach aims to reveal the temporal and cultural dimensions of the continuities that essentialists take for granted. Jonathan Katz explains this eloquently in his pioneering *Gay American History:*

I will be pleased if this book helps to revolutionize the traditional concept of homosexuality. This concept is so profoundly ahistorical that the very existence of Gay history may be met with disbelief. The common image of the homosexual has been a figure divorced from any temporal-social context. The concept of homosexuality must be historicized. Ancient Greek pederasty, contemporary homosexual "marriages" and lesbian-feminist partnerships all differ radically. Beyond the most obvious fact that homosexual relations involve persons of the same gender, and include feelings as well as acts, there is no such thing as homosexuality in general, only particular historical forms of homosexuality. There is no evidence for the assumption that certain traits have universally characterized homosexual (or heterosexual) relations throughout history. The problem of the historical researcher is thus to study and establish the character and meaning of each varied manifestation of same-sex relations within a specific time and society.[8]

In this essay we want to further the scope of social constructionist research by addressing ourselves to the subject of butch-fem roles: are they indeed constant in community culture and individual identity, and therefore subject to a fixed biological or psychological interpretation, or do they need to be seen in the total social context of a developing lesbian community? After providing some background information for our research, we will document the meaning of roles for this community and show how the specific content of roles has changed over time. We will then look at how our narrators came to their role identities and consider their understanding of lesbianism as inborn or a product of social forces.

Lesbian communities began to develop in the large industrial centers of Europe and America at the turn of the century; Buffalo was no exception.[9] Our research has positively identified an upper-class community in Buffalo during the 1920s and black and white working-class communities during the 1930s, and it suggests that these communities existed even earlier. (This difference in dates is more a reflection of the sources available for learning about each community than of age. Our data on the upper-class women come from articles about them in local newspapers, while our information on the working-class women comes primarily from their own testimonies, and therefore can go only as far back as their ages and memories permit.[10]) Our research has focused on working-class lesbians from 1930 to 1965, because we wanted to check our hunch that their consciousness, culture, and social life were formative in the emergence of the gay liberation movement of the 1960s.[11] In this article we will treat the working-class lesbian community as a unified whole, even though it consisted of separate black and white communities that overlapped only to a limited degree, and we will use material from both black and white women. Over nine years we have collected oral histories from forty-five narrators, including nine women of color, all of whom were participants in this community at some time, and some of whom were leaders. Our narrators' stories were much richer than we had ever imagined and confirmed our suspicions about their role in shaping lesbian history and politics.

Our primary concern has been to document the political and social evolution of this working-class lesbian community, looking at both its internal dynamics and its response to the changing nature of oppression. During this period the community existed predominantly in bars, since these were the only places where people could gather publicly, break the isolation of lesbian life, and develop both friendships and lover relationships. The oppressive tenor of the times is captured in a narrator's memory of what her older sister, who was already a lesbian, said to her upon learning that she was going to join the life in the early 1950s. They had gone to an after-hours club together in New York City, and a friend of her sister asked our narrator to dance. After two or three dances our narrator returned to the table and noticed that her sister was crying. When she asked why, her sister said:

"I don't like the way you're looking around here. This isn't the life for you." I said, "If it's good enough for you why isn't it good enough for me?" My sister replied, "Look around at all these people that are laughing, joking, they're having a ball—you think they are. Inside they're being ripped apart. Do you know what it's like to live this kind of life? Every day when you get out of bed, before your feet hit the floor, you've gotta say to yourself, come on, get up, you may get smacked right in the face again today, some way, somehow. . . . If you can get up everyday not knowing what this day's gonna bring, whether your heart's gonna be ripped out, whether you're gonna be ridiculed, or whether people are gonna be nice to you or spit in your face, if you can face living that way, day in and day out, then you belong here; if you can't . . . get the hell out."[12]

Although the risks involved in coming together were great, lesbians persevered and began to forge a community with a rich culture and a strong sense of solidarity and pride.[13]

Despite the fact that butch-fem roles were prominent in our narrators' memories, we at first viewed them as peripheral to the growth and development of the community. Only after several years of study did we come to understand that we could not even conceive of the transformation of the community without analyzing them. They were a complex phenomenon that pervaded all aspects of community life.[14] These roles had two dimensions: First, they constituted a code of personal behavior, particularly in the areas of image and sexuality. Butches affected a masculine style, while fems appeared characteristically female. Butch and fem also complemented one another in an erotic system in which the butch was expected to be both the doer and the giver; the fem's passion was the butch's fulfillment.[15] Second, butch-fem roles were what we call a social imperative. They were the organizing principle for this community's relation to the outside world and for its members' relationships with one another. The presence of the butch with her distinctive dress and mannerism, or the butch-fem couple, announced lesbianism to the public. The butch, in her willingness to affirm who she was and take the consequences, was the primary indicator of lesbianism to the heterosexual world. Her aggressive style set the tone of resistance to lesbian oppression. In addition, butch-fem roles established the guidelines for forming love relationships and friendships. Two butches could be friends but never lovers; the same was true for two fems. Given this social dimension of butch-fem roles, whether her identity felt like a natural expression of self or something falsely imposed, a lesbian needed to adopt a role to participate comfortably in the community and receive its benefits.

This social dimension of roles helps to explain their tenacity. But why should the opposition of masculine and feminine be woven into lesbian culture and become a fundamental organizing principle? Modern lesbian culture developed in the context of the late nineteenth and early twentieth century when elaborate hierarchical distinctions were made between the sexes, and gender was a fundamental organizing principle of cultural life. Given the nineteenth-century polarization of masculinity and femininity, Jonathan Katz argues, one of the few ways for women to achieve independence in work and travel and to escape passivity was to "pass" as men.[16] In a similar vein, Jeffrey Weeks holds that the adoption of male images by lesbians at the turn of the century broke through women's and lesbians' invisibility, a necessity if lesbians were to become part of public life.[17] Expanding this approach, Esther Newton situates the adoption of male imagery in the context of the New Woman's search for an independent life, and delineates how male imagery helped to break through nineteenth-century assumptions about the sexless nature of women and to introduce overt sexuality into women's relationships with one another.[18]

We agree with these interpretations and modify them for the conditions of the 1930s, 1940s, and 1950s. During this period an effective way for the lesbian community to express the challenge presented by its affirmation of women's sexual love of women was to manipulate the basic ingredient of patriarchy—the hierarchical distinction between male and female. Butch-fem couples flew in the face of convention and outraged society by usurping male privilege in appearance and sexuality. At a time when the community was developing solidarity and consciousness, but had not yet formed lesbian political groups, butch-fem roles were the only structure for organizing against heterosexual dominance.[19] In a sense they were a prepolitical form of resistance.[20]

The social imperative of butch-fem roles is most apparent in the evolution of lesbian bar culture even in the short period from 1930 to 1965. During the forties lesbian bar life began to flourish in Buffalo, developing a rich culture and consciousness of kind. World War II established an atmosphere where women could easily go out alone, thereby creating more space for the lesbian community. This growth in community culture and social life, in conjunction with the repression of the McCarthy era, some of which was directed specifically against homosexuals and lesbians, created a new element of defiance. Bar lesbians in the fifties went even further in asserting their identities than those in the forties and aggressively fought for the right to be themselves. Their bold rebelliousness generated the kind of consciousness that made gay liberation possible.

Butch-fem roles were the key element in this transformation of the community's stance toward the straight world. In the forties butches and butch-fem couples endured the harassment they received from being obvious lesbians with a strategy of passive resistance similar to that of "turning the other cheek." But in the fifties one segment of the community, the street dykes, aggressively fought back when provoked, defending their relationships and community standards.

Even right now it's very easy for the kids coming out now, but back then it wasn't, and I've been beaten up, I've been hit by guys. And I've fought back; sometimes I won; sometimes I lost. But I wasn't fighting to prove that I was big and bad and tough and wanted to be a man. I was fighting to survive. And I just can't see it. Things back then were horrible and I think that because I fought like a man to survive I made it somehow easier for the kids coming out today. I did all their fighting for them. I'm not a rich person. I don't even have a lot of money; I don't even have a little money. I would have nothing to leave anybody in this world, but I have that that I can leave to the kids who are coming out now, who will come out into the future. That I left them a better place to come out into. And that's all I have to offer, to leave them. But I wouldn't deny it. Even though I was getting my brains beaten up I would never stand up and say, " 'No don't hit me. I'm not gay; I'm not gay." I wouldn't do that. I was maybe stupid and proud, but they'd come up and say, "Are you gay?" And I'd say, "Yes I am." Pow, they'd hit you. For no reason at all. It was silly and it was ridiculous, and I took my beatings and I survived it.

(By acknowledging the different responses to maltreatment in the 1940s and 1950s, we do not mean to imply that the fifties butch was braver or more courageous than her predecessors. Rather we argue that each kind of butch behavior was appropriate for the general situation in the society at large, and for internal developments in the community itself. All stages of lesbian history required courage, initiative, and persistence.)

Our narrators' memories of their first impression of the bars capture vividly the differences between the butch roles in the 1940s and the 1950s. One narrator who went to Ralph Martin's, a popular lesbian and gay bar of the forties, remembers the butches she met there with affection:

And the butches were very butchie, but they were gentle, they were a gentle group. I was only fifteen when I met a lot of these real real machos, but they were gentle. Of course I had hair down to my rear end when I really went to my first club, and they accepted me, there was nothing where they . . . Hey, you got long hair, you don't belong in our group, something like that you know. They just had respect for me and I did for them.

In the fifties this mode of behavior was completely replaced by a tough image. One narrator remembers an influential conversation with two new friends shortly after entering the bars:

They were two of the, I guess, the star dykes around town, and I remember one time the three of us were together, we must have been standing at the bar, because I remember when (one) pounded her fist on the bar or table, we were talking about being gay, and she said,

"If you want to be butch you gotta be rough, tough, and ready," boom! She pounded her fist on the bar. And well, it scared me, I didn't know if I could measure up to all of that but I figured I would have to try 'cause I knew I was a butch, I knew that's what I was.

Other changes occurred in butch-fem roles that correlated with the move toward public defiance. As suggested by the quotations, the forties community adamantly refused to instruct newcomers, while the fifties community reached out to them and helped them learn their butch role. One narrator remembers a younger butch who in the early forties kept asking her questions. She always told her, "I will not tell you anything. Anything you find out will be on your own. Do what you have to do." In contrast all of our narrators who entered the bars in the fifties remember either reaching out to someone or someone reaching out to them: "With new butches you [tried] to befriend them. It ain't easy bein' alone. . . . Today it's a little more difficult. Someone walks into a bar and they're totally ignored. Before . . . you wanted to take them in for their own protection."

At the same time that the fifties community accepted the responsibility of instructing newcomers, it became less tolerant of deviance in butch-fem roles, another change from the 1940s. In the forties lesbians belonged to a role-identified community that tolerated the small number who didn't conform to roles and allowed much latitude in the way people expressed their role identity. One of our narrators said of the forties, "At that time almost everyone was in roles. For at least ninety-five percent there was no mistaking." Then she wondered out loud, "Did we do it to them, push people into roles?" She answered herself, "No they preferred it that way, we didn't do it." By the fifties those who did not conform could not be in the community. As one narrator, a well respected butch of the late fifties, remembers:

Well, you had to be [into roles]. If you weren't, people wouldn't associate with you . . . You had to be one or the other or you just couldn't hang around. There was no being versatile or saying, "Well, I'm either one. I'm just homosexual or lesbian." You know, they didn't even talk about that. It was basically a man-woman relationship. . . . You had to play your role.

Although this rigidification paralleled what was happening in the larger society, it cannot be interpreted simply as imitative. The increasingly defiant stand of the community in relation to the heterosexual world increased the pressure and strain associated with butch-fem roles and hence produced a greater concern with rules and appropriate behavior. Butches had to know how to be tough and how to handle themselves in a fight. If they didn't, they could be in great danger.

Our analysis that the powerful continuity of butch-fem roles derives from their contribution to lesbian social organization, not the inherent biological or psychological makeup of every lesbian, is also supported by our narrators' varied experiences in developing their role identities. Although some narrators knew their identity from an early age, many had to develop an identity as part of the community. Two of our butch narrators who found the bars in the thirties remember being sure of their roles as butches before finding a gay community. One remembers that she was always more masculine. She looked that way and had that air about her. The other gives many examples of her tendencies toward being butch in early life. She remembers reveling in the boyish shoes her father made her wear because she was so hard on her shoes and related a humorous tale of getting her first short hair cut in the thirties:

Then the boy's bob came out. My father took me to a barber he knew, and he got carried away and was telling the guy how to cut it up around the ears. My mother screamed, "What happened to your hair?" [Then] I used to take a scissors into the bathroom and cut my hair, and my mother would say, "How come your hair doesn't grow?" I would say, "Gee, I don't know!"

This same narrator couldn't remember a time when she wasn't "after the girls. . . . A father caught me rubbing against his daughter, standing on the running board of the car. I was sent home and forbidden to play with the girl again." When we asked if she was consciously initiating sexual contact, even though she was young at the time, she responded, "Definitely." These two women did not have to learn a role identity when they entered the bars but simply learned appropriate ways to develop and express their already established identity.

Our third narrator who came out in the thirties, however, does not emphasize her early butch identity, but rather the quest involved in finding a role. "If you're in gay life, you're in gay life, whichever—if you want to play the fem or be the butch, you certainly have to go out and find it, one way or the other, what part you are going to play." This captures the experience of those who came to the lesbian community without knowing their role identity. Since butch-fem was built on the opposition of masculine and feminine characteristics, it was harder for a fem to realize a distinctive identity while growing up in the context of customary expectations of feminine behavior. In addition, a significant portion of butch narrators also were not conscious of a role identity before entering the community. One narrator recalls that she went to her first bar with her boyfriend in the 1940s, not knowing what to expect and certainly with no preconceived idea of a butch identity. She learned from the community itself that she was butch, as is evident in her description of her first dance:

I never danced, never, not even at proms. I danced, let's face it, but I didn't follow good; so I got out and it was just a natural thing. I grabbed her and I led. She was tiny and cute, and she says, "You're gay." I says, "Oh yeh, I'm happy," and I meant it. It was sincere. She thought I was pulling her leg. And of course you're always going to try to act older because of where you are. And she said, "No," she said, "I knew you were a butch when you walked in the door. I don't care if you've got long hair or what." And I said, "Oh, I'm engaged to be married." She said, "I don't care if you're engaged, got long hair, I know you're a gay butch." I says, "Oh, no. I'm going, Oh God." Well, we finished our dance and I joined her group.

We have much more information on the complex process of creating role identity for women who entered the bars in the fifties, because we have been able to interview many more. Like their predecessors, some of our narrators knew they were butch from an early age and simply had to learn appropriate butch behavior upon entering the community:

Nine years old, I knew [I was a stud]. I used to beat up boys; girls—I would just treat them like little doll babies. But I never cared for a doll. . . . I had two brothers and a sister and my younger brother used to get cap pistols, trucks and things, I got dolls. . . . I used to beat him up and take his trucks and cap pistols and give him my dolls.

Another common memory of butch narrators who spent their childhoods in the forties is feeling comfortable in boys' clothes at an early age. One narrator remembers, ''I was under ten when I was wearing [my brother's] clothes when nobody was around. I always felt that I was in drag in women's clothing even as a child.'' This same narrator had powerful fantasies of being a cowboy:

I was a little chubby . . . so when I was in fifth grade . . . I used to have this fantasy that I was a cowboy. This excess weight I had was just sort of like props that I had on my body, and when I would leave the classroom I'd take off this excess weight and put on my cowboy suit and get on my horse and ride away.

Cowboy fantasies were common for young lesbians of this period. Another narrator who was called ''Tom'' for Tomboy, from about age six or seven, always envisioned herself as the heroic Roy Rogers. After school she would race home, take off her girl's clothes, and don her cowboy outfit. ''I was Roy Rogers.''

The clarity and forcefulness of these women's perceptions of their butch identities from an early age are striking, but their experiences were not those of all butch lesbians. Other narrators did not know their identities until they entered the community, and still others had difficulty finding the appropriate role for themselves. In some cases people came out one way and then changed their identification. One narrator remembers with humor that her mother had more insight into her developing role identity than she herself did:

She [my second relationship] was on the masculine side but I was very attracted to her, and so I naturally took the feminine approach. We started to see each other and then we started to go together and we really loved each other but we weren't making it, we were constantly hassling and fighting and arguing. And I talked to my mother and said, ''Gee I don't know what it is. I really like her'' . . . And my mother said, ''Maybe you're not happy in the way you're living your life with her.'' I said, ''What do you mean?'' She said—my mother would get embarrassed when she tried to explain things in daylight—and she said, ''Before you met [Joan] you used to dress a little different, you wore slacks and that. Now you're in dresses all the time and you put makeup on. You don't seem like you're happy. Maybe you should go back to what you were and let her be a little more feminine.'' I kind of thought about that and I talked it over with this girl, and do you know that that relationship lasted for six years?

Although lesbians only rarely switched roles during a relationship, it was common for people to change their roles after their first relationships. Such a change was associated with coming out and finding your place in the community and your sexual preferences. Coming out fem and then becoming butch was the most usual direction of this early change. There was a common saying among butches in the lesbian community, "Today's love affair is tomorrow's competition." One butch narrator remembers the pain that fems could cause by switching roles, "especially when they come back and take the girl you are with away. The only way she can get at you is that way, and it works; and then you're alone." Another narrator explains this switching as due not only to inexperience, but to the kind of vulnerability required of fems:

Some would start out real fem and the minute they got hurt by a butch . . . the next time you'd see them they'd be real butchie . . . They'd be dressed up really butchie . . . Usually the butches broke up with them. They'd start getting really butchie too. I don't know if they think butch is better.

Changing of roles even occurred after a person had been out a long time:

I've seen a lot of girls come out and be fem and wind up butch. I've seen a lot of girls that were butch turn fem . . . a lot, a whole lot. Sometimes it shocks me. Me, I could never do that. To say, well I'm gonna turn a fem, and go out with a man, or I'm gonna turn a fem and just be that. No, I couldn't do that. I've been livin' the way I am too long. But I've seen a lot do it. I've seen a lot of girls who I wouldn't even believe they could switch, turn from one side to the other.

This phenomenon of switching indicates both the power and social nature of roles. A lesbian who was not sure of her role could not simply explore. She had to take a role, and if she was not comfortable in one, then she could take the other. For many lesbians, roles had to be learned and involved an element of conscious choice. One fem who was—and still is—very famous for her beauty and attractiveness, emphasizes this element of conscious choice when explaining what she feels determines a person's role: "I don't know how they get their role because, I think it's a matter of choice, what they feel like they want to do, I suppose. It's hard to say. Because sometime, I feel like I might want to turn stud. Really!"

In addition to those who switched roles, this community also had members who were never completely comfortable in roles, even though they appeared to adapt.

I think on the surface I identified . . . when I was involved in the gay community, on the surface, you know, you either had to be butch or fem. And I was always the, I guess you'd say, the butch appearing one—back to the days when DA haircuts were popular.[21]

But this woman did a lot of joking about roles even at a time when rules were strict and serious:

Thinking back I can remember one of the things I used to say, people would say, "Are you butch or are you fem?" And I used to say, "Well, the only difference to me between the butch or a fem is when you get up on the dance floor so you don't have to argue who's going to lead." And I have another saying since then: "My biggest decision when I get up every morning is whether to be an aggressive fem or a nelly butch."

Although the women we interviewed who were uncomfortable in roles were not the majority of this community, a surprising number expressed some degree of discomfort. The fact that they adapted just enough to get by, is yet another confirmation that roles are not an intrinsic part of lesbians' biological or psychological makeup, but are a fundamental organizing principle of participation in the community.

In keeping with our narrators' varied experiences in finding their role identities, the community has not had, nor does it now have, a hegemonic view about what constitutes a true lesbian. Many narrators see the butch lesbian as the true lesbian. Other narrators consider anyone who stays with women, and is part of the community, a lesbian. Two of our butch narrators who came out in the thirties disagree with one another on the subject, and their argument, which they said was quite common among members of the community in the past, eloquently explores the central issues.

During the interview Leslie took the position that only butches are lesbians. She is a lesbian [butch] and is never attracted to another like herself. Rather, she is always attracted to a more feminine type of person. Arden, on the other hand, thought that all women who stay with women are lesbians, butch or fem, as long as they don't flip back and forth between women and men. Each tried to convince the other of the rightness of her position but neither was successful. Leslie asked Arden about two women who had been Arden's instructors in sex. These women had been married; didn't Arden consider them bisexual? Arden: "No, they didn't go back and forth. Once they were in the crowd they stayed. It was good fun and they liked it." The friends then discussed the women who had started seeing lesbians during the war while their husbands were away. Some of these women went back and forth, while others did not. Leslie again did not agree with Arden that those who stayed with women were lesbians. A final argument revolved around the identity of Ramona, a past lover of Leslie's, who was very feminine and had never been with a man. Arden saw her as a lesbian while Leslie did not. Leslie believed that her own involvement with sixteen-year-old Ramona had indelibly influenced the impressionable young woman, who might not otherwise have pursued relationships with women. It was impossible for the two friends to come to an agreement.

At another interview Leslie and Arden continued their disagreement on a different level. Leslie emphasized how the pressures of heterosexual life might influence a non-lesbian: "Women of all kinds get involved in the fun of gay life. They like the fun and freedom of gay life, and it has nothing to do with sexual preference." Arden countered, underlining the forces that encouraged lesbians to pursue heterosexual marriage: "But also there is another side. I think that there were many women who liked being with women, who preferred women, but who get the Mrs. because they wanted that status.''

The similarity of Leslie's position to that of the Kinsey reports, which were published after she came of age, is quite striking.[22] Leslie is using a continuum model in which there are ''true lesbians'' who only have sex with women, and fems whom she considers bisexuals, who can have sex with either men or women. In fact she believes that the majority of the world is bisexual. In addition her idea that only butches are true lesbians bears a striking similarity to early medical theories.[23] Arden, on the other hand, has the incipient analysis of a social constructionist. In her view, if women spend time in the lesbian community and consider themselves lesbians, they are lesbians, whether they are butch or fem. Furthermore, even though they hold these differing views about the nature of lesbianism, both women are cognizant of the social forces that influence a woman to participate in either the lesbian or heterosexual world.

In the fifties community similar disagreements existed. ''There was always that . . . jealousy. If you'd see [a fem] looking at a man, you'd think, 'What are you looking at him for?' You couldn't think of them as a lesbian—a lesbian wouldn't do that.'' When pressed further this narrator said, ''They're not as true as we are. I bet mostly all of the old [butches] feel that way.'' And to our surprise, some fems of that period concurred with this opinion. In their view, because they weren't the initiators, or because they didn't frequently make love to another woman, they weren't true lesbians. However, some fems disagreed. One fem who came out in the fifties, and left the life for sixteen years of marriage beginning in the early sixties, felt that she was a lesbian during the fifties when she moved with the crowd and is a lesbian again today.

Disagreements about what created a true lesbian went beyond this one issue of whether butches and fems were both lesbians. Women in the community also disagreed about the role of biology. Those who came to their butch identity at an early age tend to attribute it to physiological causes. Others claim that they don't know what ultimately caused their lesbianism. One respected butch humorously relates her opinion of how she became a lesbian:

I don't know. You know people ask me . . . when I tell them I've been gay all my life . . . ''How did you get to be gay all your life?'' And I tell them the story. I say, ''Well you see, the way it was with me is when I was born the doctor was so busy with my mother, it was a hard birth for her, . . . that it was the nurse that slapped my ass to bring that first breath of life into me. And I liked the touch of that feminine hand so much that I've been gay ever since.''

In conclusion, our research suggests that the reproduction of butch-fem roles involves complex issues of psychosocial identity as well as community instruction and pressure, and that the power and continuity of roles derive in part from their centrality in organizing lesbian relations with the straight world. We argue that an analysis of butch-fem roles that is located in the context of the growth and development of a specific community has more explanatory power than essentialism. In

Buffalo, as lesbians moved from a situation of relative isolation toward the political stance of the homophile and gay liberation movements, the content and meaning of butch-fem roles changed from that of building culture and community to confronting heterosexual society and fighting for dignity and respect. Some lesbians knew their role identity before entering the community, while others had to learn it, and all had to learn the content of butch-fem roles for the Buffalo community at the particular time they entered. Many members of the community adhered to essentialist explanations of their situation. This echoed essentialism in the dominant culture and provided for many a supportive sense of inescapable identity. However, others did not find essentialism a good description of their own experiences or of the variety of ways women participated in the community. They generated, from the social relations of their lives, alternative explanations that approached those of present day social constructionists.

Notes

Acknowledgments: The original version of this paper was written for the International Scientific Conference on Gay and Lesbian Studies, "Homosexuality, Which Homosexuality?" at the Free University of Amsterdam. We want to thank the conference organizing committee for granting permission to publish the paper in this volume, especially since the conference is publishing its own proceedings. We thank Christina Simmons and Kathy Peiss for their careful reading of this chapter, and helpful suggestions for revisions. We also thank Lisa Duggan, Joan Nestle, Bobbi Prebis, and David Schneider for their general support of our work and the reading of a draft of this essay.

1. See, for instance, Del Martin and Phyllis Lyon, *Lesbian/Woman* (New York: 1972); Audre Lorde, "Tar Beach," *Conditions* no. 5 (1979): 34–47; Joan Nestle, "Butch-Fem Relationships, Sexual Courage in the 1950s," *Heresies* 12 (1981): 21–24; John D'Emilio, *Sexual Politics, Sexual Communities: The Making of a Homosexual Minority in the United States, 1940–1970* (Chicago: 1983); Esther Newton, "The Mythic Mannish Lesbian: Radclyffe Hall and the New Woman," *Signs* 9 (Summer 1984): 557–75. Butch-fem roles are also apparent in twentieth-century novels and pulp fiction. For an example of the former, see, for instance, Gale Wilhelm, *We Too Are Drifting* (New York: 1935); and of the latter, Ann Bannon, *Beebo Brinker* (Greenwich, Conn.: 1962).

2. Our research is part of the work of the Buffalo Women's Oral History Project, founded in 1978 with three goals: (1) to produce a comprehensive, written history of the lesbian community in Buffalo, New York, using as its major source oral histories of lesbians who came out before 1970; (2) to create and index an archive of oral history tapes, written interviews, and supplementary materials; and (3) to give this history back to the community from which it derives. Madeline Davis and Elizabeth Lapovsky Kennedy are the directors of the project. Avra Michelson was an active member from 1978 to 1981. Wanda Edwards has been an intermittent member of the project since 1981, particularly in regard to research on the black lesbian community and on racism in the white lesbian community.

3. For a helpful overview of essentialist positions, see Diane Richardson, "The Dilemma of Essentiality in Homosexual Theory," *Journal of Homosexuality* 9 (Winter 1983): 79–90.

4. For a helpful discussion of this nineteenth- and early twentieth-century literature, see George Chauncey, Jr., "From Sexual Inversion to Homosexuality: The Changing Medical Conceptualization of Female 'Deviance,' " in this volume; and Newton, "The Mythic Mannish Lesbian," 565–68.

5. It is with hesitation that we call these psychological theories essentialist. Can there be an essentialist approach other than one that attributes homosexuality to genetic factors? Freudian theory certainly has the potential to explain the construction of homosexual identity in the context of social and cultural forces. But until recently it has only rarely been used in this way. Rather, most psychiatrists have worked with a model that dichotomized heterosexual and homosexual behavior and considered the former as normal and the latter as pathological. Carroll Smith-Rosenberg makes this point in her article,

"The Female World of Love and Ritual: Relations Between Women in Nineteenth-Century America," *Signs* 1 (Autumn 1973): 2–28. For an article that delineates some of the complex factors distinguishing an essentialist approach from a social constructionist approach and suggests some confusion in our current thinking about these distinctions, see Steven Epstein, "Gay Politics, Ethnic Identity: The Limits of Social Constructionism," *Socialist Review* 93/94 (May–August 1987): 9–56.

6. Radclyffe Hall, *The Well of Loneliness* (1928; rpt. London: 1974). For useful discussions of the novel's contribution to homosexual resistance, see Jonathan Katz, *Gay American History: Lesbians and Gay Men in the U.S.A.* (New York: 1976), 397–405; and Jeffrey Weeks, *Coming Out: Homosexual Politics in Britain, From the Nineteenth Century to the Present* (London: 1977) 107–11.

7. The dominant ideas about homosexuality are not monolithic; contradictory ideas exist alongside one another. The idea that homosexuality is a sickness, or a moral flaw, and can spread among people is also prevalent. The different ideas about homosexuality can be more or less homophobic depending on the context—the time period or the social group.

8. Katz, *Gay American History,* 6–7.

9. For a discussion of the conditions that might give rise to lesbian communities at this time, see Ann Ferguson, "Patriarchy, Sexual Identity, and the Sexual Revolution," *Signs* 7 (Autumn 1981): 158–72. The earliest references to lesbian bar communities appear in French fiction, Emile Zola's *Nana* (1880), and Guy du Maupassant's "Paul's Mistress" (1881). For a discussion of these sources, albeit a negative one, see Lillian Faderman, *Surpassing the Love of Men: Romantic Friendship and Love Between Women from the Renaissance to the Present* (New York: 1981), 282–84. For commentary on early twentieth-century lesbian communities, see Gayle Rubin's introduction to *A Woman Appeared to Me,* by Renée Vivien (Nevada: 1976), iii–xxvii; Vern Bullough and Bonnie Bullough, "Lesbianism in the 1920s and 1930s: A Newfound Study," *Signs* 2 (Summer 1977): 895–904; and Eric Garber, "'Tain't Nobody's Business: Homosexuality in Harlem in the 1920s," *The Advocate* no. 342 (May 1982): 39–43.

10. One of our narrators gave us an upper-class woman's obituary she had saved, which said that this woman was survived by a lifelong companion. From this lead we found other obituaries and learned of a group of women who had been active in business and the arts in the 1920s and 1930s. A copy of these articles is on file at the Lesbian Herstory Archives, P.O. Box 1258, New York, N.Y. 10016.

11. This hypothesis was shaped by our personal contact with Buffalo lesbians who came out in the 1940s and 1950s, and by discussion with grassroots gay and lesbian history projects around the country, in particular, the San Francisco Lesbian and Gay History Project, the Boston Area Gay and Lesbian History Project, and the Lesbian Herstory Archives. In addition we were influenced by the early social constructionist work in lesbian and gay history. See, in particular, Katz, *Gay American History;* Rubin, "Introduction" to *A Woman Appeared to Me,* Vivien; and Weeks, *Coming Out.* We want to thank all these people who have been inspirational to our work.

12. All quotations are taken from the oral histories collected for this project between 1978 and 1986.

13. For further discussion of Buffalo bar life and the development of the lesbian community, see Madeline Davis, Elizabeth Lapovsky Kennedy, and Avra Michelson, "Buffalo Lesbian Bars in the Fifties," paper presented at the National Women's Studies Association, Bloomington, Ind., May 1980, and "Buffalo Lesbian Bars: 1930–1960," paper presented at the Fifth Berkshire Conference on the History of Women, Vassar College, Poughkeepsie, N.Y., June 1981. Both papers are on file at the Lesbian Herstory Archives. We are currently rewriting them for our monograph *Boots of Leather, Slippers of Gold: The History of a Lesbian Community.*

14. For a detailed discussion of our research on butch-fem roles, see Madeline Davis and Elizabeth (Liz) Lapovsky Kennedy, "Butch/fem Roles in the Buffalo Lesbian Community: 1940–1960," paper presented at the Gay Academic Union Conference, Chicago, October 1982. This paper is on file at the Lesbian Herstory Archives.

15. For additional information on butch-fem roles and sexuality in the Buffalo lesbian community, see Madeline Davis and Elizabeth Lapovsky Kennedy, "Oral History and the Study of Sexuality in the Lesbian Community: Buffalo, New York, 1940–1960," *Feminist Studies* 12 (Spring 1986): 7–26.

16. Katz, *Gay American History,* 209–11.

17. Weeks, *Coming Out,* 89, and *Sex, Politics and Society: The Regulation of Sexuality Since 1800* (London: 1981), 115–17.

18. Newton, "The Mythic Mannish Lesbian."

19. We do not mean to relegate butch-fem roles to history. They are unquestionably meaningful for a number of lesbians today. This analytical framework explains why they continue today, as well as alerts us to expect that their current meaning is somewhat different from twenty years ago.

20. The concept of prepolitical comes from Eric Hobsbawm, *Primitive Rebels: Studies in Archaic Forms of Social Movement in the Nineteenth and Twentieth Centuries* (New York: 1959), 2.

21. The DA—the letters stand for duck's ass—was a popular hairdo for working-class men and butches during the 1950s. All side hair was combed back and joined the back hair in a manner resembling the layered feathers of a duck's tail, hence the name. Pomade was used to hold the hair in place and give a sleek appearance.

22. Alfred Kinsey, Wardell B. Pomeroy, Clyde E. Martin, Paul H. Gebhard, *Sexual Behavior in the Human Female* (1953; rpt. New York: 1965), 468–76.

23. She could have been exposed to these ideas through Hall's *The Well of Loneliness*, which she had read.

15

A Feminist Redefinition of Rape and Sexual Assault: Historical Foundations and Change

Patricia Donat and John D'Emilio

The meanings of sexual assault and women's sexuality have changed significantly since the colonial period. At that time, women were valued for their sexual purity and were viewed as the center of the family. Sexual intercourse was acceptable only within marriage for the purpose of procreation. If a woman engaged in sex outside of marriage, even against her will, she was considered a "fallen" woman and was often blamed for her own victimization. With the feminist movement of the 1960s, rape was reconceptualized as a mechanism for maintaining male control and domination, a violent means of inducing fear in women and reinforcing their subordination to men. This reconceptualization has made a clear difference in the way our culture defines and understands sexual assault, but much still needs to change.

The issues of rape and sexual assault have been major concerns of the feminist movement since its revival in the late 1960s. Because of the work of feminists, the contemporary understanding of rape and sexual assault, and the social response to sexual violence, have undergone significant revision. This paper examines the feminist response to traditional conceptualizations of rape and the impact it has had. It begins by presenting some historical background to set a context for understanding more recent events.

The Colonial Era

During the colonial period, settlers in the English colonies were influenced strongly by the church, which prescribed the behavior of its congregation. The family was defined as the central unit in society and sex roles were differentiated rigidly. Men were dominant and women were submissive. The woman was regarded "not as a person . . . but as a sexual 'type'—an inferior, a receptacle, . . . or a simple answer to his needs" (Koehler, 1980, p. 93). Sexuality was channeled into marriage for the procreation of legitimate offspring. Nonmarital sexual intercourse was immoral, an offense against both family and community (D'Emilio & Freedman, 1988).

In order to regulate deviance, the church, courts, and community joined to monitor private sexual behavior and to limit sexual expression to marriage. Colonial society held the entire community responsible for upholding morality, and sexual crimes were punished severely. Women bore the heaviest responsibility for regulating premarital sexual contact. "Church and society dealt more harshly with women . . . [because] female chastity and fidelity assured men of the legitimacy of their children" (D'Emilio & Freedman, 1988). The integrity of the family was critical to the development of community and was guarded with care. For men, the integrity of the family rested on female purity and monogamy.

A woman's value within society was based on her ability to marry and to produce legitimate heirs. The ability to attract a spouse was influenced by the woman's perceived purity. The rape of a virgin was considered a crime against the father of the raped woman rather than against the woman herself. A raped woman could not expect to marry into a respectable family and might very well remain the economic liability of the father.

During the colonial period, the rape cases most likely to come to court were those in which the perpetrator was from a lower social class than the victim or in which the victim was a married woman who physically resisted. "When men of the lower order raped women of a higher social standing, they threatened the prerogatives of other men" (Lindemann, 1984, p. 81).

Women were dependent on the courts and community (i.e., men) for their protection. In order to ensure her safety, a woman who was sexually attacked needed to comply with male standards for her behavior by proving her nonconsent through physical and verbal resistance, and through immediate disclosure of the attack to both family and neighbors. Proof of nonconsent was necessary to verify that the woman had not voluntarily engaged in sexual acts outside of marriage. If a woman could not prove nonconsent, she might be punished for the assault (D'Emilio & Freedman, 1988). Rape was therefore "an expression of male control over women, regulated by law in a way that serves the men who hold political power more than it protects women" (Lindemann, 1984, p. 81).

The 19th Century

Toward the end of the 18th century, sexual meanings began to change. Sexuality no longer was tied so closely to reproductive intentions, and more emphasis was placed on courtship and individual choice rather than on community and family control. The subsequent decline in traditional church and state regulation of morality loosened constraints on nonmarital sex.

During the 19th century, young women from the countryside and from immigrant families began to enter the paid work force and earn their livings outside the family household. Patriarchal controls over women's time, behavior, and sexuality weakened (Stansell, 1986). With increased freedom, however, also came increased vulnerability. Previously, "courtship was one part of a system of barter between the sexes, in which a woman traded sexual favors for a man's promise to marry. Premarital intercourse then became a token of betrothal'' (Stansell, 1986, p. 87). Women, however, no longer could assume that a pregnancy would lead to marriage.

Female virtue continued to be important for finding a spouse. In the 19th century women were viewed as pure and virtuous by nature, and as disinterested in sex. Women of all classes were expected to use their natural purity and superior morality to control men's innate lust. The impure woman threatened the delicate moral balance and suggested the ''social disintegration that sexuality symbolized'' (Freedman, 1981, p. 20). A woman who engaged in sexual intercourse, even against her will, was considered to be depraved—a ''fallen'' woman—and was often blamed for the man's crime and socially stigmatized as a result of the attack. ''As woman falls from a higher point of perfection, so she sinks to a profounder depth of misery than man'' (Freedman, 1981, p. 18).

The 20th Century

During the 20th century, the writings of Sigmund Freud and other psychologists and sexologists provided the foundation for reconceptualizing sexual behavior and categorizing sexual deviations. One emerging concern was an interest in understanding the causes of sexual aggression. Many hypotheses were developed, but most theories included the belief that rape was a perversion and that rapists were mentally ill (Amir, 1971). One theory of sexual aggression suggested that the rapist's behavior was the result of socialization by a strong maternal figure and a weak paternal figure. Another theory proposed that the rapist's behavior was the result of a defective superego that left the individual unable to control his sexual and aggressive impulses. Therefore, the rapist was considered to have a ''character disorder'' and was classified as a ''sick'' individual. Other theories to explain the rapist's behavior included castration fears, feelings of sexual inferiority and inadequacy, homosexual tendencies, organic factors, and mental deficiencies (Amir, 1971). All of these theories reduced the rapist's responsibility for his actions since he was considered unable to control his pathological impulses. In other words, rape was reconceptualized from the perpetrator's point of view. The focus was on understanding the plight of the man, not the woman. Her victimization was simply a by-product of his pathology.

During the 1930s, the public increasingly became interested in sex crimes committed by men against women. In 1937, the *New York Times* created a new index category of sex crimes, which included 143 articles published that year (Freedman, 1989). Due to the influence of psychoanalytic theories, sex offenders began to be considered more as deviants than as criminals. Between 1935 and 1965, several state commissions to investigate sex crimes were formed; in many places, authority for the treatment and rehabilitation of the sex offender shifted away from the penal system and toward the mental health system (Freedman, 1989). Psychiatrists began to carry more influence concerning treatment of the sex offender. The label ''sexual psychopath'' was used to describe the violent male offender who was unable to control his sexual impulses and attacked the object of his frustrated desires. Thus rape was conceptualized primarily as an act of sex rather than an act of violence.

As awareness of sex crimes increased, public concern also escalated. Several "sex psychopath laws" were passed that permitted offenders to receive indefinite commitment to state mental hospitals rather than jail sentences. This law reform, initiated by male legislators, was opposed by many women who endorsed stronger criminal penalties for rape and sexual assault. Although sexual psychopath laws were promoted as a measure to protect women, in reality these laws often resulted in White men being labeled as mentally ill and sent to state hospitals, and Black men being found guilty of a crime and sent to jail (Freedman, 1989).

Racial Aspects of Rape

In addition to oppressing women, rape served as a method of racial control. The sexual assault of minority women maintained the supremacy of White men. The experience of the Black female victim was virtually ignored (cf. Wyatt, this issue). White men used

women as verbs with which to communicate with one another (rape being a means of communicating defeat to the men of a conquered tribe). . . . Rape sent a message to black men, but more centrally, it expressed male sexual attitudes in a culture both racist and patriarchal. (Hall, 1983, p. 322)

In the post-Reconstruction South, White men used the myth of the Black man as sexually uncontrollable and as a threat to all White women as an excuse for violence toward Black men and as a means to control women through fear. Black men who were accused of sexually attacking White women received the harshest penalties. A Black man convicted of rape often was executed or castrated (D'Emilio & Freedman, 1988; Jordon, 1968; Wyatt, this issue). In the 1930s the Association of Southern Women for the Prevention of Lynching stated that the traditions of chivalry and lynching were a form of sexual and racial intimidation rather than protection.

Lynching, it proclaimed, far from offering a shield against sexual assault, served as a weapon of both racial and sexual terror, planting fear in women's minds and dependency in their hearts. It thrust them in the role of personal property or sexual objects, ever threatened by black men's lust, ever in need of white men's protection. (Hall, 1983, p. 339)

The myth of the Black rapist still lingers in more severe sentencing penalties for Black offenders (Hall, 1983). Thus rape and its legal treatment can be seen as the ultimate demonstration of power in a racist and patriarchal society.

Perceptions of the Rape Victim

In addition to changes in the conceptualization of male offenders, society's perception of the victim's role in the assault also changed during the 20th century. As female nature became sexualized and female desire for sexuality legitimated, rape became redefined as "not only a male psychological aberration, but also an act in which women . . . contributed to their victimization" (Freedman, 1989, p. 211). Many people became skeptical that a woman could be raped if she did not consent. A well-known attorney once began a rape trial by placing a coke bottle on a table, spinning it, and demonstrating to the jury his difficulty in forcing a pencil into the opening (Margolin, 1972). The implication was that a woman would be able to fend off a man attempting to rape her (Schwendinger & Schwendinger, 1983). Therefore, if a woman was raped, she must have "asked for it."

Laws requiring physical evidence of penetration, the need for corroboration, and allowing testimony about the victim's sexual history in court trials had the effect of placing the victim on trial. In addition, juries often still received the traditional instruction that an accusation of rape "is one which is easily made and, once made, difficult to defend against, even if the person accused is innocent" (Berger, 1977, p. 10). The jury was cautioned to be suspicious of the victim's testimony, much more so than in other criminal cases. As a result, prosecution rates for rape remained low.

In 1972, 3,562 rapes were reported in Chicago; 833 arrests were made, 23 defendants pleaded guilty; and 8 were found guilty and sentenced after a trial . . . fewer than 1 percent of rapes resulted in jail sentences. (Deckard, 1983, p. 433)

The Feminist Redefinition of Sexual Assault

During the 1960s, increasing numbers of women were employed. As the decade began, approximately 36% of women worked outside the home; by its end, over 50% of women were in the paid labor force (Deckard, 1983). Although women's presence in the public sphere was increasing, they rarely held decision and policy-making positions.

With women's increasing involvement in activities outside the home, the opportunity for a woman to be victimized increased (Gardner, 1980). A few men viewed women's new-found assertiveness and involvement in the public sphere as an attack on traditional roles and a defiance of chivalry. To such men, the woman who did not conform to traditional roles was relegated to the role of the "loose woman" and was not entitled to protection under the traditional guidelines for male–female relationships (Griffin, 1971). The following description of rape in the 19th century still applied:

sexual assault could be conceived of . . . as an exploitation of women's presumed dependence on men. If a woman had herself violated patriarchal norms by straying out of her dependent position—if she had fought off her attacker, asserted her rights alone in court, or behaved in too self-reliant a manner more generally—the term "rape" no longer applied, no matter how forceful the attack visited on her. (Arnold, 1989, p. 49)

Societal definitions of rape demanded adherence to traditionally defined feminine roles and behaviors. The implicit warning to women was to behave (e.g., accept traditional feminine roles) or to suffer the consequence—rape.

Women, however, began to resist traditional definitions of appropriate feminine behavior and expressed their dissatisfaction. Betty Friedan (1963), in *The Feminine Mystique,* and the National Organization for Women (NOW), founded in 1966, expressed women's changing views and interest in public reform. Women's liberationists also began to work toward changing social policies. A process called consciousness raising was used in informal women's groups to begin to empower women and to help them identify sources of sisterhood and oppression. As women began to meet, they realized that individual concerns (e.g., sexual harassment, fear of walking the streets at night) were widely shared. As a result, many women questioned the reasons for their oppression, and they began to recognize that "the personal is political." The dilemmas women were experiencing were not idiosyncratic, but were constructed socially as a result of the hierarchial gender system in our culture (D'Emilio & Freedman, 1988). Kate Millet (1970) in her landmark book, *Sexual Politics,* concluded that within our patriarchal system, force takes "a form of violence particularly sexual in nature and realized most completely in the act of rape" (p. 69).

During the 1970s, rape became an important issue within the feminist movement. Sexual assault was redefined from the victim's perspective. A woman's victimization was an "experience of helplessness and loss of control, the sense of one's self as an object of rage" (Hall, 1983, p. 342). The act of rape was seen not as an end in itself, but as a means of enforcing gender roles in society and maintaining the hierarchy in which men retained control. Feminists refuted the long-held belief that rapists were men who were helplessly controlled by their overwhelming sexual impulses. Rape was recognized as an act of violence, *not* of sex as psychoanalytic theorists had previously held. Rape was a form of domination and control, a weapon used to enforce women's subordinate role to men.

In 1971, an article by Susan Griffin described rape as the "All-American crime." She reported that "forcible rape is the most frequently committed violent crime in America today," and emphasized that all women are victims even if they are not the direct targets of the attack because "rape and the fear of rape are a daily part of every woman's consciousness" (p. 27). She held that women's behavior is shaped by their fear of attack, and as a result, women's movements are restricted. They fear to live alone, walk outside at night, smile at strangers, and leave their windows open. Psychological research has found that women's perceptions of their vulnerability to attack and their fear of being a victim of a violent crime are related to the amount of precautionary behaviors in which they engage. Women, especially those unsure of their ability to protect themselves physically, engage in isolating behavior, such as not going out at night or visiting friends (Riger & Gordon, 1981). This limits women's opportunities to be active participants in the public sphere.

The first rape crisis center was founded in Washington, DC, in 1972, and the number of centers has increased steadily since that time (Deckard, 1983). Now there are more than 550 rape crisis centers across the country, some helping as many as 1100 victims annually (King & Webb, 1981). Rape crisis centers and rape hotlines provide valuable assistance to victims of sexual assault and rape. Victims are provided with information and escorted to the police station and the hospital, and volunteers serve as advocates for the victim after the attack. Many of these centers also have educational programs in the community to help dispel rape myths and change public attitudes about rape (Deckard, 1983). Cuts in governmental funding during the Reagan administration, however, have resulted in the closing of some centers, and in an increased need for volunteers and private funding.

Susan Brownmiller (1975), in her bestselling book, *Against Our Will: Men, Women, and Rape,* reaffirmed the relationship between sexual aggression and women's fear, defining rape as "a conscious process of intimidation by which all men keep all women in a state of fear" (p. 5). Her book was crucial in the definition of rape from a feminist perspective. Brownmiller's analysis formed the foundation for numerous theoretical papers and psychological research. Her book detailed the evolution of rape in our culture and the role it has played throughout history.

Brownmiller began her analysis by considering biology. Women are physiologically vulnerable to sexual attack, and once "men discovered that they could rape, they proceeded to do it" (1975, p. 6). Rape served a critical function of domination and intimidation in primitive societies. "His forcible entry into her body, despite her physical protestations and struggle, became the vehicle of his victorious conquest over her being, the ultimate test of his superior strength, the triumph of his manhood" (p. 5). Rape, therefore, was a purposeful act of control. In some cases, rape was an act of manhood, a rite of passage, or a form of male bonding. This male bonding, on occasion, is exhibited in the form of gang rape. Examining gang rape, Brownmiller concluded that " 'sharing the girl among us fellows strengthens the notion of group masculinity and power" (p. 28). This bond between men results from their "contempt for women" and thrives in a culture of "forced and exaggerated male/female polarities" (p. 211).

The victims of rape often are portrayed as secretly enjoying their victimization—a depiction particularly common in the media. Movie images often present the woman as resisting only initially and eventually becoming overwhelmed by sexual desire despite her original protests. These images reinforce rape myths, and they prompted many feminists to speak out against the way women are portrayed in the media (Jozsa & Jozsa, 1980; Read, 1989). The images themselves represent women as inferior and as victims rather than agents in their own sexuality. Groth and Birnbaum (1979, p. 27) stated that "pornography is a media equivalent to the crime of rape. It is the sexual expression of power and anger." Women began to speculate about the relationship between the way women were portrayed in the media and the prevalence of rape and sexual assault. As a result, the phrase "pornography is the theory, rape is the practice" became a rallying cry for some radical feminists (Morgan, 1980, p. 134).

The use of coercive authority also is a component of sexual assaults in our culture. Sometimes a mere difference in status provides the necessary tool to force intercourse on an unwilling partner. Date rape, homosexual rape in prisons, and rape by police are just a few examples of this form of manipulation. In reality, however, all rapes involve status differences due to the gender-based distribution of power in our society (Box, 1983, p. 150). A woman's resistance within a dependent relationship often is weakened and she becomes vulnerable to being victimized. In addition, victimization may be facilitated by the institutional structure, which often places men in positions of authority and power over women. "Rape by an authority figure can befuddle a victim who has been trained to respect authority so that she believes herself complicitous. Authority figures emanate an aura of rightness; their actions cannot be challenged" (Brownmiller, 1975, p. 300). The victim is left with feelings of guilt and powerlessness, while the aggressor's behavior is left undisputed. For years, many women blamed themselves and did not define their sexual victimization as rape. Since the advent of feminism, and with increased research and public education, women have begun to define unwanted sexual intercourse, even contact between acquaintances, as rape (Warshaw, 1988).

Acquaintance Rape

As public discourse on sexual violence continued, it became increasingly evident that rapists were not only strangers behind bushes, but also might be dates, acquaintances, neighbors, husbands, friends, and relatives. Feminists made the case that every man is a potential rapist and all women are potential victims. Due to this reconceptualization, date rape became an area of concern. In 1972, *Ms.* magazine discussed the issue of date rape on college campuses across the country. Initial research indicated that rape between acquaintances was much more common than previously believed. Kanin and Parcell (1977) found that approximately 83% of college women had experienced male sexual aggression while dating. Research a decade later confirmed this incidence rate. Koss, Gidycz, and Wisniewski (1987) found that 27.5% of college women reported being victims of rape or attempted rape; 53.7% of women, including those who reported being raped, had experienced some form of unwanted sexual contact and/or sexually assaultive behavior. These results suggest that sexually aggressive behavior is experienced by the majority of women in "normal" dating relationships. This high incidence rate gives credence to the feminist conceptualization of rape as being supported by our culture.

Psychological Research on Rape

The views of feminists, in particular the work of Susan Brownmiller, sparked research within psychology to examine the "rape-supportive culture" that provides the context for sexual assault. Researchers made empirical studies of feminist ideas and combined these feminist views into a theoretical framework to understand and predict sexual aggression. Martha Burt (1980) hypothesized that our culture and the status of women within that culture play a significant role in the attitudes toward sexual violence held by persons, particularly rapists. She hypothesized that myths about rape (e.g., "women ask for it") might act as releasers or facilitators of sexual aggression. These rape myths were proposed as part of a larger attitudinal structure that serves to facilitate sexually aggressive acts in our culture. Attitudinal factors that were found by Burt to predict rape-supportive myths were (a) sex role stereotyping, (b) adversarial sexual beliefs, and (c) acceptance of interpersonal violence.

Sex role stereotyping refers to the appropriateness of familial, work, and social roles being based on the sex of the individual being considered (e.g., "It is acceptable for a woman to have a career, but marriage and family should come first"; Burt, 1980, p. 222). Adversarial sexual beliefs refers to the view that male–female relationships are naturally filled with conflict and competition (e.g., "Most women are sly and manipulating when they are out to attract a man"—p. 222). Acceptance of interpersonal violence refers to the belief that violence is an appropriate way of interacting with others, particularly in male-female relationships (e.g., "Sometimes the only way to get a cold woman turned on is to use force"—p. 222). These attitudes were studied by researchers (Burt & Albin, 1981; Check & Malamuth, 1983; Malamuth, 1983) as a means to understand sexual aggression using a feminist framework.

Koss, Leonard, Beezley, and Oros (1985) developed a theoretical model for characterizing nonstranger sexual aggression that incorporated Burt's findings and feminist views. They proposed a social control/social conflict model of date rape:

Culturally transmitted assumptions about men, women, violence, sexuality, and myths about rape constitute a rape-supportive belief system. Furthermore, stratified systems such as the American dating situation may legitimate the use of force by those in power and weaken resistance of the less powerful. Finally, acquisition of stereotyped myths about rape may result in a failure to label as rape sexual aggression that occurs in dating situations. (Koss et al., 1985, p. 982)

This view of a culturally based belief system that perpetuates violence against women and oppresses women has been endorsed by several feminist writers (Brownmiller, 1975; Griffin, 1971; Johnson, 1980).

Rape Within the Legal System

In the colonial period, the law conceptualized rape as the violation of a man's property. It was a man's personal privilege to have access to a woman's body. Feminist theorists have rejected traditional legal conceptualizations, which often blame the woman for her own victimization, and have refuted rape myths that women enjoy being raped, and ask and deserve to be raped by dressing provocatively. They refuse to allow women to be blamed for their own victimization. Instead, blame is placed squarely on the attacker.

Feminists have lobbied for changes in rape legislation. Previous laws considered rape an all-or-nothing crime, in which convicted offenders received sentences that ranged from 5 years to life depending on the particular state's statutes. Maximum sentences of 30–50 years in prison were not uncommon for convicted rapists (Babcock, Freedman, Norton, & Ross, 1975). Prior to the 1972 case of *Furman v. Georgia,* which "invalidated arbitrary capital punishment laws, sixteen states permitted imposition of death for rape" (Berger, 1977, p. 8). Some writers hypothesized that the severe penalties for rape may have discouraged juries from convicting a defendant because of a "perceived sense of disproportion between culpability and the prescribed sentence" (Andenaes, 1966, p. 970). Now most states have revised their laws to include several levels of sexual assault with a broader range of penalties. A perpetrator may be charged with first-, second-, or third-degree rape, with each charge varying in the maximum sentence following conviction. First degree rape is defined as forced sexual intercourse under aggravated circumstances. Second degree rape is described as forced sexual intercourse. Third degree rape is defined as nonconsensual intercourse or intercourse with threat to self or property. This calibrated system of offenses and penalties has increased conviction rates, and may therefore enhance the effectiveness of prosecution as a deterrent (Andenaes, 1966, p. 970).

In addition, the criterion of force was determined in the past by examining the victim's behavior rather than the offender's behavior. In the 1970s, women in New York needed the corroboration of a witness who saw or heard the assault to verify that it had indeed been rape, and that the woman had resisted the attack. In addition, some states viewed "no resistance" as consensual intercourse, and required the victim to have verbally said "no" or forcibly resisted or screamed (Margolin, 1972). Unless the woman exhibited these behaviors, the man's behavior was not considered rape.

In 1974, Michigan passed the first comprehensive rape reform legislation in the country (Loh, 1981). Since that time, most states have enacted similar changes. These reforms have focused on the perpetrator's behavior (e.g., use of physical force or threat of force) as the legal criterion rather than the victim's behavior alone. The context of the assault and the interaction between the victim and assailant are becoming increasingly important.

Although rape legislation has changed a great deal, many changes are still sought (see Goldberg-Ambrose, this issue). In about half of the states a man cannot be charged with sexually assaulting his wife unless they are separated legally. In six states, a husband can never be charged with raping his wife (Searles & Berger, 1987). Recently a North Carolina woman was kidnapped and raped by her husband, but since they had been separated less than one year, the separation was not yet legal and she was unable to charge him with rape. In one-fourth of the states, a man cannot be the victim of rape (Searles & Berger, 1987). In states with progressive statutes, sex-neutral terminology is used for both offender and victim. In approximately 70% of states, a victim's past sexual behavior with persons other than the defendant is admissible for determining consent, while only six states prohibit the introduction of the victim's sexual history (Searles & Berger, 1987).

Criticism of Radical Feminist Reconceptualizations

Some feminists have criticized Brownmiller's (1975) conceptualization of rape. Rather than placing all the blame on women as in the past, Brownmiller counter-blamed, condemning all men for their innate violence (Benjamin, 1983). In addition, radical feminists have ignored the "history of women's resistance to oppression" and focused on sexuality itself as the enemy—"an unchanging, aggressive male sexuality of which women have been eternally the victims" (Arnold, 1989, p. 36). Brownmiller's book also has been faulted as "supporting a notion of universal patriarchy and timeless sexual victimization; it leaves no room for understanding the reasons for women's collaboration, their own sources of power, . . . the class and racial differences in their experience of discrimination and sexual danger" (Hall, 1983, p. 341). The radical feminist view also focuses exclusively on the negative. Some writers believe that in order for feminism to persist, women must use their own strength as an energy source for reform.

Social movements, feminism included, move toward a vision; they cannot operate solely on fear. It is not enough to move women away from danger and oppression; it is necessary to move toward something: toward pleasure, agency, self-definition. Feminism must increase women's pleasure and joy, not just decrease our misery. (Vance, 1984, p. 24)

Areas of Action and Change: Then and Now

Education is still needed to help change society's attitudes about rape. In the recent past, women have been the target for increased awareness, but now men also are being included in the process of consciousness raising (Walsh, 1990). "The anti-rape movement must not limit itself to training women to avoid rape or depending on imprisonment as a deterrent, but must aim its attention at changing the behavior and attitudes of men" (Hall, 1983, p. 346). For example, the University of Florida has introduced a program called FARE (Fraternity Acquaintance Rape Education) to educate men in fraternities and on athletic teams (Walsh, 1990).

Education of women also is needed to empower them to action. In our culture, women are socialized to be submissive, but some feminists have challenged this role. "To be submissive is to defer to masculine strength; is to lack muscular development or any interest in defending oneself" (Griffin, 1971, p. 33). Women can take courses in self-defense to strengthen their bodies, and to gain the ability and the confidence to defend themselves should they be attacked. Ann Sheldon (1972) felt this solution to rape was inescapable: "there is no other way except resistance to be free" (p. 23).

Feminists clearly have made a major difference in the way sexual assault and rape are understood in our culture. Yet considering the long historical tradition of women bearing the guilt for sexual victimization, it is not surprising that much still needs to change. Over 15 years ago, Brownmiller called for action, saying, "the purpose in this book has been to give rape its history. Now we must deny it a future" (1975, p. 454). That need is still true today.

References

Amir, M. (1971). *Patterns in forcible rape.* Chicago: University of Chicago Press.
Andenaes, J. (1966). The general prevention effects of punishment. *Pennsylvania Law Review, 114,* 949–983.

Arnold, M. H. (1989). The life of a citizen in the hands of a woman: Sexual assault in New York City, 1790–1820. In K. Peiss & C. Simmons (Eds.), *Passion and power: Sexuality in history* (pp. 35–56). Philadelphia, PA: Temple University Press.

Babcock, B., Freedman, A., Norton, D., & Ross, S. (1975). *Sex discrimination and the law.* Boston: Little, Brown.

Benjamin, J. (1983). Master and slave: The fantasy of erotic domination. In A. Snitow, C. Stansell, & S. Thompson (Eds.), *Powers of desire: The politics of sexuality* (pp. 280–299). New York: Monthly Review Press.

Berger, V. (1977). Man's trial, woman's tribulation: Rape cases in the courtroom. *Columbia Law Review, 77,* 1–101.

Box, S. (1983). *Power, crime, and mystification.* London: Tavistock.

Brownmiller, S. (1975). *Against our will: Men, women and rape.* Toronto: Bantam.

Burt, M. R. (1980). Cultural myths and supports for rape. *Journal of Personality and Social Psychology, 38,* 217–230.

Burt, M. R., & Albin, R. S. (1981). Rape myths, rape definitions, and probability of conviction. *Journal of Applied Social Psychology, 11,* 212–230.

Check, J. V. P., & Malamuth, N. M. (1983). Sex role stereotyping and reactions to depictions of stranger versus acquaintance rape. *Journal of Personality and Social Psychology, 45,* 344–356.

Deckard, B. S. (1983). *The woman's movement: Political, socioeconomic, and psychological issues* (3rd ed.). New York: Harper & Row.

D'Emilio, J., & Freedman, E. B. (1988). *Intimate matters: A history of sexuality in America.* New York: Harper & Row.

Freedman, E. B. (1981). *Their sisters' keepers: Women's prison reform in America, 1893–1930.* Ann Arbor: University of Michigan Press.

Freedman, E. B. (1989). Uncontrolled desires: The response to the sexual psychopath, 1920–1960. In K. Peiss & C. Simmons (Eds.), *Passion and power: Sexuality in history* (pp. 199–225). Philadelphia, PA: Temple University Press.

Friedan, B. (1963). *The feminine mystique.* New York: Dell.

Gardner, T. A. (1980). Racism in pornography and the women's movement. In L. Lederer (Ed.), *Take back the night: Women on pornography* (pp. 105–114). New York: Morrow.

Griffin, S. (1971). Rape: The all-American crime. *Ramparts, 10,* 26–35.

Groth, A., & Birnbaum, H. (1979). *Men who rape: The psychology of the offender.* New York: Plenum.

Hall, J. D. (1983). The mind that burns in each body: Women, rape, and racial violence. In A. Snitow, C. Stansell, & S. Thompson (Eds.), *Powers of desire: The politics of sexuality* (pp. 328–349). New York: Monthly Review Press.

Johnson, A. G. (1980). On the prevalence of rape in the United States. *Signs: Journal of Women in Culture and Society, 6,* 136–146.

Jordon, W. (1968). *White over Black: American attitudes toward the Negro.* Williamsburg, VA: University of North Carolina Press.

Jozsa, B., & Jozsa, M. (1980). Dirty books, dirty films, and dirty data. In L. Lederer (Ed.), *Take back the night: Women on pornography* (pp. 204–217). New York: Morrow.

Kanin, E. J., & Parcell, S. R. (1977). Sexual aggression: A second look at the offended female. *Archives of Sexual Behavior, 6,* 67–76.

King, H. E., & Webb, C. (1981). Rape crisis centers: Progress and problems. *Journal of Social Issues, 37*(4), 93–104.

Koehler, L. (1980). *A search for power: The "weaker sex" in seventeenth-century New England.* Urbana: University of Illinois Press.

Koss, M. P., Gidyez, C. A., & Wisniewski, N. (1987). The scope of rape: Incidence and prevalence of sexual aggression and victimization in a national sample of higher education students. *Journal of Consulting and Clinical Psychology, 55,* 162–170.

Koss, M. P., Leonard, K. E., Beezley, D. A., & Oros, C. J. (1985). Non-stranger sexual aggression: A discriminant analysis of the psychological characteristics of undetected offenders. *Sex Roles, 12,* 981–992.

Lindemann, B. S. (1984). "To ravish and carnally know": Rape in eighteenth-century Massachusetts. *Signs: Journal of Women in Culture and Society, 10,* 63–82.

Loh, W. D. (1981). Q: What has reform of rape legislation wrought? A: Truth in criminal labelling. *Journal of Social Issues, 37*(4), 28–52.

Malamuth, N. M. (1983). Factors associated with rape as predictors of laboratory aggression against women. *Journal of Personality and Social Psychology, 45,* 432–442.

Margolin, D. (1972). Rape: The facts. *Women: A Journal of Liberation, 3,* 19–22.

Millet, K. (1970). *Sexual politics.* New York: Avon.

Morgan, R. (1980). Theory and practice: Pornography and rape. In L. Lederer (Ed.), *Take back the night: Women on pornography* (pp. 134–140). New York: Morrow.

Read, D. (1989). (De)constructing pornography: Feminisms in conflict. In K. Peiss & C. Simmons (Eds.), *Passion and power: Sexuality in history* (pp. 277–292). Philadelphia, PA: Temple University Press.

Riger, S., & Gordon, M. T. (1981). The fear of rape: A study in social control. *Journal of Social Issues, 37*(4), 71–92.

Schwendinger, J. R., & Schwendinger, H. (1983). *Rape and inequality.* Beverly Hills, CA: Sage.

Searles, P., & Berger, R. J. (1987). The current status of rape reform legislation: An examination of state statutes. *Women's Rights Law Reporter, 10,* 25–43.

Sheldon, A. (1972). Rape: The solution. *Women: A Journal of Liberation, 3,* 23.

Stansell, C. (1986). *City of women: Sex and class in New York, 1789–1860.* New York: Knopf.

Vance, C. S. (1984). Pleasure and danger: Toward a politics of sexuality. In C. Vance (Ed.), *Pleasure and danger: Exploring female sexuality* (pp. 1–27). Boston: Routledge & Kegan Paul.

Walsh, C. (1990, April). *FARE: Fraternity acquaintance rape education.* Paper presented at the Southeastern Psychological Association meeting, Atlanta.

Warshaw, R. (1988). *I never called it rape.* New York: Harper & Row.

16

Gay Villain, Gay Hero: Homosexuality and the Social Construction of AIDS
Robert A. Padgug

I

Patterns of disease are as much the product of social, political, and historical processes as of "natural history." From a historian's perspective, the current AIDS epidemic in the United States is "socially constructed"—the product of multiple historical determinations involving the complex social interaction of human beings over time. It is not, as the National Academy of Sciences would have it, "the story of a virus."[1] The emphasis here is on *historical* determination because AIDS, an event of the present, is imagined and dealt with on the basis of ideologies and institutions developed over time. As Marx wrote, "Human beings do make their own history, but they do not make it just as they please; they do not make it under circumstances chosen by themselves, but under circumstances directly encountered, given and transmitted from the past."[2]

The circumstances of AIDS certainly involve an epidemiologic pattern as well as associated illnesses and their effects on individual human lives; viewed more broadly these circumstances also involve beliefs, struggles, and institutions that have developed over time. That is, social, political, ideological, economic, religious, and public health realities define the meaning and treatment of AIDS both for its victims and the entire society.

AIDS, like other life-threatening diseases whose causes, means of spreading, and ultimate trajectory are not adequately known, has become, in Susan Sontag's now-classic formulation, a "metaphor," or a set of sometimes conflicting metaphors.[3] That is, most of us can comprehend and confront AIDS only if its social meaning is extended well beyond the relatively narrow spheres of medicine and epidemiology. The metaphors that have been constructed around the AIDS epidemic appear to have an unusual power for good or for evil. This power derives from the unanticipated emergence of a deadly new contagion of uncertain course and extent in an era when fatal infectious diseases were believed to have been eliminated. It is also linked to the nature of the groups first affected by AIDS, groups already included in powerful social metaphors.

As metaphor, social struggle, or disease management, AIDS is a contemporary crisis that impels us to draw upon a wide variety of historical material in the struggle to comprehend and deal with it. At the same time, however, we should recognize that such material can be interpreted differently and can be combined to form contradictory ideological and institutional responses to AIDS.

This essay develops these themes by exploring a central feature of the social construction of AIDS—sexuality, particularly, male homosexuality in the United States. Equally important aspects of the crisis, involving medical, epidemiological, economic, class, gender, and racial issues, are slighted here, although they clearly are essential elements in a full comprehension of the epidemic.

II

Sexuality is central in the social construction of AIDS in the United States because sexuality in general and male homosexuality in particular appear to play a paramount role in its etiology and spread. This distinguishes AIDS from most other diseases. As Michel Foucault and others have argued, sexuality is immensely important in the construction of personality as well as of ethics and morality in the modern world. A vast array of competing sexual ideologies, forming the basis for complicated ethical and political positions and struggles, demonstrates this in everyday American practice. In a word, sexuality is itself a set of metaphors and the product of a complicated social history.

Closely connected to sexuality, AIDS has become "moralized" to a much greater degree than, for example, tobacco- or alcohol-related diseases despite the fact they can also be seen as "self-inflicted" and devastatingly costly when measured in lives, health, and social resources. This heightened moralism is possible because AIDS in the United States has been constructed largely in the image of male homosexuality, as that image itself has been constructed in the scientific and popular mind from the mid-nineteenth century to the present.

During the first stages of the epidemic, essentially 1981 and 1982, few aside from gay men—certainly not the popular press and only to a limited degree the government and medical community—paid much attention to AIDS. The disease was happening to "them"—outsiders.[4] This silence—this absence from public discourse—is essentially the way homosexuality has been treated in our society except in periods of moral panic. The moral panic that brought AIDS to the attention of the so-called general public in periodic waves of hysteria, was the possibility that the disease might be spreading to "us," might be crossing that invisible, but ever-present ideological line that divides the normal from the abnormal, the moral from the immoral, the deserving from the undeserving. The definition of AIDS as a disease of homosexual men became entrenched in popular and medical attitudes in spite of growing evidence to the contrary and was used to describe both the disease and the majority of its sufferers. A complex history has shaped the beliefs about homosexuality that were marshalled for the AIDS crisis. The English historian Jeffrey Weeks summarizes those most often chosen:

Certain forms of sexuality, socially deviant forms—homosexuality especially—have long been promiscuously classified as "sins" *and* "diseases," so that you can be born with them, seduced into them and catch them, all at the same time.... In the fear and loathing that AIDS evokes there is a resulting conflation between two plausible, if unproven theories— that there is an elective affinity between disease and certain sexual practices, and that certain practices cause disease—and a third, that certain types of sex *are* diseases.[5]

Implicit in Weeks' description is the nineteenth-century "medicalization" of homosexuality at the hands of physicians and psychiatrists, a conception that has become widely accepted in the twentieth century. Men and women who were categorized as sodomites, practitioners of a sinful sexuality, became "inverts" and, later, homosexuals, that is, they were seen as individuals with physically or mentally diseased personalities who had, in effect, *become* their sexuality.[6] Their sexuality, and therefore their personality, bore the features of its own corruption: it was confused as to gender, it was uncontrollable, it was irresponsible, it sought ever-new pleasures[7] and it was, above all, "promiscuous" or, in more contemporary terms, "addictive."[8]

These features were used to draw the character of the person with AIDS and the person who was thought to infect others. Diseased in mind and body, the man was also "contagious" with respect to both his sexuality and his disease. AIDS was the very mark of his inner disorder, revelatory of his homosexuality as well as the "self-inflicted" result of it. As the conservative journalist Patrick Buchanan put it, "The poor homosexuals—they have declared war upon Nature, and now Nature is exacting an awful retribution."[9] Right-wing polemicists like Buchanan, followed by many ordinary citizens, used these medicalized and moralistic views of homosexuality in their most extreme and hostile forms, proclaiming AIDS a natural or divine judgment upon all homosexuals, regardless of whether they actually had AIDS. And this punishment could spread more widely if the rest of "us" were not morally careful.

The American right wing has shown an "elective affinity" for attacking homosexuality, most notably during the McCarthy period and, in response to the 1970s gay liberation movements, even before the appearance of AIDS. Aversion to homosexuality, which can be connected with a fear of social change and modernism, has its own long and complicated history.[10] But even more temperate and sympathetic observers, including some gays, have adopted two key elements of the historical indictment of homosexuality: "willful irresponsibility" and "promiscuity." Irresponsibility was linked to disregard for the effects of immoral acts, a lack of interest in dealing with the crisis that resulted from them, and, indeed, a certain *desire* to see the crisis unresolved. Thus envisioned, those who wished to "spread" their sexuality in the manner of a contagion desired to spread their contagion in the manner of their sexuality. Elizabeth Fee captures this attitude well:

It has proved an easy cultural move from the idea of populations at risk to that of populations guilty of harboring disease: from a gay plague to a plague of gays. A member of a population at risk is thus not only a potential victim but a potential villain of the epidemic: to be a member of a risk group is to be a dangerous person.[11]

Just as significantly, promiscuity—shorthand for that set of irresponsible sexual practices gay men stand accused of—is central to the entire construction of AIDS metaphors around homosexuality. In both popular and scientific fantasy over the last century, the characteristic feature of homosexuality was precisely its narrowing to pure sexuality—a sexuality lacking in order, in discrimination, in rules—a sexuality in some sense outside social institutions, and, therefore, dangerous. It is precisely this reduction that underlies the definition of homosexuality as quintessentially the "other," the utterly different, that which lies outside society. Well-entrenched in European and American culture during the nineteenth century, this definition had begun to dissipate by the 1970s, but it has been partly revived by the AIDS crisis. The "swishy queen" has been replaced in the popular and medical imagination by the dying AIDS victim as the exemplar of male homosexuality. What has not changed is the reduction of all homosexuals to the image of the supposedly most "visible" minority among them.

Many measures commonly suggested to deal with AIDS victims are patterned on those traditionally used to deal with homosexuals. Various forms of expulsion—real and symbolic—from society as a whole and, especially, from the realm of politics and public discourse have been proposed: quarantine and other forms of isolation for AIDS sufferers, public surveillance of HIV-positive individuals, HIV antibody testing without sufficient provision for confidentiality or anonymity, the general refusal to discuss homosexual sex acts publicly, as well as the strong desire of much of the population to remove AIDS patients from schools, jobs, and housing. These measures are not only entirely congruent with the definition of homosexuals as outsiders, but threaten to reinforce it significantly. As two commentators unusually sensitive to the practical effects of the metaphors of AIDS have noted: "With AIDS now regarded as manifest 'proof' of the profoundly 'diseased' and 'decadent' nature of 'queers' and 'junkies,' reactionary calls to remove gays and IVDUs [intravenous drug users] from the midst of so-called 'civil society' have truly reached new depths."[12]

The effects of such thinking have gone beyond rhetoric to produce massive discrimination against those who have contracted AIDS, inadequate funding for AIDS research and for social welfare programs for AIDS sufferers, great resistance to public health education—including an overwhelming Congressional vote on October 14, 1987, to ban federal funding for education efforts that "promote homosexuality"—and a politics of not-so-benign neglect of the epidemic by the federal government.

Ultimately, the construction of a disease from this complex, historically elaborated imagery leaves us with a view of homosexual persons with or likely to contract AIDS as either individual victims or immoral agents; they become the bearers of a disease just as they are the bearers of a psychological, social, or biologically determined (homo)sexuality. Even as an epidemiological "risk group," they tend to be considered a "group" only insofar as they share individually determined and very narrowly defined behavioral patterns (sexual acts) that bring them into contact with a specific viral agent. Such a view is insufficient on both epidemiological and historical grounds. Disease patterns are epidemiologically meaningful only when applied to groups, not to individuals. In any case, the point is not that homosexuals form a "risk group" but that certain sexual acts are "risky."[13] And whatever the biological or psychological roots of homosexuality and heterosexuality, they are historically meaningful only when viewed as socially constructed within specific societies; as such, they cannot simply be posed as opposites nor reduced to purely physical sexuality. The obsession with homosexuality, especially as a descriptor of individual personality, is seriously misleading and leaves both homosexuals and AIDS outside history.

In reality, no group has ever been outside history altogether, without rules, without internal order of some sort, except in the minds of its enemies. (This is surely as true of drug users and other groups at "higher risk" for AIDS as it is of homosexuals.) The attitudes and fantasies discussed above stem from defining homosexuals negatively by their failure to conform rather than by their actual history. This other and more complicated history involves changing social definitions of homosexuality, the emergence of homosexuals as a special class of person, and their exclusion from the rest of society. Largely in response, homosexuals have created their own communities or subcultures with specific self-definitions, institutions, and ideologies.[14]

In *this* history, the role of gay men in the AIDS crisis can be explored only insofar as we view them as a historically defined and developed group and not as predefined and ahistorical individuals. In the intersection between this history and the history of attitudes toward homosexuality it makes sense to study the AIDS epidemic as social history. Even the concept of gay men as a "risk group" ultimately is meaningful only on this wider, nonepidemiological level.

III

For gay men, the AIDS crisis has exacerbated serious problems of discrimination and homophobia. In a society that does not provide adequate funds, care, and sympathy for dealing with AIDS, the crisis means the continuation of gay men's medical and social isolation. Above all, the crisis means living with the threat and the reality of disease, death, and bereavement.

As a whole, the gay community has shown a rational fear of the disease, but it also has demonstrated a remarkably capacity to avoid panic. This relative calm undoubtedly derives from a familiarity with AIDS that is significantly greater than that of the general public, as well as the self-knowledge as a community that rejects ordinary metaphors of AIDS built on fear and loathing of homosexuality. Unlike the heterosexual world, the gay world cannot construct AIDS as a disease of "the other," but is forced to "normalize" it and to construct its own series of metaphors for so doing.

The AIDS crisis is remarkable due to the degree to which the group that appeared most affected by the disease became extensively involved in its management. Gays have been in the forefront of groups providing social aid and health care to persons with AIDS (whether homosexual or not), conducting research, lobbying for funds and other governmental intervention, creating education programs, negotiating with legislators and health insurers, and the like.[15] A recent report in the *New York Times* assesses the effort in New York City:

City officials say they shudder to think of what would have happened in New York if the homosexual community had not formed the Gay Men's Health Crisis and other spinoff organizations to care for the sick, educate the healthy and lobby for attention and funds. . . . "When the story of New York's AIDS epidemic is written, that self-help effort will be the bright part of it," said Dr. [Stephen] Joseph, the City Health Commissioner.[16]

The same could be written of other cities as well, in San Francisco, for instance, where the most successful gay "self-help" efforts to date have been carried out.

The gay community has demonstrated a remarkable willingness and ability to work within and outside the established governmental and private institutions that normally handle health emergencies. When gays have not succeeded in persuading or forcing established institutions to provide money, care, and compassion to deal with AIDS, they have provided the needed resources through their own institutions. This insistence on taking an active role in disease management serves as notice that gays will not be forced to remain outsiders, as the victims or villains of popular metaphor.

Ironically, despite the obvious danger of doing so, the gay community has in a sense embraced the identification of AIDS with homosexuality that is central to popular and medical metaphors of the disease, but has redefined this concept significantly to make effective self-management of the disease central to it. Comprehension of this effort requires a close look at the actual history of the community.

IV

The gay community—as a community of interacting and self-defining persons rather than as a pool of victims—has been noticeably and continually absent from the media and public discourse (except for the gay press). Silence about gay people and the realities of their lives is at the very center of homosexual oppression. Almost from its inception in the nineteenth century, the gay community has struggled for the right to control its own fate, to free itself from the interference of the state, the church, and the medical and psychiatric professions. The struggle has, therefore, always been about *power:* the power to define, to victimize, to deny entry into the public realm as a legitimate group.

This struggle is evident in the long history of the gay communities[17] that grew mainly within large urban centers, particularly in New York, San Francisco, and Los Angeles, precisely the communities where AIDS made its first and most deadly appearance. And the power struggle is equally apparent in the closely connected

struggle for political identity and power, beginning before World War II and growing to national significance in the period of "gay liberation" in the 1970s and
1980s.[18]

This continued struggle for political and social power molded the struggle over
AIDS; that is, gay men have fought, most often against the same groups that denied
their rights, to retain some degree of control over the definition of the disease and
the way it was combated. Refusing to see themselves as victims or to be expelled
from society again, while political, medical, and moral "professionals" determine
their fate, gay men are building on many decades of political and social organizing
and using that experience to create new forms of resistance. The speed with which
gay self-help and political organizations sprang up to meet the AIDS crisis, and
the efficiency with which they achieved their aims, was a measure of the community's organizational and institutional sophistication. The gay community, and
the so-called *gay* ghettos, had long since developed a wide variety of social, cultural, political and legal institutions—including a large number of newspapers and
magazines—that could be enlisted in the fight against AIDS. As Michael Bronski
puts it, the huge effort of AIDS organizing "is in the tradition of the gay movement—a direct response to an oppressive situation."[19] It is also a very American
response to crisis as well; this society characteristically creates a wide range of
voluntary organizations to meet social, welfare, and health needs of portions of the
population.

The gay community, of course, has never been monolithic. Like all communities
that have emerged in a context of struggle against oppression, it is highly complex
and continually developing. Not all who are homosexual in "orientation" or practice belong to it; one must embrace one's homosexuality more or less publicly for
that. People move in and out of the community as need and circumstance require.
The character and strength of gay communities differ considerably depending upon
location, with the greatest strength and development evident mainly in large urban
centers. And each has its idiosyncratic features, differences largely correlated with
the cities where they formed. Moreover, the gay community is subject to the same
differentiation across class, political, income, gender, age, ethnic, and racial lines
as the rest of American society. Insofar as it has spawned a number of political
and social movements, however, the community has tended to be white and middle
class, a characteristic that has led to significant tensions.

Most notable, perhaps, has been the tendency for contradictions to develop between gay men and lesbians. Many lesbians find an alternative political and social
practice in the women's movement and do not share gay men's way of life and
attitudes toward sexuality. What has, in fact, largely brought the varied strands of
the gay community together is an abstract "sexual orientation," originally defined
by hostile outsiders, and, above all, a common history of struggle against oppression.

Despite these internal tensions and continued hostility from outsiders, the AIDS
crisis neither destroyed nor weakened the community. In fact, its maturity enabled
the community to meet the challenge of AIDS with a noticeably strengthened sense
of identity, inner cohesion, and ability to work for common aims. Gay men and

lesbians, for example, have worked together more closely than ever in the political struggle surrounding AIDS as well as in the care of the ill and dying, mainly gay men. Lesbians have indeed performed heroically in a struggle that on many grounds need not have been theirs at all. This new cohesion is best symbolized by the march in Washington, D.C. on October 11, 1987, in which an estimated 500,000 gay men and lesbians challenged continuing homophobia and inadequate attention to AIDS in one of the most massive political outpourings in the United States in many years. These and other accomplishments resulted from fundamental changes in lesbian and gay politics, organizations, and social institutions.

On the simplest level, lesbian and gay political organizations, fundamentally oriented toward a familiar kind of pressure-group activity, have been joined or replaced by many new groups that combine health care and organizing with gay politics and legal action. Society's failure to address the health and social needs of the gay community, as well as the limitations of existing institutions, forced gays and lesbians to create their own institutions to confront the crisis. Once these community-based organizations were in place (approximately 250–300 now exist), their members realized that they had to broaden their scope by adding political goals and activities, that is, they would have to combat both homophobia and discrimination as well as AIDS. As Eric Rofes, an activist in AIDS health care issues, has noted:

If we have learned anything from AIDS, it's that you cannot separate politics from health care. They are one and the same. Women have understood that for a long time. People of color have understood that for a long time. A lot of gay white men have. But too many haven't.[20]

The new politics of AIDS has succeeded in procuring additional funding and health resources for the struggle against AIDS, as well as in combating homophobia in the government, the health sector, and the insurance industry. It is beginning to build bridges to other groups who see health care as a central issue. However, stretching itself to the limit in the struggle against AIDS, the gay community has reduced the degree to which the remainder of society is responsible for providing the money, care, and volunteers it supplies for most other epidemics.[21] Peter Arno and Karyn Feiden observe:

The fact that the SSA [Social Security Administration] has ruled that AIDS patients are eligible for presumptive disability illustrates the gay community's ability to influence public health policy. In cities with large gay populations, such as New York and San Francisco, the supportive care received by many AIDS patients is actually superior to that received by the victims of other severe chronic illnesses. The Federal Government, however, cannot take credit for this. The development and growth of community-based AIDS service organizations, largely through massive gay-organized volunteer efforts, is helping to create a high-quality integrated care delivery system. Whether the current level of voluntarism can continue to match the pace of the epidemic or serve the growing segment of IV [intravenous] drug users; whether volunteer care is viable outside major metropolitan areas and can serve victims of other diseases; and whether voluntarism allows the government to abdicate its obligations to its people, remains to be seen.[22]

Thus, the success of the gay community's crisis intervention might have the paradoxical effect of leaving most of the responsibility for care with the community and perpetuating the segregation of gay men and lesbians. One task for gay organizations is to devise ways to share the responsibility for combatting AIDS with the rest of society.

AIDS has profoundly affected the style and nature of gay politics in other ways as well. Gay political organizations originated in the context of a distinctive American political structure that has incorporated minority-group activity into political life,[23] in some circumstances, as in the AIDS crisis, a minority group largely despised by the wider society can exercise considerable political power for certain purposes. Because of this, the American gay community, unlike its counterparts in other nations, has always had a strong impetus toward seeing itself as a more-or-less typical minority demanding recognition and jockeying for position *vis-à-vis* other minorities in the political arena rather than as a part of a wider political, usually leftist, movement.

The nascent gay self-identity as a minority group that emerged in the 1950s was, however, challenged strongly after the Stonewall riots in New York in 1969. At this time a number of more radical, left-leaning groups, emerging in part from the ferment of the anti-Vietnam War movements, gained temporary domination with a political agenda aimed at broad human liberation and overcoming the homosexual/ heterosexual distinction rather than at minority rights and group privileges. Cutting across the distinction between minority-group and liberatory politics was a substantial difference in political styles that pitted pressure-group activities by representational organizations working within established American institutions against a style of protest that was street-oriented, anti-"establishment," and directly involved as many ordinary gay men and women as possible.[24]

In the late 1970s the political pendulum, influenced by the partial institutionalization of the gay "revolution" of the post-Stonewall period and by the desire to protect earlier accomplishments, swung once again toward the minority-group outlook. This shift involved a strong emphasis on membership organizations (such as the National Gay Task Force, now the National Lesbian and Gay Task Force) whose major role was to deal with federal and state legislative and judicial bodies. The notion that gay struggle aimed at *human* liberation was largely abandoned, street politics was denigrated as a sign of community immaturity, and the distinction between homosexual and heterosexual was paradoxically strengthened as a precondition for political success within, not against, the American political system.

The AIDS crisis forced another major shift in political style. The community quickly discovered that working purely within a system either unable or unwilling to meet the needs of AIDS patients and the gay community was no longer feasible. The need for direct action to procure funds, health care, and social welfare, as well as the necessity to confront a government and public that remained unacceptably homophobic, led to the revival of a more confrontational, direct-action style of politics.

The renewed politics of direct action supplemented rather than replaced a more conservative politics of membership organizations and lobbying legislatures and politicians. Both types of organization have grown in numbers and importance, and their supporters and organizers have learned to work together relatively well. They have discovered that popular demonstrations against the most blatant examples of homophobia and street actions aimed at increasing funding for AIDS work and research complement more traditional styles of politics as often as they clash. In addition, many gay organizations, most notably the increasing number that deal with the broad spectrum of legal, social, and civil rights of gay persons and persons with AIDS, have managed to combine an aggressive, confrontational style with a more traditional membership-organization structure.

This new combination of styles, although imperfect, has enabled the gay community to protect past gains while making new gains both within and opposed to established institutions. Correspondingly, the struggle between a gay minority identity and one that sees the gay community at the forefront of a radical restructuring of humanity itself has become less important and interesting in the face of the AIDS epidemic. The minority group perspective remains dominant but the outcome is still uncertain. Nevertheless, the new style of gay politics appears to be a creative response to an unusual crisis and has given the gay community a political presence and weight lacking in earlier years.

V

Like politics, gay male sexuality has substantially changed as a result of AIDS. Those gay institutions largely devoted to sexual activity—bars, baths, backrooms, public spaces—were of great importance, although they hardly exhausted the content of gay community life. The fundamental link among gay persons was, after all, sexual, but these institutions have represented far more than sites of sexual activity. Such places have developed a far greater symbolic and social significance to the gay community than is readily understood by non-gays.[25] For decades they represented the only public spaces that could in any sense be termed homosexual and where homosexuals could discover each other as well as a wider homosexual world, in spite of frequent police raids and moral crusades against them. Outsiders probably cannot imagine the significance of these spaces in the complicated double process of ''coming out''—that is, entering the homosexual world as well as publicly committing oneself to one's homosexuality.

Not surprisingly, when gay people asserted their right to exist in the gay liberation period that began in the 1960s, sexual institutions expanded astronomically. The room for sexual experimentation and creativity also expanded immensely, as an expression of gay identity, as a protest against the earlier suppression of homosexuality, and as a genuine, although sometimes utopian, attempt to fashion a society under new conditions of freedom. And the public nature of much of this sexuality became another expression of the fact that gay sex was a product of a community, not merely of a group of pre-existing homosexual individuals.

Gay men, like feminists, have been quite aware for some time that sexuality has a deeply political aspect. Because of its role in their identity, this sexuality was central to their political struggles against the oppressive institutions of society. The rightists who chose the gay community as one of their primary targets appear to have comprehended this as well.

Gay identity itself may be said to have been built largely on sexual identity and sexual institutions. But in the context of the gay liberation movements of the late 1960s and 1970s, the existence of sexual institutions and identity encouraged the expansion of nonsexual institutions, including political and protest groups, self-help groups, and cultural institutions. In the 1970s both sexual and nonsexual institutions grew in importance as a real gay community emerged in the wake of gay liberation. It was, however, precisely the sexual institutions and the role of sexuality within the gay community that were most definitively shaken by AIDS, a disease spread, at least in part, through some forms of sexual intercourse. The gay community is still struggling to cope with the challenge of AIDS to its sexual beliefs and practices. But the strong emphasis on sexuality in its multiple forms is too deeply rooted in gay history simply to be abandoned. The forces—church, state, or medical—that seek to use the AIDS crisis to restore their authority will not easily banish all homosexual acts. Certainly the gay community's efforts to repeal all sodomy laws, especially on the federal level, have been impeded by AIDS (see the Supreme Court's decision in *Bowers v. Hardwick* in June 1986, declaring that sodomy laws are constitutional and that the private practice of gay sexuality is not protected by the United States Constitution[26]). But the struggle for control of sexuality is only in part a legislative or judicial struggle; it also encompasses the community's struggle to control its own sexuality and the ability to control, through sexuality, such disparate aspects of human life as health care, the body, and the family. The gay community well recognizes the nature of this struggle and its implications for the community's ability to survive the challenge of AIDS.

Under the impetus of AIDS, sexual institutions themselves have declined in importance within the gay community. They are increasingly being replaced by nonsexual social, cultural, and political institutions, including the community-based health, social welfare, and related organizations mentioned earlier. The nature of the gay community, the institutions that provide its cohesion, and the way gay people deal with one another have all changed considerably. At the same time, gay sexuality has increasingly been reconstructed under the impetus of AIDS along the lines of sexuality found in the majority heterosexual world. This has, for example, meant a new emphasis on "dating" and on longer-term, more monogamous relationships among gay men. The new sexuality is perhaps symbolized by the "wedding" ceremony that brought together thousands of gay and lesbian couples to reaffirm their commitment to each other on October 10, 1987, as part of the activities that led up to the massive march in Washington, D.C. But change has also meant a decline in the various forms of sexual experimentation, spontaneity, unorthodox relationships, community "flamboyance," willingness to cross social boundaries, and sense of "celebration"—the "Dionysian" aspects of life—that made the gay community so interesting and creative in the 1970s.

Gay men will need many years to come to terms with the current realities of sexuality and its place within their community and self-identity. In the meantime they need to undertake the serious theoretical work—lesbians and the women's movement in general have done far better in this sphere—of understanding sexuality in an age of crisis and reconstructing its role within gay identity. Broadly theoretical concerns have attached themselves to narrowly defined issues such as the debates, both within and outside the gay community in San Francisco and New York in 1984 and 1985, over whether gay baths should be allowed to operate in a time of epidemic. But the largely symbolic nature of these concerns ultimately makes them poor arenas for elaborating a new gay sexuality. The debates fed on the rhetoric of "promiscuity" among non-gays as well as old and not particularly well-conceived arguments over the role of monogamy and multiple sexual partners among gay men. In fact, only a minority of gay men regularly used the baths, and there was never substantial evidence to suggest that closing the baths would decrease the spread of HIV infection. Closing baths and similar institutions in many cities represents less a restructuring of gay sexuality than a partial defeat for the gay community's control over its own sexuality.

To date, the major changes in gay male sexual practice are mainly the product of a practical need to meet the AIDS crisis directly. A significant "safe-sex" movement, largely staffed, operated, and funded by the gay community, has been created to carry out the necessary work of educating gay men (and others) regarding sexual practices in a crisis, using pamphlets, discussion groups, safe-sex pornography, and the like. Substantial evidence suggests that this movement has helped change the behavior of the majority of gay men.[27] While some gay men are evidently abandoning sex altogether—a few even appear to have accepted the assertion that all gay sex equals death—most are adapting to the crisis by building new sexual identities around safe-sex activities.

This restructuring of gay institutions and deeply rooted sexual practices may reflect a certain malleability that enables the gay community to respond rapidly to external changes. This malleability appears to be conditioned by a long history of oppression and by the fact that gay traditions are not passed on through the family. A history that at first sight seems to demonstrate significant weaknesses may turn out in retrospect to offer important advantages as well.

And, in fact, gay men were never as "obsessed" with sex as their enemies and even many in their own community believed. A significant proportion of gay men never made sex central to their lives, and the main gay tradition, which did privilege sexual relations especially in the 1970s and early 1980s, did not sexualize the entire world or foster an obsession with sex. Ironically, sex became tame, an ordinary part of everyday life, and necessary changes became easier.

VI

In contrast to its surprising development of strength in other areas, the gay community has been less successful and shown more ambivalence in relation to medicine. Ronald Bayer perceptively suggests that gay men find themselves "between the specter and the promise of medicine."[28] Medicine offers both the promise of solutions to AIDS and the danger that physicians and medical researchers will reassume control over the gay community or work with the state to do so. After all, physicians and psychiatrists "medicalized" homosexuality in the first place, and only in 1973, after a long struggle, was the American Psychiatric Association "persuaded"—some would say forced—to remove homosexuality from its list of mental disorders.[29]

The AIDS crisis has rekindled much of that long history of hostility between the homosexual community and the medical world. Physicians and other health workers have not been notably sympathetic to gay men or persons with AIDS. Homophobia has risen dramatically as AIDS threatens to link gay men permanently with a specific, deadly disease, thought to be of their own making.[30] The association of gay men with other "medicalized" risk groups, such as illicit drug users and prostitutes, has similar effects. In addition, gay male health—like that of other oppressed or poor groups in our society—has been neglected by the medical community. When gay men receive excellent medical treatment, they do so as middle-class men, rarely as gays. Not until the mid- to late 1970s did anyone recognize that the gay male community might suffer from specific diseases that would best be treated in the context of the community. This recognition, which grew out of the liberation movement and the sense of community that accompanied it, was largely confined to gays.[31]

Before the 1970s most physicians and psychologists refused to recognize the existence of a gay community, insisting that gay people were merely individuals with certain medical or psychological characteristics. For the medical establishment gay men were mentally or physically sick and their other diseases were the expected byproduct of their homosexuality. With a heavy dose of moralism, the medical profession acted as if—and often stated that—it preferred to see people suffer from venereal disease than commit acts it did not approve.[32] Moreover, many gays feared that seeking treatment for particular sexually transmitted diseases would, in effect, be an admission of their homosexuality before a hostile world—precisely what happens when gay men are diagnosed as suffering from AIDS or AIDS-related complex (ARC). And, finally, the neglect of gay men's health derived also from gay men's willingness to accept the typical twentieth-century emphasis, especially in the age of antibiotics, on curative medicine rather than preventive measures, particularly condoms and other devices that might have prevented the spread of infectious disease through sexual contact. This multi-sided mismanagement of the gay community's health left it peculiarly vulnerable to new diseases, among which AIDS is only the most devastating example. As Cindy Patton notes:

The opportunistic infections (other than KS [Kaposi's sarcoma] and PCP [*Pneumocystis carinii* pneumonia]) that accompany AIDS in gay men are precisely those minor infections that have, at least for the last few decades been a part of the gay male health picture. . . . Yet the historical relationship between lesbians and gay men and their physicians has been hostile and fraught with deception and fear.[33]

The new emphasis on self-management of health and illness among feminists, poverty advocate groups, and, in somewhat different ways, middle-class people in general, has contributed to the determination of the gay community and particularly people with AIDS to play a significant role in the medical management of AIDS.

Gay persons with AIDS have undertaken to educate themselves in technical matters relating to their disease and its possible cures and treatments. They have actively demanded services from the medical and epidemiological establishments and have even occasionally provided them directly. Especially in San Francisco and New York, these services are, arguably, superior to those available for most other types of patients in the United States. As Richard Dunne, executive director of the New York–based Gay Men's Health Crisis, recently put it:

What's happening today is something that has not happened before in modern medicine— maybe never before. The patient walks in to see the doctor and says, "I'm on AZT and I'm having some side effects. What do you think of my taking cyclovir?" Physicians are overwhelmed that the P.W.A. [person with AIDS] is the expert. A P.W.A. said to me recently that his physician is someone he consults but that he makes the decisions.[34]

In a closely related development, the gay community has been forced to pay particular attention to the private health insurance industry. In America, unlike almost every other industrial nation, private health insurance represents health care access to all but the elderly or very poor. Gay men, never in favor with the insurance industry,[35] are in danger of being denied adequate insurance against illness. The gay community, largely through its legal organizations, has actively combated discrimination that would deny them health insurance or employee benefits. While not uniformly successful, its efforts have helped ensure that gay men and others thought to be at risk for AIDS will not automatically be denied access to insurance and, therefore, to health care itself. For example, the National Association of Insurance Commissioners, whose regulations are usually accepted by the various state insurance departments, was persuaded to adopt guidelines banning inquiries into applicants' sexual orientation and any use of information regarding sexual orientation in insurance underwriting.[36] That the gay community, whose legitimacy is barely recognized, should be able to "negotiate" with the powerful insurance industry is impressive evidence of its ability to intervene in all aspects of the AIDS epidemic and alter the terms in which they are discussed and managed.

The gay community, however, has tended to remain aloof from other groups (many of the poor, the aged, and a substantial number of health care workers) who are pressing for a national health care system. This is a surprising development in that it is precisely minority-group members who are, in addition to gay men, those most at risk for AIDS and AIDS-related conditions.

Many middle-class, white gay men have been surprised to discover the substantial inadequacies of the private health insurance system in meeting the AIDS crisis and in meeting their personal needs for access to health care. However, their organizations have neither joined the struggle to reform it in more than essentially minor ways, nor demanded in a forthright manner a system of nationally provided health care or insurance. Perhaps the reason the gay movement has been unable to work fully with minority and other protest groups for common aims is the continuing racism among white, middle-class gays and homophobia among other minorities as well as belief on each side that they compete for limited resources. A significant exception was the boycott of Coors Beer that began in San Francisco and brought together gays, women, unions, blacks, and other minorities, was spearheaded partly by the gay community, and at the beginning was led by Harvey Milk.[37] And recent developments, including the courting of the gay movement by Jesse Jackson's Rainbow Coalition, may yet bring major changes.

In health-related activities the gay community has begun to move closer to the heterosexual world in general. Many gay health organizations, caring agencies, and related institutions have become large and successful bureaucracies, dispensing hundreds of thousands of dollars and becoming attentive to public fund-raising and government grants. In addition, they are becoming integrated into the wider health-care world. Some radical gay political groups, however, see such mainstreaming as political timidity, an overemphasis on the purely clinical aspects of the epidemic, and too great a willingness to cooperate with governmental bodies, which are thereby allowed to escape justified charges of having done too little to meet the crisis.[38] Such tensions are probably inevitable as the gay community's position on the complicated problems of medicine and health care involved with AIDS continues to evolve.

VII

The detailed responses to AIDS coalesce into two complex and parallel sets of metaphors—two types of discourse, two varieties of practice—built on the relationship between AIDS and homosexuality. Both sets of metaphors accept the reality of that relationship, resting upon the complicated ideological and institutional history of American homosexuality. But they draw on different aspects of that heritage, reconfigurating them in response to the AIDS crisis and creating significantly different amalgams of past and present. In fact, they form the materials for two sides of a massive political and ideological struggle that extends far beyond the reality of AIDS as a disease.

The two discourse do not speak directly to one another, but they "echo" each other strongly. Both regard AIDS as a moral crisis, but where the first defines AIDS as the breakdown of the dominant "traditional" morality of sexual behavior and social organization, the second considers it the breakdown of a new "social contract" that includes all people as full members of the body politic. Where the first seeks to exclude homosexuality from public view and shroud it in silence, the second argues that "silence is death" with respect to both AIDS and homosexuality.[39] Where the first finds sexual irresponsibility and lack of self-control at the heart of homosexuality, the second demonstrates an unusual capacity on the part of gay people to alter their own sexual behavior. Where the first sees victims and villains, the second sees actors and heroes.

The gay community, in an ironic reversal of popular views of AIDS, constructed the AIDS crisis and its metaphors in the image of its own history. But the metaphors we find here, unlike those of homophobic approaches, are socially, institutionally, and ideologically rich, because they build on the history of a real community coming to terms with its past and its need to take control of its present and future. They are also useful metaphors, in that they allow for a rational intervention in the management of the disease while they let us remove at least some of the hysteria that has prevented us from treating AIDS like any other disease.

The gay community has largely succeeded in removing AIDS from the category of the new, the terrifying, and the special and made it more ordinary, normal, and therefore, manageable. In the same manner, people with AIDS have shown that it is possible—indeed necessary—to live with AIDS and not merely die from it.

The best summation of this story can perhaps be found in the moving remarks of Paul Monette in the preface to a cycle of poems on the death of his lover from AIDS:

The story that endlessly eludes the decorum of the press is the death of a generation of gay men. What is written here is only one man's passing and one man's cry, a warrior burying a warrior. May it fuel the fire of those on the front lines who mean to prevail, and of their friends who stand in the fire with them. We will not be bowed down or erased by this. I learned too well what it means to be a people, learned in the joy of my best friend what all the meaningless pain and horror cannot take away—that all there is is love. Pity us not.[40]

Notes

Acknowledgments: This essay is a considerably revised version of papers presented at the annual meeting of the American Historical Association in December 1986; at the Marxist School in New York City in April 1987; at the Socialist Scholars Conference in New York City in April 1987; and at a panel organized by the Association of Social Scientists in Health Care at the October 1987 annual meeting of the American Public Health Association in New Orleans. It has been much improved by the generous comments of Gerald Oppenheimer (Brooklyn College), in dialogue with whom many of my views on AIDS have been developed.

1. Institute of Medicine, National Academy of Sciences, *Mobilizing Against AIDS: The Unfinished Story of a Virus* (Cambridge, Mass.: 1986).

2. Karl Marx, *The 18th Brumaire of Louis Bonaparte* (New York: 1963), 15. I have altered the customary translation from "men" to "human beings," a change I feel is warranted by the German "menschen."

3. Susan Sontag, *Illness As Metaphor* (New York: 1978).

4. Cf. Ronald Bayer, "AIDS and the Gay Community: Between the Specter and the Promise of Medicine," *Social Research* 52 (Autumn 1985): 581–606 at 587ff.

5. Jeffrey Weeks, *Sexuality and Its Discontents* (London: 1985), 45–46.

6. On the process in general, see Jeffrey Weeks, *Coming Out* (London: 1977); Jonathan Katz, *Gay American History* (New York: 1976), 129–207; and *Gay/Lesbian Almanac* (New York: 1983), 1–19. For further details: Vernon L. Bullough, "Homosexuality and the Medical Model," *Journal of Homosexuality* 1 (1974): 99ff; George Chauncey, Jr., "From Sexual Inversion to Homosexuality: The Changing Medical Conceptualization of Female 'Deviance,' " in this volume; Georges Lanteri-Laura, *Lecture des perversions: histoire de leur appropriation médicale* (Paris: 1979); Peter Conrad and Joseph W. Schneider, *Deviants and Medicalization: From Badness to Sickness* (St. Louis: 1980), ch. 7. Cf. Michel Foucault, *The History of Sexuality,* vol. I, *An Introduction* (New York: 1978), 44.

7. Cf. Philippe Ariès, "Thoughts on the History of Homosexuality," in *Western Sexuality: Practice and Precept in Past and Present Times,* ed. Philippe Ariès and André Béjin (Oxford: 1985), 62–75.

8. Cf. Patrick Carnes, *The Sexual Addiction* (Minneapolis: 1983); Craig Rowland, "Reinventing the Sex Maniac," *The Advocate,* 21 Jan. 1986, 43–49; Daniel Goleman, "Some Sexual Behavior Viewed as an Addiction," *New York Times,* 16 October 1984, C1. Not surprisingly in light of the historical associations of this concept, it turns out that women and gay men are the groups most at risk for this supposed "addiction."

9. *New York Post,* 24 May 1983.

10. Cf. the material collected in Jonathan Katz, *Gay American History* and *Gay/Lesbian Almanac.*

11. Elizabeth Fee, commentary on the session "AIDS in Historical Perspective," annual meeting of the American Historical Association, Chicago, Ill., December 1986.

12. Nancy Krieger and Rose Appleman, *The Politics of AIDS* (Oakland, Calif.: 1986), 18. See most recently Randy Shilts, *And the Band Played On: Politics, People, and the AIDS Epidemic* (New York: 1987); and Daniel M. Fox, "AIDS and the American Health Polity: The History and Prospects of a Crisis of Authority," *Milbank Quarterly* 64 (1986), Supplement I, "AIDS: The Public Context of an Epidemic," ed. Ronald Bayer, Daniel M. Fox, and David P. Willis, 7–33.

13. See William H. McNeill, *Plagues and Peoples* (New York: 1976), for a good historical overview.

14. See the works cited in note 6 and Dennis Altman, *The Homosexualization of America and the Americanization of the Homosexual* (New York: 1982); John D'Emilio, *Sexual Politics, Sexual Communities: The Making of a Homosexual Minority in the United States, 1940–1970* (Chicago: 1983), and "Gay Politics, Gay Community: San Francisco's Experience," *Socialist Review* 55 (Jan.–Feb. 1981): 77–104; and Toby Marotta, *The Politics of Homosexuality: How Lesbians and Gay Men Have Made Themselves a Political and Social Force in Modern America* (New York: 1981).

15. On all these aspects and the reaction of the gay community in general to the AIDS epidemic, see Shilts, *And the Band Played On;* Dennis Altman, *AIDS in the Mind of America* (Garden City, N.Y.: 1986); "AIDS: The Politicization of an Epidemic," *Socialist Review* 78 (November/December 1984): 93–109; "The Politics of AIDS," in *AIDS: Public Policy Dimensions,* ed. John Griggs (New York: 1987), 23–33; and, in some ways most perceptively, Cindy Patton, *Sex and Germs: The Politics of AIDS* (Boston: 1985). In addition, it is important to look at coverage of AIDS in the gay press from 1981 on in some detail, particularly the *New York Native,* the (national) *Advocate,* and the San Francisco *Bay Area Reporter.*

16. *New York Times,* 16 March 1987, 17. On the Gay Men's Health Crisis and its role in the crisis in New York, cf. Richard Dunne, "New York City: Gay Men's Health Crisis," *AIDS: Public Policy Dimensions,* ed. Griggs, 155–69.

17. On the gay ghettoes in general, see: Martin P. Levine, "Gay Ghetto," *Journal of Homosexuality* 4 (1979): 363–78; Martin P. Levine, ed., *Gay Men: The Sociology of Male Homosexuality* (New York: 1979); Manuel Castels, *The City and the Grassroots: a Cross-Cultural Theory of Urban Social Movements* (Berkeley: 1983).

18. An overview of the various gay liberation movements can be found in Barry Adam, *The Rise of a Gay and Lesbian Movement* (Boston: 1987).

19. Michael Bronski, "Death and the Erotic Imagination," *Gay Community News* (Boston), 7–13 Sept. 1986, 8–9 at 8.

20. Quoted by Mark Vandervelden, "Gay Health Conference," *The Advocate,* 28 April 1987, 12. The occasion for Rofes' statement was the eighth annual "National Lesbian and Gay Health Conference," held in Los Angeles on 26–29 March 1987, and attended by representatives of more than 250 organizations.

21. On the limits of voluntarism, cf. Peter S. Arno and Karyn Feiden, "Ignoring the Epidemic: How the Reagan Administration Failed on AIDS," *Health-PAC Bulletin* 17 (December 1986): 7–11, and Peter S. Arno, "The Contributions and Limitations of Voluntarism," in *AIDS: Public Policy Dimensions*, 188–92.

22. Arno and Feiden, "Ignoring the Epidemic,"11.

23. Cf. Altman, *AIDS in the Mind of America,* who strongly argues for the unique nature of the AIDS crisis in the United States, due in part to this peculiarly American type of political system.

24. On the general development of gay politics and gay self-identity, see the works cited in notes 14 and 18 and, in particular, the works listed by John D'Emilio and Barry Adam.

25. Cf. Dennis Altman, "Sex: The New Frontline for Gay Politics," *Socialist Review* (September/October 1982).

26. 106 S.Ct. 2841, 2842–56 (1986).

27. The increasingly large literature on changes in gay sexual behavior due to AIDS is summarized and discussed in Marshall H. Becker and Jill G. Joseph, "AIDS and Behavioral Change to Reduce Risk: A Review," *American Journal of Public Health* 78 (April 1988): 394–410.

28. Bayer, "AIDS and the Gay Community: Between the Specter and the Promise of Medicine."

29. See Ronald Bayer, *Homosexuality and American Psychiatry: The Politics of Diagnosis,* 2nd ed. (New York: 1988).

30. See, in general, Dan DeNoon, "AIDS Takes its Psychological Toll on the Health-Care Community," *In These Times,* 14–20 October 1987, 6–7.

31. The first relatively thorough and scientific survey and analysis of diseases specific to the gay community that I am aware of appeared in 1981: William W. Darrow, Donald Barrett, Karla Jay, and Allen Young, "The Gay Report on Sexually Transmitted Diseases," *American Journal of Public Health* 71 (Sept. 1981): 1004–11; cf. the accompanying editorial of H. Hunter Handsfield, 989–90, who cites other, less complete studies.

32. Cf. Allan M. Brandt, *No Magic Bullet,* 2nd ed. (Cambridge, Mass.: 1987).

33. Patton, *Sex and Germs,* 8.

34. Quoted in Anne-Christine D'Adesky, "Breaking the F.D.A. Drugjam," *The Nation,* 17 October 1987, 405. See also the various PWA (persons with AIDS) newsletters, magazines such as "AIDS Treatment News," and the pages of the gay press, in particular the *New York Native,* all of which provide substantial coverage on AIDS treatments (in addition to AIDS politics and organizing). For work by PWAs themselves, see Michael Callen, ed., *Surviving and Thriving with AIDS* (Boston: 1978) and Peter Tatchell, *AIDS: A Guide to Survival* (Boston: 1987).

35. Cf. the 1906 remarks of Dr. William Lee Howard, "The Sexual Pervert in Life Insurance," quoted in Katz, *Gay/Lesbian Almanac,* 318f.

36. See *New York Native,* 5 January 1987, 7; *National Underwriter,* 29 December 1986.

37. Cf. Randy Shilts, *The Mayor of Castro Street: The Life and Times of Harvey Milk* (New York: 1982).

38. The most notable example of such an attack was by Larry Kramer, "An Open Letter to Richard Dunne and Gay Men's Health Crisis, Inc.," *New York Native,* 26 January 1987, 1ff., which in part led to a slightly more activist stand by the GMHC as well as to the formation of several direct action groups in New York City, most notably the civil disobedience–oriented group ACT-UP.

39. "Silence = Death" is the organizing slogan of the New York–based ACT-UP, an AIDS activist group that uses street demonstrations to demand more funding for AIDS-related treatment.

40. Paul Monette, *Love Alone: Eighteen Elegies for Rog* (New York: 1988), xii–xii.

An Ending: Stalking
"The Other Americans"

Writing about sexual deviance, as opposed to prosecuting (or persecuting) it, is a relatively recent phenomenon in the United States, dating back no farther than circa the opening of the present century. What *has* occurred over most of the period has been in the domains of anthropology, medicine, psychology, and sociology. Only in the last twenty-five years or so have historians taken an interest in sexuality in general, or deviance in particular. This volume has sought to deal with sexual variance as a dimension of American social history. For these purposes, sexual normality is defined simply as a set of standards that inform and characterize behavior (or is thought to do so) in any given society or social group. Deviance is the opposite. It is practice that falls or, more properly, is socially placed outside the boundaries of normality, real or imagined. Deviance is a social construct that changes over time and place.

The definition of social deviance points directly to social origins of that behavior. It is not only what we say it is; deviance is also a necessary commodity in societies. Definitions of it and deviant actors supply important services to social settings by clearly marking the outer limits of acceptable behavior. Deviance provides needed contrast for normality and gives it scope as well as dimension. In this sense, it is possible to argue that deviance is a product of normative structuring. Of deviance in general, and sexual variance specifically, it may be argued that were such practices not around, social imperative would require their creation. In brief, deviance is here to stay. Not only is it necessary, but deviance is likely to remain more or less constant in a society over time. If it were suddenly banished, were it possible to rid a social setting of the most unacceptable population, very little would change. *Either* new ranks of deviant actors would move in to fill the vacuum; *or* agencies of control (if only out of self interest) would work more diligently and in a more sophisticated fashion to fill the void; *or* targets of concern would shift and new categories of deviance would be defined. Most probably a combination would ensue. One way to approach and examine sexual deviance (it has been used here interchangeably with the term variance) in America is in two ways. One is chronological and through periodization. A second is through categories of stigmatized practice. This volume has sought to combine them.

The sexual order of early America was, of course, an import from Western Europe. Despite diversity in other aspects of lifestyles, there was general consensus, at least in theory, on appropriate and improper sexual expression. Agreement held that marriage was the only acceptable place for sexual union to occur. It admitted to the existence of female sexual desire, a matter denied, at least theoretically, in Victorian America. It assumed that women's desire was stronger and less controllable than that of men. It held that coitus should be pleasurable for both spouses. The possibility of sexual union was created by God and thus could not be evil per se. Married couples were cautioned, however, against excess or overindulgence, which would be abuse of God's gift and could lead to a variety of ills, even death. The primary purpose of intercourse was procreation. Sexual expressions outside marriage and not directed toward procreation were sin.

The last assertions suggested that sexually stigmatized behavior included, historically at least: masturbation, same-sex relations, bestiality, prostitution, adultery, fornication, and every form of contraception including coitus interruptus. All could be construed to carry negative Biblical injunction (the spilling of seed and the failure to multiply). Masturbation deserves more specific comment in the American history of sexually variant behavior. In the first instance, its most heinous and well-recognized threat lay in the autoerotic nature of that practice. Abuse was virtually unlimited because it did not require a coconspirator and was, of course, by its low visibility not subject to social control. More pertinent here, prior to the eighteenth century, that practice was cast essentially as "sin." Both Judaic and Christian tradition regarded masturbation as evil because it denied the natural function of sexuality, namely procreation. By the middle of the eighteenth century, the practice was becoming medicalized, that is, alleged to have deleterious physical consequences. By 1800 that assertion was not only accepted by many physicians, but it had added the new etiology of causal relationship to mental illness, specially labeled "masturbatory insanity." These notions would prevail and prosper through most of the nineteenth century, though masturbation never completely escaped moral censure. In its transformation from moral issue to medical issue, masturbation was a prototype for similar transition in same-sex relationships at the end of the Victorian era.

While not related directly to the issue of procreation, sexual assault or rape was, of course, also stigmatized and in some cases obtained criminal punishment. It was defined generally as "carnal knowledge of a woman, forcibly and against her will." But this matter was not a simple one. For one thing, in that period women were held to be dominated more than males, generally wanton, and largely unable to control their "lustful" insatiability. In cases of alleged rape, proof of nonconsent was necessary on the part of the woman or the likely conclusion was that she invoked the assault. On the other hand, rape was conceptualized essentially as a violation of a male's property. The crime, if there was one, was against a father or husband rather than the female victim. Her immediate well-being was at least a secondary concern.

The matter of using law in early America as a form of negative sanction against sexual deviance, warrants further comment. English heritage imposed initially on the colonies an intimate relationship between law and morals. "Moral law" was the base upon which civil law was justified. Nor was enactment of morality into law done so simply to establish community ideals. In varying degrees of rigor throughout the Colonial Period enforcement was attempted, but it was always a troublesome matter. In the first place, the colonists found it difficult, even irrelevant, at least in the seventeenth century, to assign gradations of sins, to separate out categories of "disorder" as especially abominable or to establish a hierarchy of evils among moral malpractices. They were all violations of God's law. They were all acts to which every individual was capable given the natural depravity of human beings. In the eighteenth century, zeal for successful implementation of "morals" legislation weakened. Growing secularism played a part in this. This law tended to shift in purpose, away from enforcement of social etiquette with individuals toward general preservation of order in society. In part, this shift may well have been the result of recognition that legislating and enforcing private moral standards were not particularly effective. This was especially the case with sexual standards because breeches were so common and unlikely to surface sufficiently to be detected, much less prosecuted.

Still, sexual deviance as a distinct category of disorder did develop and gradations of social threat within deviant categories were made at a "gut" level. Most fearful were masturbation, bestiality, and male homosexuality. On the latter behavior, popular view held that there were only homosexual acts, not identities or personalities. Any male might be tempted into such an interlude. That it could be a lifestyle would not be recognized until the last years of the nineteenth century. Lesbianism received no recognition, privately or socially. Rape and prostitution were condemned and unlawful, but public concern was less than with the above. In the former case, conviction in courts was most difficult to obtain even where children were involved. Indeed, male gender bias was so embedded in that society that the act of rape was not always perceived as such by either participant. Prostitution was too uncommon to obtain serious concern, though it did become so in seaport cities after circa 1750. Moreover, the relative scarcity of women even into the eighteenth century meant that marriage (if only that) was generally a viable and better option to life on the streets.

Finally, antideviancy enforcement mechanisms, principally the wrath of God and/ or that of community pressure and to a lesser extent law, were sufficiently effective, in most deviant categories, to keep such behavior at a low level. Arguable exceptions, while clearly stigmatized, were adultery and fornication. Both were ordinarily low visibility infractions and difficult to identify unless they resulted in pregnancy. Fornication and even out-of-wedlock pregnancy were forgivable if the end result was marriage. Social and official concern were both lessened in the eighteenth century and even bastardy was less a moral issue than an economic question of who would provide financial support. Of the four traditional negative sanctions against sexual transgressions: God's wrath, peer pressure, law, and assignment of social taboo, only the latter was not employed in early America. Sexuality was always open to discussion, even with children. In New England, Puritan fathers and mothers could contemplate and converse readily on the most heinous forms of sexual transgressions.

On the other hand, this was not the case in Victorian America. Michel Foucault may well be correct in the notion that the volume of discourse on sexuality increased as all social relationships became sexualized. Under a concept known as "delicacy," however, every reference to things sexual, as well as all "morally" offensive aspects of life, were highly structured or heavily euphemised. While premarital sex was condemned certainly prior to circa the 1820s, that condemnation was characterized by a calmness of tone, perhaps suggesting tacit if unspoken recognition that after puberty some breeches were likely, even necessary. Beginning in the latter part of that decade condemnation became sharper and more shrill. The range of acceptable premarital sexual expression tightened and nonmarital intercourse became more heavily stigmatized, dramatically excluded from even the continuum of sexual expression. The new limit of the premarital continuum on sexual behavior became "petting," a relatively new concept. For the great majority of Americans who stayed within developing rigid mores, "petting," which stopped short of coitus, did provide substantial latitude in acceptable sexual behavior. Bestial sexual lust in males might be grudgingly tolerated if such lapses were limited and continued within the marital setting. Sexual desire in women was to be publicly denied or admitted to only as abnormality in need of correction, though actual behavior on this point is debatable. The only legitimate ground for sexual union was within marriage and the only acceptable purpose was procreation. Finally, the cult of respectability, which descended on the American middle class, required that all social behavior be filtered for evaluation through the eyes of others. Conventional behavioral appearance became more important than actual practice.

Using procreation as the measure of sexual legitimacy, birth control practice was, of course, stigmatized behavior. Knowledge of it was common despite the best efforts of Victorian antagonists. This awareness combined with the private nature of sexual intercourse made use of birth control difficult to suppress. But because it carried public stigma, women and men were forced to go underground in search of reproductive control. Essentially this meant transformation of desire for family planning and recreational sex into disreputable, even criminal behavior. Rumors of its use abounded in the Colonial Period if only in the form of the presumed effect of prolonged breast feeding. Utilization was widespread in one form or another in the nineteenth century and has been generally acknowledged as a primary factor in reduced fertility during that period. The most common contraceptive forms were coitus interruptus, the condom, douching (especially popular because it had multiple forces, some respectable), and intravaginal methods. The latter was marked by a middle-class bias because use required generally significant reliance on assistance of physicians.

Contraception was, of course, only one form of birth control, and across all social classes not the most prevalent. There was also infanticide and abortion. Economic factors certainly had causal relationship in the decision to exercise such practice, but surely in the case of unmarried Victorian women the stigma of illegitimacy could drive them also to such action. Infanticide was a violation of morality and law but was a regular occurrence in urban America by the mid-nineteenth century. One indicator of this was extensive sale of the drug laudanum sold ostensibly to relax and quiet crying children but which had the capacity also to kill painlessly. Abortion was much more common. Until the latter part of the century there were no laws against this practice if it was done in the early months of pregnancy. It should be added that the reversal of this tradition and the coming of anti-abortion legislation after mid-century did not immediately alter customary belief that early abortion was a woman's right. The less dangerous tools of abortion were mechanical ones, e.g., scraping the uterus. The more dangerous were chemical with their potentially harsh disruption of the body system. Yet despite physical threat and public condemnation, advertisements for abortifacient were plentiful. A common ploy in ads was something of the following, "Portuguese Female Pills, not to be used during pregnancy for they will cause miscarriage." Even without the "tag line," however, the purpose was clear to potential buyers in use of the key word *Portuguese*. Abortion was the most prevalent or common form of birth control across all social classes in America.

The most blatant affront to the imperatives of heterosexual respectability in the century was certain communitarian experiments and, for that matter, Mormon polygamy. Both were openly sexual alternatives at odds with that of the larger society. One matter that bound such challenges together was dissatisfaction with the traditional family unit. In approaching that concern, management of sexuality was a threshold issue. It was met in different ways, from celibacy to group marriage. The most notorious and the epitome of sexual challenge was John Humphrey Noyes' Oneida Community in upstate New York established during 1848. Its centerpiece was "complex marriage"; critics called this "free love" though this was hardly the case. Provision for multiple sex partners was highly encumbered in bureaucratic specifications. Social affront to the larger society was compounded by the use of "male continence" and "stripiculture." The former was a form of coitus reservatus that severed the connection between intercourse and procreation. The latter was a rudimentary type of eugenic manipulation that dictated which couples in the community might have children. In all this Oneida did march to a different drummer *but* clearly there was a drummer.

The challenge of elective communal living versus the traditional nuclear or even extended family was the former's potential, if not imperative, for multiple sex partners. It surfaced once more in the so-called counter culture of the 1960s. Affront of such behavior to the larger society was less threatening than in antebellum America but not without social disruption. It was understood as one more part of the heterosexual "revolution," and was met with the same public hostility directed toward all "radical" sexual change assigned to the "baby boom" generation. Communitarianism in the 1960s with all its sexual overtones, differed dramatically from its antebellum counterpart. In the latter, sexual variation was instrumental in nature, meaning that it was one aspect of larger lifestyle practice, which has been labelled "patent office models of the good society." The goal was conversion of the larger society. Communes of the 1960s and early 1970s turned inward. Rather than concern with the larger society, participants sought merely self-realization or actualization of members. Sexual variance was basically one avenue in reaching this goal. Clearly the most offensive commune forms begun in the decade of the sixties, it should be noted, were interracial and, even more so, homosexual. The latter was one inverted expression of the growing outwardly expressive homophile movement in the period.

At any rate, as the nineteenth century moved on, Americans heavily sexualized many aspects of their lives, which was previously not the case. They also lost tolerance toward heterosexual variance. Adultery had long been and continued to be heavily stigmatized. Fornication, especially as it became evident in out-of-wedlock pregnancy, became outrage, whatever the outcome of such relationships. Premarital pregnancy was a much more traumatic event for affected women than had been true in the previous century. It generated a condition filled with guilt, shame, and fear about the future as it had never been so before. Redemptive and rescue care for those who had "fallen from grace" remained largely in the hands of middle-class women's organizations operating within an evangelical context until the turn of the century. Involvement in these efforts by middle-class matrons served not merely the ends of benevolence, but also as a warning and a reminder of behavioral boundaries.

That adultery and seduction were intolerable matters was demonstrated in the so-called unwritten law that sanctioned the assassination of "libertines" by husbands, fathers, and brothers of female victims. That "law," it might be noted, was not without its complications for Victorian culture. It meant at least the implicit and awkward acknowledgment that female sensuality did exist, contrary to proscription in the period that held that women were pure and without sexual desire. In this sense the "unwritten" code was in fact a warning to females about the consequences of sexual misconduct. Secondly, the doctrine raised the very real question of exactly whose honor was avenged by these murders. One reading was surely that the act of seduction was a property crime against the would-be assassin more than a dishonor to the victim.

Moral fervor as well as the cult of respectability combined to denounce sexual deviance and demand its eradication. All four norm enforcement mechanisms were employed against such variance, though peer pressure and law became the leading forms of sanction. Social taboo was solidly in place also but, after all, such practice did not eliminate deviancy; it merely hid it from view. At best, this mechanism might make some forms of stigmatized behavior more difficult to pursue. A case in point was restrictions on the spread of information on contraceptive techniques. Aside from the force of moral condemnation and the imperative of social respectability however, one additional measure of deviance in Victorian America came in the form of physiological theory.

It was commonly held in the nineteenth century that the body was a closed energy system at any given time. This meant that heavy energy outlay in any one area of the body took place at the expense of other areas. In terms of sexuality, male orgasm became very serious business. It severely diminished all bodily energy available for some period of time. The implication for overindulgence, some said even excessive preoccupation with sexual expression, was obvious. Utilizing a crude form of sublimation, Victorian Americans concluded that sexual activity took place at the expense of higher creative endeavor and vice versa. Society could not have it both ways. Surely then in this context, the *only* justification for orgasm was procreation. "Waste" of sperm in other purposes was of course socially unacceptable, deviant, and stigmatized. Arguable, sexual prudery and asexuality were male inventions forced upon women by men to minimize their gender threat in society. Women were, after all, "sperm absorbers." At least as a legacy of thought in early America, female sexuality, or properly, alleged lack thereof, was always a matter of suspicion in this century. On the other hand, the positive sanction and assumed respectability of close, intimate, and long-term same-sex relationships among women could have been socially provided as an alternative to the constraints on heterosexual intimacy. At least the former did not involve the potential for loss of valuable male sperm. By the close of the nineteenth century, it should be noted such same-sex female "friendships" had lost a priori innocence.

To the extent that sexually deviant or so defined behavior involved "sperm waste" it could only be harshly condemned, above and beyond the weight of Victorian morality and respectability, be it the "solitary vice" of masturbation, the social vice of prostitution, or structured lifestyle among homosexuals. The latter used as a noun rather than an adjective was significant. By the end of the nineteenth century, homosexual behavior had been medicalized and recognized as a sexual identity preference. It was alleged to be congenital by some medical professions and also later given a competitive psychological causation. Prostitution increased greatly in the century, a corollary of urban growth and the conclusion among some poverty-ridden working women that the "wages of sin" were better than those of the market place. Public distress over prostitution took two forms. One was a more traditional moral condemnation of such practice that held that prostitution was an evil to be eradicated and that this ideal could be realized. The second was resignation that prostitution would not be vanquished. It should therefore be recognized as a public health problem, regulated, segregated, and treated medically. In any event, efforts to cope with causation turned gradually from emphasis on individual moral choice to causation in environmental ills.

Understanding of sexual assault did not change substantially in Victorian America from what it had been previously, with two exceptions. More central to the sexual script of the period than before was the idealization of female virtue. Impurity in women was a threat to the delicate moral order and sexual balance of the day. Secondly, proscription became that females were "blessed" with a natural frigidity and lack of sexual desire, though deep within this assumption was a lurking fear of women's potential for sexual boundlessness. In terms of sexual assault, this meant that even a forced "fall from grace" left heavy social stigma, leaving moral damage that might not be correctable. It meant also a general proclivity to somehow blame the victim for the act of the perpetrator. Rape as a specific sexual act was one of several feminists' targets under the label "crimes against women." Enthusiasm for even the larger general cause tended to wane in the last decade of the century.

The American sexual order altered significantly in the twentieth century from what it had been previously. Change was not abrupt, contrary to loose use of the label "sexual revolution." Attempts to locate it in limited chronological spans of time do not ring viable. The more meaningful approach to changes is to simply recognize that sexual expression circa 1970 was a form of social construction quite different from what it had been at the opening of the century. This was true especially in the case of "accepted" heterosexual practices. Responsible social forces are not yet completely clear, though some factors are apparent. One was the increasing effectiveness in contraceptive techniques that finally severed any necessary connection between coitus and procreation. A second was the collapse of physiology that viewed the body as a closed energy system along with its corollary of necessary limitation on semen loss. Yet another was the scientific assault on a world of absolute standards. More specifically, there was the growing appearance of modern "sexology" a la Alfred Kinsey and those who followed. They pointed out a substantial disparity between moral injunction and actual public practice, then invited the public to measure its normality against empirical behavioral data.

In the end, however, the most important factor in change was the "resexualization" of women in the early years of the new century. Not only was there recognition of female desire, albeit not without significant trepidation and some consternation, but acknowledgment also that women could play a positive role in initiating sexual encounters. The result could be dramatic and surprising. Mary Odem (*Delinquent Daughters . . .* , 1995: See Bibliography Cit.) has illustrated that point well in her examination of strategies in the management of adolescent female sexuality, 1885–1920. In the 1880s purity activists sought to make sex with these females a criminal offense by raising the age of consent. The underlying assumption was that male vice and exploitation were the essential forces behind the moral ruin of otherwise virtuous young women. Progressive period reformers, on the other hand, replaced the model of female victimization with one of female sexual delinquency. Their posture in the early years of the twentieth century was to use civil authority to regulate behavior of the adolescents themselves and their environment rather than assault on male partners. The "blame-the-victim" motif in rape cases was as will be noted another curious consequence of "resexualization."

At any rate, the "sexual revolution" (whatever the chronology) was first and foremost a heterosexual one. Heterosexual change took the form of extension and elaboration of previously stigmatized behavior: nonmarital coitus, anal and oral sex, mutual masturbation, and even deviations from the traditional so-called missionary position. Further proof of heterosexual emphasis may be found in examination of sexology targeted at women and female sexuality, which was published in circa the three decades after 1950. The classic marriage manual was eroticized, made more daring, and as Meryl Altman put it, "brought out of its plain brown wrapper onto the mass-market shelf." In her 1984 essay, "Everything They Always Wanted You to Know: The Ideology of Popular Sex Literature" (See Bibliography Cit.), Altman demonstrates that sex manuals of the 1960s and 1970s uniformly affirmed the essential worth of varied erotic experience. That experience on the other hand meant heterosexual, if not solely marital unions. One general theme was that dysfunctional female sexuality required therapeutic resocialization, which is followed by successful marriage. Marriage aside, the male-female relationship was always dominant. An illustration would be Alex Comfort's *The Joy of Sex* (1972), which, as Altman observes, should more aptly be titled "The Joys of Heterosexual Sex." It contains not a single reference to homosexuality. David Reuben's *Everything You Always Wanted to Know About Sex, But Were Afraid to Ask* (1969) repeats conventional stereotypes about gay men and very briefly comments on lesbianism. It is located in the section on prostitution. "J," *The Sensuous Woman* (1969), while endorsing "swing" (group sex), warns that lesbians may be present and advises discouraging their advances. So it goes. Enhanced and accepting emphasis on heterosexual behavior may well have been purchased then at the cost of marginalizing relations which do not meet that measure of normality.

Innovation and liberalization in heterosexuality did, of course, have consequences for sexual deviance. They tended to blur the boundary between accepted and stigmatized behavior. Increasing tolerance toward variance in sexual expression was also facilitated by other previously noted forces operating on heterosexual change. Disappearance of assumptions regarding bodily harm as a consequence of unlimited sperm loss surely made some difference. Partly as a result of decline in belief of physical damage from semen loss, it may be said that masturbation passed out of the category of deviance altogether. Scientific assault on moral absolutes re Kinsey et al. surely helped also. Moral rigidity must have been sorely tested by Kinsey's observation that over 90 percent of men had broken at least one law on the way to orgasm. Moreover, his research into homosexuality and the population figures it produced reassured gays, providing statistical support for the integrity of the budding homophile community. (This research fueled also, of course, cultural panic of the early 1950s over "sexual perverts.") It would be improper and oversimplified, of course, to understand liberality toward variant sexual practice as merely a "spin-off" of social forces acting on heterosexuality, but they surely cannot be discounted.

At any rate, liberalization has occurred at least in two forms of historically defined variant practice, namely homosexuality and prostitution. In the case of the former, a first step was medicalization of that activity, which led to assertion that homosexuality was a personal identity or lifestyle and not merely "acts." In the last two decades of the nineteenth century, that recognition asserted congenital causation. Somewhat later, a rival view advanced psychological causation. In both cases it could be argued that such behavior was not merely an act of criminal choice and should not be treated as such. Beyond this, homosexuality became a more complicated issue (e.g., what behavior really fell properly under that label) and went through "revolutionary" periods of its own. Most favored candidates are: the late nineteenth century when homosexual social structure began to appear in large urban centers; the 1940s when World War II mobilization requirements tolerated, even encouraged, "coming out." This culminated symbolically in the 1950 organization of the Mattachine Society whose purpose was freedom for the nation's major "sexual minority." Finally came the 1960s, which witnessed origination of a civil-rights style Gay Liberation Movement. Failure on the part of identified celebrities to "come out of the closet" and to "go public" tended to be grounds for serious criticism by fellow homosexuals and lesbians. This was especially so when AIDS was involved. In brief, homosexuality, not unlike heterosexuality, was in a very different social state in the 1970s than was the case in late Victorian America.

Prostitution also changed status in this period. The assumption of environmental and economic causation begun in the nineteenth century persevered and grew from that time on, moderating condemnation of prostitutes themselves. The old debate over elimination versus regulation continued. The so-called Progressive period in the opening years of the twentieth century witnessed a new eradication assault on prostitution, an effort that combined traditional moral "purity" reformers with reformers concerned primarily with social hygiene issues. In the end, the old urban Red Light districts essentially passed into history. Prostitution, of course, did not, but rather was transformed into geography nonspecific brothels, "street walkers," and "call girls."

The introduction of male prostitution brought additional deviant actors onto the scene. The practice had precedents on the American frontier and in isolated military garrisons of the nineteenth century, but the volume was new. Insofar as limited evidence indicates, there does not seem to be substantial demographic or environmental differences between men and women entrepreneurs. Even identified categories within male prostitution distinguished by some researchers appear not dissimilar to those female counterparts, namely: "street hustler," "bar hustler," "call boy," "kept boy." Not unlike structured deviance in women of that trade, the male component also tends to operate within its own community, that is, homosexual social structure. Whether there is significant division within that social structure between commercial and "amateur" participants remains unclear. Female prostitutes began to ply that trade at much younger ages, indeed, not uncommonly, in early adolescence. The movement toward legalization gained new momentum from the 1960s on. Not unlike homosexuality, that momentum was fueled by insistence that prostitution was a "victimless" crime. Also, and not unlike homosexuals, prostitutes rode the wave of the civil-rights activities and took on the political overtones of a "liberation" movement. Such posture never approached, however, the level of homosexual and lesbian political force.

On the other hand, rape or sexual assault obtained increasing condemnation by the 1960s especially under the impact of the feminist movement. The Victorian concept of female purity, sexlessness, and fragility, which posed at least symbolic protection against male brutish passion, disintegrated in the 1920s. "Resexualization" of women eliminated this appeal to male honor. As noted earlier, the issue of sexual assault as psychopathology surfaced strongly in the 1930s along with increased public awareness of sex crimes. Discussion of the sexual psychopath lead not only to the understanding of such acts as male psychological aberration, but also to the notion that women, even children, contributed to their own victimization. By the 1950s, women were clearly paying a high price for modern recognition of their sexuality. Female victims were construed somehow as willing participants or at least predisposed to participation in their own sexual assaults. This theme of "blaming-the-victim" was played out across the 1950s. Only in the next decade and driven by the force of feminism, did it lose effectiveness. The notion of rape as a crime of passion, of uncontrollable desire, was called into question. Feminists sought with some success to reinterpret rape (the threat as well as the act) as a male weapon of control over females. It was, they charged, the cement of patriarchy, and was intended to reinforce women's dependence on men. In the end, rape was at least as much a political affront as sexual victimization.

Incest, at least in the form of male abuse of female blood relatives, followed a not dissimilar tangled path in the twentieth century. It too was "discovered" as a form of serious abuse in the sixties. Previous limited concern was premised on the assumption that, even granting the heinous nature of this crime, victims were not totally innocent. This view was in turn encouraged by alleged recognition by child care professionals of a connection between incestuous molestation in childhood and subsequent later sexual misbehavior. That connection pointed not only to "pollution" of victims from the act of incest, but brought many professionals to conclude that contamination was transmittable to other young females. The brutal nature of incestuous behavior was further diminished in force by shifting public attention from it to sexual misconduct on the "streets." The result was lessened concern with the incestuous male in favor of more interest in the nature of childhood delinquency. Not unlike the case of rape noted above, a central theme in this issue became one of "blaming the victim." This matter of incest in twentieth-century America is thoroughly discussed by Linda Gordon in " 'Be Careful About Father': Incest, Girls' Resistance, and the Construction of Femininity" (See Bibliography Cit., Chapter 7). The author concludes quite correctly that the "blame-the-victim" interpretation of incest ceased only when that experience was situated finally within the context of the feminist critique on male dominance in society.

What then may be said finally of sexually stigmatized behavior in America? At least this: The nation is only slightly over the five-hundredth anniversary of sexual "deviance" in America, that is dated from the day in 1492 when Columbus' crew first discovered native women and sought to use them sexually. In a sense little has changed. Sexual deviance is alive and well. Certain behavior is still separated out and stigmatized. Variance and tensions over it were present in the Colonial Period and remain so today. Verily it shall always be and perhaps must be so. We might hope, however, that the criteria for selection will become "victimization." Granted, determination of exploitation is not a simple matter. Arguable, the case for social harm could be made against prostitution. Child molestation appears to be a clear enough matter. Yet, more recently, divisions have developed on this issue within the homosexual community relative to voluntary man-boy relationships. What does one make of voyeurism or occasional instances of bestiality? Many issues related to the appropriate application of the label "stigmatized" to specific behavior have yet to be resolved.

Still, just perhaps, harsh strictures heretofore hurled at sexual variance can be softened, and defined categories of stigmatized sexual behavior could be measured against whether or not particular behavior is harmful to others, to unwilling victims, to willing participants and/or to society at large. Perhaps Americans could come to see that it is no longer reasonable to use marital sex and procreation as the gage against which sexually respectable behavior is defined. A first step would be our recognition that, as earlier suggested, the "Other Americans"—the enemy—have in significant degree always been "us."

Bibliographical Essay:
Writing the History of Sexual
Variance in America

Only in the last twenty-five years or so have historians given serious attention to human sexuality. Some corrective work has since taken place. Products range from sophisticated historical treatment, such as John D'Emilio's and Estelle Freedman's *Intimate Matters: A History of Sexuality in America* (1988), to more popularized renditions such as Milton Rugoff's *Prudery and Passion* (1971) and, finally, to the complex theorizing of Michel Foucault in *The History of Sexuality,* Vol. 1 (1978), Vol. 2 (1985). The latter has become so significant among American scholars in the area that at least passing reference to it is almost mandatory in most serious historical efforts. A most helpful guide to recent historical literature is Lisa Duggan, "From Instinct to Politics: Writing the History of Sexuality in the United States," *Journal of Sex Research,* 27 (1990), 95–109. Its focus is on the influence of feminism on recent approaches to the history of sexuality. See also Ruby Rich, "Feminism and Sexuality in the 1980s: Review Essay," *Feminist Studies,* 12 (1986), 525–561 and Susan Cahn, "Sexual Histories, Sexual Politics: Review Essay," *Feminist Studies,* 18 (1992), 629–647.

As a general statement sexual deviance (used as a synonym for the more value-free term, *variance*) when treated in texts has been peripheral to the larger and more inclusive matter of human sexuality as a whole. A still useful framework for historical study of sexual and social deviance in general in America is Kai T. Erikson, *Wayward Puritans: A Study in the Sociology of Deviance* (1966). His insights into the purposes of deviance for the larger society are extremely important. The dean of historical studies into sexual deviance in America and otherwise has been Vern Bullough, who with and without collaborators has done substantial pioneering work in the area. See, for example, his *Sex, Society and History* (1976), ed., *Sexual Variance in Society and History* (1976), and with Bonnie Bullough, ed., *Sin, Sickness and Sanity: A History of Sexual Attitudes* (1977). His most recent work is *Science in the Bedroom* (1994). It is a highly comprehensive and thoughtful history of sex research, beginning with such thought in classical Greece. A curiosity of historical coverage in America is that it clusters essentially in the decades of the 1970s and 1980s. Little was done before the former decade, except on the issue of dating chronologically the "sexual revolution." Insofar as journal essays after 1990, those pertinent to discussion of sexual deviance in America are few. This observation is based on a 1989–1995 run of volume contents of the following: *American Historical Review, American Quarterly, Journal of American History, Journal of American Studies, Journal of Social History,* and *Signs: Journal of Women in Culture and Society.* Given the surprising outcome of the investigation, a search was made of the *Social Sciences Index* and a computer data base for the years 1989–1995 titled *Index America: History and Life* held at the John Hodges Library, The University of Tennessee, Knoxville. The data base is comprised of two-thousand, one-hundred journals and unpublished dissertations, nine-hundred of which are published in the United States and Canada. All told the total search turned up no more than a dozen germane essays.

It is possible to approach survey and interpretation of sexual deviance across the American past in at least two ways. One is chronological and through periodization. A second is by categories of stigmatized behavior. The attempt in this essay is to combine them. The focus is on: stigmatized heterosexual behavior excluding prostitution; sexual assault; prostitution; and same-sex intimate practice. Periodization is: Early America, Victorian America, and twentieth-century America. While notice is taken of pertinent published monographs, primary concern is on journal articles because in deviance, treated historically, the better coverage is that of periodical coverage, and because reader usefulness is enhanced by identification of this less visible material. References included in the essay are cited less for currency of publication than their judged usefulness to the topic. The most useful journals and the most commonly cited in this essay are the *Journal of Social History,* the *Journal of Homosexuality,* and *Signs: Journal of Women in Culture and Society.* They are hereafter abbreviated as *JSH, JH,* and *Signs.*

For a brief summary of the Colonial sexual order see Vern Bullough's "An Early American Sex Manual, Or Aristotle Who?" in his edited *Sex, Society and History* (1976), 93–103, and D'Emilio/Freedman, *Intimate Matters* op. cit. Chapters 1–3. Useful introductions to early categorization of deviant practice are Vern Bullough, "Europeans in a New Setting: Colonial America" in his *Sexual Variance in Society and History* (1976), 504–529, and Carol Bingham, "Seventeenth Century Attitudes Toward Deviant Sex," *Journal of Interdisciplinary History,* I (1979), 447–472. That the Puritans had to struggle mightily with sexual temptation is examined in Kathleen Verduin, " 'Our Cursed Natures': Sexuality and the Puritan Conscience," *New England Quarterly,* 56 (1983), 220–237. A pertinent community study concerning deviance in seventeenth-century New England is Roger Thompson, *Sex in Middlesex: Popular Mores in a Massachusetts County,* 1649–1699 (1986). The latter suggests that community social controls kept violations at a low level. See especially Chapter four. Effectiveness of controls over moral infraction is discussed also in David Flaherty, "Law and the Enforcement of Morals in Early America" in David Fleming and Bernard Bailyn, eds., *Perspectives in American History,* V (1971), 203–253.

The common corpus of social history research suggest that premarital coitus and premarital pregnancy rose from the seventeenth century across much of the eighteenth century, especially in New England. One illustrative reference is D'Emilio/ Freedman, *Intimate Matters* op. cit., 23–43. See also Daniel Smith/Michael Hindus, "Premarital Pregnancy in America 1640–1971: An Overview and Interpretation," *Journal of Interdisciplinary History,* 5 (1975), 537–548. Sweeping general studies that discuss the issue of illegitimacy are Maria Vinovskis, "An Epidemic of Adolescent Pregnancy? Some Historical Considerations," *Journal of Family History,* 6 (1981), 205–230, and Daniel Smith/Michael Hindus, "Premarital Pregnancy in America, 1640–1941," *Journal of Interdisciplinary History,* 5 (1975), 537–570. A form of heterosexual deviance, especially identified with what became the southern United States, was black-white intimate contacts. That phenomenon has long attracted historical attention, but an exceptional and brief statement on it is Winthrop Jordan, "The Dynamics of Interracial Sex in Colonial America," in his *White Over Black: American Attitudes Toward the Negro,* 1550–1812 (1969), 136–150. Such sexual contacts, he concludes, were inevitable, but public disdain toward such contacts went beyond simple racism. Antebellum interracial sexual tensions in the American South, especially as they were related to the issue of slavery, are explored in Ronald Waters, "The Erotic South: Civilization and Sexuality in American Abolitionism, *American Quarterly,* 25 (1973), 177–201. See also Steven Brown, "Sexuality and the Slave Community," *Phylon,* 42 (1981), 1–10. Finally that adultery was a very serious matter tied ultimately to the virtue and perpetuation of the Young Republic is explored in Jan Lewis, "The Republican Wife: Virtue and Seduction in the Early Republic," *William and Mary Quarterly,* 44 (1987), 687–721.

In the seventeenth and eighteenth centuries abortion in the early stages of pregnancy was neither a crime nor sin, as it would later become. Infanticide was both, but not uncommon, commensurate with the very limited social importance assigned to infants and young children, given mortality rates of the time. See Peter Hoffer and E. H. Hull, *Murdering Mothers: Infanticide in England and New England* (1981) for further discussion. Sexual assault is examined from two quite different perspectives, one in Barbara Lindemann, "To Ravish and Carnally Know: Rape in Eighteenth Century Massachusetts," *Signs,* 10 (1984), 68–82. The other takes a more narrow yet quite useful focus, Marybeth H. Arnold, "The Life of a Citizen in New York City, 1790–1820," in Kathy Peiss, Christina Simmons, and John Padgug, eds., *Passion and Power: Sexuality in History* (1989), 35–56. Virtually nothing of significance has been done on prostitution in this period. The combination of limited female immigration to "sinful" cities, tight family community supervision of women, and female scarcity that dictated better economic and sexual prospects, at least in marriage, kept levels of such activity quite low. An interesting exception to the above observation is Timothy J. Gilfoyle's "The Urban Geography of Commercial Sex: Prostitution in New York City, 1790–1860," *Journal of Urban History,* 13 (1987), 371–393. Finally, homosexual and bestial contacts were sorely condemned and severely punished, at least in the seventeenth century. Severity of response in the case of the latter is examined in Louis Crompton, "Homosexuality and the Death Penalty in Colonial America," *JH,* 1 (1976), 277–293. On the other hand, bestiality in that century invoked more official concern than did the above. See Robert Oaks, "Things Fearful to Name: Sodomy and Buggery in Seventeenth-Century New England," *JSH*, 12 (1978), 268–281. Roger Thompson takes issue with Oaks's argument that homosexuality obtained some degree of tolerance in the former's "Attitudes Toward Homosexuality in the Seventeenth Century New England Colonies," *Journal of American Studies*, 23 (1989), 27–40. Lesbianism was not apparently a matter of any social concern in the period under discussion and may not have been even recognized in law as sexual deviance. See Lillian Faderman, "The Morbidification of Life Between Women by Nineteenth-Century Sexologists," *JH*, 4 (1978), 75 and N–1.

The need for sperm conservation is crucial to the understanding of stigmatized sexual behavior in nineteenth-century America. See for example G. J. Barker-Benfield, "The Spermatic Economy: A Nineteenth Century View of Sexuality," *Feminist Studies*, I (1972), 45–72. For an excellent study of female sexuality and behavioral assumptions see Cynthia Russett, *Sexual Science: The Victorian Construction of Womanhood* (1991). Sperm "waste" was stigmatized and surely the most degenerate form was the "solitary vice" or "secret sin"—masturbation. A valuable general statement that examines evils of the practice with emphasis on the nineteenth century is Vern and Bonnie Bullough, "The Secret Sin" in their volume *Sin, Sickness and Sanity* (1977), chapter five, 55–73. A rather different approach to masturbation across nineteenth-century America is R. P. Neuman, "Masturbation, Madness and the Modern Concept of Childhood and Adolescence," *JSH*, 8 (1976), 1–27. Biblical authority might also imply negative sanction against birth control techniques, but the horror of wasted semen loss did the same. On birth control as deviant practice see appropriate sections (especially chapter three) "The Criminals" in Linda Gordon, *Woman's Body, Woman's Right: Birth Control in America* (1977), and James Reed, *From Private Vice to Public Virtue: The Birth Control Movement in American Society Since 1830* (1978), more particularly Part One, "Birth Control Before Margaret Sanger," 3–63. It should be noted, however, that energy theory taken to its extreme could discount even actual semen loss itself. See for example Stephen Nissenbaum's *Sex, Diet and Debility in Jacksonian America: Sylvester Graham and Health Reform* (1980). Graham, a popular health reformer, concluded that "lust in the heart" was as injurious as ejaculation (correctable by diet) and therefore deviant in itself.

Whatever the issue of "energy" even heterosexual relations were a major management problem in Victorian society, as it is in all social groupings. An example of efforts at orthodoxy, though loosening "respectable" boundaries a bit, is Ellen Rothman, "Sex and Self Control: Middle Class Courtship in America, 1770–1870," *JSH*, 15, (1982), 409–425. For those males who dared to stray beyond proper boundaries to adultery and seduction, there could be harsh recompense. See R. M. Ireland, "The Libertine Must Die: Sexual Dishonor and the Unwritten Law in the Nineteenth Century United States," *JSH*, 23 (1989), 27–44. Institutions of assistance for women who did "fall" at the close of the century are examined at one locale in Marian Morton, "Seduced and Abandoned in an American City: Cleveland and Its Fallen Women, 1869–1936," *Journal of Urban History*, 11

(1985), 443–469. See also Joan Brumberg, "Ruined Girls: Changing Community Responses to Illegitimacy in Upstate New York, 1890–1920," *JSH,* 18 (1989), 247–272. A different perspective on rescue of "soiled women" is Steven Ruggles, "Fallen Women: The Inmates of the Magdalen Society Asylum of Philadelphia, 1836–1908," *JSH,* 16 (1983), 65–82.

There were those who rejected openly the orthodox measure of monogamous marriage altogether, developing at least in the Victorian mind their own particular deviant brands of sexuality management. Such deviance was probably a potential in much of Antebellum humanitarian reform, e.g., Hal D. Sears, *The Sex Radicals* (1977), especially Chapter one, "Love Worketh No Ill: Free Love and Spiritualism," 3–27. It was necessarily prominent in communitarian experiments of the period as examined so well in Raymond Muncy, *Sex and Marriage in Utopian Communities in Nineteenth Century America* (1973), and Lawrence Foster, *Religion and Sexuality: Shakers, the Mormons and the Oneida Community* (1984).

Sexual assault in Victorian America has as yet obtained only limited attention by historians. A notable exception is Elizabeth Pleck, "Feminist Responses to 'Crimes against Women,' 1868–1896," *Signs,* 8 (1983), 451–470. Hints of incestuous proclivities within the context of nineteenth-century sexual constraints is examined in Bryan Strong, "Toward a History of the Experiential Family: Sex and Incest in the Nineteenth Century Family," *Journal of Marriage and the Family,* 35 (1973), 457–466. Much more attention has been given to prostitution. The link between the antiprostitution movement and Progressive social hygiene reform is examined in David Pivar, *Purity Crusade: Sexual Morality and Social Control, 1868–1900* (1973). The most valuable framework within which to examine prostitution is on a continuum of belief in the feasibility of abolition to, resignation to, and segregation of such practice. The transition in perception of the prostitute from that of victimized "fall from grace" to product of environmental deficiency is traced in Robert Riegel, "Changing American Attitudes Toward Prostitution, 1800–1920," *Journal of the History of Ideas,* 29, (1968), 437–452. Exceptionally insightful interpretations are provided in Leslie Fishbein, "Harlot or Heroine? Changing Views of Prostitution, 1870–1920," *Historian,* 43 (1980), 23–35 and Neil L. Shumsky, "Tacit Acceptance: Respectable Americans and Segregated Prostitution, 1870–1910," *JSH,* 19 (1985), 665–680. The latter is more valuable. On prostitution in the Progressive period see Ruth Rosen, *The Lost Sisterhood: Prostitution in America 1900–1918* (1983).

Three particularly interesting local studies are Jeffrey Adler, "Streetwalkers, Degraded Outcasts, and Good-for-Nothing Huzzies: Women and the Dangerous Class in Antebellum St. Louis," *JSH,* 25 (1992), 137–155, Joel Best, "Careers in Brothel Prostitution, St. Paul, 1865–1883," *Journal of Interdisciplinary History,* 12 (1982), 597–619, and Neil Shumsky/Larry Springer, "San Francisco's Zone of Prostitution, 1880–1934," *Journal of Historical Geography,* 7 (1981), 71–89. A fourth quite local study on regulation is John Burnham, "The Medical Inspection of Prostitutes in the Nineteenth Century: The St. Louis Experiment and its Sequel," *Journal of the History of Medicine and Allied Sciences,* 45 (1971), 208–218. An ethnic perspective is provided in Lucie Hirata, "Free, Indentured, Enslaved: Chinese Prostitutes in Nineteenth Century America," *Signs,* 5 (1979), 3–29. A more general study is Judith Walkowitz, *Prostitution and Victorian Society* (1980).

Same-sex intimate relations in Victorian America are complex historical issues. For most of the nineteenth century, male homosexual behavior was just that—acts but not identities. Lesbianism was easily denied in a society where women who were believed devoid of heterosexual desire could hardly be tempted by other women. In the case of the latter, close, intimate, and long-term relationships between females were held to be not only "respectable" but were essentially encouraged by social restrictions on cross-gender relationships. See Carroll Smith-Rosenberg, "The Female World of Love and Ritual: Relations Between Women in Nineteenth Century America," *Signs,* I (1975), 1–29. Better these associations should exist than the dreadful heterosexual threat to men of desirous women. They were, after all, "sperm absorbers." See A. J. Barker-Benfield, "The Spermatic Economy: A Nineteenth Century View of Sexuality," *Feminist Studies,* I (1972), 45–74. The presumption of innocence began to change significantly toward the end of the century. An overall starting point on this transition is George Chauncey, "From Sexual Inversion to Homosexuality: Medicine and the Changing Conceptualization of Female Deviance," *Salamagundi,* 58/59 (1982), 114–146.

As Vern Bullough and Martha Voght point out, identification, understanding, condemnation, and even causation of male homosexuality was complicated in the Victorian mind by its confusion with masturbation (parenthetically both involving wasted semen). See "Homosexuality and its Confusion with the 'Secret Sin' in Pre-Freudian America," *Journal of the History of Medicine and Allied Sciences,* 28 (1973), 143–155. On the general evolution of male same-sex behavior to that of pathology and the province of physicians see Vern Bullough, "Homosexuality and the Medical Model," in his collection *Sex, Society and History* (1976), 161–172. Finally Bullough provides a broad coverage of homosexuality as deviance in "Stigmatized Sexual Behavior in Nineteenth Century America" in Chapter two of his *Sexual Variance in Society and History* (1976), 587–631.

The social organization of sexual expression changed significantly in the twentieth century from what it had been previously. That change was not abrupt, contrary to what has been suggested over recent decades by the loose use of the label "sexual revolution." Favored chronological candidates for that "revolution" have been several: the first decade of the century, the 1920s, the period of World War II, and belatedly, the 1960s. On sexual change in the Progressive period see James McGovern, "The American Woman's Pre–World War I Freedom in Manners and Morals," *Journal of American History,* 55 (1968), 315–353. On the 1920s see Ira L. Reiss, "The Sexual Renaissance: A Summary and Analysis," *Journal of Social Issues,* 22 (1966), 123–137, and Erwin Smigel and Rita Seiden, "Decline and Fall of the Double Standard," *The Annals of the American Academy of Political and Social Science,* 376 (1969), 6–17. Consequences of sexual liberalization specifically on women, which began to occur in the late 1950s, are examined in Barbara Ehrenreich, Elizabeth Hess and Gloria Jacobs, *Remaking Love: The Feminization of Sex* (1986).

The more appropriate label is "sexual evolution" and the changes involved predate in origin the present century. Discussion of the "longer view" may be found in Robert Bell, *Premarital Sex in a Changing Society* (1966), and Paul Woodring, "Some Thoughts on the Sexual Revolution," in Gerald Winter and Eugene Nuss, eds., *The Young Adult: Identity and Awareness* (1969), 16–19. A quite interesting approach to sexual changes, or the lack thereof, in the Progressive period is Howard I. Kushner, "Nineteenth Century Sexuality and the 'Sexual Revolution' of the Progressive Era," *Canadian Review of American Studies,* 9 (1978), 34–49. Drawing on a view of the Victorian sexual order that questions the real extent of repression in that period, he goes on to minimize change in the years as conservative attempts to channel and limit innovation.

Two matters related to change in sexual expression require comment here. One is that the primary direction of change was in heterosexual behavior. The extent of that change is well demonstrated in the published findings of Alfred Kinsey et al. On Kinsey's work see Paul Robinson, *The Modernization of Sex* (1976), Chapter two, "Alfred Kinsey," 42–119, as well as Regina M. Morantz, "The Scientist as Sex Crusader: Alfred C. Kinsey and American Culture," *American Quarterly,* 29 (1977), 563–589. That sexual liberalization was channeled toward heterosexual behavior over other sexual expressions is well illustrated in the work of William Masters and Virginia Johnson as pointed out in Robinson op. cit., Chapter three, 120–190, and by Michael Gordon/Penelope Shankweiler, "Different Equals Less: Female Sexuality in Recent Marriage Manuals," *Journal of Marriage and the Family,* 33 (1977), 459–466. The implications for sexual variance as a consequence of that channeling in sexology of the 1960s and 1970s is examined in Meryl Altman, "Everything They Wanted You to Know: The Ideology of Popular Sex Literature," in Carol Vance, ed., *Pleasure and Danger: Exploring Female Sexuality* (1984), 115–129. One of her conclusions is that such work elevated the worth of heterosexual pleasures while marginalizing other forms of sexual expression. A thorough study of the nature of impact of sexology in recent decades is Janice M. Irvine, *Disorders of Desire: Sex and Gender in Modern American Sexology* (1990).

A second matter related to changes in heterosexual behavior was the separation of a previous connection between coitus and procreation, indeed sexual expression and coitus. The former was essentially a matter of increasing effectiveness in birth control techniques and the social acceptance of such practice. Classic texts on this issue are David M. Kennedy, *Birth Control in America: The Career of Margaret Sanger* (1970), Linda Gordon, *Woman's Body, Woman's Right,* op. cit., and James Reed, *From Private Vice to Public Virtue,* op. cit. (1978). Once taboo but now accepted, if not warmly so, elaboration in heterosexual practices has yet to be explored in historical perspective. That such elaboration does exist was borne out in the work of Alfred Kinsey as well as that of Masters and Johnson. A pertinent interpretation of this work is Paul Robinson, op. cit. An example of contemporary analysis is J. H. Gagnon and W. Simon, "The Sexual Scripting of Oral-Genital Contacts," *Archives of Sexual Behavior,* 16 (1987), 1–25. An interesting examination of concern with masturbation especially across the nineteenth century is R. P. Neuman, op. cit. See also Annie Reich, "The Discussion of 1912 on Masturbation and Our Present Day Views" in her *Psychoanalytic Contributions* (1951),

157–178. Its value is as a document in history contrasting views of masturbatory practice in the opening of the twentieth century with those of the immediate post–World War II era.

What is clearly the case with respect to liberalization in heterosexual intimacy in the first two decades of the present century, particularly with females, is that it took place against a backdrop of serious tensions over sexual expression in general. That turn-of-the-century behavioral change was conservatively channeled and contained and is illustrated in Howard I. Kushner, "Nineteenth Century Sexuality and the 'Sexual Revolution' of the Progressive Era," op. cit. Barbara Epstein suggests more significance in "Family, Sexual Morality and Popular Movements in Turn-of-the-Century America," in Ann Snitow, Christine Stansell, Sharon Thompson, eds., *Powers of Desire* (1983), 117–129. Indication of sexual ill ease and male-female relations in general is provided in William O'Neill, *Divorce in the Progressive Era* (1967), and in Joe L. Dubbert, "Progressivism and the Masculinity Crisis," *The Psychoanalytic Review,* 61 (1974), 443–455. Changing strategy to contain and limit sexual expression that speak in part to the consequences of "re-sexualization" and adolescent females circa turn-of-the-century years is Mary Odem's excellent volume, *Delinquent Daughters: Protecting and Policing Adolescent Female Sexuality in the United States, 1835–1920* (1995). Efforts to "save" heterosexuality in the 1920s are examined in Christina Simmons, "Companionate Marriage," *Frontiers,* 4 (1979), 54–59, and Lisa Duggan, "The Social Enforcement of Heterosexuality and Lesbian Resistance in the 1920s," 75–92, and Rayna Rapp and Ellen Ross, "The Twenties' Backlash: Compulsory Heterosexuality, the Consumer Family, and the Waning of Feminism," 93–107, the latter two in Amy Swendlow and Hanna Lessinger, eds., *Class, Race and Sex: The Dynamics of Control* (1983). The relationship between sexuality and radicalism, the "libidinal left" in the 1920s, is examined in Leonard Wilcox, "Sex Boys in a Balloon: V. F. Calverton and the Abortive Sexual Revolution," *Journal of American Studies,* 23 (1989), 41–62. While more concerned with same-sex intimacy, a useful essay on the whole matter of sexual privacy is A. S. Cohan, "The State in the Bedroom: What Some Adults May Not Do Privately After Hardwick v. Bowers," *Journal of American Studies,* 23 (1989), 41–62.

A must essay on sexual violence in the twentieth century is Estelle Freedman, "Uncontrolled Desire: The Response to the Sexual Psychopath, 1920–1960," *Journal of American History,* 74 (1987), 83–106. Also valuable because it discusses somewhat unique assault concerns of Afro-American females is Darlene Hines, "Rape and the Inner Life of a Black Woman in the Middle West," *Signs,* 14 (1989), 912–920. Rape and the threat of rape as a form of social control by males is examined in Susan Brownmiller's classic study, *Against Our Will: Men and Rape* (1975). A brief and important statement on rape's changing social meaning is Patricia Donat and John D'Emilio, "A Feminist Redefinition of Rape and Sexual Assault: Historical Foundations and Change," *Journal of Social Issues,* 48 (1992), 9–22. Sexual abuse against children has not as yet obtained historical coverage. A useful contemporary analysis is David Finkelhor, *Sexually Victimized Children* (1979). A bit of historical insight into incest is Linda Gordon, "Be Careful About

Father: Incest, Girls' Resistance and the Construction of Femininity," in her *Heroes of Their Lives: The Politics and History of Family Violence,* Boston 1880–1960 (1988), 204–249. An interesting discussion of tensions among homosexuals over adult-adolescent intimate contact is David Thorstad, "Man/Boy Love and the American Gay Movement," *JH,* 20 (1971), 251–274. Prostitution in this century is a long-time matter of historical interest. Classic and still valuable statements on the early years of the period are Egal Feldman, "Prostitution, the Alien Woman and the Progressive Imagination," *American Quarterly,* 19 (1967), 192–206, and David Pivar, "Cleansing the Nation: The War on Prostitution, 1917–1921," *Prologue,* 12 (1989), 29–40. See also Ruth Rosen, *The Lost Sisterhood: Prostitution in America, 1890–1918* (1984). Significant level of male prostitution is a rather recent phenomenon, another field yet to be tilled historically. That it is worth concern is demonstrated in Christopher Earls, Helene Davis, "A Psychosocial Study of Male Prostitution," *Archives of Sexual Behavior,* 18 (1989) 401–419, and D. K. Weisberg, *Children of the Night: A Study of Adolescent Prostitution* (Toronto, 1985). An important and provocative discussion of law and prostitution as well as homosexuality is the Church of England's sponsored study, *The Wolfender Report: Report of the Committee on Homosexual Offenses and Prostitution,* 1959, published in the United States by Stein and Day Publishers (New York, 1963). It should be viewed, of course, as a document of history in its own right.

An interesting introduction to behavioral characteristics in identification of homosexuals is Henry L. Minton, "Femininity in Men and Masculinity in Women: American Psychiatry and Psychology Portray Homosexuality in the 1930s," *JH,* 13 (1986), 1–21. A dramatic change occurred in the "innocence" once ascribed to female same-sex relationships as described by Carroll Smith-Rosenberg, op. cit. An outstanding examination of that change is Lillian Faderman, "The Morbidification of Love Between Women by Nineteenth-Century Sexologists," *JH,* 4 (1978), 73–90. Faderman provides a full history of lesbianism in this century in *Odd Girls and Twilight Lovers: A History of Lesbian Life in Twentieth-Century America* (1991). Ann Ferguson discusses societal conditions in turn-of-the-century America and Europe that gave rise to lesbian communities in "Patriarchy, Sexual Identity and Sexual Revolution," *Signs,* 7 (1981), 158–172. An interesting perspective on the concept of "companionate marriage" is Christina Simmons, "Companionate Marriage and the Lesbian Threat," *Frontiers,* 4 (1979), 54–59. Less useful, but noteworthy, is Vern and Bonnie Bullough, "Lesbianism in the 1920s and 1930s: A Newfound Study," *Signs,* 2 (1977), 895–905.

On "Butch" relationships see Joan Nestle, "Butch-Fem Relationships: Sexual Courage in the 1950s," *Heresies,* 12 (1981), 21–25, and on a more analytical level Elizabeth Kennedy's and Madeline Davis's study of Buffalo, New York, "The Reproduction of Butch-Fem Roles: A Social Constructionist Approach," in Peiss, Simmons, Padgug, eds., *Passion and Power,* op. cit., 241–256. The nature of lesbianism through the eyes of novelist Radclyffe Hall (e.g., *The Well of Loneliness*) is examined in Esther Newton, "The Myth of the Mannish Lesbian: Radclyffe and the New Woman," *Signs,* 9 (1984), 557–575. Adrienne Rich provides a provocative and bibliographic essay on the nature of the lesbian experience and on belief in "natural" heterosexual inclinations of women in "Compulsory Heterosexuality and Lesbian Existence" in Snitow, Stansell, Thompson, eds., *Powers of Desire,* op. cit., 177–205. A related discussion is Ann Ferguson, Jacquelyn Zita, Katherine Addelson, "On Compulsory Heterosexuality and Lesbian Existence: Defining the Issues," *Signs,* 7 (1981), 158–173.

The primary text for examination of homosexuality in the twentieth century is John D'Emilio, *Sexual Politics, Sexual Communities: The Making of a Homosexual Minority in the United States,* 1940–1970 (1983). A statement on the early history of that "homosexual minority," that is before the Stonewall riots, is Foster Gunnison, "The Homophile Movement in America," in Ralph Weltge, ed., *The Same Sex: An Appraisal of Homosexuality* (1969), 113–128. The whole of the Weltge volume still remains useful. Homosexuality as an identity obtained recognition only in the last years of the nineteenth century. The complexities of defining the label is examined in George Chauncey, "Christian Brotherhood or Sexual Perversion: Homosexual Identities and the Construction of Sexual Boundaries in the World War I Era," *JSH,* 19 (1985), 189–211. Homosexuality also has its historical watersheds, notably the late nineteenth century when visible social structure began to appear in cities, and the 1969 Stonewall riots, which can be identified, if a bit arbitrarily, as the beginning of the Gay Liberation Movement. Allan Bérubé makes an argument for the World War II era as an equally important fault line, "Marching to a Different Drummer: Lesbian and Gay GIs in World War II" in Snitnow, Stansell, Thompson, eds., *Powers of Desire,* op. cit., 88–99. See also *Coming Out under Fire: The History of Gay Men and Women in World War Two* (1990). Bérubé's thesis receives additional support in John D'Emilio, "Forging a Group Identity: World War II and the Emergence of an Urban Gay Subculture" in his *Sexual Politics, Sexual Communities,* op. cit., Chapter two. See also D'Emilio, "The Homosexual Menace: The Politics of Sexuality in Cold War America" in Peiss et al., ed. *Passion and Power,* op. cit., 226–240.

Discussion of the relationship between gender and homosexuality in the first half of the present century is explored in Karin A. Martin, "Gender and Sexuality: Medical Opinion on Homosexuality, 1900–1950," *Gender and Society,* 7 (1993), 246–260. Finally Robert Padgug discusses the social, political, and moral consequences of AIDS within and without the homosexual community, "Gay Villain, Gay Hero: Homosexuality and the Social Construction of AIDS," in Peiss, Simmons, Padgug, *Passion and Power,* op. cit., 293–313. Needless to say, the AIDS "crisis" has generated substantial interest in its social meaning. One valuable example is John H. Gagnon, "Disease and Desire," *Daedalus,* 118 (1989), 47–77. Another in which AIDS is considered in the realm of concepts and definitions within sexology literature is Chapter five, Janice Irvine, *Disorders of Desire: Sex and Gender in Modern American Sexology* (1990). While not the main concern of the essay, interesting comment with regard to AIDS and condoms is provided in Joshua Gamson, "Rubber Wars: Struggles Over the Condom in the United States," *Journal of the History of Sexuality,* I (1990), 262–282, as well as commentary on that essay by Scott Bravman in that same journal, Vol. 2 (1991), 98–102.

With respect to the overall matter of law and sexual variance, a vital beginning still is "Sex Offenses," an exploration of this relationship in *Law and Contemporary Problems,* 25 (Spring, 1960). Finally it should be noted here again that citations in this bibliography are selective and are only those deemed especially useful to the present volume. Volume comments made by the editor draw collectively and directly on these sources.

Index

About the Editor

CHARLES O. JACKSON is Associate Dean and a professor of History at the University of Tennessee, Knoxville. He is the author of four earlier books, including *Passing: The Vision of Death in America* (Greenwood Press, 1977).